Britannica
Review
of Foreign Language
Education

Britannica Reviews in Education

Advisory Board

Britannica Review
of Foreign Language Education

Edited by Dale L. Lange

Volume 2, 1970

Sponsored by the American Council
on the Teaching of
Foreign
Languages

Encyclopædia Britannica, Inc. *Chicago*

William Benton *publisher*

American Council on the Teaching of Foreign Languages

Preface

The *Britannica Review of Foreign Language Education*, proposed in 1968 by Encyclopædia Britannica and published for the first time in 1969, has met with an enthusiastic reception. ACTFL is proud that the review has been the most successful in the Britannica Reviews in Education Series. By responding to the proposal and by making the *Britannica Review of Foreign Language Education* a benefit of Comprehensive Membership in ACTFL, the ACTFL Executive Committee has also responded to the need to make available a resource that collects, catalogs, and analyzes basic information needed to improve foreign language instruction in American education.

The combined resources of the MLA/ERIC Clearinghouse on the Teaching of Foreign Languages, the ACTFL Annual Bibliography, and the *Britannica Review of Foreign Language Education* are a continuing response to the need for providing to the profession the essential information for wise decision-making.

C. EDWARD SCEBOLD
Executive Secretary, ACTFL

American Council on the Teaching of Foreign Languages

Officers for the Year 1970

President
Lester McKim
Bellevue, Wash., Public Schools

President-Elect
Lowell Dunham
University of Oklahoma

Executive Secretary
C. Edward Scebold

Treasurer
Kenneth W. Mildenberger

Executive Committee

Clara W. Ashley
Auburndale, Mass.

Edward H. Bourque
Fairfield, Conn., Public Schools

Jean Carduner
University of Michigan

Frank Grittner
*Wisconsin Department
of Public Instruction*

Kai-yu Hsu
San Francisco State College

Gail Hutchinson
Atlanta Public Schools

Mari-Luci Ulibarri
*Minority Group Cultural
Awareness Center,
University of New Mexico*

Constituents

Alabama Association of Foreign
Language Teachers

Alaska Foreign Language
Association

Arizona Foreign Language
Association

Arkansas Foreign Language
Teachers Association

California Council of Foreign
Language Teachers'
Associations

Colorado Congress of Foreign
Language Teachers

Connecticut Council of
Language Teachers

Delaware Council on the
Teaching of
Foreign Languages

Greater Washington Association
of Teachers of Foreign
Languages

Florida Foreign Language
Association

Classical and Modern Foreign
Language Association of
Georgia

Hawaii Association of
Language Teachers

Idaho Foreign Language
Teachers' Association

Illinois Foreign Language
Teachers' Association

Indiana Foreign Language
Teachers' Association

Iowa Foreign Language
Association

Kansas Foreign Language
Association

Kentucky Council of Foreign
Language Teachers

Louisiana Foreign Language
Teachers Association

Foreign Language Department,
Maine Teachers' Association

Maryland Foreign Language
Association

Massachusetts Foreign
Language Association

Michigan Foreign Language
Association

Minnesota Council of Teachers
of Foreign Languages

Mississippi Modern Language
Association

Foreign Language Association
of Missouri

Montana Foreign Language
Teachers Association

Nebraska Foreign Language
Association

Nevada Foreign
Language Teachers'
Association

New Hampshire Association for
the Teaching of Foreign
Languages

New Jersey Foreign Language
Teachers Association

New Mexico Foreign Language
Teachers Association

New York State
Federation of Foreign
Language Teachers

Modern Language and Latin
Sections, North Dakota
Education Association

Ohio Council on the Teaching
of Foreign Languages

Oklahoma Foreign
Language Teachers'
Association

Ontario Modern
Language Teachers'
Association

Oregon Association of
Foreign Language Teachers

Pennsylvania State Modern
Language Association

Rhode Island Foreign
Language Association

Association of Foreign
Language Teachers of
South Carolina

South Dakota Foreign
Language Association

Texas Foreign Language
Association

Utah Foreign Language
Association

Vermont Foreign Language
Teachers' Association

Modern Foreign Language
Association of Virginia

Washington Association
of Foreign Language
Teachers

Wisconsin Association of
Foreign Language Teachers

Wyoming Language Teachers'
Association

Affiliates

American Association of
Teachers of Arabic

American Association of
Teachers of French

American Association of
Teachers of German

American Association of
Teachers of Italian

American Association of
Teachers of Slavic and East
European Languages

American Association of
Teachers of Spanish and
Portuguese

American Classical League

American Philological
Association

Association des Professeurs
Franco-Américains

Association of Teachers of
English as a Second Language
(NAFSA)

Association of Teachers
of Japanese

Central State Conference on
the Teaching of Foreign
Languages

Chinese Language Teachers
Association

Classical Association of the
Atlantic States

Classical Association of the
Middle West and South

Classical Association
of New England

Classical Association of the
Pacific Northwest

Colleges of
Mid-America, Inc.

Department of Foreign
Languages, National Education
Association

Linguistic Society of America

Middle States Association
of Modern Language Teachers

Modern Greek Studies
Association

National Association of
Language Laboratory Directors

National Association of
Professors of Hebrew in
American Institutions of
Higher Learning

National Council of State
Supervisors of Foreign
Languages

New England Foreign
Language Association

Northeast Conference
on the Teaching of Foreign
Languages

Pacific Northwest Conference
on Foreign Languages

Rocky Mountain Modern
Language Association

Société des Professeurs
Français en Amérique

South Atlantic Modern
Language Association

Southern Conference on
Language Teaching

Teachers of English
to Speakers of Other
Languages

Foreword

Although for obvious reasons the *Britannica Review of Foreign Language Education, Volume 2,* did not have the initial birth-pains of Volume 1, nevertheless it could never have been completed without the help of many people. The editor would especially like to thank the staff at Encyclopædia Britannica for its guidance and help in the specific details in the preparation of the chapters for final printing: J. Thomas Beatty, Lorene Lawson, Richard O'Connor, Keith Snyder, and undoubtedly many others who have contributed their time and knowledge.

To the chapter authors, who have provided the substance of this review, the editor owes a special debt of gratitude because they had to meet an almost impossible schedule of deadlines for the submission of manuscripts. The Editorial Board for *BRFLE* 2 provided invaluable support to the editor by giving its counsel in the selection of the major topic, the suggestion of authors to write the various chapters, and the reading and evaluation of manuscripts. The immediate past and present Executive Secretaries of ACTFL, F. André Paquette and C. Edward Scebold respectively, have been especially helpful in working out the necessary arrangements between ACTFL and Encyclopædia Britannica for the publication of an annual review in foreign language education.

A special word of thanks is due to Barbara Bentz and James Hammers, my secretary and assistant on this project. And most of all, without the complete understanding of his family, the editor would never have been able to perform his role.

The editor would especially wish to dedicate this volume to the memory of Donald L. Ehrlichmann, a German teacher in the Minneapolis public schools, recently killed in an unfortunate series of events, who used his own classrooms to pilot work in the individualization of instruction and who spent much of his career thinking and working with that particular concept.

Dale L. Lange
University of Minnesota

Contents

1 Introduction: Theme and Overview, Dale L. Lange   1

2 A Rationale for the Individualization and Personalization of Foreign Language Instruction, Lorraine A. Strasheim   15

3 Behavioral Objectives and Evaluation, Florence Steiner   35

4 Strategies of Instruction for Listening and Reading, Gilbert A. Jarvis   79

5 Strategies of Instruction for Speaking and Writing, Alfred N. Smith   113

6 Curricula for Individualized Instruction, Gerald E. Logan   133

7 Media in Foreign Language Teaching, Jermaine D. Arendt   157

8 Language Learning Laboratory, W. Flint Smith   191

9 Recent Developments in the Training and Certification of the Foreign Language Teacher, Howard B. Altman and Louis Weiss   239

10 Classics: The Teaching of Latin and Greek and Classical Humanities, Gerald M. Erickson   275

11 TESOL, Bernard Spolsky   323

12 Trends in Foreign Language Enrollments, Richard I. Brod   341

Index   363

Introduction: Theme and overview

Purpose of the Review

Dale L. Lange

University of Minnesota

In the year since the writing of the chapters of the first *Britannica Review of Foreign Language Education*, forces and events in this country and abroad have brought into focus and produced, among more noticeable outcomes, unrest with some tragic results on college and university campuses, demonstrations in secondary schools, and political and social alienation and polarization in the general public. The mores, values, and institutions of American society are being challenged from many segments of the population for a number of reasons, among which are: an unending, seemingly unjustifiable war in Southeast Asia, unequal treatment of minority groups in all parts of the country, lack of attention to problems of urban areas, pollution of natural resources, and a general inability of society's leaders to formulate goals in order to attempt solutions to major domestic problems.

These forces, events, and challenges to our society almost require each individual to face the issues and determine his relationship to them. Foreign language educators, like other groups in our society, have been forced to react to events which have affected them. The cancelling of the Foreign Language Basic Studies Institutes under the Education Professions Development Act (EPDA) in October 1969 and virtual elimination of federally sponsored foreign language research programs, caused by budget cuts in federal spending in order to finance our military commitments in Vietnam and later Cambodia, resulted in the expression of deep concern on the part of some individuals and professional foreign language associations to members of Congress as to the seriousness of the federal government's commitment to education programs.

In this disturbed period of our history, the individual is testing his rights as a citizen under a democratic philosophy. He is asking his government and other social institutions to become humanized, to react to his needs and goals as well as those of other individuals no matter what their ethnic background, political and religious beliefs. Since the schools, colleges, and universities represent institutions of this society for youth, they are demanding that these institutions become humanistically responsive. Students are asking the schools and colleges to provide for the education and learning that each individual requires to achieve his own personal goals. The educational institutions have begun to respond and will continue to respond, shaping and changing curricula, requirements, and instruction to more closely approximate individual necessities.

In relating to the present educational scene, the main theme of the second volume of the *Britannica Review of Foreign Language Education* is "Individualization of Instruction." The presentation of a major theme in foreign language teaching and learning in the second volume represents a departure from the overview of the professional literature provided in the first volume of the *Review*. The theme is still in keeping with the intent of the *Review* which is "to describe and appraise all the important work of the year" (Birkmaier, 1). The theme was chosen by the editor and the Britannica Review of Foreign Language Education Advisory Committee, as listed in the front pages of this volume, because of the emphasis that foreign language educators seem to be placing on the value of and necessity for individualized instruction. Furthermore, the theme seems to be widely discussed in the literature of foreign language pedagogy in the past year, making it even more appropriate.

Main theme of Volume II

As in the first volume, the authors in the second volume, within the confines of their tasks, have been asked to analyze, synthesize, evaluate, and interpret the literature they are reviewing. Thus each chapter contains a meaningful review, not a dry, objective presentation of a topic.

The *Review* continues to be supported by the *ACTFL Annual Bibliography* (Lange, 3) and by MLA/ERIC (Mildenberger & Satlin, 4; Mildenberger & Wood, 5). Each author, however, has been asked to use his own sources and reading within the topic to add to the provided sources.

As the development of individualized programs takes place, we must also appreciate the fact that individualization of instruction is not new to American education, as witnessed by works of other decades in this century (Henry, 2; Whipple, 6). Hopefully we can build on these ideas rather than rediscover them, thereby making foreign language programs truly innovative and productive.

The second chapter of this review, "A Rationale for the Individualization and Personalization of Foreign Language Instruction," by Strasheim, sets the tone for the discussion of individualization of instruction. She points out, among other things, the effects of college requirements, of programs, and of teacher attitudes toward all students as "majors" in language in language programs. *But times are changing.* These past procedures are no longer appropriate. Strasheim points out that perhaps the most important reason for individualization of instruction lies in the recognition of each individual's worth. Such a rationale is carefully documented and explained through persons and events in our changing world.

A rationale for the individualization and personalization of foreign language instruction

In describing the student's world, Strasheim relates how the individual has begun to question his world and his education. He wants to be able to cope with his world and desires that his education provide him with necessary information, tools, and processes to do so.

Foreign languages have a role to play in this world if they provide diversity for the student. Strasheim reviews some of the conferences, publications, and curricula which have attempted to indicate the necessity for the individualization and personalization of instruction for the "new" student. The propositions for planning individualized instructional programs that she offers in the final pages of her chapter require a response from each teacher in terms of the most important element of any instructional model, the individual.

Steiner follows the discussion of a rationale for individualized and personalized instruction with a careful analysis of the use of behavioral objectives in building curricula and in testing and evaluating student performance and curriculum. Like Strasheim, she relates the necessity for behavioral objectives and a performance curriculum to the attitudes and demands of the "new" student for a more "relevant" curriculum. Other factors such as motivation and aptitude, and inherent qualifications of students, also have a role to play in terms of objectives for foreign language instruction.

Behavioral objectives and evaluation

The definition and discussion of behavioral objectives Steiner provides indicate how objectives are obtained and formulated for a performance curriculum. If such objectives are used, the literature indicates that teachers will have to reorient their behavior more toward the students.

The advantages and disadvantages for the use of behavioral objectives are discussed at length, providing a useful display of both sides of the issue. But before behavioral objectives can be formulated, they must be situated within a taxonomy for the specific discipline. Steiner reviews those taxonomies that apply to foreign languages and English as a second language, in particular.

Performance or behavioral objectives are the determining factors for curricula. Steiner indicates a wide use of objectives within curricula for total programs, for teaching culture within individualized programs, for preassessment of knowledge, and in building materials.

Within this context Steiner clarifies the role of the teacher toward performance objectives only suggested in the early part of the chapter. She also reviews the implications for the classroom that a performance curriculum may require: grouping, scheduling, time and space allotments.

The evaluation of student performance, abilities, and attitudes is important for a performance curriculum. Steiner points out the progress in testing and evaluation of performance in the areas of achievement motivation, aptitude, and criterion reference tests. Suggestions for new concepts of grading are also considered.

Program evaluation is quite obviously tied to the program's objectives. Steiner indicates how performance objectives are being used to account for success or failure of projects in education. Specific evaluative instruments in the foreign language field are still lacking, although progress in measuring student attitudes is particularly noted.

The two chapters which follow Steiner's examination of performance objectives review strategies of instruction in the receptive skills of listening and reading and the productive skills of speaking and writing, the former written by Jarvis and the latter by Alfred N. Smith.

Jarvis's chapter is a careful review of the literature on the listening and reading skills in terms of their relationship to the productive skills as being easier to develop in terms of learning conditions. Some of the quantitative approaches used in schools are reviewed for the listening skill including practice in listening, contextual procedures, media, exchange programs, and

Strategies of instruction for listening and reading

4

bilingual programs. Very little research is indicated for the qualitative variables of the listening skill although some literature is reviewed in discrimination, language aptitude, physical response, achievement, and use of media. Some particular classroom techniques are also noted.

The review of the reading skill examines the differences between first and second language reading, reading within the audiolingual model, reading outside the audiolingual model, and literature related to first language learning. Again strategies are presented in different contexts, but little evaluation of their effectiveness is available.

In the conclusion to the chapter, Jarvis is particularly critical of the lack of strategies for individualized instruction with the receptive skills, not to mention empirical research in general within foreign language learning. Some of the programs which do offer individualized learning opportunities are reviewed in the chapter, but as Jarvis points out they offer nothing new. As will be related in another chapter, student self-pacing seems to be the main technique in individualizing instruction in beginning and intermediate programs. Thus his statement regarding lack of innovation in terms of strategies for the receptive skills with individualized instruction may be quite appropriate.

Alfred N. Smith's chapter on the speaking and writing skills confirms to a large extent the conclusion of Jarvis's chapter in terms of specific strategies for individualizing the speaking and writing skills. In reviewing recently revised beginning language learning materials, Smith finds little reference to individualized learning. It seems mainly up to the teacher to devise ways of using these materials to develop the productive skills on an individual student basis. Some of the procedures to develop these skills show a modification of audiolingual practices, but little if anything startling. Even programmed learning has little to offer for the development of the speaking skill. It may be conceived that really free speaking and writing are nonprogrammable.

Strategies of instruction for speaking and writing

A review of the specific programs which do individualize instruction reveals no real new approaches to the learning of the speaking and writing skills except that more avenues of approach are open to their development than previously under more strict audiolingual procedures: group work in terms of conversation seems to be more applicable; reward and motivational activities in terms of writing are suggested; the use of the computer for the development of the writing skill is evaluated;

general approaches to curriculum are considered as having a positive effect on speaking and writing.

A review of the general methodological literature also reveals little in the individualized learning of speaking and writing skills. However, strategies for the "liberated" use of speaking are especially highlighted by Smith.

Together, these two chapters indicate that the development of truly individualized strategies for the development of language skills is as yet some time removed. At least they were not developed sufficiently in 1969 to see a particular trend. Perhaps, when individualization of instruction in foreign language has sufficiently evolved and has become mature, a comparison between the minimal kinds of strategies for skills development available today and those of the future will reveal extensive progress. The two chapters do provide, however, background which teachers and administrators might use in preparing for individualization of instruction.

In contrast to the Jarvis and Smith chapters, Logan's chapter on curriculum reveals much literature specific to individualized curricula. Although they are not extremely numerous, Logan cites those programs which have come to his attention. They represent all sections of the country, thereby indicating that individualization is not a localized phenomenon, but rather a widespread one. Logan's review of the kinds of individualization used in such programs is useful to their understanding: pacing, independent study, interest and ability grouping, remedial or enrichment grouping, specific interest grouping, interdisciplinary courses, and combinations of any of these. He also examines other elements in individualized programs such as materials, scheduling, and staff and room utilization.

Curricula for individualized instruction

The most important part of the chapter is the survey Logan provides of some of the problems which have been encountered in individualized programs. The individualization of content is perhaps the most difficult task because teachers do not have appropriate materials to work with, especially at beginning levels. At advanced levels, however, a variety of materials can be collected for individual topics. Examples are cited of the use of materials at all levels of learning. The problems of oral work, packaging the program, variety of materials, scheduling, articulation, and use and arrangement of space as well as staff indicate areas in which the profession has made some progress in individualizing instruction. Further concentration of effort in

6

these areas is dictated by the many unresolved questions that remain.

The next two chapters, by Arendt and W. Flint Smith respectively, review the literature on media and software *and* the language learning laboratory. These two chapters complement each other in showing what is being done with media and language learning laboratories that can be applied to individualized learning.

Arendt, in the introduction to his chapter, indicates how electric media have changed the students' "real world." He uses this emphasis to suggest how electric and other media are being and might be used in the classroom. He reviews the use of television and the tape recorder, and overhead, motion picture, and slide projectors. He also touches on the use of the language laboratory within the context of the Pennsylvania study.

Media in foreign language teaching

In a major section dealing with software, Arendt pays much attention to the criteria for the development of classroom materials containing a mixture of software elements. Examples of such programs are outlined. In this same section, Arendt reviews the use of software in smaller multimedia packages, where he concentrates on the contextual drill. He also analyzes the use of software in independent study, concentrating on the Unipac, programmed learning, and some of the "plans" for use of independent study.

Minor sections of the chapter, although certainly not less important, review the role of the teacher in the use of media and the importance of the learning environment in individualized programs, including the classroom, the resource center, and language center on the university level, as developed in England.

The discussion of the application of the systems analysis approach to integrated materials in foreign languages leads Arendt into a discussion of the use and benefits of the computer as a factor in language learning. Criteria for and uses of computer-assisted instructional programs are outlined and reviewed. The relationship between programmed learning and computer-assisted instruction is also probed.

In the present foreign language situation no chapter on media could avoid teacher education. Arendt reviews the use of media in helping the prospective teacher learn the second language and the effectiveness of the use of media in his own teaching.

In addition to reviewing the literature on the language learning laboratory, W. Flint Smith was given the responsibility by the editor of providing a comprehensive review to date of the Pennsylvania studies and the literature generated by them. This task is completed in the first part of the chapter. Smith's review and perspective on these studies reveals how they have jarred foreign language educators loose from complacency and forced them to look at foreign language learning elements from a more analytic and yet creative point of view.

Smith also describes some of the small-scale research projects in machine-aided second language learning. One of the studies indicated the effectiveness of record-playback equipment when used to greatest advantage. Another evaluated the results of a classroom-laboratory instructional system in an intensive learning situation. The results of the study indicate the effectiveness of media in language learning if well planned for and systematically used with appropriate materials. Other studies describe the development of auditory comprehension and the effects of short-delayed feedback using electromechanical equipment.

Another major section of Smith's chapter is devoted to the use of equipment in audio-tutorial learning and simulated tutoring. After providing the necessary definitions of the terms, which reveal their close relationship to individualized learning, Smith provides numerous examples of such strategies aided by machines: the correcting of themes and teaching of compositions, conversation with the tape recorder, recording of student dialogues, and computer-aided testing and instruction. Smith's review of the general pedagogical literature also reveals some specific uses of technology in individualized learning.

Some of the newer developments in machine learning are reviewed in the final portion of the chapter. A discussion of the use of portable laboratory systems, instant playback equipment, experimental language laboratories, radio, and cassette tape recorders makes the chapter complete. Smith, however, indicates the need for evaluation of these and other elements as well as their distribution in providing for individualized learning.

Some of the chapters in this volume are only marginally associated with the theme of individualized instruction. Their intent however is to continue the reporting of literature in specific areas such as teacher education, the teaching of classical languages, and enrollments, *or* to carry out a promise of the editor of the first volume of the *Review* by including an overview chapter on the teaching of English to speakers of other languages.

Altman and Weiss review developments in teacher education from the first volume of the *Review* through the first half of 1970 essentially. They find the profession talking about teacher education but little action seems to result.

Some trends are noticeable in terms of temporal and spatial arrangements in foreign language teacher education in the demand for longer periods of student teaching, longer professional preparation, study abroad, and the movement of methods courses out of the college and into the schools.

Another kind of use of time and space in teacher education has evolved through such experience- or performance-oriented activities as microteaching. The authors review the content of performance programs as well as the content of language-specific methods courses and other preservice curricular aspects.

In-service programs for teachers under NDEA are described by the authors as being largely demoralizing because of the "re-training" aspect. The term "advanced study" is used to describe programs which fill in gaps in basic training, which refresh knowledge about the language, and which develop the particular interests of the teacher. At least one performance-oriented program is discussed in this category.

Altman and Weiss discuss in some detail the teacher training programs for TESOL (Teaching English to Speakers of Other Languages) and SESOD (Teaching of Standard English to Speakers of Other Dialects). Qualifications, theoretical models, and a practice-centered curriculum are reviewed for teachers of SESOD. They also suggest some of the areas necessary to the preparation of teachers for bilingual programs: linguistics, psycholinguistics, developmental psycholinguistics, sociolinguistics, and social psychology. Large numbers of teachers are needed in the latter area, but few institutions prepare qualified personnel.

In the discussion about the training of college teachers of foreign languages or the lack of the same, the authors analyze a very recent survey by Hagiwara of colleges and universities regarding the training of teaching assistants. The same author and others provide examples of some of the kinds of programs which do exist for the training of such personnel. In the same vein, the training of teachers for FLES has received about as little attention as for college teachers. Programs are suggested, but they provide little if anything new.

Another important survey by Sheppard is discussed in terms of the certification of foreign language teachers. Altman and Weiss

9

point out that critics wish to remove licensure or certification of teachers from the state boards of education and allow local school boards or professional organizations to license teachers according to predetermined criteria. Sheppard's survey shows so much complexity in licensing procedures as to make inter- or intra-state standardization almost an impossibility. Teachers are still basically certified by number of hours in approved programs rather than by performance. In this area as well as others, little movement seems apparent other than more diversity in certification practices, with even more diversity proposed.

The authors' review of the training of foreign language supervisors reveals the complexity of the position and the need for a broad preparation. Their main preparation might most profitably be in methodology as well as supervision and evaluation.

Some of the graduate programs in foreign language education are also reviewed by Altman and Weiss. These programs, about eleven in number, provide the leadership and graduates capable of training FLES and secondary teachers, supervisors, and even college teachers. The programs and their diversity are underlined in the discussion of their specific characteristics.

The authors' glimpse into the future includes more realistic preservice and in-service teacher preparation programs; domination of foreign language teacher training programs by specialists; continued support of teacher training programs by the federal government; more realistic and relevant certification procedures; and coordination of programs for training teachers at all levels.

Erickson's review of the teaching of the classics, Latin and Greek, initially reveals the frustration of classicists in the decline of enrollments in Latin and Greek in all levels of formal education. He devotes much of the first part of the chapter to a review of statistics and the multiplicity of reasons for the almost disastrous decline of classics enrollments. Erickson does indicate, however, some of the support that the teaching of the classics has been given by other foreign language groups outside classics. But even more important, he reveals a militant attitude and determination on the part of classicists that the classical heritage will continue to have a place in the curricula of schools and colleges.

Classics: The teaching of Latin and Greek and classical humanities

The outline of curricula in the classics which Erickson provides shows that this determination has resulted in concrete action. Programs in the classics are being developed and tested for

10

varieties of populations. Inner-city schools in Washington, D.C., Cleveland, Detroit, and Philadelphia are examples of programs where the teaching of Latin has been particularly successful. Other programs such as an extended classics curriculum beginning in the elementary school and "spinning off" into modern Italian and classical Greek seem to be revitalizing programs in more academically oriented schools. The Latin advanced placement program for more advanced students continues to be a part of the now more diversified curriculum for secondary schools. Classical humanities and literature in translation courses on the college level are being broadened to make them more relevant to today's education scene.

In methods of teaching classical languages, Erickson notes the resistance of classics teachers to change their approaches to teaching languages. Regardless of the intransigence of some teachers, changes in methodology are taking place. Programmed learning, computer-assisted instruction, independent study, and multisensory instruction reveal new approaches to the teaching of Latin and Greek. He also discusses some of the developments in the teaching of reading and literature which are not extensive for reading, but which for the teaching of classical literature indicate some useful contributions.

Erickson's review of teacher education in the classics shows how important the EPDA Basic Studies Institute and Fellowship Programs were to the development of classics programs in secondary schools. He describes several programs which received funding from this program as well as the few "privately" sponsored ones.

The chapter closes with an exhortation to teachers of classics to look at the value of their study as a humanizing element which can contribute much to present-day life.

Developments in TESOL (Teaching English to Speakers of Other Languages) are discussed in a chapter by Spolsky. Such a review was promised for Volume Two by Birkmaier in the introduction to the first volume of the *Review*. This chapter provides an understanding of the acronym, moving on to explore a theory *TESOL* of TESOL. This exploration reveals literature which discusses the relationship of linguistics, psychology of learning, and pedagogy to the teaching of English as a second language. From the presentation of such literature the emerging view of language, language learning, and language teaching is one of complexity. The simple solutions to language learning suggested

11

by the audiolingual approach have been replaced by new understandings of language and its acquisition, which, because of
their complexity, have not yet formed a theory of second language learning. Spolsky suggests that such a theory may be
some distance in the future.

Spolsky reviews the relationship of TESOL to the national
scene. He indicates a very direct relationship with bilingual programs and teaching of English to speakers of other languages.
He reviews Mackey's bilingual model, Fishman's work in the
study of a bilingual community, and Galvan and Troike's development of curriculum materials based on a study of languages and dialects in East Texas as examples of useful kinds
of research. He also draws attention to the teaching of English
to American Indians, the curricula developed for them, and the
attention to the contrastive studies completed in Navajo, Cree,
Choctaw, and Papago. The relationship between TESOL and
the teaching of Standard English to speakers of other dialects is
presented. Spolsky discusses the major issues involved: How
different is standard English from nonstandard dialects? To
what extent are principles and practices of TESOL applicable to
SESOD?

In reviewing TESOL literature in methods and testing, Spolsky indicates that there is little new in methods. What has been
written either develops earlier notions and techniques or
modifies standard teaching practices. Methods of teaching, he
suggests, are being consolidated with no one method found superior. The developments in testing TESOL parallel somewhat
those in other foreign languages, with emphasis being placed on
testing for specific objectives.

In a final section, Spolsky reviews the programs suggested or
those in operation to find guidelines for the development of
TESOL teachers. Some commonalities exist between the two, but
some rather important differences are indicated by the variety of
programs. Spolsky relates the intention of the TESOL organization to develop guidelines for teacher training to countermand
the variety of programs as a step toward professionalization of
the field.

The chapter on "Trends in Foreign Language Enrollments" by
Richard Brod brings into focus ten years of foreign language
enrollments, from 1958–1968, for secondary schools. The base
year for reporting college enrollments was 1960, so that enrollment figures reported for higher education reflect only an eight-

year period. However, enrollments on both levels show a leveling off and in some cases serious decline as especially noticed in the Latin and Russian enrollments on the secondary school level.

Brod carefully analyzes the studies of secondary school and college enrollments showing both the kinds of information offered by them as well as the many inadequacies and differences in reporting they contain. He concludes that regardless of the faults such surveys possess, they are nevertheless useful in terms of decision-making.

In order to make secondary school foreign language census reports more meaningful and complete, Brod recommends that such studies be supplemented by periodic sampling of a limited number of schools which could provide more precise information affecting enrollments. Quality of teaching, method, patterns of administrative policy, and community attitudes, among others, might be some of these factors. He presents several studies which attempt to go beyond the mere collection of numbers of students, but which do not really evaluate or collect information about student reaction to the instructional milieu.

Trends in foreign language enrollments

The author isolates some of the more innovative aspects of the college studies, including their wide distribution and inclusion of summer school data and the number of student contact hours. In turn, he compares general college enrollment figures between 1965 and 1968 with enrollments in the major foreign languages studied at that level during the same period. The result indicates very clearly that enrollments in these languages are on the decline. Some of this decline, perhaps a major portion of it, is traced to the reduction of the B.S. and B.A. entrance and degree requirements.

The decline in enrollments relates to the supply and demand for teachers on all levels. Brod points out the relationship between economic factors and the cutbacks in foreign language programs. Among other factors, relatively large numbers of teachers on all levels were "produced" in the early sixties, making the supply greater than the demand at the end of the decade. The projection for the future is not clear, but from the present trend the future of foreign language enrollments appears ominous. Brod suggests that means other than entrance and degree requirements will have to be found on the secondary and college level as a means of keeping a captive audience. And with that statement, the necessity for more individualized instruction arises as a possibility for keeping an audience.

It is hoped that the main emphasis of this volume will provide an understanding of individualized instruction and contribute in even a small way to the reversal of the trend away from foreign language study in our schools and colleges.

References, Introduction: Theme and overview

1 Birkmaier, Emma M. "Introduction," 1–12 in Emma M. Birkmaier,ed., *Britannica Review of Foreign Language Education, Volume I.* Chicago: Encyclopaedia Britannica, 1968[1969].

2 Henry, Nelson B.,ed. *Part I. Learning and Instruction.* The Forty-Ninth Yearbook of the National Society for the Study of Education. Chicago: Univ. of Chicago Press, 1950.

3 Lange, Dale L.,ed. "1969 ACTFL Annual Bibliography of Books and Articles on Pedagogy in Foreign Languages." *Foreign Language Annals* 3(1970):627–73.

4 Mildenberger, Andrea S., and Simi Satlin. "ERIC Documents on the Teaching of Foreign Languages:List Number 2." *Foreign Language Annals* 2(1969):361–68.

5 _____ and Carol Wood. "ERIC Documents on the Teaching of Foreign Languages:List Number 3." *Foreign Language Annals* 3(1969):113–27.

6 Whipple, Guy M.,ed. *Part II. Adapting the Schools to Individual Differences.* The Twenty-Fourth Yearbook of the National Society for the Study of Education. Bloomington, Illinois: Public School Publishing Company, 1925.

2

A rationale for the individualization and personalization of foreign-language instruction

Introduction

Lorraine A. Strasheim
Indiana University

Instruction, as Marker & Mehlinger (30) point out in their article "School, Politics, Rebellion, and Other Youthful Interests," has historically been controlled by the teacher.

The details for carrying out the primary task of the schools — instruction — are left to the teacher. In this role, he may expect a number of conflicts. First of all, he is likely to face students who have no special desire to learn what he wishes to teach. They did not choose his course but were assigned to him by a counselor, a member of the administrative team. While a teacher has some flexibility regarding how the course will be taught, he is expected to cover specified content during the year in order that his students will be ready for the courses that lie ahead. Even the books he will use often have been chosen by others, perhaps a state textbook committee, an administrator, sometimes a committee of teachers.

Teacher-centered instruction

In foreign language instruction, whatever the prevailing philosophy or objective priorities, students have been called upon to "sit and listen to the teacher" and are "required to *remember*" (Postman & Weingartner, 35) in what Hocking (24) calls teaching "in single formation, by one person facing and haranguing 25 to 30 younger persons who are lined up like a glee club." The result is what Goodman (13) terms an "inflexible lock-step." The student never takes notes or listens very carefully to the recitation of his peers. The "core" of the course is not to be found in the words of other students — the words of other students are not to be found on tests (35).

The principle underlying what Shepherd (39) identifies as the "teacher-centered class" is that there is some defined corpus of basic and static facts which must be mastered before the student is ready for activities which are personally interesting and meaningful (Barber, 2). The curriculum guides underscore this principle that there is a sort of "ideal" sequence and content, or at least that there is a single sequence and a single basic content to be recommended (*Minnesota Guide for Instruction in*

Modern Foreign Languages Grades 4–12, 21; Grittner, 16,17, 18,19). This assumption of a "recommended" sequence and a "recommended" content has been accompanied by a "recommended" set of teaching methods. There is a single philosophic and "mechanical" thrust in the books published about foreign language teaching in the mid- to late sixties (Grittner, 20; Rivers, 36). Methods has been the area of concentration of foreign language meetings and considerations since the immediate post-Sputnik years. The author told the first meeting of the reorganized Central States Conference on the Teaching of Foreign Languages in 1969 that "our methods convictions have not only dictated our 'how's' but also our 'what,' the content, more often than not. The rationales we talk about are more appropriately rationales for certain methods than for foreign-language study itself" (Strasheim, 42). In this authoritarian atmosphere, individualized instruction consists of giving the high achiever an extra book to read, an extra assignment to complete, or an extra report to make. The low achiever, in this model, is given additional help with the prescribed work of the course. Foreign language educators in the "lockstep" instructional process, whether traditional or audiolingual in orientation, have tended to behave "as if the sole function of the elementary school were to prepare the student for the secondary school and the secondary school only to meet the 'requirements' of the college or university" (42).

A great deal of what has happened in foreign language instruction (and what has *not* happened) is directly attributable to the constraint of the college requirement. Hocking (24) points out that "millions of dollars of public funds, and millions of children in public schools, are subordinated to two archaic assumptions by higher education: first, that the principal function of the schools is college-preparatory: and second, that the advanced study of 'language' must in fact be the study of literature. The acceptance of these assumptions distorts language teaching in general, and teacher training in particular." In what the author calls "tunnel vision," the focus of all foreign language teaching has been upon the actual or assumed requirements of college and university departments. In "What the Colleges Expect of the High Schools," Hartwig (22) asks: "But should there be a placement problem at all? If we told the high schools what levels of achievement their pupils need to reach in order, later in college, 'to make the grade' and if at the same time we helped them push

The effects of college requirements on secondary school FL programs

16

their charges to the expected achievement levels, then there would be no placement problems for us to struggle with. And the old formula might work again, to wit: 'Two years of high school foreign language training equals one year of F.L. college work!' " This definition of what high school foreign language instruction and learning should be came at a time when colleges and universities were assessing their requirements and revamping them, often drastically; it was formed at a time when school foreign language educators were being asked to defend foreign language's legitimacy in the curriculum. The foreign language teacher in the elementary or secondary school has historically been more closely related to the college professor than to his colleagues in the school in which he teaches. This approach has meant that the college requirement imposed, very subtly but very effectively, many restrictions upon the lower levels of the sequence. The objective priorities and the content of the school offerings were of necessity directed toward the "advanced study" prescriptions of the college or university and an "elite" student population, the college bound, was admitted to study. The greatest cost of this orientation has been that foreign language teachers have not participated in the curricular innovations that have been taking place in the schools—the varied time scheduling arrangements, the experimentation with varied types of grouping for instruction, and interdisciplinary planning for integrated course offerings.

Because foreign language instruction had a single direction, FLES (foreign language in the elementary school) was almost destroyed. FLES educators had to turn to other elementary educators in an effort to give FLES a broader curriculum base in the elementary school. It became apparent that FLES could not survive in this environment unless, like all the other offerings of the elementary school, it could be integrated horizontally as well as vertically in the curriculum. Every foreign language student, no matter where he began his studies, as a third grader, a junior high or middle school student, or as a high school freshman, has been treated as a "major" from the day of his enrollment (Strasheim, 41). The prevailing atmosphere in foreign language education, until the mid- to late sixties, was not one in which the individualization of instruction could be discussed. During the sixties, however, the school, the college and the university, and society were changing and being changed in radical and dramatic ways.

How does FLES fit?

17

Change changed

Heraclitus wrote that "nothing endures but change," but, as Postman & Weingartner (35) point out, *change changed*—in our time the *degree of change* is what is really different. The questions which arose in American society in the sixties found every possible divisible segment of society trying to determine *how* it was valuable; no segment was interested in being told *how valuable* it was. Friedenberg's discussion of self-appraisal as a qualitative rather than a quantitative question began to apply to all societal groupings as well as to the adolescent (10). *The best rationale for the individualization or personalization of all instruction lies in the demands for recognition of individual worth being made by all the various segments of society.* President John F. Kennedy (27) in an address at American University in Washington, D.C., in 1963 said: "Let us not be blind to our differences—but let us also direct attention to our common interests and the means by which those differences can be resolved. And if we cannot end now our differences, at least we can help to make the world safe for diversity." Today Black Panthers, student dissidents, Mexican-Americans, Indians, women—every possible societal group—are pleading for a life "safe for diversity." Weisbord (43) points out that black students, Mexican-Americans, and American Indians want recognition of their unique origins and identities. Postman & Weingartner suggest that the violence often associated with one or another of these groups' attempts to win recognition stems from the fact that frustration makes violence the only possible form of statement (35). In any event the questions which Shane (38) identifies as the queries of basic importance in education have assumed basic importance for every man, of every age, in every walk of life, in our society:

1 Who am I? (self-identity)
2 What am I doing? (self-orientation)
3 Where am I going? (self-direction)

In the societal upheaval that has resulted from the attempts of the various segments of the whole to assert their right to diversity and the worth of diversity, the Melting Pot ideal in the United States came to an end. The student's role in an environment of accelerated change becomes more complex than ever before in

Best rationale for individualization of instruct

18

history, for, as Becker (3) says, "Society no longer lets the young stay naive. Informed by the mass media, urged by parents and teachers to question, the students are more sensitive to the larger world than were previous generations." Add to that group of "more sensitive students" the disadvantaged children Smith (40) identifies as "not clear [about] what their lives are for and what is worth working for" and who are not given the chance to "experience success, realize [their] own worth, and be equipped to make choices from the alternatives available to [them]" and the societal-educational challenge becomes almost beyond mental grasp, much less actual solution.

Societal upheavals have caused great tumult for the schools and colleges. This tumult has resulted from what Barber (2) identifies as a narrowly conceived concept of education.

Effects of societal changes on education

Introducing change into complex social systems is always difficult, but I suspect that the hiatus that presently exists is due at least in part to the fact that the practice of teaching is based on a narrow, constrained concept of education. The concept of education dominant in our society and reflected in the practices of our schools is that of the traditional formal training in the academic disciplines. This system hands down to the student the knowledge and values accumulated by the culture. We have, in a sense, talked *at* the student about the knowledge and values of the culture instead of talking *with* him. The pupil becomes a passive recipient of the culture instead of an active participant in its examination, evaluation, and change. The natural product of such a system is usually an informed, conforming individual who is a "cultural product" in the passive sense. This cultural product is turned out by a teacher who can bring together the necessary information that the culture wants passed on and who then presents the material and evaluates whether or not students can take it in and re-present it.

This concept of education does not allow for what Mark Twain called the "Master Passion" and what he defined as the "hunger for self-approval." This concept of education makes all students undergo some indoctrination and some alteration to fit the pattern established in the culture. It does not recognize (Marker & Mehlinger, 30) "that teen-agers are a remarkable subgroup in American society, perhaps unique in human history. It is a group with its own symbols, language, values, status system,

19

interests, and activities. A flow of children move through this adolescent society before they emerge to accept roles as adult citizens. The culture of American teen-agers is not only influenced by the total American society, but it in turn influences the total society." Against a backdrop of "changed change," this narrow concept ignores Goodman's argument that "it is not necessary to plan for Society," that "society is inevitably present in any school in how the children are, what the youth aspire to, what the teachers have mastered and can teach." He contends that the problem is to outgrow this society through scholarship (13). So narrow an interpretation of education's purpose in the whole of society assumes that society has ready answers for the problems confronting it, not, as Greenleaf suggests, that the United States has no clear-cut definitions even of its priorities (15): "Today, several things come first, hundreds second, and tens of thousands third as the United States—rich, powerful, yet deeply troubled—tries to thrash its way through a jungle of competing, conflicting needs and desires to reach Utopia which, we want to believe, lies within a day's or a decade's march." Becker (3) suggests that today's societal environment requires that education move from a relatively passive role to one of leadership in the process of social change if the current demands for both equality of opportunity and social justice are to be met. The Honorable Robert H. Finch, former secretary of the Department of Health, Education and Welfare, underscores Becker when he says that "too often we are stuffing the heads of the young with the products of earlier innovation rather than teaching them how to innovate," that we are treating student minds "as storehouses to be filled rather than as instruments to be used" (9). Educators must be concerned with the movements and concerns of society as they plan for the future if their "clients" are to avoid future shock. Postman & Weingartner assert that the consequences of future shock are as destructive for society as for the sufferers of this phenomenon (35).

"Future shock"

Future shock occurs when you are confronted by the fact that the world you were educated to believe in doesn't exist. Your images of reality are apparitions that disappear on contact. There are several ways of responding to such a condition, one of which is to withdraw and allow oneself to be overcome by a sense of impotence. More commonly, one continues to act *as if* his apparitions were substantial, relentlessly pursuing a course of action that he knows will fail him. You may have noticed that there are scores of political, social, and religious leaders who are clearly suffering from advanced cases of future shock. They repeat over and over again the words that are supposed to represent the world about them. But nothing seems to work out. And then they repeat the words again and again. Alfred Korzybski used a somewhat different metaphor to describe what we have been calling "future shock." He likened one's language to a map. The map is intended to describe the territory that we call "reality," i.e., the world outside of our skins. When there is a close correspondence between map and territory, there tends to be a high degree of effective functioning, especially where it relates to survival. When there is little correspondence between map and territory, there is a strong tendency for entropy to make substantial gains. In this context, the terrifying question, What did you learn in school today? assumes immense importance for all of us. We just may not survive another generation of inadvertent entropy helpers.

Birmingham would contend that these questions are particularly vital in regard to the high school, for the high school activists believe that their movements will have greater impact on education *and* society than the college movements, pointing out that "high school is responsible at one time or another for the education of all young people in America" (4). In order to make decisions about the individualization and personalization of instruction, we must know more about the individuals we are discussing and much more about their world. As we look at the student's world, however, we must keep Dennison's comments in mind, for the student has the same reservations as the scientist and the philosopher: "For given the current crisis in education, the question, How can we improve our schools? would satisfy neither the scientist nor the philosopher. Both would ask instead, How can we educate our young?" (8).

How do we educate our youth?

The student's world

Holt contends that we have separated learning and living in our schools to such a degree that the child's self-concept is virtually destroyed in the process. " 'You come to school to learn,' we say, as if the child hadn't been learning before, as if living were out there and learning were in here and there were no connection

21

between the two," implying that "he cannot be trusted to learn and is no good at it" (25). If this dichotomy of school and life is related to the concept that the pupil must be imbued with the culture, we find that we are ignoring the impact of the mass media, an impact which McLuhan says has been a kind of "release" of monoculturism. Simultaneously with the minority's rejection of the tacit direction to become part of the American majority's monoculturism, there is McLuhan's assertion that in the past "most people have accepted their cultures as a fate, like climate or vernacular; but our emphatic awareness of the exact modes of many cultures is in itself a liberation from them as prisons" (32).

Not only is the student's world filled with "mass" media—it is filled with "mass" everything. Hills & Hills (23) make this abundantly clear:

The "mass" in the student's world

> The central forces at work in contemporary American society —industrialization, urbanization, and bureaucratization—all tend toward standardization and depersonalization of our lives. The agents of these forces—mass production, mass marketing, mass communication, mass education, and so on—all lead us rapidly toward the evolving mass society. But while the nation as a whole may be becoming less diverse, each individual's experience is of a greater variety of worlds and ways, confronting him with more choices but many fewer reasons, codes, and norms to guide him to any particular choice. Against the tendencies toward standardization stand such forces of discrimination and differentiation as religion, race and class—all aspects of a social order that is in the process of disintegration.

Clark (7), however, points out that there are simultaneously people who have no rights in any real sense, people who seemingly have no choices.

People without rights and choices

> There are places in each city where people have no rights in the real sense. A right is not what someone gives you but what no one can take from you. There is an uneasy order in these places, but little law. If the poor save up and buy a television, as they do, and if when they get it home the tube does not work, and the person who sold it to them knew it when he sold it, what can they do? Sue? How? If they are lucky they may find a Neighborhood Legal Services Office or legal aid, but

22

the chances are very slim. The people who live there have no power.

For the middle class student and above the world is full of norms and codes that no longer serve; for the lower class student and the disadvantaged of every type the world is without options, without hope. Today's student, says Gossage (14), is smarter than the older generations: ". . . what the hell, I was young once myself. I *was* — but not like that. For one thing I wasn't as smart as that. Also, this teen-age revolution has been going on for quite a few years now and the early crop is getting up in its late twenties. And I wasn't like them when I was twenty-six either."

The world of the student is populated with adults who stand *The generations* with one foot in each of two worlds — one that once existed and one that is coming into existence, a kaleidoscopic existence that alters just as one grasps it. The older generations "practice" one world and "intellectualize" the other, while the student *lives* in the single world available to him, a world which has forced him to come to grips with some realizations about his society that the adults in his life space have not yet grasped — and may never. One such concept is Boyd's "community" which "isn't a *place* but a state of being, fluid and on-going, marked less by a post-office address than [by] an attitude shared by persons." Like Boyd, the student is convinced that "no one makes a community; he accepts community where and as it *is*" (5).

Bruner has called for the end of what he calls the "non-controversial and banal" and attacks the "embarrassment of passion" which leads to the banal in teaching. He says that the Old *Schools for what?* Testament, the Greek myths, the Norse legends, and such writings are the chronicles of men of passion (6). In this same regard, Leonard (29) suggests what students *"already need"* while asking "Schools for what?":

— To learn the commonly-agreed-upon skills and knowledge of the ongoing culture (reading, writing, figuring, history, and the like), to learn it joyfully and to learn that all of it, even the most sacred "fact," is strictly tentative.
— To learn how to ring creative changes on all that is currently agreed upon.
— To learn delight, not aggression; sharing, not eager acquisition; uniqueness, not narrow competition.
— To learn heightened awareness and control of emotional,

sensory and bodily states and, through this, increased empathy for other people (a new kind of citizenship education).

— To learn how to enter and enjoy varying states of consciousness, in preparation for a life of change.

— To learn how to explore and enjoy the infinite possibilities in relations between people, perhaps the most common form of ecstasy.

— To learn how to learn, for learning — one word that includes singing, dancing, interacting and much more — is already becoming the main purpose of life.

Nyman, writing in the underground high school paper *Smuff* in New Jersey (34), makes some of the following suggestions for an independent student study program. They do not differ substantially from Leonard's above.

The student and the schools — an individual's view

— . . . we see that what is palmed off as an education is largely a collection of fact and information, a collection of required readings and required subjects and electives that have no meaning to our lives. Physics, French, U.S. history, English all being taught (with the emphasis on the teaching not the learning) to get people into college, to complete requirements, to proliferate lies; being taught because they "have" to be taught, and being taught not to help us cope with and try to save the dying world we will take over or to help us cope with and save each other, but because they are on a list of "available subjects."

— In Philadelphia there is a full-fledged program of independent studies — a school without walls — which has been a great success. There the Students learn U.S. history in the ghetto where history manifested itself, biology in the concrete jungle, on the banks of the polluted rivers where man has destroyed the biological balances, English from people who've lived. No one forced a course on them and no one deprived them of courses they wanted, because somebody out there understood that no one learns something he has no interest in. And if you say that Students won't learn something when they're out of the cage, it becomes obvious you were wasting your time with him in it.

— "Supplementary studies," being anything that the group felt was not being given in their regular courses and which they wanted. . . . The group could then publish a paper so that

24

the Students (especially the Students in the classes that were not getting the truth) would have available to them an objective (or clearly opinionated) and well researched challenge to what the teacher(s) said was truth.

— Independent studies can go in two directions: they can be individuals learning on their own, or they can be study groups who communicate as Students and learn together. . . .
— The debate (an informal, un-ruled debate) is sadly ignored by many teachers even though it is undisputably the easiest to arrange and the most productive of all variations on the teaching method. Everyone has opinions and no one's opinions are so sacred and perfect that they can't be argued and possibly altered (I wonder how certain teachers would fare in a debate where they couldn't "give notes" and had to support their filthy prejudices).
— "Communication games" would be a real test of the viability of the group and their own ingenuity: Communication between the "groupers" is artificially impeded in some way (just as there are barriers in our society between people that aren't real; for instance, if you're black or Puerto Rican you're suddenly "one of them," you're different and though we might talk we can't communicate, or you look like a crew-cut fascist to me, or you're old, or talk with a Southern drawl or for gawd's sake you're a hippy and I can't make somebody like you understand) and to achieve the goals of the group the impediments have to be overcome, put aside or obliterated. . . .
— . . . *We hope* that even if you're skeptical or think *Smuff* is a dirty rag or think I'm a dirty rag or you lean heavily to the "right"—no matter where your head is at—we hope you'll be with us, we need you to work with us, not for *Smuff* or us, but to prove something, to let *them* know that Students aren't mindless, unimaginative, plastic robots who have to be led around by teachers to produce, to learn.
— Just this once prove you're not apathetic—you'll make or break student power.

What the students are trying to communicate is what Holt responds in answer to a question from the editors of *Education News* in New York City that asks what American schools might do to "take a giant step forward this year toward a better tomorrow." His response is "to let every child be the planner, director,

The student as planner

25

and assessor of his own education, to allow and encourage him, with the inspiration and guidance of more experienced and expert people, and as much help as he asked for, to decide what he is to learn, when he is to learn it, how he is to learn it, and how well he is learning it" (25). The same basic opinion of what can be done to help the student in his world is expressed by Gibbons (12).

> A stifling educational program can be ventilated by an explosion (and likely will be at the present rate of revolution), but how much more profitable to do now what should have been done long ago—open up alternatives, giving students choice, greater control over their schooling, and a greater measure of freedom. But it would likely be a mistake to substitute one fixed program for another. Is there any reason why several routes and rates through any course or program cannot be tolerated within the same structure (except that it is administratively easier not to)? Try substituting diversity for singularity.

Lawson (28) makes an effort to keep foreign languages in the student's world when he challenges the foreign language profession with: "Your response to diversity may well determine whether foreign languages will be part of the curriculum of the future."

Foreign language diversity

In the mid-sixties all schools and all education fell under critical eyes; students called for "relevance" and all other segments of the population demanded "accountability." Because FLES was the newest entry into the whole of foreign language education, it was the most vulnerable and suffered almost immediately from the intense scrutiny. In November 1968, the American Council on the Teaching of Foreign Languages and the Indiana Language Program cosponsored FLES Symposium I in Minneapolis, Minnesota. Allen & Paquette assembled the papers presented at this conference into a document entitled *The Student's World Is the World: New Dimensions in the Teaching of FLES* (1). The Symposium brought together FLES and foreign language specialists with elementary educators to explore the possibilities for the evolution of a broader rationale for FLES programs integrated into elementary education. The publication is somewhat a departure in professional publication, for it does not give guide-

The FLES Symposium

lines or prescriptions. It is a discussion document designed to extend the dialogues begun in Minneapolis. It provides reports of trends in American elementary education, including psychology and learning, curriculum, organization, administration, supervision, the emerging language arts curriculum, and the developing social studies program. The section on "Managing Change" defines a single school approach to an extension of the dialogue begun in the publication and represents both diversity and individualization; "Managing Change" (1) includes the following topics for team planning within the elementary school.

1 What are the objectives of the FLES program as it now exists?

2 What are the needs of the student population we are trying to reach?

3 What is the overall school design and teaching philosophy?

4 What kinds of content and what instructional strategies are the other subject-matter areas employing in their efforts to fit into a total curriculum responsive to student needs?

5 What kinds of foreign-language learnings best relate to the student needs and/or complement and reinforce his other learnings?

6 What kind of foreign-language program, incorporating the identified learnings, must be designed to be well integrated into the total curriculum?

FLES team planning for the individual school

This approach to the structuring of FLES programs is designed to provide *school individualization*. The result should be a diversity which does not presume that all enrollees are to become college and university majors in foreign language. Much the same approach is taken in *Modern Foreign Language in Ohio Elementary Schools* (33), although in a more modified fashion. In this publication, it is pointed out that the present mobility of the U.S. population precludes the continuous sequential learnings most long sequences assume, recommending that the experience offered should be meaningful in and of itself, especially in cultural studies and in the study of language as an entity. Masciantonio (31) outlines a Latin FLES program which has as its objectives: "To extend the verbal functioning of children in English through a study of Latin roots and affixes and a contrastive analysis with a classical language; To broaden the cultural horizons of children through the comparison of classical civilization to their own; To teach children to understand and speak

An example of individualized school objectives

Latin; eventually to read and write it." Individualization and personalization of instruction can relate to the needs of student populations as well as to the needs of individuals.

Secondary school foreign language curriculum, too, is being diversified. The American Council on the Teaching of Foreign Languages, the Indiana Language Program, and the National Association of Secondary-School Principals cosponsored a Secondary-School Symposium on Foreign-Language Curricula in Bloomington, Indiana, in 1969. Although the symposium was intended to focus on curricular innovation, it soon became apparent that the program participants were all involved with the individualization and personalization of instruction. The Mc-Cluer Plan in St. Louis County, Missouri, is experimenting with team teaching, differentiated learning experiences, flexible scheduling, and nongraded curricula. The Nathan Hale High School Program (Seattle) emphasizes independent study and FL seminars in conjunction with a contract plan. Part of the presentation of the Foreign Language Innovative Curricula Studies (FLICS) project of the state of Michigan discussed Afro-French studies. Marshall-University High School personnel (Minneapolis) explained their use of "individualized" modules (minicourses) and individualized instruction which permit students to approach language study through materials of their choice, materials responsive to individual learning strategies.[1]

The Secondary School Symposium

Both Samuels (37) and Jakobovits (26) warn of the dangers of seeking justification for teaching methods used in *scientifically* based learning theories. Samuels (37) says that "it would seem that the best justification for an educational method should rest not on theory but on empirical investigations that provide information on the efficacy of the method in terms of helping students to achieve the course objectives." Jakobovits (26) provides a series of guidelines to the corrective measures that are needed.

1 There is no single "proper" goal for FL study that can "logically" be demonstrated.
2 The goals of a particular course in a FL program must be clearly defined in specific terms that specify the terminal knowledge and skills to be reached.

Guidelines for objectives in individualized programs

---

1 All of these programs are reported in the Indiana Language Program publication, *Foreign Language in a New Apprenticeship for Living*, now in press. This report of the ACTFL, ILP, NASSP secondary symposia will be available in fall 1970.

3 Not only must we recognize variable goals and interests in FL study, but also variable abilities and FL aptitude.

4 The question of when FLs are to be taught within our educational system is a complex problem that involves political, social, philosophical, and psychological considerations and should not be reduced to a matter of neurophysiology, as it has become fashionable to do in recent years.

5 More serious attention must be given to the sociopsychological ramifications of FL study.

6 Global comparisons between "methods of instruction" are unrealistic.

7 It is necessary to take seriously the oft quoted distinction between competence and performance, between knowledge and behavior.

8 The instructional process involved in the teaching of a FL must take proper account of the existence of a "folk linguistics," a term used here to refer to assumptions that individuals hold about language and language acquisition.

Samuels compensates for many of these cautions with a Model of the Teaching Process (37).

Diversity is developing in foreign language education. It has risen out of dissatisfaction with the outcomes of past instruction and out of the demands all segments of the population are making of their schools. The removal of the college-requirement constraint makes possible (and imperative) the development of programs responsive to the students being served if foreign language is to remain a part of the curriculum of the American school. In considering ways and means of diversification, however, foreign language educators must be well aware of some of the most vital reasons for reassessing and restructuring foreign language offerings. Lawson (28) says: "It is becoming increasingly difficult for administrators to document the accelerating need of funds for a discipline that affects so few." He adds a question to which FL specialists must find an answer: "Is it not possible to have 75 to 100 percent of our secondary students studying a foreign language at the end of the next decade?" The author reminded the administrator-teacher teams present at Secondary Symposium I in Bloomington, Indiana, that in Indiana, 65% of all beginning foreign language students enter second year; 29% of these second year students continue into third year; only about 31% of those in third year will enter the fourth.

The development of diversity in foreign language education

29

At the present time 65 of a beginning 100 students enter second year; 19 of the original 100 survive into the third year and 6 into the fourth. She called upon the participants to devise foreign language programs that will have intrinsic holding power, to devise foreign language programs that will be addressed to the 92 of every beginning 100 who are not college bound foreign language majors. Gardner (11) provides another reminder that foreign language specialists have required over and over again in the past: "In the United States, college professors who look at secondary education with a critical eye almost invariably start from the mistaken assumption that the highest function of the secondary school is to prepare youngsters for college. That isn't true. The first purposes of American education are to foster individual fulfillment in all children and to nurture the free, rational, responsible men and women without whom our kind of society cannot endure." Shane's questions (38) are inherent in diversification, individualization, and personalization, but the answers to "Who am I?" "What am I doing?" and "Where am I going?" are not to be *provided by* the school or the subject-matter area —only the opportunity to find the answers is to be *provided to* the student.

Conclusion

Individualized instruction has been used as a cover term for a more precise prescription of the work to be done or the provision of the freedom to do the work at one's own pace. Either of these two approaches might be better termed *individualized pacing*. In using this term, no value judgment of either performance criteria defined in foreign language offerings or continuous or nongraded programs is intended. It is used here only to clarify the goals of a foreign language program. Individualized pacing provides activities, tasks, and instructions which are teacher imposed. Individualized "instruction" implies provision for varied learning strategies and varied modes of attack. *Personalized instruction* provides the student with the opportunity to utilize the school's totality to construct his own instructional program. As Shane says (38): "The individualized, and sometimes nongraded, approach to instruction was a distinct improvement, since it endeavored to shorten or lengthen the Procrustean bed to fit the child. The personalized curriculum continuum, on the other hand, is one in which the child, with teacher guidance, is

Individualized instruction an pacing; personalized instruct

encouraged—indeed expected—to *build his own bed*."

There is certainly room in American education for a myriad of foreign language programs, each with its own objective priorities and expected learning outcomes, so long as the guidelines of Jakobovits cited earlier or some comparable set of guides are used. Throughout, the teacher or the "head" teacher must serve as the "quality control." No real learning will be sacrificed unless the programs, whatever their goals, are permitted to become something other than what they profess to be by the teachers in command. There are several "propositions" which may be useful in planning whatever form of individualized instructional plan is being considered.

1 Foreign language is *one* of the vehicles by which *some* students can be given greater options in their environment and be taught to control their environment more fully.

Propositions for planning individualized instruction

What kind of options can foreign languages give students who are not willing to continue study for protracted periods of time? Can foreign language offerings be devised by which some change of behavior or some knowledge is imparted *through* the foreign language—either other subject matter in the foreign language or societal-attitudinal change through the foreign language experience?

2 Foreign language curricula cannot be predicated wholly upon college and university requirements as in the past.

What expertise can our college and university personnel offer the schools in devising curricula other than that for the college preparatory student? Should all first year (and second year) offerings be taught solely from the first-step-in-a-long-sequence standpoint or can there be provision for the types of learnings that make any experience of any duration worthwhile as an independent entity?

3 Strong efforts should be made to involve 65 to 75% of the total school population in foreign language studies by 1980.

Can we continue to fight for a place in the curriculum for a discipline which only 30% (or less) of the total population of the school ever study in any way? What segments of the school population who have never been interested in foreign languages can we reach through offerings deliberately designed for them?

4 The rationale for foreign language should be developed through team planning by foreign language specialists, with their colleagues in other subject-matter areas and

31

with students, to broaden the curriculum base for foreign languages in the schools.

5 Every avenue leading to curriculum improvement should be explored: interdisciplinary approaches, interdisciplinary planning, methods studies to determine method efficacy in accomplishing objectives, attitude studies to determine student reaction to the ideas in the course content, time and space organizational plans, grouping for instruction, and teaching models.

In the entire process the teacher must be prepared to change himself or herself and some of his or her most cherished ideas about what "keeping school" really means and what constitutes real learning.

The author (41) suggests that FL specialists will have to learn to accept objective hierarchies of this sort:

For All Students

To contribute to the student's intellectual, social, aesthetic, and emotional growth through foreign language study in an effort to assist the student toward a more positive approach to other peoples through in-depth experiences with the thought processes and social behavior of native speakers and thus help him to interpret and cope with the societies he will encounter in life.

Goals for students

For Some Students (Some will achieve all, some one, some varied combinations)

To provide the student with skills that will enable him to communicate orally with speakers of another language and with people of other nationalities who have also learned this language, taking great care to attribute cultural meaning to all learnings.

To provide the student with skills which will enable him to communicate in writing with speakers of another language and with people who have also learned this language, taking great care to attribute cultural meaning to all learnings.

| To teach the student to read the foreign language so that he may keep abreast of modern writing, research, and information. | OR | To provide the student with an introductory knowledge and personal experience of the literature of the speakers of the foreign language. |

To increase the student's understanding of how language functions and to bring him, through the study of a foreign language, to a greater awareness of the functioning of his own language.

Ideally, of course, at the head of the priority list there should be recognition of the student's motivation in objectives labeled *For Me*.

References, A rationale for the individualization and personalization of foreign language instruction

1 Allen, Virginia G., and F. André Paquette,eds. *The Student's World Is the World:New Dimensions in the Teaching of FLES*. Bloomington: The Indiana Language Program, Indiana Univ., 1969

2 Barber, William H. "Keynote Address, San Francisco, 1965–66 TEPS Conference," 30–42 in Roy A. Edelfelt,ed., *Remaking the World of the Career Teacher*. Washington, D.C.: National Commission on Teacher Education and Professional Standards, National Education Association, 1966.

3 Becker, James M. "A Course in Questions Without Answers," 101–07 in *The School and the Democratic Environment*. Papers and other materials drawn from a Conference sponsored by the Danforth Foundation and the Ford Foundation. New York: Columbia Univ. Press, 1970.

4 Birmingham, John,ed. *Our Time Is Now*. New York: Praeger, 1970.

5 Boyd, Malcolm. *Free to Live, Free to Die*. New York: New American Library, 1969.

6 Bruner, Jerome S. "Learning and Thinking," 70–77 in Editors of *Teachers College Record* and *Harvard Educational Review*,comps., *Problems and Issues in Contemporary Education*. Glenview, Illinois: Scott Foresman, 1968.

7 Clark, Ramsey. "It's Time for Change; Are Schools Up to It?" 29–37 in *The School and the Democratic Environment*. Papers and other materials drawn from a Conference sponsored by the Danforth Foundation and the Ford Foundation. New York: Columbia Univ. Press, 1970.

8 Dennison, George. *The Lives of Children:The Story of the First Street School*. New York: Random House, 1969.

9 Finch, Robert H. "That Question of Relevancy," 17–28 in *The School and the Democratic Environment*. Papers and other materials drawn from a Conference sponsored by the Danforth Foundation and the Ford Foundation. New York: Columbia Univ. Press. 1970.

10 Friedenberg, Edgar Z. *The Vanishing Adolescent*. Boston: Beacon Press, 1964. [Introd. by David Riesman.]

11 Gardner, John W. *No Easy Victories*. New York: Harper and Row, 1968.

12 Gibbons, Maurice. "Changing Secondary Education Now." *The Bulletin of the National Association of Secondary School Principals*. 54,342 (1970):30–40.

13 Goodman, Paul. *Compulsory Mis-education and the Community of Scholars:* New York: Vintage Books, 1964.

14 Gossage, Howard L. "You Can See Why the Mighty Would Be Curious," 20–30 in Gerald E. Stern,ed., *McLuhan:Hot and Cool*. New York: New American Library, 1967.

15 Greenleaf, Warren T. "Humanities and the Culture-Hungry American." *American Education* 6, i(1970):7–11.

16 Grittner, Frank M.,ed. *French Curriculum Guide*. Madison, Wisconsin: State Department of Public Instruction, 1968.

17 _____ *German Curriculum Guide*. Madison, Wisconsin: State Department of Public Instruction, 1968.

18 _____ *Russian Curriculum Guide*. Madison,

Wisconsin: State Department of Public Instruction, 1968.

19 _____ *Spanish Curriculum Guide*. Madison, Wisconsin: State Department of Public Instruction, 1968.

20 _____ *Teaching Foreign Languages*. New York: Harper and Row, 1969.

21 *Guide for Instruction in Modern Foreign Languages Grades 4-12*. St. Paul: State of Minnesota Department of Education, 1965.

22 Hartwig, Hellmut. "Teaching Advanced Language:What the Colleges Expect of the High Schools." *Modern Language Journal* 53(1969): 485–91.

23 Hills, Penney C., and L. Rust Hills,eds. *Contemporary Life in Contemporary Fiction*. New York: Macmillan, 1968.

24 Hocking, Elton. "The Schools Take Over Foreign Languages." *Journal of Secondary Education* 39(1964):243–50.

25 Holt, John. *The Underachieving School*. New York: Pitman, 1969.

26 Jakobovits, Leon A. "Physiology and Psychology of Second Language Learning," 181–227 in Emma M. Birkmaier,ed., *Britannica Review of Foreign Language Education, Volume 1*. Chicago: Encyclopaedia Britannica, 1968 [1969].

27 Kennedy, John F. Address, American University, Washington, D.C. (June 10, 1963).

28 Lawson, John H. "Should Foreign Language Be Eliminated from the Curriculum?" in Lorraine A. Strasheim,ed., *Foreign Language in a New Apprenticeship for Living*. Papers from a Symposium sponsored by ACTFL, NASSP, and the ILP. Bloomington: The Indiana Language Program, Indiana Univ., in press.

29 Leonard, George B. *Education and Ecstasy*. New York: Delacorte Press, 1968.

30 Marker, Gerald W., and Howard D. Mehlinger. "School, Politics, Rebellion, and Other Youthful Interests," 38–54 in *The School and the Democratic Environment*. Papers and other materials drawn from a Conference sponsored by the Danforth Foundation and the Ford Foundation. New York: Columbia Univ. Press, 1970.

31 Masciantonio, Rudolph. "Innovative Classical Programs in the School District of Philadelphia." *Foreign Language Annals* 3(1970):592–95.

32 McLuhan, Marshall. *The Gutenberg Galaxy*. New York: New American Library, 1962.

33 *Modern Foreign Language in Ohio Elementary Schools*, Revised Edition. Columbus, Ohio: Department of Education, 1969.

34 Nyman, Stephen. "The Student Independent Study Program," in John Birmingham,ed., *Our Time Is Now*. New York: Praeger, 1970.

35 Postman, Neil, and Charles Weingartner. *Teaching as a Subversive Activity*. New York: Delacorte Press, 1969.

36 Rivers, Wilga M. *Teaching Foreign-Language Skills*. Chicago: Univ. of Chicago Press, 1968.

37 Samuels, S. Jay. "Psychological and Educational Considerations in Early Language Learning," 9–18 in Virginia G. Allen and F. André Paquette, eds., *The Student's World Is the World:New*

Dimensions in the Teaching of FLES. Bloomington: The Indiana Language Program, India Univ., 1969.

38 Shane, Harold G. "A Curriculum Continuu Possible Trends in the Seventies." *Phi De Kappan* 51(1970):389–92.

39 Shepherd, W. Everitt. "An Experiment in dividualized Advanced French." *Foreign L guage Annals* 3(1970):394–99.

40 Smith, William L. "Cleveland's Experiment Mutual Respect," 83–93 in *The School and t Democratic Environment*. Papers and other m terials drawn from a Conference sponsored the Danforth Foundation and the Ford Found tion. New York: Columbia Univ. Press, 19

41 Strasheim, Lorraine A. "Foreign Langua Part of a New Apprenticeship for Living." *T Bulletin of the National Association of S ondary School Principals* 54,342(1970):87–1

42 _____ "Where from Here?" *Modern Langua Journal* 53(1969):493–97.

43 Weisbord, Marvin R. "What Do We Want fr Our Schools?" 1–16 in *The School and the De cratic Environment*. Papers and other materi drawn from a Conference sponsored by the D forth Foundation and the Ford Foundation. N York: Columbia Univ. Press, 1970.

3

Behavioral objectives and evaluation

Introduction

Florence Steiner

*Glenbrook South High School,
Glenview, Illinois*

During recent years increasing attention has been focused upon behavioral objectives. A new terminology has inundated our professional literature with such phrases as educational accountability, systems approach, relevant curriculum, performance objectives, purposes, instructional objectives, teacher effectiveness, educational responsibility, accessibility, individualized instruction, behavioral engineering, performance criteria, educational assessment, independent educational accomplishment audit, baseline measures, cost effectiveness, etc. Each of these terms reflects a growing concern for the *educational product.*

Behavioral objectives and other new concepts

Drastic changes grow out of great needs. The past decade has focused upon the teacher—increasing teacher competency, both in language skills and in methodology, providing the teacher with materials that draw upon the competencies of specialists such as the anthropologist, linguist, historian, and psychologist, among others. This present decade is focusing upon the learner, the reasons for which grow out of the times.

Change: needs, students, forces

Many colleges and secondary schools are noticing a new brand of student—one who demands a share in planning his curriculum, one who demands "relevant" learning, and one who demands that all students be admitted to all learning experiences. This new student includes the disadvantaged, the ghetto child, both rural and urban children (Delco, Matthews, & Rogers, 23), and many of our typical students of the past.

Another factor forcing change is the federal government. Educational accountability has become a common term in studies of evaluative criteria and is influencing the specifications drawn up for governmental programs. The examiner or critic can now be expected to ask what the teacher was trying to do, how he did it, whether he achieved the desired results, and, if not, why not.

School boards and administrators, upset over referenda that fail to pass, are also turning with renewed attention to the product of education. They are asking how students can be given more individual attention in an era when salaries are at an all-time high; they are seeking new ways to eliminate educational waste.

The emergence of minority groups that demand their rightful place in our educational system creates a problem of individual differences unlike those of the past. If all students are admitted to language study, then the curriculum must change drastically. How can this be accomplished?

The year 1969 saw the implementation of many ideas proposed previously. Criterion-referenced tests began to appear in California (Damore, 21), districts began to put performance curricula into operation (Laleike, 46; Moreno, 57). The area of performance objectives is too new to have many research results as yet. Not all who considered the issue were in favor of behavioral objectives; some writers even raised the question as to whether or not they would be harmful to the schools. *Appearances of change*

The purpose of this chapter is to examine the professional literature, with special attention to the year 1969, to ascertain what were the findings of both the modern language specialists and the generalists as to the area of behavioral objectives and evaluation. These terms are clearly intertwined and for purposes of this paper evaluation will be considered in both its aspects: testing and program evaluation. The article will be divided into the following sections: *Purpose of the chapter*

Introduction

The case for behavioral objectives: the relevant curriculum and the "new" student

Definition of the performance curriculum: implications for change

Implementation of the performance curriculum: upsetting the educational applecart

Testing and evaluation: its role in the performance curriculum

Program evaluation: educational accountability to learner and taxpayer

Conclusion

The case for behavioral objectives:
the relevant curriculum and the "new" student

Foreign language educators are becoming increasingly aware of a new breed of student. In opening the 1970 Northeast Conference, Remunda Cadoux stressed the theme of the "new" student and his demands for a relevant curriculum (15).

She stated that this new student is demanding:

The new student

1 participation in determining the curriculum (Should foreign language requirements be abolished?)
2 relevant education—an education meaningful both to the student and the world
3 sharing of the good effects of education by all

Conversely, Professor Cadoux pointed out the negative aspects of this new student:

1 he refuses to accept absolute values
2 he refuses to look to the past for models of the future
3 he is globally concerned because he has been exposed to mass media

In her preface to the conference report, Professor Cadoux (14) indicated that foreign language teachers must ask themselves:

1 What shall we teach him?
2 How shall we teach him?
3 Will he let us teach him?

This "new" student might also be called the "now" student, for he is demanding relevancy and meaning in his work *now*; he is not content to wait years for his work to bear fruit. Valette (89) states that students who cannot keep up with the class usually lose motivation and as a result experience a decline in attitude. She says that most statements made by foreign language teachers reflect long-range affective components such as:

The "now" student

1 The student will grow to like language.
2 The student will grow to appreciate culture.
3 The student will grow to be more tolerant of other cultures, etc.

Yet reality shows that many businessmen, educators, and even administrators look back upon language learning with distaste.

Kersten & Ott (43) describe the new student. They observe that the students in the secondary schools today find a great disparity between their daily life activities and much that goes on in the classroom. With the demands of home and society, and the great personal importance of a relationship to a peer group which is constantly pressuring him, the present-day adolescent resembles only slightly his predecessors of two or three generations ago. The emphasis upon the individual's right to choose a course of action which his nature dictates, and the resulting resistance to any superimposed instruction interfering with it, has disastrously hampered learning for many confused teen-agers. Kersten & Ott recommend that the material to be studied and the presentation must be geared toward achieving a twofold aim: it must be relevant to the student's immediate needs and interests and it must have appeal in those areas of interest where curiosity reaches out for a satisfying experience so that language information can be used immediately in the student's daily life.

Student attitudes

We have not done an adequate job of promoting foreign language study to our students. Reinert (69) reports on student attitudes. In a survey conducted in Edmonds, Washington, a fairly typical suburban town, students indicated that the main reason *A survey* they took a foreign language was for college entrance. This fact was borne out in the tables that showed student reasons for not continuing beyond the second year. The vast majority (approximately 70% of each language enrollment) listed "requirements completed" as their reason for not continuing. They bypassed such attractive reasons as "class is boring" and "dislike the teacher." Some did indicate that their grades were too low (about 18% in French and German). According to Reinert the teachers still need to do a better job of communicating with parents since parents influence the students' choice of subjects. Also the teacher has to persuade these students that foreign language study has some intrinsic value.

Accessibility

Grittner (29) maintains that all students should be encouraged to study a foreign language, not only the college-bound. He says that the objectives should be realistic and there should be individualized units according to student interests. Strasheim (86) emphasizes that we aim only at the college-bound student, that we do not study our customer, that materials are written by *The client* college professors who pay little attention to the interest of the student or to his learning level. She also indicates that foreign languages are not made a part of the total education of the youngster and suggests that in the future they be integrated with other subject areas to give them greater relevancy in the mind of the learner. Objectives for foreign language study must be realistic, achievable, and humanistic. She reports that there is much that foreign language teachers might learn from colleagues in other subject areas in this regard. Further she adds that foreign language students must have a sense of accomplishment *now*, not at some point in the future.

Although as Professor Cadoux states, some suburban educators hope the problem will go away, the evidence is to the contrary. Since foreign language requirements *are* being dropped, the planning of new curricula within the range of all students—not only of the elite—must be considered.

Sandstrom & Pimsleur (73) set forth the idea that all students should have an opportunity to study a foreign language since it is a humanizing experience, a system of verbal communication in a social situation. If this premise were to be accepted, different kinds of programs to fit the needs of different types of students should be made available.

All students should study a foreign language

Motivation

Many writers see relevance associated with motivation. If the student wants to study the subject, if he believes that his efforts are producing a measure of success, if he feels that the work is worthwhile, he will definitely consider the subject relevant. Nelson & Jakobovits (59) propose that the student must have a realistic sense of accomplishment that comes not only from traditional evaluative practices such as grades, praise, and critical appraisal, but also from a course of study that allows him to see his own progress. The "new" student does not readily accept vague reassurances of success indefinitely if they are not accompanied by visible evidence of his own achievement.

Relevance and motivation

Jakobovits (41) presents the psychologist's point of view by stating that in general we know little concerning how people learn but that we do know enough to examine individualization of instruction as a possible means for solving some learning problems. Jakobovits designed an interest questionnaire which was distributed at the 1970 Northeast Conference. From results of this questionnaire teachers may be able to determine the type of curriculum that will have the greatest interest for their students. Serafino (77) and his associated committee presented some scant data from a study in which the instrument was initially used, but he indicated the results could not be broadly interpreted because of an insufficient sample.

Nelson & Jakobovits (59) emphasized that students should be encouraged to set realistic goals for themselves. The student must be made to see that practical mastery of a second language is a large task. Further, not all students possess the same goals. Therefore a teacher should not make the mistake of thinking he has the right or the power to set the goals for his student even though, at the secondary school level, the student's goals may be ill defined and the teacher may offer radically different ones that may help a student to exploit his own identity. *Realistic student goals*

Mager (51) suggests approaches we can use to encourage positive attitudes in our students. He outlines two kinds of student attitudes. The first one he labels "approach tendencies," that is, here the student tends to move toward the subject, to show interest by spending more time than necessary on it, to talk to the teacher, to try to get into advanced courses. The second, or opposite, attitude he calls "avoidance techniques," that is, here the *Two kinds of student attitude* student is late to class, fails to do assignments, tries to get out of the course. Mager states that we can act to develop and strengthen approach tendencies toward any subject and then evaluate the success of such moves. He concludes that people tend to like or dislike a subject because of: (*1*) the conditions that surround it; (2) the consequences of coming into contact with it; (3) the way that others react toward it. Mager would use observable behavior to measure the success of the strengthening of approach tendencies to determine the success of the development of positive attitudes in our students.

Some educators believe that the role of testing must change and that both testing and classroom situations must be structured to reveal what the student does know and what he can do. *Role of testing* Brooks (12) concurs that measurement should be a positive, not a negative, element of instruction.

Valette (91) proposes that tests be devised that will help teachers determine student knowledge. Those tests which diagnose student knowledge according to predetermined criteria are called criterion-referenced tests. Valette asserts that criterion-referenced tests, essential tools in individualized instruction, must be thoroughly investigated in that particular framework.

Sandstrom & Pimsleur (73) suggest that one step which must be taken to make learning accessible to all students is to abandon lockstep language programming in the secondary schools *Lockstep programming* and actively publicize new developments in multilevel programming that enable each student to proceed at his own rate of

40

learning. They quote Michael E. Hernick of the Oxon Hill Senior High School where on-level and sublevel groups were set up for each year of language study. Parallel scheduling made easy transfer between on- and sublevels possible. They further state that behavioral objectives must be precisely described in step-by-step fashion so that student progress can be measured. Such evaluation will give students and teachers a continuous achievement record. Such evaluative tests must be criterion referenced and must serve as milestones of progress. They should test passive as well as active knowledge.

Performance objectives

Educators are also clamoring for clarification of goals and objectives. Brooks (12) maintains that we must be more explicit in defining certain terms that are in wide and constant use, terms like method and approach, culture and civilization. We must not offer our students courses whose very titles we ourselves are unable or unwilling to define. Strasheim (86) calls attention to the plight of the student of the seventies, pointing out that each time he has a decision or a choice to make and each time he applies the criteria he has been taught, he is frustrated. Many students, from the dissatisfied in the ghetto to the restless in suburbia, are refusing to listen to our promises of the future because our preparation for the present is proving ineffectual. The student is trying to manufacture a way to live in the only world he knows, the world in which he lives.

Clarification of goals and objectives

Samuels (72) proposes that prior to implementing the teaching aspect of a FLES program teachers should have constructed an articulated program of objectives and unit tests. Thus, when actual teaching begins, teachers could devote their time to planning, teaching, diagnosing, and remediation. Tests also would provide a target that would aid in unit planning. Samuels, like Nelson & Jakobovits, cautions that goals should be realistic since unrealistic ones bring student disillusionment. A further point is made that where mastery is the objective, provision must be made for different rates of student learning.

Joyce (42), speaking of the elementary school curriculum, states that until very recently a teacher who wished to individualize instruction was frequently frustrated because he could not even process the information about his students that is necessary to make wise decisions about objectives for individualizing instruction.

41

Role of aptitude and achievement tests

Pimsleur & Struth (64) advocate the use of aptitude tests so that teachers may know their students in advance and can thus place them in proper learning situations. Valette (92) cautions against the use of aptitude tests for excluding students from foreign language study since research shows that students who score low on aptitude tests, but are motivated to language study, can be successful.

Aptitude tests

The Pennsylvania Report, now many times digested, has raised questions about achievement tests that linger in the minds of all. Hocking (37) asks if we have made the best use of the language laboratory. Valette (90) inquires if we have the proper testing devices for undertaking a major research project. Are we able to state objectives clearly enough that all evaluators will know exactly what is meant? While Valette stated the case for criterion-referenced tests (89), others such as Herbert (35) are saying that student progress should be evaluated at intermediate levels of proficiency so that the teacher may discover what levels have to be attained in certain behaviors before the student can proceed effectively to others. The teacher will then develop criteria or guidelines for measuring the progress of the learner in the instructional program.

Achievement tests

Historical development of objectives

Certain writers are interested in the historical development of performance objectives. James Hoetker (38) quotes from Elliot Eisner, who traced the concern with specifications of objectives back 50 years to the "scientific movement in education" and to Franklin Bobbitt. According to Eisner (in Hoetker) the movement was revived in the late forties and early fifties by such influential writers as Benjamin Bloom, Ralph Tyler, and Virgil Herrick. Hoetker also quotes Ray Callahan who showed that "the scientific movement in education" was one manifestation of a broad social movement (originating in industry) toward efficiency, rationalization, and human engineering. Hoetker further states that the turn-of-the-century efficiency expert was resurrected in the guise of a systems analyst. He sees the first evidence of the computer revolution, systems analysis, and cost effectiveness procedures applied to the armed services and to defense industries. Like others he notes the influence the systems analysts exercise upon public education, primarily through

The industrial model applied education

the U.S. Office of Education, in the interests of evaluation, efficiency, and accountability. This influence was furthered through the more prestigious graduate schools of education, in the interests of rigor in research and efficiency in school administration. Hoetker questions whether an approach that is quite applicable to the military would be applicable to democratic civilian institutions, whether it might not produce and exaggerate the most grotesque features of our schools — standardization, rigidity, regimentation, and authoritarianism.

Summary

Many factors seem to be creating a climate for change: the new student who wants a share in his own learning, the government which wants evaluative proof that schools with funded programs are accomplishing their aims with students, administrators and parents who are demanding more individual attention for students, and voices within the profession which are clamoring for clarification of goals and ordered sequences of learning with demonstrated proof that each goal has been achieved. It must be stated, however, that while yet few in number there are voices on the other side challenging the claims of the advocates of behavioral objectives.

Definition of the performance curriculum: implications for change

The definition of terms is essential in any discussion. A performance curriculum is one which includes purposes (broad statements of goals or objectives), objectives (defined in terms of student behavior), and criteria for measuring the success or lack thereof in changing student behavior. Such a curriculum has the advantage of communicating to both student and teacher exactly what the student is to learn and to what extent it should be learned.

Definition of terms

Many authors provide their own definitions of behavioral objectives. Mandel (53) states that basically an objective is a statement of instructional goals specifying which behavioral changes in the learner are sought by the teacher. He implies that it is necessary to distinguish between operational objectives and procedural statements. A procedural statement is not really an objective but a declaration of what content the teacher intends to use to bring about this change; it is a statement of

43

teacher *activity* whereas an operational objective states what change is to take place in the behavior of the learner. One source (1) indicates that it is "the precise statement of educational objectives in language which specifies expected responses, performance and outcomes which can be measured as accurately or objectively as possible." Most writers, including Seelye (75) and Steiner (84), start with Mager's book, *Preparing Instructional Objectives* (52).

Other writers have been interested in the principles of learning that underlie performance objectives. Popham (67) lists five generally accepted principles of learning:

Principles underlying performance objectives

1 Appropriate practice
2 Individual differentiation
3 Perceived purpose
4 Knowledge of results
5 Graduated sequence

Popham also pleads that all objectives should be exposed to the psychology of learning and the philosophy of education. He also asks for the use of taxonomies so that all objectives would not be at the same level. As stated above, not all critics are in agreement about performance objectives. Bruner (13) sets forth the idea that what is learned is *competence*, not particular performances. In broad outline, skilled action requires *recognizing* the features of a task, its goal and means appropriate of attainment; a means of *converting* this information into appropriate action; and a means of *getting feedback* that compares the objective sought with present state attained.

Some writers see in performance objectives a greater end than the objectives themselves. They regard them as a means to help people teach themselves. According to Parker & Rubin (61) the school cannot hope to produce an educated adult unless it ensures through its curriculum both the desire and the wherewithal for carrying on self-directed learning after school days have come to an end. Whatever the nature of the curriculum it must provide each individual with a number of different ways of learning and with an opportunity to cultivate his personal potential for excellence. Borton (10) considers the processes of an educated mind, processes for handling information and for responding to others, a primary concern. He also believes in sharing the process of education with the learner—of giving him some choices.

Objectives: a means to teach oneself

44

Priorities

Members of the profession have been concerned with establishing priorities. Certain steps seem to precede others.

Mowrer (58) gives priority to preassessment, stating that the behavior a child possesses must be analyzed when he comes to us. Then the learning task must be divided into small teaching units called steps or en route behaviors. These steps can be written as a set of carefully sequenced instructions. A system of precision recording must also be available so that we can know both the error rate and the total response rate.

Preassessment

Banathy (6) suggests that the design of a teacher training program should commence with a detailed description of the on-the-job performance of the foreign language teacher. Training programs as they now exist are usually based on some vague generalized goals, rather than on a detailed analysis of the actual performance of the teacher. Such a description of the job performance becomes the basis for formulating training objectives. Banathy describes the formulation of objectives: first, some broad statements are framed which then can be refined even more specifically, until the task level has been reached.

Detailed description of on-the-job performance

Teacher trainers need to state in terms of the smallest independent unit of performance whatever the future teacher is expected to be able to do, know, and feel. They need to state in measurable terms how well the teacher is expected to perform. The stimuli which are to evoke the teacher's performance, the circumstances and constraints under which he is expected to perform, should also be described. Banathy pleads for a teacher training curriculum that is based on what the teacher does in the classroom, not what he does outside it.

Pillet (62) states that current methods courses are attempting to integrate into the foreign language teaching techniques those educational innovations which have application to foreign language teaching. It is important, he continues, for many of our teachers in the schools to have some understanding of flexible grouping, modular scheduling, interaction analysis, differentiated staffing, and systems analysis. He sees this last mentioned as having possible serious consequences for the foreign language curriculum.

Teaching techniques and educational innovation

Politzer & Bartley (65) include a section on performance criteria in their syllabus for the training of teachers of Standard English as a second dialect. The section consists mainly of a systematic listing of behaviors of the good language teacher. The listing is accompanied by discussions of teacher methodology. The performance criteria are used as an instrument for the training as well as for the evaluation of the teacher.

Listing of teacher behaviors

Priorities in the use, description, and development of performance objectives in foreign language education have at this point not completely permeated the field.

Changing teacher behavior

Melvin Smith (79) explores behavioral objectives as a means of changing teacher behavior. He says that teachers usually select a learning activity first and, then, after it has been presented, decide what has been taught. He implies that an unwillingness to state objectives first arises from ignorance or insecurity on the part of the teacher. According to him behavioral objectives change the focus of attention from the learning activity to the end or resultant behavior desired. He also has used performance objectives to establish a proper order of priorities.

Objectives focus on desired behavior

Herbert (35) states that objectives must specify the content, degree of skill to be attained, and the means for measuring achievement. What is it that we want the student to learn? What is the best way for him to learn it? How will we know when he has learned it?

Moore (56) shows that the mind should develop better retrieval procedures; he says that teachers must be constantly aware of the importance of organizing and classifying all information to be taught. The teacher must generate and test productive instructional hypotheses. The careful sequencing of objectives will provide a basis for generating and testing such hypotheses. He lists the types of performances as:

Classifying and sequencing objectives

1 Definitional items
2 Generation-of-new-instance items
3 Discrimination items
4 Comparison items
5 Creative items

According to Moore (56) the primary emphases in instructional design include:

1 Classification, organization and evaluation procedures which will increase the probability of retention, learning how to learn, etc.

2 Observational procedures which will increase the probability that productive instructional hypotheses can be generated and tested; thus instructional procedures can be modified accordingly.

Moore describes the effective teacher as capable of applying research to instruction as well as carrying out the program listed above.

Disadvantages and some advantages of performance objectives

Some writers express negative opinions or grave doubts about the system. Grittner (29) reports that the weakness of a systems curriculum is that by its nature it includes only that which can be quantified and objectively tested. This approach does not cover the full range of the humanities. He also states that creative performance cannot be reduced to measurable overt behaviors. And since it cannot be tested, it cannot be taught by the systems approach. Grittner also states that unless foreign language educators accept for foreign language instruction a rationale which is limited to mere training in routine behaviors it is difficult to see this approach as more than a partial solution to instructional problems.

Weakness of a systems curriculum

James Hoetker (38) expresses the sentiments of many humanists when he speaks of the advantages and the limitations of behavioral objectives in the arts and humanities. He does not quarrel with the fact that specific objectives have their place in the curriculum, but he gives three interesting categories of behavior: "can-do" behavior, "may-do" behavior, and "will-do" behavior. He finds that traditional education has occupied itself with the "can-do" behaviors, that progressive education concentrated on "may-do" behaviors, and that no one really knows what will happen to the "will-do" behavior. "Can-do" behavior is concerned with skills and knowledge; "may-do" behaviors involve what a student may be able to do in a novel or unfamiliar situation because he has mastered certain "can-do" behaviors; "will-do" behaviors are the choices and preferences that describe the quality of an adult's life, and which are present only fractionally during the school years.

Limitations in the arts and the humanities

Hoetker suggests that the humanists and artists not neglect the advantages of behavioral objectives but that they approach the writing of the same from a different point of view. They

47

should start by asking themselves, "What are the things a liberally educated man does that are not done by the uneducated? What are his preferences, responses, pastimes, expenditures, companionships, activities that distinguish him from those who have not had his advantages?" Next he exhorts humanists to adopt the following rules in writing behavioral objectives:

1 Never write behavioral specifications having to do with can-do behaviors. Work only with high-level behavior to avoid being trapped in the lower level.
2 State all behavioral objectives in binary terms: pass or fail; happen or not happen; present or absent.

With the constraint of these two rules may-do behaviors are the ones to be specified. They may be thought of as fractional components of will-do behaviors. He also suggests a third rule:

3 Do not define behavior too narrowly.

He gives several examples which might be acceptable under certain circumstances, e.g., "the students will cut class less often; the students will express enjoyment . . .; the students will try to help or protect younger or weaker students . . .; the students will ask to do additional work of a certain kind." According to Hoetker these objectives help teachers measure their own performance; the same criteria will be used to judge them that are used to judge coaches, who win or lose so many games. With the use of objectives there is no room for self-deception. Teachers can no longer blame students for the teachers' failures.

Tyler (88) lists eight reasons why teachers generally are reluctant to accept performance objectives:

Reasons why teachers are reluctant to accept performance objectives

1 Teachers are accustomed to thinking in terms of what they do.
2 Teachers are convinced that the difficult task in teaching is to motivate students.
3 Teachers think behavioral objectives are overly specific and usually insignificant.
4 Teachers believe it is an overwhelming task to formulate objectives for all the students in classes.
5 Teachers believe that what is presented is less important than how it is presented.
6 Prespecification of objectives makes it difficult for a teacher to pursue ideas which emerge spontaneously in a classroom.

7 If objectives are prespecified, learners are not involved in the formulation and they should be.
8 Some objectives do not lend themselves to measurement yet they may be more important than those that are measurable.

Tyler then proceeds to build the case for behavioral objectives and summarizes the objections given by teachers as being predicated upon inadequate conceptions of education, curriculum, or instruction.

Eiss (25) lists four hazards in the use of behavioral objectives:

Hazards in using behavioral objectives

1 As behavioral objectives are now written, many, if not most of them, tend to be trivial.
2 The list of objectives may become encyclopedic.
3 There are too many examples of objectives at the lower levels of the cognitive domain, and too few examples of objectives in the affective domain.
4 Developing a catalog of objectives may limit the goals of teaching, with the result that some of the spontaneity and value of education may be lost.

One of the most interesting treatments of performance or behavioral objectives is found in a monograph of the American Educational Research Association (Popham, 66). In this volume, four educators, W. James Popham, Elliot W. Eisner, Howard J. Sullivan, and Louise L. Tyler, discuss behavioral objectives from four points of view. Each author has prepared a chapter dealing with a specific topic. The four discuss each chapter, raising questions and challenging certain points of view. Eisner divides objectives into two sections, instructional and expressive. Instructional objectives, which we commonly refer to as behavioral objectives, should describe what the student should be able to do, the context in which the behavior is to be displayed and identified, and the context for assessing the behavior. These objectives should refer to observable behavior. Expressive objectives is a new concept which Eisner describes as encounters that students are to have in educational settings. Such encounters are intended to relate to the "creative" aspects of learning. The expressive objectives could only be provided after the encounter has taken place and were not to be specified in advance.

Popham pleads for instructional objectives in behavioral terms and says that a properly stated behavioral objective must

AERA monograph on behavioral objectives

describe without ambiguity the nature of learner behavior or product to be measured. It is also desirable, he continues, to distinguish between statements which could be used to describe learner behavior which occurs during an instructional sequence and those post-instruction behaviors toward which the instructor is aiming. Popham points out that we find an increasing number of instructional schemes which are essentially means referenced (norm referenced) rather than goal referenced (criterion referenced). He cites the interaction analysis model of Flanders as illustrative of the means-referenced scheme. Sullivan (87) treats behavioral objectives and evaluation. He includes a section on prescribing individualized instruction with regularly administered tests to diagnose each learner's particular difficulty.

Tyler treats the area of psychoanalysis as a source for behavioral objectives. She also has an interesting chapter on the reasons why some people are resistant to the notion of specifying objectives. Parker & Rubin (61) suggest that the process of learning is actually a part of the content of learning. The goal of the educational process *is* the process.

In another article, Popham (67) states that those instructional outcomes which cannot be behaviorized are usually the most trivial. He explains that many teachers cover all the material but there is no change in behavior on the part of the student.

The case for performance objectives in the teaching of foreign languages has been presented in different forms by numerous writers. Seelye (75) stresses the idea of educational accountability, going so far as to raise the question about paying teachers in relation to the success of their students. He further proposes that culture can be taught and tested via performance objectives and criterion-referenced testing. Steiner (84) pays attention to the teaching of grammar and the structuring of the learning process. Banathy (5) sees the objectives growing out of the goals which change according to the needs of society. Both he and Valette (92) emphasize that a high degree of specification of objectives enables the construction of criterion-referenced tests. According to Banathy an objective in speaking proficiency should state: (*1*) the context in which the student is expected to operate; (2) the kinds of language features to be acquired; (3) the degree of accuracy and fluency; and (4) the types of tasks the learner is expected to perform.

Banathy (6) applies the principle of objectives and learning tasks to contrastive linguistic analysis.

Behavioral objectives and FL teaching and evaluation

Taxonomies

Taxonomies of learning experiences have been considered essential by many writers.

A taxonomy, according to the dictionary, is a classification especially of animals and plants according to their natural relationships.

A definition

Valette states (89) that as early as 1949 a group of college and university examiners began work on a system of classifying educational goals. The first volume, *Taxonomy of Educational Objectives: Cognitive Domain* (1956), was edited by Benjamin Bloom (9), and this classification system became known simply as the "Bloom Taxonomy." The second volume, *Taxonomy of Educational Objectives: Affective Domain* (Krathwohl, Bloom, & Masia, 45) appeared in 1964. The third volume, yet to appear, deals with the psychomotor domain.

Cognitive, objective, and psychomotor taxonomies

Bloom (9) states that his taxonomy is intended to provide a classification of the goals of educational systems. It should help educators discuss curricular and evaluation problems with greater precision. The use of the taxonomy can help one gain a perspective on the emphasis given to certain behaviors by a particular set of educational plans. Bloom claims that it should help curriculum builders to specify objectives so that it becomes easier to plan learning experiences and to prepare evaluation devices.

Various authors have adapted the Bloom taxonomy to a classification of foreign language learning objectives. Certain authors proposed their own psychomotor domain, as did Valette (89). Gronlund (32) has, in general, not only suggested categories for the psychomotor domain, but also establishes a process for writing instructional objectives which is different from that of Mager (52). The differences occur in the practicality of the Gronlund process, whereas the Mager process requires almost literary skill for writing objectives. Gronlund also suggests the use of objectives for all levels of the learning domains: cognitive, affective, and psychomotor.

Certain writers see the use of a taxonomy as guaranteeing better results. Moreno (57) proposes that the use of the taxonomy, performance objectives, and tests will guarantee success by 80% or more of the class. Other writers see in taxonomies a safeguard that objectives will not be written only in the low-level learning areas.

Usefulness of taxonomies

Behavioral objectives/Steiner

Melvin Smith (79) lists taxonomies for the four language skills. He suggests that they serve as a guide so that objectives may be developed for more than one level of a specific skill. In listening comprehension, for example, we should develop objectives for: *Taxonomies for the four language skills*

1 Discriminating between phonemes of a language
2 Understanding the semantic and structural meaning of words
3 Understanding the meanings of entire sentences

In speaking, we should develop objectives to develop the ability

1 To imitate words and sentences
2 To respond to a linguistic stimulus with an appropriate response
3 To initiate a conversation

As objectives are developed, they should be compared to each other and to the taxonomies in order to make sure that higher as well as lower level objectives are developed. Smith maintains that teaching toward these objectives can:

1 Facilitate better communication of the purpose of the course to the students and to other teachers
2 Improve articulation between grade levels because the objectives set up an acceptable standard against which the students can be measured
3 Increase the efficiency of the teacher in selecting learning experiences for the students

Valette (89) finds nine types of explicit language objectives which she draws from the broad aims of second language learning as they have appeared in the literature over the past fifty years: *Nine types of language objectives*

1 Vocabulary knowledge
2 Grammar knowledge (including morphology and syntax)
3 Knowledge of the sound system and the writing system (phonology and orthography)
4 Translation into English
5 Translation into the second language
6 Listening comprehension
7 Speaking ability
8 Reading comprehension
9 Writing ability

She then considers these aims against Bloom's taxonomy and finds much of language learning is in the psychomotor domain while another portion of it falls in the cognitive domain. Hence vocabulary knowledge, grammar knowledge, knowledge of phonology, and spelling fall, in part, in the cognitive domain. As the student practices speaking and writing he moves to the psychomotor domain. Valette finds the six categories of the cognitive domain listed by Bloom pertinent to language teaching:

Language learning and two domains: cognitive and psychomotor

1 Knowledge
2 Comprehension
3 Application
4 Analysis
5 Synthesis
6 Evaluation

Also pertinent to language study are the parts of the psychomotor domain which she creates for language use:

1 Perception
2 Conscious production—mimicry and memorization
3 Manipulation
4 Free production
5 Internalization

Valette indicates that an element such as translation can exist at various levels in the taxonomy although it remains in the cognitive domain.

The categories of the affective domain are also important to language teaching. They relate to motivation and attitudes toward foreign language learning and toward the foreign culture. The categories useful for foreign language learning according to Valette (89) are:

The affective domain

1 Receiving
2 Responding
3 Valuing

Herbert's (35) *Behavioral Objectives for English as a Second Language* includes the following taxonomy:

Behavioral objectives and ESOL

1 Phonology
2 Morphology
3 Structure
4 Vocabulary

5 Culture

6 Interrelated learnings

These content items are then paired with the four skills as follows:

1 Listening

2 Speaking

3 Reading

4 Writing

5 Combined skills

Each area is developed into specific categories with demonstrable performances.

Summary

In formulating performance objectives educators stipulate the order and variety of the learning tasks. The purposes or goals grow out of the needs of society and include student needs as well. Before formulating objectives many educators construct a taxonomy of educational objectives for their particular discipline. Objectives are then formulated around each appropriate classification or level of learning; in this way one avoids writing only psychomotor or low-level cognitive objectives. Such a process contributes to the careful development of curricular offerings.

Implementation of the performance curriculum: upsetting the educational applecart

Spanish and ESOL via performance objectives

In many schools 1969 was a year for implementing performance objectives. Administrators, curriculum designers, teachers all came face to face with the real problems of putting the performance curriculum into action. Stanislaus County in California was in the vanguard and published "Criterion-Referenced Tests for the Teaching of Spanish by Specific Objectives" (79).

Examples of performance curricula

Herbert (35) developed a program for the teaching of English as a second language in which he developed a taxonomy and then formulated objectives for each classification. He followed Hoetker's (38) suggestion of a pass/fail criterion which he used for certain objectives. Herbert's program is one of the most completely developed projects in behavioral objectives that has ap-

54

peared. It can be extremely useful to anyone writing performance objectives in foreign languages. The Stanislaus County
project (79) is also an excellent model because it provides the
teacher with everything needed to make the testing program
work, including answer keys, records, etc.

French at the secondary level

Steiner (84) sketches the daily management of the classroom
in which one teacher runs the program alone. Her objectives are
in the cognitive domain and centered around the second level of
French at the secondary school. She provides information on
classroom management, record keeping, and student reaction to
the program. She offers the suggestion that schedules and calen-
dars be established in the early stages of teaching with performance objectives so that the teacher has a period of transition.
Steiner also proposes that while students work independently,
time criteria should be established to enable both students and
teachers to know what is expected of them.

Use of objectives in daily program management

Culture

Seelye (75) suggests a classification of objectives for teaching
culture. He points out that a subject such as culture, while usually considered to be in the affective domain, can actually be
measured in behavioral terms. In this article, Seelye gives examples of objectives for teaching culture which fit his classificatory
system and which can be measured.

Cultural objectives

From time to performance

Laleike (46,47) lists as one of the objectives of his project the
attempt to change the foreign language program from one based
on time criteria to one based on performance. The program is
individualized to a high degree and offers flexibility in scheduling. The student's work is carefully detailed in a step-by-step
process although his work is not stated in terms of performance
objectives. The teacher guide gives specific directions to the
teacher on the use of check lists in evaluating student achievement. This project employs several teaching strategies and
learning situations: (1) large group instruction; (2) small group
instruction; (3) one-to-one instruction; (4) independent study;
(5) the independent study group.

Continuous individual progress programs have caught the attention of educators. Some educators such as Kittel (44) fear,

Continuous progress programs

55

however, that the same old material will be served up under new labels; he states that in the elementary school only reading is taught by continuous individual progress in sequenced levels when all agree that mathematics should also be so taught.

Individualizing instruction

Not all individualized programs operate on performance criteria. In Rice Lake, Wisconsin, Grittner (30) reports that there is individualized pacing of instruction in the teaching of Russian. The language laboratory is utilized to send eight different programs; when the student has practiced sufficiently in the laboratory to be tested he raises his hand and the teacher gives him the oral test. After the laboratory practice and testing, the student returns to the conventional classroom where he contributes what he can to a group conversation.

Individualized pacing

Language laboratories have also been used for a kind of individualization of instruction in the LaFollette High School where underachievers, i.e., those who achieved less than C, were assigned an additional hour of lab work per week.

Hoye (39) pleads that school buldings be constructed more for instructional efficiency than for maintenance. He proposes that new buldings have movable walls, that individual study and classroom areas be centered around resource centers instead of around gyms, that noisy learning situations be separated from quiet areas, that teachers be given offices so that they have some place to meet students.

Use of facilities

Ruplin & Russell (71) propose structuring the student's non-class hours. In essence they are removing from the college level classroom all homework correcting, all presentation of grammar, and all laboratory work. They are structuring these activities for the student to accomplish outside the three contact hours. These contact hours are to be used for recitation and conversation in the language, for the study of culture, perhaps for philology. The professor's main task would be to motivate the student and to stimulate conversation.

Use of time

Preassessment

Many writers are showing signs of recognizing the barriers to completing behavior objectives because difficulty frequently arises when the practical matter of implementation faces the teacher. Interest has centered on various areas. First, in importance, is the matter of preassessment.

Moreno (57) has designed a program of performance outcomes for sixth grade Spanish programs in the El Rio Elementary School District. This program is highlighted by its practicality and by the involvement of the staff in its delineation. His project uses teacher aids. Pupil performances are what the aids have determined are important and accomplishable within the conditions existing in the classroom. The writers repeatedly ask themselves this question: "Are the expected student performances realistic for this instructional time provided and with the present competency of the aids?"

How preassessment may be used

Valette (89) cautions that clarification must precede the writing of objectives. Page, in Matranga (54), notes the time spent in assessing the needs and determining the direction of the project. He also pleads for teacher time in summer curriculum projects, pointing out the hours needed to implement a program.

Preplanning was also essential at West Bend, Wisconsin, according to Laleike (46,47). Program implementation has proceeded according to plan although some thought has been given to augmented planning periods for languages other than Spanish. (Spanish was the first language to be put on the program.) The year 1969–70 saw Spanish classes continuing into a second year of the program and implementation of German and French classes at the beginning level. Early feedback indicates that students in the project classes are experiencing less boredom than their counterparts in traditional classes.

Preplanning

Materials

Others have pleaded for materials that would be teachable under existing conditions. Sharp (78) feels that the materials must be: (1) self-directing; (2) self-initiating; (3) self-implementing; and (4) self-evaluating. He argues that programs must not require direct supervision for prolonged periods of time. Geis (28) pleads for the innovative materials to come from the school and not to be imposed upon it. He cites the need for good teacher manuals, for expertise to be made available through specially trained personnel. He argues that efforts to change teacher behavior do not reflect the growing sophistication that we have used in changing student behavior. Macías (50) reports on the use of programmed homework in the Tacoma public schools suggesting that traditional student attitudes toward responsibility for their own learning must change. Teachers must learn not to reteach programmed materials or the student will

Characteristics of needed materials

57

not bother to master them. The teachers must also learn different techniques of presentation in conjunction with programmed instruction.

Teacher behavior

Most authors agree that orientation, preservice and in-service training, consultant help, and favorable teacher attitudes are essentials to success. Money and time create special problems. Teachers are busy with their current jobs, and while objectives should meet *their* aims it is hard for them to get time to write the objectives without the help of summer curriculum projects or released time. Also many teachers must be convinced of the necessity for change.

Teacher preparation for performance curricula

Geis (28) cites continuing support, financing, and teacher training as some of the problems working against innovation. He poses the question, "Why should teachers change? What does it cost the teacher? What does she gain?" He suggests that the school environment be one of innovation and that the teacher assume a more dignified and more rewarding role as manager and investigator of student learning. There should be systematic, progressive, and cumulative change. If the teacher can see the need for change, the change will be more readily accomplished.

Damore (21) states that because of the needs shown last year for a keener insight into behavioral objectives his district instituted a series of monthly in-service meetings to increase teacher awareness of the advantages of preparing objectives in terms of student behavior. Consultants were available at these meetings so that each teacher who attended could be provided with direct consultant service.

In-service meetings to increa[se] teacher awareness

In Connecticut, Page (Matranga, 54) pleaded for more time for teachers, stating the purpose of a ten-semester continual program: (1) improving teacher-student communication; (2) reversing the motivation lag; (3) preventing proliferation of levels and courses; (4) avoiding student dropout or attrition after two years; (5) escaping fallout from involvement in the audio-lingual vs. more conventional methodologies controversy. This school system established two tracks and separate courses for a ten-semester period. A student who lacked the proficiency needed to proceed to the next full level of learning could elect a half-step course in which he could review the material previously introduced and cover half of the new material. The courses were

A ten-semester curriculum

numbered in such a way as not to seem pejorative. Although the work was heavy, Page stated that students came to the conclusion that "learning is continuous and unavoidable." She felt that she could now use textbooks and not have textbooks use her.

Hoetker (38) rejects many of the techniques of the so-called change agents, saying that teachers show hostility to the proponents of behavioral objectives because the advocates of behavioral objectives are arrogant, badly educated, and clearly of the opinion that anyone who "cannot" sit down and write behavioral objectives for his discipline is a fraud and an incompetent. To avoid this Hoetker shuns the jargon common to this area and presents the behavioral specifications of objectives within the context of a particular sequence of work.

Change agents, "arrogant?"

Mowrer (58) sees the role of the teacher shifting from taskmaster to central intelligence officer. Popham (67) sees the teacher as an artist and the teaching act as amenable to rigorous empirical involvement. Markle, in Brodinsky (11), describes the teacher as a prescriber of instruction basing this instruction on his knowledge of each student. She sees the teacher as a programmer in a sense who will have to know considerably more about kinds of learning. Sharp (78) describes the personnel needed to help the teacher keep records. These persons will review the success, the needs, the interests, desires, and progress of the students. They can also help the teacher keep current on the availability of new materials.

Clark (19) experimented with using programmed foreign language courses in secondary school with specially trained teachers. He found that teachers with nonfavorable attitudes are unlikely to get good results. Successful teachers are both competent in their field and know what they are doing with programmed materials. Clark suggests that the teachers should have some programming experience so that they may know they can control it. Further research in this area would combine programmed learning and individualized instruction.

Grouping and scheduling

The time-honored problems of grouping and scheduling received attention in this year's literature. Grittner, in Rose (70), was asked whether various levels of achievement could successfully work together in a single group. He answered that total self-study programs require many paraprofessional assistants and money for materials development. When asked about schedules

Grittner replied that it was better to modify schedules rather than to eliminate pupils. He questions whether or not it is necessary to have full programs at every level, implying that some students want only to retain their skills without further development and that less scheduled time is needed for them.

Modify schedules; don't eliminate students

Allen & Politzer, reviewed in Hoye (39), report that foreign language teachers in flexibly scheduled schools have difficulty defining the performance criteria necessary to facilitate the desired individualization of instruction. Indeed the problem seems prevalent in areas where the schedule has preceded the writing of behavioral objectives. Wilmoth & Ehn (93), writing of the Franklin High School in Livonia, Michigan, question whether the flexible modular schedule is really flexible. They ask if it may not be more rigid than traditional scheduling. They point out that while the traditional schedule repeats itself each day, the flexible schedule repeats itself each week. They also report teachers' attitudes toward such scheduling schemes. Most teachers feel the type of teaching they are doing is far different from the traditional classroom situation. Certain teachers feel themselves unsure of handling the new and unfamiliar groupings. In spite of some positive attitudes toward flexible scheduling, Cawelti (17) suggests:

Flexibility of new schedule formats?

> Despite much involvement in planning for the technical aspects of the flexible schedule, it appears that in many instances not much change in teaching occurred except that traditional teaching was done for different lengths of time in different sized groups.

Hoye (39) indicates that the solution to the use of different kinds of scheduling arrangements is for teachers to work in teams with groups of students so that they can modify the schedule each week. In this way large groups, regular classes, seminar groups, tutoring, and automated self-teaching can be scheduled for the learning activities which contribute to the meeting of objectives. He further proposes that modules of time be organized into large fluid time blocks that can easily be rearranged by teachers.

Teacher teams

Sharp (78) advocates scheduling students in ten half-hour segments per week. The teacher would make out a schedule for each student every two weeks. This procedure guarantees that the teacher must interview the student at least once every ten days. The student, in this case, is working independently.

Hibbard (36) recounts an interesting experiment at White Bear Lake, Minnesota, in the secondary schools. Large groups are used when the teacher wishes to introduce grammatical structures or aspects of culture or to present the background of problems about to be studied. They are useful also for exercises in choral response, for testing, for film presentations, and when guest speakers are available. Small groups are used for conversational practice, dialogue adaptation, and directed dialogue. The laboratory is scheduled for library use while a resource center provides the proper atmosphere for the individualization of instruction.

Examples of use of flexible schedules

Elsass (27) suggests that the French system illustrates one means of flexible scheduling since the European plan does not schedule each subject for the same amount of time each day.

Demuth (24) states the case for flexible scheduling well when he says that the use of the different modes of instruction (small group, large group, independent study, laboratory) "requires that the subject and the curriculum must be carefully scrutinized and that the activities which are appropriate for each of these modes of instruction must be determined."

Scheduling may also influence the individualization of teacher training programs on the college level. Langer (49) reports on minicourses in teacher training. He suggests that a program should be defined in terms of pupil outcomes, not teacher outcomes. His minicourses are based on the process of microteaching. Autoinstructional and self-evaluation forms are included. In the process, as he illustrates it, the student (a teacher trainee) taught a lesson which was taped, then critiqued the lesson, next restructured the lesson, and finally retaught it. In this program each minicourse centers around one particular problem such as higher-order questioning techniques.

Student-teacher responsibility

A problem considered by very few writers is the question of how to motivate the student who remains unmotivated when working with a performance curriculum, or of what to do for the good student who lets freedom go to his head. Is it appropriate to let the students accomplish little or nothing during a year if that is their choice? Many teachers will say that students are already doing just this in a traditional classroom; others will say that certain students work when the teacher puts pressure on them each day but will not work without the presence of the teacher.

Motivating students

61

Page, in Matranga (54), remarks that some students are too immature to profit from the program since they do not exhibit sufficient self-discipline. Educators, however, frequently point out that today's student demands the right to make his own decisions and that he must therefore learn from those choices. Perhaps the next few years' research will verify such assumptions and offer findings about the number of such students as well as the various techniques that have proven successful with them.

Students learn from their choices

Summary

Implementation of a performance curriculum does not imply only the act of writing behavioral objectives. Time, space, and materials are involved, and, most importantly, teacher behavior must change before student behavior can be allowed to change. This year (1969) saw the beginnings of implementation of performance curricula and individualized programs but good commercial materials structured on performance objectives have not yet appeared on the market. Perhaps they will become available in the early 1970s. Schools are finding out that flexible scheduling alone can create problems but that when coupled with curriculum change and performance objectives it can be a boon. Space for individualized programs is being created, but teachers are not waiting for old facilities to be remodeled. Rather they are changing the *ways* in which available space is used. The implications for changes in space and use of space will grow as programs are implemented. Also, teacher assignments, including instructional time, will have to be reevaluated, as will teacher load.

Testing and evaluation: its role in the performance curriculum

This portion of this article considers testing and measurement and the evaluation of student performance, that is, what is normally called "grading." Program evaluation is discussed later.

College Entrance Examination Board changes

There were two significant developments in testing and evaluation during the past year: the appearance of some criterion-referenced tests and the announcement by the College Entrance Examination Board that on May 1, 1971, new listening-reading achievement tests in French, German, Italian, Russian, and Spanish will be introduced. These composite tests will only be given in May. No foreign language achievement tests will be

New tests

offered in December 1970, March 1971, or July 1971. There will be an administration of the reading test only in January 1971. Although these composite examinations represent a giant step forward in the minds of most foreign language educators, there is a problem of securing tape recorders at the various test centers and also one of obtaining sufficient proctors. Woodford (94) reported on these examinations in a speech before the Northeast Conference. Another encouraging development is the recurring theme in the professional literature that testing should be shaped to demonstrate *what the student knows*, not how he performs in relation to other students. There is a further thought expressed that testing should both reinforce the student's knowledge and should be the means whereby the teacher diagnoses the student's difficulties and prescribes further instructional activities for him.

Mastery tests

Valette (90) links tests to performance objectives when she states that according to research, student learning can be significantly enhanced if teachers focus on specific linguistic objectives and insist that a high percentage of those objectives be mastered before the student proceeds to the subsequent lesson.

Tests and performance objectives

Although the past year did not see the emergence of learning packages with specific objectives, pretests, and self-evaluation materials, such packages have now appeared in the area of mathematics (Arena, 4) and one may assume that they will soon be available in foreign language study.

Aptitude tests

The area of aptitude testing was explored by Valette (90) and Pimsleur (63). Both feel that factors other than aptitude are involved in language success. Pimsleur sees the tests as basically useful for the placement of students. Delco, Matthews, & Rogers (23) plead for more reliable instruments for identifying potential aptitude and achievement than the "quite inadequate predictors of success now employed." They consider the construction of such instruments essential for the education of the disadvantaged.

Aptitude tests used for various reasons

Scholars are asking that tests be used as motivating factors. Pimsleur (63), in a speech at the Northeast Conference, suggested that no grade lower than a *B* be assigned and that students have whatever time is needed to master material sufficiently to score at such a level. This suggestion is indeed in keeping with the idea that foreign languages be accessible to all students.

En route measurement

There is also interest in intermediate measures of student progress. Herbert (35) points out that mastery may take years and that student progress should be evaluated at intermediate levels. The teacher, then, determines what levels must be attained in certain behaviors before the student can proceed effectively to others and develops criteria or guidelines for measuring the learner's progress in the instructional program. Since the teacher must deal with a variety of individuals she will also deal with variations in pupil abilities. Carroll, in Valette (90), equates aptitude with the time needed to master a task; so in this sense students with a high aptitude are those who learn more quickly. Herbert suggests that the writers of objectives specify that 75% of the class should score 60% or higher for an objective to be achieved. As mentioned earlier, some writers question whether certain students have the maturity to keep working on a particular objective to the point of mastery. Other writers maintain that the student should remain on the particular unit until mastery has been attained.

Measurement of student progress

Project Cram (DeLay, 22) is a project designed to give continuous sampling of student achievement throughout the year. One might think of it as a process whereby one administers several variants of the final at various times during the year to see whether or not the students are making progress toward achievement of the desired objectives. This project was undertaken at Stanford University by Dwight Allen, Donald DeLay, William Gorth, and Lee Popejoy (DeLay, 22). Such "Comprehensive Random Achievement Monitoring" can, according to its proponents, provide evaluation of individual student performance, teacher performance, and the evaluation of a total school program. It also monitors in terms of final criteria rather than intermediate criteria and should indicate whether or not the final criteria are being met by means of the intermediate criteria. It is a basic sampling design implemented in four procedural phases: (1) preparation of instructional objectives and performance criteria; (2) establishment of performance tests; (3) diagnosis of initial student achievement; and (4) application of random achievement sampling. One form of the final testing instrument should be given before the course begins to determine

CRAM

exactly where the student is. This preassessment of student needs can then be documented from the test itself. Students would be cued to the scope of the learning expected; major issues and principles would be exposed to the student. Armed with this information the student could then plan his attack on the objectives of the course. Data could be gathered from this first test for grouping students so that learning would be at a maximum.

Grading

Not much attention has been paid to grading except that several writers have pointed out the negative influence of grades, among them Pimsleur & Struth (64), Valette (90), Markle in Brodinsky (11), and Donald Stewart (83). Stewart points out that when a professor at the University of California at Santa Barbara gave 200 A's in an introductory course a regent of the university stated that the action of awarding that many A's was "outrageous and indefensible" and demanded a study of the university's grading system in order to identify if there had been a decline in grading "standards" in recent years. A statewide faculty group had just completed such a study and found no evidence of declining "standards." Stewart then discusses this phenomenon by pointing out that when the grades of a class approximate a "normal curve," it is evidence that the degree of learning which took place in the course occurred by *chance*, i.e., the teacher neither tried to facilitate learning nor to inhibit learning. When students are getting more A's and B's than normal, the indication is that the teacher is trying to improve learning beyond mere chance. Conversely, when students are getting more D's and F's than normal, the indication is that a teacher is trying to inhibit learning beyond mere chance. Stewart then makes the point that the students attending the University of California (in a vast majority) represent "the cream of the crop" and therefore a normal curve for grading these students would be highly inappropriate.

Influence of grades

Misuse of grades in regard to learning

Pimsleur & Struth (64) suggest that the schools give thought to setting goals that most students can achieve, such as the receptive skills of listening and reading in low-aptitude classes. They state that the present system of giving all the C's, D's, and F's a bad language experience so that the happy few A's and B's can learn a language is as wasteful as it is undemocratic.

Popham (67) wishes to improve teacher behavior by acquainting prospective teachers with terms of testing such as (*1*) validity;

(2) reliability; (3) correlation; (4) item analysis; (5) standardized test; and (6) percentile. His book, which is written using performance objectives, sets as terminal behavior for teachers the ability to carry out a simple item analysis operation and the rating of answers in such a way as to reveal an attitude toward measurement as something less than perfect and grading as highly subjective and value laden.

Grading is subjective

Measurement and performance objectives

In a document published by the U.S. Office of Education (1), reference is made to the relationship between well-stated performance objectives and measurement. The former make both measurement and audit of performance more objective, reliable, and valid. The measurement will be objective and reliable because anyone using the evaluation technique under the same conditions would tend to get the same or almost the same results. It will be valid because it will measure what it was intended to measure, i.e., the relative attainment of performance objectives.

Educational audit

Sharp (78) suggests that the testing program should be divided into two phases: (1) standardized instruments, some of which will be commercial and some of which will be especially constructed; and (2) a battery of diagnostic tests that will help the teacher pinpoint the specific difficulty students may be encountering.

Two phases of a testing program

Seelye (74) attempted to measure the cognitive changes that are associated with confrontation with another culture. He measured the extent to which a national group (North American) is familiar with the patterns of the host country (Guatemala). As a result of his work, he suggests that it is feasible to employ an objective instrument to measure the cultural understanding of a highly literate group living in a second culture. Seelye & Brewer (76) also measured the effect which a number of emotional states, such as ethnocentrism, authoritarianism, and attitudes towards deviants, have on adjustment to a second culture.

Testing of cultural awareness

Meiden (55) writes that testing plays a part in the training of teaching assistants and graduate students. He points out that while many handle all aspects of the major language competently there are some who are surprisingly deficient in certain aspects of the language. Thus, all graduate students and teaching assistant candidates are given an entrance test before entrance into the M.A. or Ph.D. programs at Ohio State University.

Use of testing in the training of teaching assistants

The test consists of a dictation, a conversation with the examiner, the reading aloud of a passage in the foreign language, a translation from English to the foreign language, and one from the foreign language to English. Candidates with deficiencies are required to take appropriate courses to remedy the deficiency. It seems to this writer that if more universities were to adopt such a policy the quality of graduate assistant teaching would most certainly improve; many of us have had students return from college complaining that they knew more about structure or pronunciation than the teaching assistant.

Placement tests

The issue of the placement test appeared in certain writings. Hartwig (33) feels that college professors must take the leadership in articulation and must tell the high schools what is expected of them. He states that placement tests imply that the high schools are not doing a good job. Ultimately he would like to see them abolished if a common curriculum can be set up. Grittner, in Rose (70), suggests that if standardized objectives could be maintained then placement tests would be unnecessary, but since levels of achievement vary they are needed. Damore (21) used criterion-referenced tests for placement purposes and found them as reliable as teacher recommendations.

Different points of view

Teacher-made tests

Certain writers prepared material primarily for the classroom teacher. A new trend in these articles was the accent on testing with visuals and testing the audiolingual skills without involving reading and writing. Woodford (95) has prepared a practical guide for new and prospective teachers of Spanish and Portuguese. His principles of testing reflect both the expertise of years spent at Educational Testing Service and the practical experience of the classroom. All beginning teachers of any language should study his suggested techniques for evaluating speaking and listening. Also, his section on the scoring of essay questions would be of use to many experienced teachers. Woodford makes the point that if the teacher gives no tests during the first few weeks of the course the student will in all probability not take the subject seriously and will devote his energies to those areas where he receives grades. Woodford also covers other aspects of testing such as the placement test, aptitude test, and a survey of the nationally administered tests.

A practical guide

Steiner treats teacher-made tests (85) and concentrates on helping the classroom teacher separate the testing of the four skills.

Although 1969 did not bring to the commercial market any criterion-referenced tests, it did see the publication of such tests in California (Damore, 21) in the teaching of Spanish. It now remains the task of some state to sponsor a conference or assume a statewide project of writing criterion-referenced tests for one level of one language following preestablished state guidelines. Such guidelines are appearing in various states such as Illinois and Wisconsin and they make excellent precursors for criterion-referenced tests.

Criterion-referenced tests

Summary

1969 saw the following emerge in the area of testing: (*1*) a new awareness of the role of testing in motivation; (2) an assertion that low aptitude scores should not exclude a student from the study of a foreign language; (3) a recognition that well-stated performance objectives facilitate the making of criterion-referenced tests and a plea for this type of test; (4) the introduction of the composite achievement test in French, German, Italian, Russian, and Spanish by the College Entrance Examination Board; (5) new concepts of grading such as offering grades of *A* and *B* only; (6) various processes of obtaining intermediate measurement when mastery has not yet been achieved, such as continuous sampling of student achievement; and (7) the appearance of criterion-referenced tests in Spanish. In short, the year has been fruitful.

Program evaluation: educational accountability to learner and taxpayer

Purposes

Program evaluation includes all aspects of the teaching-learning process and encompasses both curriculum and instruction. Evaluation, according to Hatfield (34), implies the collection, processing, and interpretation of data pertaining to an educational program. The area of evaluation includes four basic types: (*1*) program evaluation; (2) student evaluation; (3) teacher evaluation; and (4) research evaluation.

Sullivan (87) states that evaluation should improve instruction and student achievement or there is no justification for the

Relationship of evaluation to instruction

money spent on it. He suggests that the essential criterion for evaluating educational experiences is the extent to which they produce desired learner behaviors that previously were not performed under the same conditions. Sullivan cautions that many evaluations of schools are based on content and classroom conditions instead of objectives. He adds that those who oppose goals want to introduce content and let changes (whatever they may or may not be) occur. In dealing with evaluation Sullivan says that assessment based on performance objectives is a good part of formative evaluation. He treats both summative and formative evaluation.

Grobman's (31) basic treatise covers many of the traditional aspects of evaluation and is valuable for the practitioner. Grobman points out that decision making is ever present, that the decision to continue using a text or to continue operating on a traditional schedule is an evaluation. She defines curriculum evaluation as reflecting all systematic efforts of a project to assess the strengths and weaknesses of its activities and their use-*Curriculum evaluation* fulness. She points out that more change has occurred in curriculum during the last ten years than in any previous decade in the history of the United States. Such change would only underline the need for proper evaluation procedures. Many materials that have been designed are experimental. The word *experimental* implies that the activities or materials may not fully achieve the intended results and that feedback may indicate changes that are necessary to improve them. She feels that evaluation instruments should be designed at the same time that the project is designed so that immediate feedback may be used to correct any deficiencies.

Ethics

Grobman (31) indicates that there are certain ethics in evaluation. She discusses the observation of a person or a group when that person or group does not know it is being observed, the release of information or data that identifies schools or individual teachers with the result that this information reflects pejoratively on the schools. Grobman, like Sullivan, discusses two types of *Formative and summative* evaluation—formative evaluation, which occurs during the per-*evaluation* iod of the classroom tryout, and summative evaluation, which is written after the project is completed. She discusses the merits of the project evaluator from within and the project evaluator who comes from the outside. The former is able to communicate the findings to the project staff much more conveniently than the latter. She does not feel that objectives stated in behavioral terms are necessary for project evaluation. She sees Mager's approach to objectives as differing from Bloom's classification or taxonomy since she feels that most behavioral objectives are to be found in the cognitive domain.

Involving the authors of materials in the evaluation project — having them make classroom visits so that they can see what is being done to and with their materials, so they can see what youngsters are really like — is a valuable evaluation procedure. Grobman points out that many authors are college professors who have not been inside a school for years. She delineates the differences between short-run and long-run evaluation. One must be cautious for, even though funders are often interested in short-run information, *it is long-run information that will have the most lasting value.* She proposes that new materials should be viewed and evaluated not only by interested teachers but by disinterested and even hostile teachers. Grobman pleads that tests not be the only means of evaluation, that there be other techniques such as structured observations, classroom visits, reviews of materials, teacher feedback, questionnaires, etc., that would support test data. She finally points out the necessity for the project evaluator to establish rapport with the project personnel and with the school systems involved.

Teacher involvement

One writer, Moore (56), would involve the teacher actively in the research process. He says, "The program requires first-rate teacher-scholars who are productive researchers in the teaching-learning process." He continues, " . . . they [teachers] must acquire competencies necessary for developing and applying an effective instructional design. Instructional objectives are only the starting point in developing these competencies."

Mandel (53) finds evaluation essential for determining whether or not a program is successful in achieving its goals. He points out that in certain guides for evaluating the effectiveness of a program, the emphasis is on what the teacher does and the techniques he uses. The fault of this emphasis, he implies, is that the discussion usually revolves around how a supervisor would have handled a problem or taught a class. A nonsubjective point of view would derive from observable and measurable data which could be agreed upon and substantiated by the su-

Involvement of the teacher in the research process

Evaluating the teaching-learning process

pervisor and the classroom teacher. Such data are most easily gathered when objectives for each lesson are determined in advance and are stated in terms of terminal student behavior. The objective, rather the achievement of the objective, then becomes the focal point for discussing classroom practice and ultimately for determining the value of a given program.

Mandel proposes that in evaluating an entire program the supervisor is interested not only in how well the students perform on tests but also in the nature and quality of the teacher activity. He is interested in analyzing the activities of the teacher in order to raise the achievement level. Although achievement may be only related to a teaching activity, nevertheless, the evidence for the success of the activity is drawn from pupil performance.

Accountability

The year 1969 was the year of educational accountability. Extensive cuts in federal funds produced greater emphasis on the evaluation of those projects that were funded. Not only were many projects required to measure their own aims, but independent educational accomplishment auditors were sent in to measure the evaluation as well as the project. The clear, precise statement of performance objectives was requested in most literature published by the U.S. Office of Education. One document (40) stated that accountability "means that the agent accepting a grant will be held responsible for performing according to the terms of the grant, particularly in accomplishing the objectives of the project within the time period or periods specified, within the budget limitations designed, and according to the standards established." The document continued by stating that this concept requires the agent to keep records or accounts of the progress of the grant in the above area and to make these records available for outside scrutiny and audit by the Office of Education or other legal authorities. The evaluators and auditors were to be carefully trained to evaluate baseline data, as another document published by Behavior Systems Corporation indicated (68).

Requirements of the U.S. Office of Education

Evaluative feedback was also considered essential. One should not wait until the end of a project (or until the end of a school year) to evaluate the process and the content. Cohen (20) writes of the problem and concern over the time lag between rescarch findings and their application to the classroom. ESEA Title VII or Title VIII evaluators give day-to-day or week-to-week

Evaluative feedback

71

reports of program progress and achievement. These reports must also contain diagnoses for current program problems and suggestions for program revisions.

Becker (8) describes the accountability concepts worked into the various dropout and bilingual projects that were developed. He listed four main headings of provisions for accountability: (1) applicants were asked to state their general and specific objectives in measurable terms; (2) applicants had to make provisions for use of good management techniques in planning, installing, and operating projects; (3) applicants were required to develop an evaluation design that would measure the results, processes, and management of their projects; and (4) applicants had to make provisions for an outside independent educational accomplishment audit of projects. In addition there was to be a thorough needs assessment and the use of technical assistance in developing, managing, and evaluating projects: the latter included a performance contract. These contracts are the bases for grants which require local educational agencies to accomplish what they intend to accomplish during a specified period of time.

Headings of provisions for accountability

According to Becker the best proposals spell out in detail their structuring of the classrooms, giving the activities in each class, the composition of the class, and the time allotted for the use of each language in instructing the children. Special evaluation instruments are being designed to meet the needs of these projects in cases where these needs cannot be met by existing instruments. One dropout prevention project has entered into a performance contract with private industry to operate a learning center for potential dropouts. The contractor will be reimbursed on the basis of each student's achievement and the efficiency of the approach taken. Becker describes this project as an exciting approach to accountability. He feels that these efforts to move toward greater accountability should greatly affect education in the future.

Some projects and details

Kittel (44) indicates that more and more frequently all aspects of education will be evaluated by the criterion of pupil performance rather than by criteria of provisions for teaching, learning, administration, supervision, and so forth.

Stake (82) has developed an evaluation form that can be used by schools connected with the program for gifted students in Illinois. This form describes and evaluates the classroom and the learning activities that take place there. Little attention is paid

An evaluation form for learning activities

to the individual student's performance, but background information about the students in the class is provided. This evaluation instrument asks outside evaluators to describe the three best things about the classroom and the three features that most need changing. A circle is provided for the teacher to indicate how much class time was spent on individual work, teacher explanations, exchange of ideas, social matters, or administrative matters. There is a section for the teacher, individual student, or group to select the most appropriate descriptions of the classroom. Each statement is phrased positively. There is a further section that describes how work in a particular class differed from work in an average class. The form is innovative and might indeed provide parents with more information about the experience the youngster is having in the classroom.

The Pennsylvania Report (Smith, 80) is a magnificent example of a profession evaluating itself—its goals, its ambitions, its strategies. From the project certain interesting revelations have appeared. For instance, there seems to be no relationship between teacher proficiency as demonstrated on the MLA Foreign Language Proficiency Test for Teachers and Advanced Students and class performance of students as evidenced by achievement tests. (Philip Smith (81) makes this point, but Carroll (16) takes issue with it.) The Pennsylvania Report was also evaluated as a research project by a number of very distinguished members of the profession. Questions have been raised about the tests used in the project by Valette (90) and by Carroll (16), the use of language laboratories by Hocking (37), the role of the teacher by Otto (60), the research design and interpretation of results by Aleamoni & Spencer (2), the bias due to school, teacher, and student variables by Clark (18), and about the evaluation of different strategies involved in audiolingual and traditional approaches by Lange (48). This project which attempted to *evaluate* will doubtless continue *to be* evaluated for years to come.

The profession evaluating itself

Summary

Program evaluation was closely tied to behavioral objectives during the year 1969. The U.S. Office of Education, with its accent on educational accountability and on the independent educational audit, gave impetus to this move since many documents stated that precise behavioral or performance objectives would facilitate evaluation and audit. Teachers were urged to make feedback and evaluation part of their educational process so that change could occur before the end of the school year. The Pennsylvania Report served as an example of evaluation being evaluated and weighed to determine whether or not the conclusions it presented were valid. Guidelines were established by authors such as Grobman to aid the school district beginning an innovative project so that proper evaluation mechanisms might be built into the project at its conception. There now appears to be a need for specific evaluative documents in the foreign language field because the teacher is too busy to design them. There did appear the questionnaire on attitudes distributed at the 1970 Northeast Conference (Serafino, 77) that can be used by teachers in the field. More documents of this type are needed.

Conclusion

The three areas of behavioral objectives, testing, and evaluation are closely interwoven. The past year has seen greater emergence of performance curricula than ever before. Many authors stressed the need to state educational objectives in terms of observable, measurable behavior. Although some expressed reservations about teaching everything by means of behavioral objectives, most agree that a part of the curriculum should be so organized. Insistence on a new type of curriculum grew out of several societal concerns: (1) the new student who no longer accepts docilely tasks given to him but who demands a share in creating the type of experience in which he is to participate; (2) the demand for relevancy for knowing what one is doing and why; (3) the demand for all to be admitted to study in any area; (4) the decrease in funding of projects that brings with it a concomitant scrutiny of the effectiveness of those projects that are funded.

If student behavior rather than teacher behavior is to be judged, then there must be tests that measure the changes in student performance. These would be criterion-referenced tests that could be used for preassessment of student learning, for measuring en route behavior changes, and for measuring mastery. Some such tests have been prepared, but no commercial publishing house has yet put such tests on the market. Aptitude tests were questioned as a means of eliminating students from foreign language study, but for purposes of diagnosis or grouping they still have acceptance. Teacher proficiency tests were challenged since the Pennsylvania Report gave rise to the claim that there was no relationship between teacher proficiency as measured on the MLA Foreign Language Proficiency Test for Teachers and Advanced Students and on class achievement; others refuted the claim, stating that other factors were involved here. Grading came under scrutiny; if performance objectives were established for each course and if each student had his own time criterion then indeed all students might earn an *A* in the course. Some challenged the profession to justify the numbers of *D*'s and *F*'s given so that the happy few could receive their *A*'s and *B*'s.

The same factors which prompted the growing acceptance of performance objectives have influenced the area of evaluation. The U.S. government, administrators and school boards, and students have all demanded greater accountability from the schools. This worries some serious educators who see in this tendency a threat to the freedom to explore, to let students read a book with no purpose in mind but to enjoy it and to learn from it whatever they can learn. Most writers did agree that the formulation of specific objectives, the use of criterion-referenced tests and the formulation of proper and appropriate evaluative instruments should help education to improve and make the educational experience a more exciting one for its customers — our students.

References, Behavioral objectives and evaluation

1 *Accountability:The New Concepts and Terminology Affecting the Dropout Prevention and Bilingual Evaluation Programs*. Washington, D.C.: Division of Plans and Supplementary Centers, Bureau of Elementary and Secondary Education, U.S. Office of Education, 1969. [Mimeo.]

2 Aleamoni, Lawrence M., and Richard E. Spencer. "An Evaluation of the Pennsylvania Foreign Language Project." *Modern Language Journal* 53(1969):421–28.

3 Allen, Virginia G., and F. André Paquette,eds. *The Student's World Is the World:New Dimensions in the Teaching of FLES*. Bloomington: Indiana Language Program, 1969. [Invitational conference on FLES, Minneapolis, Minnesota, November 1968.]

4 Arena, John E. "An Instrument for Individualizing Instruction." *Educational Leadership* 27 (1970):784–87.

5 Banathy, Bela H. "Current Trends in College Curriculum:A Systems Approach," 105–40 in Emma M. Birkmaier,ed., *Britannica Review of Foreign Language Education, Volume 1*. Chicago: Encyclopaedia Britannica, 1968[1969].

6 ——— "The Design of Foreign Language Teacher Education." *Modern Language Journal* 52 (1968):490–500.

7 ——— "The Potentials and Limitations of Con-

trastive Linguistic Analysis," 1–7 in Jerrold L. Mordaunt, ed., *Proceedings:Pacific Northwest Conference on Foreign Languages, Twentieth Annual Meeting, April 11–12, 1969.* Vol. 20. Victoria, B.C.: Univ. of Victoria, 1969.

8 Becker, Ralph J. *Role of the Division of Plans and Supplementary Centers in Implementing Accountability.* Presented at the Institute on Independent Educational Accomplishment Auditing, Washington, D.C., 16–18 October 1969. [Mimeo.]

9 Bloom, Benjamin S.,ed. *Taxonomy of Educational Objectives, Handbook I:Cognitive Domain.* New York: David McKay, 1956.

10 Borton, Terry. "What's Left When School's Forgotten?" *Saturday Review* 53(18 April 1970): 69–71.

11 Brodinsky, Ben. "Trends and Issues." *Education Summary* 3(1970):5.

12 Brooks, Nelson. "The Rung and the Ladder," 135–47 in Joseph A. Tursi,ed., *Foreign Languages and the "New" Student.* Reports of the Working Committees of the Northeast Conference on the Teaching of Foreign Languages. New York: MLA Materials Center, 1970.

13 Bruner, Jerome. "The Skill of Relevance and the Relevance of Skills." *Saturday Review* 53(18 April 1970):66–68.

14 Cadoux, Remunda. "Foreword," 5 in Joseph A. Tursi,ed., *Foreign Languages and the "New" Student.* Reports of the Working Committees of the Northeast Conference on the Teaching of Foreign Languages. New York: MLA Materials Center, 1970.

15 ———Speech at the 1970 Northeast Conference. Boston, March 1970.

16 Carroll, John B. "What Does the Pennsylvania Foreign Language Research Project Tell Us?" *Foreign Language Annals* 3(1969):214–36.

17 Cawelti, Gordon. "Does Innovation Make Any Difference?" *Nation's Schools* 82,v(1968):60–63.

18 Clark, John L. D. "The Pennsylvania Project and the 'Audio-Lingual vs. Traditional' Question." *Modern Language Journal* 53(1969):388–96.

19 Clark, William H. *Using Programmed Foreign Language Courses in Secondary School with Specially Trained Teachers.* Final Report. Rochester, New York: Univ. of Rochester, 1968.

20 Cohen, Bernard,ed. *Objectives.* Darien, Connecticut: Dunlap and Associates,n.d. [Mimeo.]

21 Damore, Anthony P. *Teaching Spanish by Being Responsible for Specific Objectives.* Modesto, California: Stanislaus County Schools, 1968.

22 DeLay, Donald. *Cram:Random Testing Gives Steady Feedback on Pupil Progress.* Stanford, California: Stanford Univ., n.d. [Mimeo.]

23 Delco, E.A., George T. Matthews, and Robert W. Rogers. "Opportunities and Responsibilities for Developing Human Resources." *Liberal Education* 55(1969):235–43.

24 Demuth, Jerry. "Exciting Experiment at West Leyden." *Chicago Sun-Times* (26 October 1969).

25 Eiss, Albert F. "Performance Objectives." *The Bulletin of the National Association of Secondary School Principals.* 54,342(1970):51–57.

26 Ellert, Ernest E. *The Concept of Directed Program.* Presented at 21st Univ. of Kentucky Foreign Language Conference, Lexington, April 1968.

27 Elsass, Ray. "French Education." *Foreign Language Speaker* (November 1968):2–28.

28 Geis, George L. *Developing a Strategy for Innovation.* Presented at a symposium on the Associated Staff Training Program for the American Educational Research Association, Chicago, February 1968. [ERIC Documentation Reproduction Service: ED 024 295.]

29 Grittner, Frank M. "A Critical Re-Examination of Methods and Materials," in Robert F. Roeming,ed., "Proceedings of the Central States Conference on the Teaching of Foreign Languages, 1969." *Modern Language Journal* 53(1969): 467–77.

30 ——— "What's New in Wisconsin:Innovative Foreign Language Programs." *Voice of the Wisconsin Foreign Language Teacher* 7,i(1967): 33–42.

31 Grobman, Hulda. *Evaluation Activities of Curriculum Projects:A Starting Point.* Chicago: Rand McNally, 1968. [AERA Curriculum Evaluation Monograph 2.]

32 Gronlund, Norman E. *Stating Behavioral Objectives for Classroom Instruction.* New York: Macmillan, 1970.

33 Hartwig, Hellmut A. "Teaching Advanced Language:What the Colleges Expect of the High Schools," in Robert F. Roeming,ed., "Proceedings of the Central States Conference on the Teaching of Foreign Languages, 1969." *Modern Language Journal* 53(1969):485–91.

34 Hatfield, William N. "Foreign Language Program Evaluation," 375–88 in Emma M. Birkmaier,ed., *Britannica Review of Foreign Language Education, Volume 1.* Chicago: Encyclopaedia Britannica, 1968[1969].

35 Herbert, Charles. *Behavioral Objectives for English as a Second Language.* San Bernardino, California, 1969. [Mimeo.]

36 Hibbard, Allen. *Modular Scheduling and Modern Foreign Languages.* Presented at Spring Conference of North Dakota Foreign Language Association. [ERIC Documentation Reproduction Service: ED 030 353.]

37 Hocking, Elton. "The Laboratory in Perspective: Teachers, Strategies, Outcomes." *Modern Language Journal* 53(1969):404–10.

38 Hoetker, James. "The Limitations and Advantages of Behavioral Objectives in the Arts and Humanities:A Guest Editorial." *Foreign Language Annals* 3(1970):560–65.

39 Hoye, Almon G. "Let's Do Our Thing:Flexibly," in Robert E. Roeming,ed., "Proceedings of the Central States Conference on the Teaching of Foreign Languages, 1969." *Modern Language Journal* 53(1969):481–84.

40 *Interpretation of New Concepts and Terminology for the Dropout Prevention and Bilingual Education Programs.* Washington, D.C.: U.S. Office of Education, n.d. [Mimeo.]

41 Jakobovits, Leon A. Speech to the 1970 North-

east Conference. Boston, March 1970.

42 Joyce, Bruce R. "The Emerging Elementary School as a Setting for Foreign-Language Instruction," 19–29 in Virginia G. Allen and F. André Paquette,eds., *The Student's World Is the World:New Dimensions in the Teaching of FLES*. Bloomington: Indiana Language Program. [Invitational conference on FLES, Minneapolis, Minnesota, November 1968.]

43 Kersten, Caesar S., and Vesperella E. Ott. "How Relevant is your Foreign Language Program?" *Modern Language Journal* 54(1970):9–13.

44 Kittel, Jack E. "Goals and Trends of Administration, Organization, and Supervision in Elementary Education," 41–56 in Virginia G. Allen and F. André Paquette,eds., *The Student's World Is the World:New Dimensions in the Teaching of FLES*. Bloomington: Indiana Language Program. [Invitational conference on FLES, Minneapolis, Minnesota, November 1968.]

45 Krathwohl, David R., Benjamin S. Bloom, and Bertram B. Masia. *Taxonomy of Educational Objectives:The Classification of Educational Goals. Handbook II:Affective Domain*. New York: David McKay, 1964.

46 Laleike, Fred H. *Individualized Foreign Language Program*. Application for a Continuation Grant Under P.L. 89–10, Title III. West Bend, Wisconsin: Joint School District No. 1. n.d. [Mimeo.]

47 —— *Individualized Foreign Language Program:An Outline of Objectives, Procedures and Emphasis*. West Bend, Wisconsin: Joint School District No. 1. [Mimeo.]

48 Lange, Dale L. "Methods," 281–310 in Emma M. Birkmaier,ed., *Britannica Review of Foreign Language Education, Volume 1*. Chicago: Encyclopaedia Britannica, 1968 [1969].

49 Langer, Philip. "Minicourse:Theory and Strategy." *Educational Technology* 9,ix(1969):54–59.

50 Macías, Cenobio C. "Programmed Learning as Used in the Tacoma Public Schools," 160–62 in Jerrold L. Mordaunt,ed., *Proceedings:Pacific Northwest Conference on Foreign Languages, Twentieth Annual Meeting, April 11–12, 1969*. Vol. 20. Victoria, B.C.: Univ. of Victoria, 1969.

51 Mager, Robert F. *Developing Attitude Toward Learning*. Palo Alto, California: Fearon, 1968.

52 —— *Preparing Instructional Objectives*. Palo Alto, California: Fearon, 1962.

53 Mandel, E. Jules. *Foreign Language Program Evaluation Based on a Definition of Objectives*. Ellensburg, Washington: Central Washington State College, 1967.

54 Matranga, Edward C. *The Ten Semester Continuum*. Stratford, Connecticut: Stratford Town Schools, 1970. [Mimeo.]

55 Meiden, Walter. "Training the Inexperienced Graduate Assistant for Language Teaching." *Modern Language Journal* 54(1970):168–74.

56 Moore, J. William. "Instructional Design:After Behavioral Objectives What?" *Educational Technology* 9, ix(1969):45–48.

57 Moreno, Edward V. *Performance Outcomes for 6th Grade Spanish Program*. Ventura County, California: El Rio Elementary School District, 1969. [Mimeo.]

58 Mowrer, Donald E. "The Language of Behavioral Engineering." *Educational Technology* 9,ix (1969):34–36.

59 Nelson, Robert J. and Leon A. Jakobovits,eds., "Motivation and Foreign Language Learning; Working Committee II," 34–104 in Joseph Tursi,ed., *Foreign Languages and the "New" Student*. Reports of the Working Committees of the Northeast Conference on the Teaching of Foreign Languages. New York: MLA Materials Center, 1970.

60 Otto, Frank. "The Teacher in the Pennsylvania Project." *Modern Language Journal* 53(1969): 411–20.

61 Parker, J. Cecil, and Louis J. Rubin. *Process as Content:Curriculum Design and the Application of Knowledge*. Chicago: Rand McNally, 1966.

62 Pillet, Roger A. "Teacher Education in Foreign Languages:An Overview." *Modern Language Journal* 54(1970):14–19.

63 Pimsleur, Paul. Speech before the Northeast Conference. Boston, March 1970.

64 —— and Johann F. Struth. "Knowing Your Students in Advance." *Modern Language Journal* 53(1969):85–87.

65 Politzer, Robert L., and Diana E. Bartley, "Practice-Centered Teacher Training:Standard English as a Second Dialect." *Modern Language Journal* 54(1970):31.

66 Popham, W. James,ed., *Instructional Objectives*. Chicago: Rand McNally, 1969. [AERA Monograph Series on Curriculum Evaluation, Monograph 3.]

67 —— *The Teacher Empiricist:A Curriculum and Instruction Supplement*. Los Angeles: Tinnon-Brown, 1965.

68 *Projects for "Baseline Measures."* Salt Lake City: Behavior Systems Corporation, 1969.[Mimeo.]

69 Reinert, Harry. "Student Attitudes Toward Foreign Language—No Sale!" *Modern Language Journal* 54(1970):107–12.

70 Rose, Theodore E. "Recorder's Report." *Modern Language Journal* 53(1969):477–80.

71 Ruplin, Ferdinand A., and John R. Russell. "Towards Structural Foreign Language Study:An Integrated German Course." *Modern Language Journal* 54(1970):174–83.

72 Samuels, S. Jay. "Psychological and Educational Consideration in Early Language Learning." 9–18 in Virginia G. Allen and F. André Paquette,eds., *The Student's World Is the World: New Dimensions in the Teaching of FLES*. Bloomington: Indiana Language Program, 1969. [Invitational conference on FLES, Minneapolis, Minnesota, November 1968.]

73 Sandstrom, Eleanor L., and Paul Pimsleur,eds., "Foreign Languages for all Students?" 105–33 in Joseph A. Tursi,ed., *Foreign Languages and the "New" Student*. Reports of the Working Committees of the Northeast Conference on the Teaching of Foreign Languages. New York: MLA

Materials Center, 1970.

74 Seelye, H. Ned. "An Objective Measure of Biculturation of Americans in Guatemala, A Case Study." *Modern Language Journal* 53(1969): 503–14.

75 —— "Performance Objectives· for Teaching Cultural Concepts." *Foreign Language Annals* 3(1970):566–78.

76 —— and Marilynn B. Brewer. "Ethnocentrism and Acculturation of North Americans in Guatemala." *Journal of Social Psychology* 80(1970): 147–55.

77 Serafino, Robert. "A Relevant Curriculum:An Instrument for Polling Student Opinion:Foreign Language Attitude Questionnaire," 7–30 in Joseph A. Tursi,ed., *Foreign Languages and the "New" Student*. Reports of the Working Committees of the Northeast Conference on the Teaching of Foreign Languages. New York: MLA Materials Center, 1970.

78 Sharp, Gerald V. "Individualized Study Programs in the General Secondary School Curriculum." *Educational Technology* 9(1969):45–47.

79 Smith, Melvin. *Teaching Spanish by Being Responsible for Specific Objectives*. Modesto, California: Stanislaus County Schools, July 1969.

80 Smith, Philip D., Jr. *A Comparison of the Cognitive and Audiolingual Approaches to Foreign Language Instruction:The Pennsylvania Foreign Language Project*. Philadelphia: The Center for Curriculum Development, 1970.

81 —— "The Pennsylvania State Foreign Language Research Project:Teacher Proficiency and Class Achievement in Two Modern Languages." *Foreign Language Annals* 3(1969):194–207.

82 Stake, Robert. *Classroom Report*. Urbana, Illinois: Univ. of Illinois, Center for Instructional Research and Curriculum Evaluation, 1969.

83 Stewart, Don. *Dial-Access Information Retrieval and Systems for Education Newsletter*. 20(1970):n.p. [Systems for Learning by Application of Technology to Education. Westminster, California.]

84 Steiner, Florence. "Performance Objectives in the Teaching of Foreign Languages." *Foreign Language Annals* 3(1970):579–91.

85 —— "Teacher-Made Tests Vital in the Foreign Language Classroom," 75–78 in Pat Castle and Charles Jay,eds., *Towards Excellence in Foreign Language Education*. Springfield, Illinois: Office of the Superintendent of Public Instruction, State of Illinois, 1968.

86 Strasheim, Lorraine A. "Where from Here?" *Modern Language Journal* 53(1969):493–97.

87 Sullivan, Howard J. "Objectives, Evaluation, and Improved Learner Achievement," 65–99 in W. James Popham,ed., *Instructional Objectives*. Chicago: Rand McNally, 1969. [AERA Monograph Series on Curriculum Evaluation, Monograph 3.]

88 Tyler, Louise L. "A Case History:Formulation of Objectives from a Psychoanalytic Framework," 100–29 in W. James Popham,ed., *Instructional Objectives*. Chicago: Rand McNally, 1969.

[AERA Monograph Series on Curriculum Evaluation, Monograph 3.]

89 Valette, Rebecca. *Directions in Foreign Language Testing*. New York: MLA/ERIC Clearinghouse on the Teaching of Foreign Languages and of English in Higher Education, 1969.

90 —— "The Pennsylvania Project, Its Conclusions and its Implications." *Modern Language Journal* 53(1969):396–404.

91 —— Speech to the Northeast Conference. Boston, March 1970.

92 —— "Testing," 343–74 in Emma M. Birkmaier,ed., *Britannica Review of Foreign Language Education, Volume I*. Chicago: Encyclopaedia Britannica, 1968[1969].

93 Wilmoth, Juanita, and Willard Ehn. "The Inflexibility of Flexible Modular Scheduling." *Educational Leadership* 27(1970):727–31.

94 Woodford, Protase. Speech to the Northeast Conference. Boston, March 1970.

95 —— "Testing Procedures," 89–107 in Donald Walsh,ed., *A Handbook for Teachers of Spanish and Portuguese*. Lexington, Massachusetts: D. C. Heath, 1969.

4

Strategies of instruction for listening and reading

Introduction

Gilbert A. Jarvis
Ohio State University

The purpose of this chapter is to review and interpret recent professional literature dealing with the learning and teaching of listening and reading skills in the second language situation. The review focuses primarily upon material published in 1969. Some work from 1968 is included, as are a few highly pertinent items of either pre-1968 or early 1970 publication. Attention has been given not only to publications dealing with second language listening and reading skills, but also to seemingly pertinent first language development of these skills, in the hope that cautious generalizations may be helpful to the practitioner and may serve as indicators of areas for future foreign language consideration and research. The consumer of this chapter who wishes to pursue topics noted here but not sufficiently developed, or which are peripheral to the bibliography at the end of this chapter, is directed to the following sources: Lange (63,64), *Education Index* (28), and *A Language-Teaching Bibliography* (65).

Relationships between language skills

To say that the four language skills are different actualizations of the same underlying phenomenon, sometimes called "thought," would be in accord with many definitions of language (Hughes, 43), but such a notion would contribute little useful information to the language teacher. It is only recently that the separation of language and thought as distinct entities (Ausubel, 6) has been more generally accepted. Thought, the covert phenomenon, does not have the same form as language, according to some. Lado (59) describes thought as "multidimensional"; it may simultaneously encompass space, movement, color, sound, touch, smell, or subjectivity. Language, in contrast, is linear in all the skills. When one thinks of a particular house, the thought can include simultaneously many characteristics, such as size, location, style, color, ownership, or value, according to Lado. But in talking about it one must refer to these features separately and report them in words that follow one another.

Language and thought separated

Even if this formulation were not accurate, and the thought aspects were found to occur serially, the rapidity of their occurrence distinguishes this covert phenomenon from the language skills. The four skills, thus, have an affinity merely through the abstraction called "language."

The four skills are often considered in terms of pairs. Speaking and listening are frequently called "oral" skills. They are linked, of course, on the basis of audible language. Likewise, reading and writing are linked on the basis of written language. In other words, these pairings of the skills are founded upon an extra-human factor—the form or medium of the language message after it has been produced. The affinity between listening and reading and between speaking and writing, however, is based upon what occurs *within* the language user. Speaking and writing are frequently referred to as "active" or "productive" skills; listening and reading as "passive" or "receptive." The label "receptive" seems to be much more descriptive. The listener or reader is far from "passive"; indeed, he must perform many operations which can properly be described as "active." He must deal with an indefinite number of sentences which he has never previously encountered. The number of sentences possible in any language has, in fact, been called "infinite" (Alexander, 2). Ohman (75) makes the same point with the arresting example of a simple drawing placed before 25 persons. The drawing shows a bear in a phone booth while a man stands outside the booth. When asked to describe in a sentence the situation portrayed, the 25 persons would be expected to give 25 different sentences, each adequately describing the drawing. Moreover, it is unlikely that any of the speakers would have ever previously produced or heard his sentence. Using the vocabulary and structures actually supplied in 25 sentences, and permuting them in all possible ways, Ohman found that it was possible to construct 19.8 billion sentences, all describing this one drawing and all described as grammatical. One need only consider that there are merely 3.2 billion seconds in a century to recognize that the learner cannot master a finite corpus of language which will serve as a mirror to which all future language data can be passively matched or compared. He must actively make classifications and apply principles to the novel language data which continually impinge upon him in these skills.

While it is true that listening and reading do share many characteristics, it is also true that differences between them extend

Four skills in pairs

Speaking and writing

80

beyond the physical factors of sound waves vs. light waves and the involvement of different sense modalities. The differences are particularly significant in the teaching-learning process.

Listening and reading

Listening depends upon the speaker's effectiveness in presenting the material to a much greater degree than does reading. In listening, the rate of presentation is normally controlled by the speaker. In reading, however, the rate is directly controlled by the reader. He can reread portions at a speed of his own choosing and in whatever sequence he wishes. The listener does not have this option in normal speech. The message with which he must cope is not preserved. Indeed, the necessity for speed in listening comprehension distinguishes this skill from the other three.

Debate has continued in the recent literature about primacy and priority among the language skills. Feldman & Kline (32) stand firm in the belief that human communicative behavior is first of all spoken and only secondarily written. This conception has through steady repetition, they claim, become almost a platitude. The history of man's use of language is postulated as evidence for the belief. Brooks (12) reiterated his belief that language is, at bottom, a phenomenon of sound. He cites the great number of people on this planet for whom language is a matter of sound only. The historical development of the belief in the primacy of speech has been traced by Banathy & Sawyer (7).

Priority among language skills

Unfortunately, even definitive answers to questions of primacy do not necessarily yield information that is of direct use to the practitioner. That man spoke for centuries before he wrote tells little *per se* about the way any *individual* learns a language.

Receptive skills as principal objectives

Because the utilitarian goals of FL instruction have usually been stated in terms of language skills, recent questioning of the role of foreign languages in the total curriculum inherently involves questions about individual skills. The tendency to speak of differential emphasis upon the skills is not a new phenomenon, nor can it be phrased as a question of which skill is most "important." Importance must be considered in terms of importance for what.

Jakobovitz (45) holds that the traditional goal of reading capacity sufficient to serve library research requirements and to provide the possibility of enjoying major literary works in a language other than one's own remains dominant in the minds of undergraduate and graduate university students. Teachers, on the other hand, when time is short and a choice has to be made, place emphasis on the development of oral skills. He believes that insistence on this goal is felt to be unwarranted by many students in our educational system and may be responsible in large measure for a lack of high motivation in foreign language study. If so, the solution would be student choice of skill on the basis of felt need.

In general, the recent literature indicates an inclination toward reducing the number of skills emphasized or included in an instructional program. There appear, however, to be distinctly different rationales underlying the views of various authors. Some of the views seem to reflect the frustration of the teacher who has established program objectives, has failed to reach them, and solves his dilemma by changing the objectives. Klin (58), for example, argues that "we must be honest with ourselves and with our students and set only goals that have a chance of fulfillment. . . . That means we must abandon all attempts to achieve speaking fluency." He believes the only meaningful goal we can set for the college non-major is a reading knowledge. The belief is based on the fact that reading comprehension can be learned privately and on the view that language is a skill and, as such, the study of a language is justified only if it becomes operative. This view apparently excludes cross-cultural understanding as a valid objective of foreign language study.

Rationales for reducing the number of skills

Bennett (9) believes that every language teacher needs to compromise both by restricting the number of language skills and by limiting the lexical and grammatical items in the course on the basis of comparative usefulness. He reasons that restrictions of this kind allow a higher standard of proficiency to be maintained than if the range of work were not thus limited.

Usefulness of skills, lexicon, and grammar as criteria for compromises

The usual school situation has had minimal effectiveness, according to Asher (3), perhaps because the foreign language program has tended to be overambitious. Even the objectives of listening and speaking may be unrealistic expectations with the limited time available. He presents a rationale for sole stress upon listening skill in the first level of language instruction.

Grittner (39) considers the incongruity between objectives and accomplishments to be a function of two factors. He notes, first of all, that some teachers have set the achievement of full "coordinate bilingualism" as their goal. To this he suggests that the profession might begin by openly admitting that it really cannot be accomplished in the classroom situation. Secondly, Grittner takes note of the fact that the college or high school program is unlikely to produce either a great number of bilinguals or literary scholars. The sensible alternative to a four-skill mastery approach would seem, then, to be a scaling down of objectives to a more realistic level, but without reverting to the single reading skill orientation of the past. He maintains that students can develop considerable skill in listening and reading with somewhat lesser achievement in speaking and writing skills.

Incongruity between objectives and accomplishments

Such views are not new. Darian (23), in reviewing the work of certain significant early 20th-century FL educators, mentions that Palmer (79) contrasted receptive and productive work and advocated that teachers in elementary courses spend considerably more time on receptive skills.

It is interesting to note that most of these writers seem to conceive of the language teaching-learning process as occurring only in the traditional classroom situation where a teacher meets with perhaps 25 students, and, according to their views, concentrates upon listening and reading skill development. The notions of other writers would probably have the same net result of reducing the number of skills studied by a student. The rationale seeming to underlie their notions is, however, quite different. They advocate modifying the curriculum so that skill emphasis is matched to learner characteristics, purposes, and interests. They would tailor the instructional program to individual learners—in a word, "individualize" the instruction, but *in terms of language skills*.

Pimsleur & Struth (80), for example, observe that many believe low-aptitude students cannot possibly pursue the same goals of four-skill mastery that high-aptitude students can pursue. In order to set goals that students can achieve, the authors suggest that those who make curricular decisions consider only reading and listening as goals for low-aptitude classes.

Everett (30) has described experimentation in intermediate-level language instruction at Gustavus Adolphus College. The approach recognizes, firstly, that not all students can or want to achieve the same goal in language study. Secondly, it attempts to answer the question of how so many individual needs can be satisfied without just as many individual teachers. The program gives the student substantial responsibility for his education.

Programs where skills are reduced

83

The role of the teacher is not that of a master but that of a guide who surrounds the student with an environment within which opportunities to develop language skills are provided. The effort is pertinent to this chapter because the pivotal concept seems to be that of language skills. Briefly, each class period is totally devoted to a single language skill. But the various language skills are all going on simultaneously in different classrooms. The student is free to move from room to room as he wishes, or as he feels the need. In reading, for example, the student can select his reading material from an extensive list. During the class he may obtain aid or advice from the assistant in the reading room. Media are used for other aspects of the teaching-learning experience according to their suitability for the particular purpose.

Listening comprehension and speaking skill are separated also in the McCluer Plan, a nongraded performance curriculum (Wood, 113). The strategy demands that the neophyte concentrate on one skill at a time.

A further generalization can now be made about the limitation of skills. The tendency is to limit instruction to the receptive skills, either for all students or for those for whom these skills are more appropriate. General agreement seems to exist that these skills are more easily developed than are the productive skills. It should be noted, however, that "easily" does not imply any inherent simplicity, but rather that the conditions which result in learning are more facilitating. For example, the learner can more easily practice the receptive skills while unassisted; moreover, they inherently provide him with greater feedback about his accuracy or progress.

Listening skill learning conditions

Listening behavior is an amalgamation of physical and mental events. In order to listen one must be receptive to the physical sound waves which impinge upon the auditory organs. Listening can then be defined as the organism's response to that which is heard. Duker (25) describes the relationship as one of dependency. "Hearing involves the conversion of pressure waves into neural impulses which move to the brain for interpretation. Listening is the process of interpretation." Exactly what constitutes the mechanism of attention and the neurophysiology is not known (Witkin, 112).

Listening behavior

A segment of spoken language contains sequences of sounds which are peculiar to any given language. Because the number of sounds is finite, and the potential number of combinations of sounds is limited even further, anticipation of sounds becomes a significant factor in coping with the stream of sounds. Rivers (87), whose chapter on listening comprehension is probably the best single recent source of information, discusses the implications of the conventional phonic patterning in FL teaching. In learning his native language the child comes to expect certain patterns of sounds but not others. In the foreign language the student will require extensive practice in order to develop such a frame of expectations. Only after considerable practice will he be able to anticipate sounds and "know" that after a given combination of sounds only certain others can occur.

Listening: combinations of sounds

This concept of "likelihood of occurrence" also has utility at other levels of linguistic units. Here the application comes directly from communication theory. If a speaker were to stop abruptly in the middle of an utterance, there are times when we could with near certainty correctly supply the following word. At other times we could predict the next word with varying probabilities. But there would occur some instances where the next word would be totally uncertain and indeterminable. The range of possible alternatives is referred to as "information." If the item is nearly certain, it is said to contain little information. If it cannot be predicted, it is said to contain or convey considerable information. Information is, then, a measure of one's freedom of choice in selecting a message component. If, for example, a speaker points to a new automobile across a street and says, "Look at that beautiful new red _____," the completion contains little information. Situational and visual clues delimit the alternatives. Many times clues are linguistic. Particular categories of words are likely to occur in certain linguistic environments. As Rivers emphasizes, the FL student requires considerable practice to develop these necessary sets or frames of expectations which will aid him in comprehension.

Information

Recognition of the large amount of practice necessary to develop listening skills is a common theme in recent literature. Many efforts are essentially directed toward quantitatively increasing the amount of listening practice which the student has available.

Two recent studies (Purdom, 84; Van Valkenburg, 110) in developing first language listening skills indicate that listening ability, as measured by comprehension of material heard, can, in fact, be improved by systematic programs of instruction and by practice in listening. Van Valkenburg (110) noted, moreover, increases in reading comprehension as a result of such a program. Students of "low socio-economic status" gained more than "high socio-economic status" students. Taylor (104) reaches a related conclusion after reviewing the literature. He finds that, in general, less competent students, those judged to be scholastically below average, show a marked preference for listening over reading in most learning situations and do retain more from listening. The slower student seems to depend on the special attributes of listening for much of his understanding. In listening, his comprehension is facilitated by the phrasing and expression of the speaker, while in reading he must construct his own linguistic units in order to realize meaning. The speaker's appearance adds listening clues; in reading the print is non-committal. When related to the foreign language situation the phenomenon may be the same observed in methodological comparisons (Chastain & Woerderhoff, 18) where low-aptitude students achieved more success in an audiolingual methodology than in other approaches.

Studies of listening in first language learning

One recent approach to increasing the amount of practice, in particular in listening, has been the teaching of other subject-matter areas in the foreign language. Ort & Smith (78) compiled descriptions of innovative programs. Many of the programs involved social studies courses being taught in the foreign language. Lectures, class discussions, and textbooks in the target language are usually a part of the programs.

Listening in foreign language programs

A course in world cultures which was developed and offered in German has been described by Keitel (52). Students had completed two years of audiolingual German before the world cultures course. When compared to control groups the participating students scored significantly better (p < .01) in all the language skills.

Reports by Lambert & Macnamara (61) and Samuels (92) are available which indicate very good results from teaching the lower elementary curriculum in a foreign language. Particularly good mastery was noted in the receptive skills.

Jarvis (47) compared practice procedures in beginning college French. A "contextual" procedure in which practice involved particularized referents was contrasted with a "drill" procedure where practice was with language forms having generic meaning. When, for example, the French word *maison* occurred in the contextual classes, it always referred to a particular house, whereas in the drill classes it referred to *maison* in general. While results favored the contextual classes significantly in the productive skills, there was little difference between the treatment groups in the receptive skills. Noteworthy in this context is the fact that listening skill was the only criterion measure in which there were significant instructor differences. The most plausible explanation is that the seven instructors did vary in the total *quantity* of practice utilized. Some used more English explanation than did others.

Other programs have been described which, among other considerations, do increase student contact (practice) with the foreign language. Coleman (19) describes the use of a film each week in the third trimester of college study. Scripts are also provided. Testing is largely aural comprehension. Coleman believes the approach helped the student realize that the target language is alive and dynamic. Slightly increased aural comprehension was observed.

Renshaw (86) describes the program of Escola de Português e Orientacão at Campinas near São Paulo, Brazil. The program is designed to prepare foreigners in 44 weeks to be able to live and work with the Brazilian people. The author stresses that the program is founded upon the principle that the first and continuing task of the instructors is to develop the learner's auditory discrimination and comprehension.

The "twinned classroom" approach (Jonas, 50) is another program which has as one of its features the increase in student contact and practice with the language. An American FLES class and a class of boys and girls of the same age in France exchange tapes, slides, and other materials each month. The students involved have scored slightly higher in listening comprehension than similar students in control groups. The program and the evaluation of its effects are continuing.

The Applied Language Research Center of the El Paso, Texas, Public Schools (Saavedra, 91) has been conducting experimental classes in bilingual education. One of its more novel techniques results from the necessity of bussing culturally deprived elementary children to the language center for sessions. The bus has been wired for sound so that tape-recorded songs, stories, and other cultural material in both languages can be played. Both listening practice and information transmission would seem to be enhanced. A loudspeaker arrangement permits the teacher to point out and discuss items of interest along the bus route.

Thus, while many varied purposes may be served by the above programs, they all do imply efforts to increase quantitatively student contact with the language. When that contact is with spoken language it inherently results in greater listening practice. The most optimistic view of the importance of quantity has been presented by Newmark & Reibel (72) who contend that, to be effective, language teachers need not wait for the development of a theory of language acquisition based on a theory of the structure of the language. They state (72): "We believe that the necessary and sufficient conditions for a human being to learn a language are already known: a language will be learned by a normal human being if and only if *particular, whole instances of language use are modeled for him and if his own particular acts using the language are selectively reinforced.*"

Contact with spoken language helps listening

Accepting this view, one might assume that the conditions are best fulfilled by studying the foreign language in its own environment—in a land where it is spoken natively. Jaekel (44) has cautioned, however, that assumptions of greater learning potential in this "ideal way" may have been accepted too quickly without substantial evaluative results. The environment does not automatically produce its good works. Being surrounded by the language is not sufficient in all cases.

Belief in the efficacy or sufficiency of quantity of exposure to a language is often generalized from the fact that first language acquisition is *accompanied by* considerable contact. Jakobovitz (46), however, has recently emphasized three relevant differences between first and second language acquisition:

Differences between first and second language learning

1 The notion of FL aptitude has no parallel in first language acquisition during infancy. The latter appears to be a maturational process whose development is universal and regular throughout the human species.
2 It is highly probable that unless a first language is acquired by adolescence, the capacity to acquire a language is lost forever. No such effect is true of second language learning.
3 The acquisition of oral fluency in second language learning under intensive training conditions by a well-motivated, high-aptitude adult is achieved in the order of 400–600 hours and in slightly less than two months. The time factor in infancy is about nine times larger.

If quantity of listening practice is important, but is far from the sole consideration, one is led to question what qualitative variables influence the acquisition of listening skill. Here, as in other aspects of second language acquisition, research results are sparse. Both specific and general deficiencies in various areas of research have been recently indicated (Jakobovits, 46; Lane, 62; Schramm, 94). Much of the literature involves theorizing and conjecture rather than empirical results.

Politzer & Weiss (82) have discussed the auditory discrimination aspect of listening ability. They note that it is almost a "common sense" assumption that auditory discrimination and pronunciation ability are related to each other. Accurate pronunciation depends upon the speaker's ability to monitor the accuracy of his own utterance. The student who cannot discriminate between the sounds of the target language and differentiate them from native language sounds will likely confuse them when he pronounces them. The authors observe that auditory discrimination training is often used as a first stage in pronunciation training, despite the fact that past research results have been ambiguous on the question. One recently reported study is somewhat pertinent to this aspect of listening ability. Westphal (111) investigated the relationship between certain psycho-acoustic factors, intellectual abilities, and achievement in second language learning. One of the investigator's findings was that listening to and imitating the sounds of German throughout the school year seemingly improved most students' ability to hear those differences in sound which are measured by the Seashore Measures of Pitch and Timbre.

Auditory discrimination as an aspect of listening

Politzer & Weiss (82) also attempted to determine whether foreign language aptitude could be significantly increased by specific training and whether increases in language aptitude brought about by such training resulted in better achievement in foreign language study. In the first phase of the experiment some auditory discrimination was included in the training. Among their conclusions the authors expressed the belief that the rather short period of auditory discrimination training which was included in the training was ineffective in improving aptitude if compared with the many hours of such training inherent in intensive audiolingual language courses. All the subjects who were studying a foreign language made gains which were not observed in a comparable group which had received no language training. The investigators inferred from their data some

Auditory discrimination and FL aptitude

evidence that the first year of audiolingual training in high school may by itself constitute aptitude training. It seems, however, that the nature of the languages involved is a significant factor.

Several research efforts, while being more global in scope than a single skill, are relevant to listening skill development. Asher (3) has developed a teaching-learning strategy which is based on the primacy of listening skill. He cites his earlier work (4,5) as evidence that the skill of listening comprehension has high positive transfer, especially to speaking a foreign language. The transfer to reading and writing is partly dependent upon the fit between the phonology and orthography of a specific language. Pursuing this rationale, Asher affirms that for at least one semester in college or six months to a year in high school the goal of foreign language learning should be listening fluency only. The listening fluency should be so keen that the student can understand almost anything he hears. The strategy (which has some similarity to how children seem to learn a first language) is called the Total Physical Response Technique. It requires the student to listen to a command in a foreign language and immediately obey with a physical action. The training begins with brief one-word utterances, but within thirty minutes, the morphological and syntactical complexity of the commands has been increased to utterances such as "Stand up and erase your name from the blackboard." Asher does present some empirical data about the effectiveness of the strategy. He cites data showing that when students learned to understand Russian through the approach, their comprehension was accelerated far beyond (p<.001) that of students who tried to learn with translation methods. In 21 experiments to determine what factors within the approach were producing the acceleration in learning, the following observations were made:

Research in FL listening

Primacy of the listening skill

1 It did not matter whether students listened to the command and acted along with a model or listened and observed a model perform the action. What was important was that each student perform motor acts during the retention tests.
2 Only as the complexity of the foreign utterance was increased did the motor act become a variable producing a dramatic change in learning.
3 When the students attempted to learn both listening and speaking together, the comprehension of Russian was sig-

nificantly reduced. If a high level of listening comprehension is achieved, there may be a "perceptual readiness" to begin making the foreign utterances. Future studies will be needed to show how much listening training is necessary to produce "perceptual readiness."

Among other empirical studies involving listening skill, Mueller (71) has reported positive results in all the skills for a programmed French course when compared to a traditional audiolingual course.

Connor (20) compared high IQ nonachievers in foreign languages with achievers. Among the conclusions was the observation that some otherwise able students do fail in audiolingual foreign language classes. These nonachievers were poorer than achievers in audio and verbal learning skills, but they were more able than achievers in visual and spatial organization. The investigator recommends that audiolingual teachers maintain both audio and visual attention during class. The nature of optimal visual support and identification of its appropriate role in instructional strategy remains, however, a matter in need of considerable research.

Receptive skills were included in the Pennsylvania Project. Because of the complexity of the findings one runs the danger of being simplistic and inaccurate in summary statements. Several discussions and reports (Carroll, 17; Smith, 100,101; Valette, 108,109) seem to be most helpful, if the reader is concerned with listening and reading aspects of the study. An excellent treatment of the study also appears in the chapter on the language learning laboratory by W. Flint Smith in this volume.

One of the promising recent developments in the area of listening skill is the commercial availability of devices which permit alteration of the rate of recorded speech. The devices permit an increase or decrease in the rate of the recorded message without the accompanying changes in vocal pitch which occur when one changes the speed of a conventional tape recorder or phonograph. Sticht (103) has described the operation of the device. Increasing the speech rate is accomplished by periodically deleting small temporal segments of the speech signal while the remaining speech segments are connected to produce continuous discourse. Through this deletion and sampling technique the time required to present the speech is reduced. Hence, the speech is called "time-compressed" speech. "Time-expanded" or

Devices for alteration of rate of recorded speech

decelerated speech is produced by reversing the procedure. In other words, small temporal segments of the recorded message are periodically repeated. This produces the perceptual effect of a reduction in the speech rate. No reports of work in foreign languages with compressed speech were discovered. Several areas of work in native language comprehension were noted. A crucial research question, according to Witkin (112), is how fast individuals can track and process information presented orally. Is there a built-in limitation to the amount of information per unit of time that can be comprehended or retrieved? Speech typically ranges from 125 to 175 words per minute. Speech compressors can retard the speech to one half of its original rate or accelerate it to about three times the original.

Witkin has reviewed the literature. She finds indications that practice does result in considerable improvement in ability to comprehend compressed speech. Up to a certain amount of compression, practice improved both speed and comprehension. Spaced practice was generally better than massed.

Sticht (103) notes that some distortion inevitably occurs as the rate is increased. He cites research indicating that when speech is accelerated over 250–300 words per minute, comprehension declines at a very rapid rate. Efforts were made to determine whether it was the signal distortion or the speech rate which diminished the listening comprehension in highly accelerated speech. It was found that both factors contributed. However, it appears that for normal orally read prose materials comprehension is limited more by speech rate than by signal distortions. The barrier to the comprehension of fast rates of speech appears, therefore, to be in the information-processing capacities of the listener, not in the fidelity of the time-compressed signal.

Speech acceleration

Orr et al. (77) compared comprehension when the speech rate was established at 1.5 times the original with comprehension when subjects could freely vary the rate. Subjects varied the rate from 1.16 to 2.05 times the original with a mean of 1.45. Comprehension was equal, perhaps because subjects chose a rate nearly equal to the fixed rate.

What extrapolation in rate research can be made from first language research to the second language learning situation is not certain. Perhaps insights, heretofore unavailable, might be provided by future FL research in this area. One might wonder, for example, if the comprehension difficulties of the foreign language student when hearing normal-speed target language speech are similar to the comprehension difficulties in first language highly compressed speech. Perhaps internal rate may be a less significant variable than length and frequency of pauses between segments of speech. One might speculate that the devices could be used to provide some information on the efficacy of "normal-rate" language presentation vs. a slowed rendition in the early stages of instructional strategy. Many methodologists in the 1960s advocated normal-speed rendition, believing that slowing the rendition distorts it. This view is not easily reconciled with the long-standing principle that one simplifies in the early stages of a learning task and that this simplification in no way delimits or vitiates the terminal behavior.

Classroom techniques in listening

The recent literature contains several discussions about classroom considerations. Most are personal viewpoints about techniques the authors have found successful, or they are expressions of pertinent concern about aspects of classroom behavior.

Hamilton (41) perceives the "standard" procedure for dictation as a memory test from preassigned material. He feels this procedure involves little reliance on auditory comprehension *Dictation* and suggests that, by using lengthy selections which students have never previously seen or heard, the teacher can make the dictation a comprehension rather than memory task. The author does not make reference to the view that in dictation one need know only associational rules for linking orthography to the sound system. Consequently, auditory comprehension is not inherent regardless of student familiarity or lack of familiarity with the material.

Kirch (57) has advocated the use of visuals to "provide the bridge" between sound and meaning. They can be used for either lexical or grammatical meaning. Hughes (43) argues that *Use of visuals* there are practically no techniques for teaching vocabulary. Teachers have concentrated their attention on teaching grammar. Hughes apparently chooses to ignore the relative cognitive complexity of grammar learning when compared to that of vocabulary learning as a factor in this alleged classroom emphasis.

Nixon (74) attempted to test the hypothesis that students in audiolingual classes using visual aids would be superior to students who did not use visual aids. Four skills were tested. The hypothesis was not confirmed, but there was some confounding of results due to teacher differences and small class sizes.

Sources of information about the use of games in the foreign language classroom have become available (Buckby, 13; Mac-Laughlin, 68; Shankman, 96). Buckby (13) points out that games can link language to action to an extent at least equal to any other type of activity. The learner practice is almost invariably accompanied by understanding.

Games

Edgerton (27) includes, among many ideas on using media, advice on preparing students carefully for listening experience with taped materials. Preparation should include the following considerations:

Use of media

1 New vocabulary and structure that cannot be easily guessed with the help of the context must be previewed.

2 The setting should be described, characters listed, and a general statement of the subject given.

3 The purpose of the listening exercise should be made clear to the students and a specific assignment made.

Unfortunately commercially prepared taped materials continue to be stereotyped in the mold of materials of ten years ago. Most are merely recordings of printed textbook content.

Grittner (40) advocates the need for flexibility in the development of true listening ability. By using rearrangements of familiar lexical items, he notes, the teacher can expose students to listening experiences of increasing complexity. Any unfamiliar items must be taught in advance so that student attention is not drawn toward puzzling new vocabulary items and away from the message.

Development of flexibility in listening

In the area of testing listening skill, Valette (106) has expanded some of the material in her earlier book on testing (107). Kirch (56) has presented some ideas for testing listening comprehension. He gives examples in German. Educational Testing Service is preparing to incorporate a listening section into the College Entrance Examination Board's Achievement Test Program in Foreign Languages. This inclusion should improve the face validity of the tests in the eyes of all status groups involved with it. Tentative plans call for its inclusion during the 1970–71 academic year.

Advances in testing listening

The status of knowledge about reading skill

Because reading is a type of behavior and a behavior which is very important to modern man, it is logical to assume that psychologists have given a great deal of time to its study. Indeed, the research is voluminous. Nevertheless, it is also true that few, if any, researchers have devoted their entire professional careers to the study of the reading process (Kingston, 55).

Farr (31) echoes the sentiments of Harris (42), who believes that "reading as a psychological process, either in its beginning or in its later, more refined stages, is poorly understood in the sense that a common understanding of the reading process is accepted and translated into instructional practice."

Controversy continues regarding many crucial aspects of both first and second language reading. Varied viewpoints continue to be expressed, for example, about such questions as "phonics" approaches vs. so-called linguistic approaches (Seymour, 95) and about the merits of alphabets which provide better fit between orthography and phonology (Robinson, 88). Differences and similarities between first and second language reading remain undetermined. While there seems to be a growing recognition that the corpus of knowledge about first language reading should yield insights for the FL situation, there is reason to wonder whether most foreign language students are ever "taught" to read. Very frequently students are simply assigned material (even on the first day of foreign language study) and expected to return the next day and recite in some way about the material. This practice implies that the ability to read in one's native language automatically transfers to the second language. Indeed, it would be reasonable to expect transfer in some aspects of the phenomenon. Physical aspects, for example, would seem to be similar, particularly in alphabetic languages written in a similar way.

What is reading in a first and in a second language?

Grittner (40) lists the following advantages accruing from having already learned to read English:

Advantages and disadvantages of reading English for reading in a second language

1 The student has already gone through the difficult process of learning to associate graphic symbols with sounds and their meanings.
2 The alphabet he has learned is the same for many languages.
3 The habit of scanning from left to right is an advantage in languages which so operate.

The disadvantages are:

1 English pronunciation habits strongly influence articula-

95

tion of foreign language phonemes when reading aloud or in subvocalization.

2 Students may be inclined to think of foreign language words as symbols which stand for English words and which have similar semantic ranges.

The first language situation always implies an oral proficiency. In the second language, the range of proficiency may vary from near zero to a level of good competency. Whether one has or has not developed an oral command of the language would seem to be a significant factor in aspects of both instructional and learning strategies. The foreign language pedagogical literature is, therefore, viewed as dichotomous. It is grouped in this chapter into that which necessarily implies prior oral training (the "audiolingual paradigm") and that which may or may not presume the paradigm. Any literature which seems pertinent to reading but which does not necessarily imply the rather well-defined theory and procedures of the audiolingual paradigm is included in this latter category.

Reading in the audiolingual paradigm

Within the audiolingual approach there exists a generally agreed upon body of principles and procedures. If the student has a considerable oral skill foundation, "the precepts of the audiolingual theory clearly point the way" (Rosenbaum, 89). Descriptions of the process and procedures have continued to appear in recent literature.

Feldman & Kline (32) describe learning to read as the process of transfer from the auditory language signals, which have already been learned, to the new visual signs used to represent those same auditory signals.

Transfer of auditory symbols to visual ones

Politzer (81) writes that probably the most important aspect of the initial phase of the teaching of reading is simply that it should consist primarily of a process of tying orthographic representation to audiolingually familiar material. Thus, the pupil should not learn "how to pronounce letters" but should learn which written symbols correspond to sounds, words, and utterances which he can already pronounce. The author notes that this procedure implies that the initial phase of reading instruction should not be used to introduce new vocabulary or structure. The goal is the establishment of sound-symbol correspondence

Sound-symbol association

which will enable use of a visual image to reinforce the "acoustic memory." Color or underlining can be used to call attention to the important orthographic features being learned. (One might suggest the use of "highlight" pens, so popular with college students.)

The audiolingualists continue to emphasize a distinction between reading and translation. Explanations in the native language and translation are tolerable, according to Politzer, only as a last resort and strictly for the sake of economy.

Reading and translation

King (54) agrees with the conclusion that listening to a foreign language is a very similar skill to reading the language. Theoretically, then, the student with an audiolingual background has a double advantage over the traditionally trained reader. He has the pronunciation skills necessary to read for meaning, and he has listening-comprehension skills for additional language contact of a type very similar to reading.

Smith (98), in his doctoral dissertation, analyzes the literature in reading and uses the audiolingual basis to make recommendations which might be summarily stated as:

Recommendations for audiolingual reading

1 An extended audiolingual period prior to reading instruction. During this period the student develops a fluent pronunciation, acquires a sight vocabulary containing sufficient examples of sound-symbol relationships, and becomes familiar with sufficiently varied structure to permit the composition of interesting recombined materials.
2 First reading activities are the whole sentence reading of memorized materials. The activity is immediately extended to include the oral reading of recombined sentences.
3 Whole words from context are isolated, drilled, and returned to appropriate contexts to develop rapid sight recognition.
4 Words containing a certain sound-symbol relationship are taken from context and grouped. Sound-symbol association is made inductively.
5 Practice in the use of context clues is begun as soon as new words are encountered.
6 Structural analysis at beginning levels is restricted to the development of rapid recognition of inflected forms.
7 Activities in checking literal meanings should be purposeful and always lead to higher levels of comprehension.
8 Training in interpretive reading should begin with the first experiences and continue to play an increasingly important role.

Rivers (87) has delineated six stages in reading training which fit the audiolingual paradigm quite closely.

1 Reading of memorized dialogues (chorally, at first). The teacher must be sure the student is not reciting. Some here advocate direct teaching of sound-symbol relationships, particularly with older learners.

2 Students read memorized material in rearrangements and recombinations. Students must here be taught to read in word groups, to look ahead.

3 More sustained reading. The student is introduced to the pleasure of reading simple narrative and conversational material which develops an uncomplicated but entertaining theme. He is not yet left on his own.

4 Students do intensive and extensive reading (discussed below).

5 Foreign language material which has not been adapted in any way is read.

6 The student has reached a level of confidence where he can pick up an FL book or paper, even after his formal training.

Six stages in reading training

The audiolingual approach to reading has not been without detractors. The first recommendation of Bundy et al. (14), in the report of the Colby College Conference on the Undergraduate Major in French, had stated:

> Emphasis on the audiolingual approach, we think, has seriously devalued ability to read a foreign language. The primacy of the oral threatens to produce a generation of illiterates and makes impossible any serious intellectual work in a foreign language either at the undergraduate level or at the graduate, either in literature or in any other subject. . . . We suggest that the order of priority should be altered and that the present primacy of speaking and understanding yield to the primacy of reading.

A detractor to audiolingual reading

Dannerbeck (22) has taken exception to parts of the report. He points out that no evidence or plausible arguments were presented to support the contention that the audiolingual approach has seriously reduced reading ability. He cites evidence to the contrary, indicating that the approach is not detrimental. Dannerbeck does remind the reader, firstly, that the teacher must guide the learner from the audiolingual foundation to reading and, secondly, in order to do this, he must have a clear idea of how

A defense

the transition to future learning will occur. How will the learning in his course be complemented in intermediate and advanced courses?

In the continuum of reading skill development which begins at the zero point and proceeds upward, it is at this point of the transition to liberated reading that opinions, rationales, research results, and pronouncements become increasingly sparse, fragmentary, and less specific. Rosenbaum (89) defines the point of difficulty as that time "when reading matter is no longer identical with, nor an extension of the spoken language." It must be remembered that the above discussion of reading is limited to the audiolingual paradigm. If this paradigm, particularly the early insistence upon spoken language, is not utilized, the point at which reading matter differs from previously spoken material is, in the most extreme instance, on the first day of class.

Non-audiolingual reading and first language research

Researchers in general reading skill have recently made progress in cataloging and disseminating information. The ERIC/CRIER Center (29) has now prepared indexes to more than 3,500 documents (dissertations, articles, conference papers) relevant to reading and published since 1950.

Laffey et al. (60) provide a recent comprehensive listing, with descriptions, of reading-related projects and reports (primarily first language) during 1967 and 1968.

Research results pertaining to FL reading treat a broad range of aspects and all levels of instruction.

Kaufman (51) studied the effects of three hours of instruction in reading Spanish upon 75 seventh-grade New York students who were reading two to four years below grade level. Students in a control group attended extra health and art sessions during this time. Spanish was spoken in the homes of all students. Results indicated a positive transfer from learning to read in Spanish to learning to read in English. The experimental group was also superior in reading Spanish.

Lipton (67) compared FLES groups which were taught reading activities from the second day with FLES groups which had only listening and speaking activities. The group which had experienced the reading activities was superior (p<.01) on auditory comprehension tests.

Reading in FLES

99

A comparison of the effects of FLES foreign language vs. no foreign language upon the reading proficiency and general school achievement of primary grade children is reported by Potts (83). The "experimental" group was given 15 minutes daily of audiolingual French instruction during the entire school year. The "control" group was given dance instruction during this time. Sophisticated data analyses revealed no significant differences.

In a small-scale study Shawl (97) found that students who were given explicit statements about syntactic composition and interrelationships performed noticeably better (p<.01) in reading than students who did not receive these statements.

Burkholder (15) investigated relationships between underlying psycholinguistic, cognitive, and other mental abilities and first language reading ability. After identifying deficiencies in underlying abilities such as perception, memory, closure, and classification, she devised methods and materials for improving the abilities. After training, the experimental group did significantly better in measures of the underlying abilities and in measures of reading (without specific training in reading) than did a matched group who merely took the tests. The differences in the underlying abilities remained six months later. One might interpret the results as supporting the view that there are, indeed, very specific components in the reading process which can apparently be modified.

Reading and underlying abilities

Samuels (93) studied the effect of pictures upon the acquisition of reading responses. In an experiment in which 26 matched pairs of first-grade students were given reading instruction with and without pictures as prompts for meaning, there was no general difference between the groups. But when below-average subjects were compared, the no-picture group had learned more vocabulary. Results were interpreted as raising questions about the desirability of providing pictures in beginning reading instruction.

Use of visuals in reading

Periodic overt responding to questions imbedded in standard textbook format promoted greater retention for specific information, according to the research of Banks (8).

Several recent investigations have surveyed students to learn about their reading habits and preferences when they can choose material (Alderson, 1; Gallo, 37; Gottsdanker & Pidgeon, 38). Results are pertinent to upper level foreign language courses. Among their findings, fiction was the most popular choice among

Reading habits and preferenc

college seniors with more than one half of the material mentioned being from the post-World War II period. Nevertheless, among 309 books mentioned, only two authors (Camus and Hesse) were mentioned by more than 10% of the students. There were 227 books which were mentioned only once and 42 only twice. Hence, the diversity of interests is large. Among high school students reading habits of boys and girls were found to be different in every age group. Boys' interests varied more than did girls', and all students had a strong aversion for "book-report" assignments. A substantial number do engage in free reading.

Robinson (88) investigated the use of the Initial Teaching Alphabet (ITA) in the teaching of English as a second language to adults. A group using the ITA was compared to a group learning with traditional orthography. Both made significant gains in reading, but there were no significant differences between groups. Through use of selected ITA symbols pronunciation skills increased significantly (p<.001).

Use of ITA in TESOL

No work was apparent in the area of developing "readability" formulas for foreign language materials, despite continuing first language work in the area. Maginnis (69), for example, has described and praised the time-saving Fry formula. It judges readability on the basis of sentence length and word length in terms of syllables. Whether such criteria are relevant to the difficulty of foreign language reading material is not clear. The availability of such an instrument, even if crude, could permit comparisons of *relative* difficulty between textbooks, literary selections, or other foreign language reading material. Presently little information is available. Even where students read large enough numbers of works, student input about difficulty, time spent, etc. has not, apparently, been systematically recorded and reported.

"Readability" in native language

Visual fatigue is a physical factor which would seem to be equally a factor in first or second language reading. Demilia (24) has presented an excellent discussion of factors involved. Fatigue, which is characterized by an increased number of fixations per line of print, more regressions per line, slower rate of reading, less accuracy, and diminished comprehension, results from lack of legibility in the written materials. Illegibility can stem from the printed page itself.

Physical factors

Reading is aided by certain perceptual "cues." The cues permit the organization of letter units into higher order units so that more can be perceived at a glance (Kingston, 55). The cues considered most significant are initial and final letters, ascenders and descenders (parts of letters extending up or down from the central ribbon of print), letters with large enclosed white space, groups of letters which lead to the recognition (or preconceived notion) of ensuing letters, and word form. Illegibility is, then, any condition which interferes with the effectiveness of the cues, particularly lack of distinctive and distinguishing shape. Uniformity of type design, effective use of space, and the highest degree of brightness contrast between the color of ink and the tint of the page without producing glare all contribute to clarity. Demilia uses the following kinds of examples to show what happens when one interferes with the cues. ALL CAPS READ LESS EFFECTIVELY THAN TEXT PRINTED IN UPPER AND LOWER CASE LETTERS. In A mOrE eXtReMe FoRm, WoRd ShApE iS hErE bEiNg LoSt By AlTeRnAtInG uPpEr AnD lOwEr CaSe LeTtErS. Legibility must, therefore, be a significant concern in selecting reading materials.

Perceptual cues

The distinction between "intensive" and "extensive" reading continues to be made in the literature, both within and without the audiolingual paradigm (King, 54; Light, 66; Oliva, 76). The use of the concept dates back further than most believe. It appears, for example, in the 1931 Syllabus of Minima of the New York City Schools (73).

King (54) has updated and modified the concept. She notes that audiolingual practices have not altered the fact that students must do a considerable amount of reading. A dilemma results from this need for a large quantity of practice and the excessive time demands which such a quantity of reading would place upon a student. The preparation time is dictated by the usual practice of basing classroom oral skill practice on the assigned reading material; thus, the concept of two to four pages to be handled in class "intensively" by question-and-answer practice, vocabulary drill, word study, dictation, and discussion. The "extensive" or "outside" reading assignment is an entire play, short story, or short novel assigned sometime in advance of a terminal date, to be read from the standpoint of overall comprehension of characters and events rather than precise details of language or content. It is here that King makes her modification. Both types of reading should be from the same text, according to her strategy. The intensive reading should be limited to: (*1*) a paragraph which the student is to master almost as he masters a dialogue in an audiolingual approach; and (2) a translation assignment of approximately a paragraph in length

Intensive-extensive reading

which the student should be able to render orally into good English without a prepared written version or extensive marginal gloss.

What advantages are offered by this approach? Because the same text is used, the student can familiarize himself with one aspect of the text in depth and apply these learnings to the rest of the assignment. Moreover, if a key passage is chosen, it alone can help in the comprehension of the entire work.

The biggest obstacle facing the class is that students will approach extensive reading as they do the intensive assignment. The previous exact learning experience establishes a set to do so. Students must be made explicitly aware of what is expected of them and what strategies should be employed.

One such strategy is contextual guessing of unknown vocabulary. The procedure has been advocated by Joll (49) and Rosenbaum (89) and described by Dulin (26), who recommends making students explicitly aware of the processes. The learner must be trained *not* to stop at the unfamiliar word, but to read on, according to Rosenbaum. He must be aware of the fact that the context often permits him to "guess" the meaning of the unknown item. This is the procedure usually used with unknown items in first language reading. Dulin has described several of the various types of syntactical and structural processes which elucidate meaning.

Contextual guessing

1 Contrast: the development through specific antonyms or definitive words and phrases of the exact opposite or logical antithesis of the new word; e.g. "Instead of the even, regular beat usually found in such music, this selection was quite *syncopated*."

2 Linked synonyms and/or appositives: pairing of synonyms in a series or linking item with a synonym by commas or a dash; e.g. "The *weir*, a fence-like device placed in the river to lead the fish into a trap, provided a ready landmark for measuring the canoe's progress upstream."

3 Direct description: process of definitively describing what the word's meaning must be; e.g. "All chances for agreement were now gone, and compromise would now be impossible; in short, an *impasse* had been reached."

4 Cause-effect relationship: setting up a cause-effect relationship from within which the meaning of the new word can be logically inferred; e.g. "Strength and size seemed to be

the key qualities needed; therefore, a *leviathan* of a man was chosen."

A technique which would seem to facilitate this ability has been described. Culhane (21) writes, "There are no new methods for _____ or testing comprehension. Those that are _____ use don't seem to do the _____. I've tried everything I know but _____ pupils don't seem to be able _____ understand. Isn't there a better way _____ teach and test comprehension?" Besides being representative teacher statements, this is a sample of a method which Culhane believes is generally unknown to teachers. It is called the CLOZE procedure. Infrequently used as a teaching device (more frequently in testing), it is a word deletion process whereby words are removed from a printed passage. The student's task is to predict or identify the word which was removed and replace it. In making his predictions the student must utilize prior knowledge, general understanding of the material, context clues, and knowledge of word usage. Moreover, the student is forced by the very nature of the task to pay attention to the message of the passage without unnecessary translation coding.

The CLOZE technique

Rosenbaum (89) feels that some marginally prepared teachers favor translation because it clarifies the meaning for them as much as for the students. "If the teacher would apply time, diligence and imagination in preparing questions and simple explications on vocabulary, syntax, and thought content in the target language, specific and general understanding could almost always be elicited without the use of English." (One might add that such procedures have the concomitant benefit of increasing the quantity of practice in oral skills, particularly listening comprehension.) Rosenbaum further provides descriptions of specific and useful classroom procedures in developing reading. One of these techniques, oral reading in class, has been seriously questioned elsewhere (81) on the basis that if the student can do it well, he doesn't need it; if he cannot do it well, he should not become a model for the entire class.

Oral reading

The question of whether literary material is appropriate reading material continues to be debated. If program objectives specify reading skill development, but do not include literary objectives, the answer is simple: Literary works are inappropriate. If, however, objectives do include learnings in the literary domain, decisions must be made about selecting the works. Stewart (102)

Reading of literature

believes that three points should be kept in mind in deciding when and how literature should be studied: (1) Will the student enjoy it? (2) Is it relevant to his needs? (3) Is it within the range of his linguistic competence? Bradford (10) maintains that literature can aid language learning by building vocabulary, by presenting syntactical patterns unique to written language, and by fostering understanding of the society in which the work is set.

Programmed materials, particularly reading materials, are not new in foreign language education. Their use remains, however, strikingly limited. An up-to-date view on programmed materials focuses on individualization of training for maximum accommodation to individual student characteristics as well as subject-matter characteristics (Fiks, 33). According to this view, no single teaching strategy is best for everyone, in all subjects, at all stages. Fiks lists 48 commercially available programs.

Programmed reading?

Valdman (105) has differentiated "guided learning" from "programmed instruction." The former he defines as the type of learning where the subject matter has been reduced to manageable steps and in which most of the learning will be acquired by the learner himself by way of self-instructional activities. The differentiation from programmed learning is based upon his hesitancy to attempt to specify the terminal behavior of a complete foreign language course in terms of finite sets of elements.

Programmed materials, readers in particular, and taped listening materials are occasionally being placed in "resource" or "learning" centers. Two such facilities have been described (Fleury, 34; Rallo, 85).

Kendall (53) has offered another alternative to leaving students to struggle with and recite upon a reading assignment. He suggests that when students arrive in class they find a list of the important words from the passage on the chalkboard. The list is, in a sense, a schematic version of the story. The words serve as memory prompts during teacher questioning. As the student develops facility in retelling the story, words are gradually erased.

The classroom teacher is not without other recent descriptions of "cookbook" ideas and techniques. Darian (23) describes amazingly modern reading procedures advocated by Jespersen (48) near the turn of the century. Young (114) describes classroom procedures for a reading class, using examples from the French novel *Les Misérables*. Meiden & Murphy (70) have described question-and-answer techniques which permit use of the

"Cookbook" ideas

language laboratory for reading lessons. Ryding & Sareil (90) have offered suggestions for developing transformation exercises from reading materials. Breitenstein (11) provides a transcript of a question-and-answer strategy in an English-as-a-foreign-language class using Christina Rossetti's sonnet "Remember."

Burling (16) makes what he calls "outlandish" proposals about language learning. Using reading skill as an example, he envisions separating different aspects (grammar, lexicon, phonology) of the new language. One might begin by having the student read the equivalent of a word-for-word translation of the foreign language. He would learn a good deal of syntax without worrying about the lexicon. Gradually foreign language material is introduced. Smith (99) has expressed opinions which are somewhat contrary. He believes that it is impractical to postpone "vocabulary enrichment." The student is hampered by limitation of vocabulary.

Conclusions

This chapter has reviewed recent literature relating to FL listening and reading skill strategies. The list of references at the end of the chapter is not otherwise selective; the absence of any items related to the topic is only a result of their unavailability at the time of preparation.

Four characteristics of the literature should strike the reader:

1 There remains a great paucity of empirical research in this area of FL education. In fact, a substantial part of the reported research is extrapolated from *seemingly* related first language investigation. Consequently, teachers teach, methodologists teach teachers, graduate programs prepare methodologists, all while very little is known about the *learning* at the end of the chain.

2 The literature evokes an overwhelming sensation of *déjà vu*; there is little in this chapter which has not been said previously. Foreign language education is, perhaps, becoming too accustomed to very slow progress in developing insights into second language learning. Contrastingly, we live in an era of telescopic progress in knowledge.

3 In a volume whose theme is "individualization of instruction" the term is strikingly absent from the literature. The only use of the concept is in the restriction to receptive skills for some learners and in the use made of some media in the

development of these skills. Indeed, the focal point in the literature is not truly the learning. The literature on the whole reminds one of the teacher who makes a detailed lesson plan of her activities for the day, proceeds efficiently from one to the next, finishes the last activity just at the sound of the bell, sighs and says, "What a great class this was! I accomplished everything I wanted to!" But not a thought has been given to student learning.

4 Paradoxically, in spite of the absence of efforts toward individualization, listening and reading skills offer unique opportunities for relating the entire methodology for individualization to language learning. Individualization implies maximizing the conditions for learning, conditions which vary for each learner. What is implied by individualization has been documented elsewhere in this volume and should not be repeated here. Suffice it to mention several key considerations in the receptive skills. Individualization always implies specificity. One must be able to identify learning outcomes, specific components of skills to be learned, and the absence or presence of component skills in a learner. Foreign language educators have, perhaps, become smug in their satisfaction with the specificity achieved by viewing language learning in terms of four skills. Such specificity is primitive in terms of what will be necessary. If one were to utilize, for example, the highly respected procedures outlined by Gagné (36), two tasks would have to be accomplished. Terminal behaviors would have to be specified, and component skills would have to be identified. The latter task is analogous to tasks being done in all disciplines, and its difficulty appears to be merely a function of research time and effort. Specifying terminal behavior, however, requires a rationale because the meaningfulness of specifying terminal behavior has been seriously questioned (Politzer, 81; Valdman,105) on the basis of the near-infinite (for practical purposes) variety in language. How can one specify outcomes and components for anything so complex as language?

It would seem that an answer to this question could come from the statistical concept of *sampling*. The population or universe ("knowing" French, Spanish, etc.) is unmanageable. What knowing French, Spanish, etc. means in terms of behavior must be stated. It is here that the sampling procedure is useful. One chooses (samples) from all possible behaviors which could mean "knowing the language" the one which will satisfy this meaning for the particular instructional setting. For example, a teacher may determine that being able to read *Le Petit Prince* means knowing French for his program. By using the procedures outlined by Gagné this entire task is eventually analyzed. Instructional strategy could then be devised which would permit total mastery of the task by each *individual* learner.

The unique contribution of receptive skills is one of facilitation. Approaches such as this, or others, require specification of the goal or terminal behavior as the *sine qua non* of the strategy. While specification of productive skill behavior is equally possible, there seems to be inherent facilitation in the existence of an extant representation of the content of the goal *prior to* the performance by the learner. One has, for example, a written message or an audible message with which the learner is to cope. In the productive skills, if one specifies, for example, that the learner is to be able to say where he lives, it is more difficult to specify components because the behavior is not totally predictable. There are alternative ways of saying nearly anything. It would seem, therefore, that it might be less complex to do initial work in receptive skills.

Perhaps, efforts in such literally untried areas will result in progress. We cannot be content with matching global entities like language skills with learner characteristics and considering it "individualization." Foreign language education must reach a status where it no longer merits being one of the "last to respond" to changes in curriculum (Foshay, 35).

References, Strategies of instruction for listening and reading

1 Alderson, Connie. *Magazines Teenagers Read.* Oxford: Pergamon Press, 1968.

2 Alexander, L. G. "The New Grammarians and the Language Teacher." *English Language Teaching* 24(1969):5–11.

3 Asher, James J. "The Total Physical Response Approach to Second Language Learning." *Modern Language Journal* 53(1969):3–17.

4 ——— "Vision and Audition in Language Learning." *Perceptual and Motor Skills* 19(1964):255–300.

5 ——— "Toward a Neo-Field Theory of Behavior." *Journal of Humanistic Psychology* 4(1964):85–94.

6 Ausubel, David P. *Educational Psychology:A Cognitive View.* New York: Holt, Rinehart and Winston, 1968.

7 Banathy, Bela H., and Jesse O. Sawyer. "The Primacy of Speech:An Historical Sketch." *Modern Language Journal* 53(1969):537–44.

8 Banks, Michael E. "An Application of Some Programming Variables To Standard Textbook Prose." *Dissertation Abstracts* 30(1969):481A (Kansas).

9 Bennett, W.A. *Aspects of Language and Language Teaching.* New York: Cambridge Univ. Press, 1968.

10 Bradford, Arthur. "Reading Literature and

Learning a Second Language." *Language Learning* 18(1968):199–210.

11 Breitenstein, P. H. "How to Start Reading Poetry in Class." *English Language Teaching* 23(1969): 283–89.

12 Brooks, Nelson. "The Meaning of Bilingualism Today." *Foreign Language Annals* 2(1969):304–09.

13 Buckby, M. "The Rôle of Games in Language Teaching." *Audio-Visual Language Journal* 6(1968):125–28.

14 Bundy, Jean D.,et al. "The Colby College Conference on the Undergraduate Major in French." *French Review* 42(1968):66–73.

15 Burkholder, Rachel B. "The Improvement in Reading Ability through the Development of Specific Underlying or Associated Mental Abilities." *Dissertation Abstracts* 29(1968):1157A–58A(Arizona).

16 Burling, Robbins. "Some Outlandish Proposals for the Teaching of Foreign Languages." *Language Learning* 18(1968):61–75.

17 Carroll, John B. "What Does the Pennsylvania Foreign Language Research Tell Us?" *Foreign Language Annals* 3(1969):214–36.

18 Chastain, Kenneth D., and Frank J. Woerderhoff. "A Methodological Study Comparing the Audio-lingual Habit Theory and the Cognitive Code-Learning Theory." *Modern Language Journal* 52(1968):268–79.

19 Coleman, Ben C. "A Clinical Report of the Use of Motion Pictures in Foreign Language Teaching." *Hispania* 51(1968):291–94.

20 Connor, Marjorie W. "Learning Characteristics of Able Nonachievers in Audiolingual Foreign Language Classes." *Dissertation Abstracts* 29(1968):1446A–47A(Cincinnati).

21 Culhane, Joseph W. "CLOZE Procedures and Comprehension." *The Reading Teacher* 23 (1970):410–13.

22 Dannerbeck, Francis J. "Audio-Lingual Teaching and Reading." *French Review* 43(1969):265–68.

23 Darian, Steven. "Backgrounds of Modern Language Teaching:Sweet, Jespersen, and Palmer." *Modern Language Journal* 53(1969):545–50.

24 Demilia, Lorraine. "Visual Fatigue and Reading." *Journal of Education* 151,ii(1968):4–34.

25 Duker, Sam. "Listening," 747–53 in Robert L. Ebel,et al.,eds., *Encyclopedia of Educational Research*. New York: Macmillan. [4th ed.]

26 Dulin, Kenneth. "Using Context Clues in Word Recognition and Comprehension." *The Reading Teacher* 23(1970):440–46.

27 Edgerton, Mills F., Jr.,ed. *Sight and Sound:The Sensible and Sensitive Use of Audio-Visual Aids*. Reports of the Working Committees of the Northeast Conference. New York: MLA Materials Center, 1969.

28 *Education Index*. Bronx, New York: H. W. Wilson. [monthly.]

29 ERIC/CRIER [Educational Resources Information Center/Clearinghouse on Retrieval of Information and Evaluation on Reading.] School of Education, Indiana Univ., Bloomington, Ind.

30 Everett, Aaron B. "A New Look for Intermediate French." *French Review* 43(1969):72–80.

31 Farr, Roger. *Reading:What Can Be Measured?* An IRA Research Fund Monograph from the ERIC/CRIER Reading Review Series. Newark, Del.: International Reading Association, 1969.

32 Feldman, David M., and Walter D. Kline. *Spanish:Contemporary Methodology*. Waltham, Massachusetts: Blaisdell, 1969.

33 Fiks, Alfred I. *Foreign Language Programmed Materials:1969*. MLA/ERIC Focus Report 7. New York: MLA/ERIC, 1969.

34 Fleury, Dale F. "Independent Study:Foreign Language Seminars." *National Association of Secondary School Principals Bulletin* 53,338 (1969):90–99.

35 Foshay, Arthur W. "How Fare the Disciplines?" *Phi Delta Kappan* 51(1970):349–52.

36 Gagné, Robert M. *The Conditions of Learning*. New York: Holt, Rinehart and Winston, 1965.

37 Gallo, Donald R. "Free Reading and Book Reports—An Informal Survey of Grade Eleven." *Journal of Reading* 11(1968):532–38.

38 Gottsdanker, Josephine S., and E. Anne Pidgeon. "Current Reading Tastes of Young Adults." *Journal of Higher Education* 40(1969):381–85.

39 Grittner, Frank M. "A Critical Re-Examination of Methods and Materials." *Modern Language Journal* 53(1969):467–77.

40 ⸺ *Teaching Foreign Languages*. New York: Harper and Row, 1969.

41 Hamilton, Stanley, "Using the 'Dictée' for Aural Comprehension." *French Review* 42(1968):279–82.

42 Harris, Theodore L. "Reading," 1069–1105 in Robert L. Ebel,et al.,eds., *Encyclopedia of Educational Research*. New York: Macmillan, 1969. [4th ed.]

43 Hughes, John P. *Linguistics and Language Teaching*. New York: Random House, 1968.

44 Jaekel, Hugo. "The Study of Foreign Language and Culture in the Host Environment:Prefatory Note." *Modern Language Journal* 53(1969):305.

45 Jakobovits, Leon A. "Research Findings and Foreign Language Requirements in Colleges and Universities." *Foreign Language Annals* 2(1969):436–56.

46 ⸺ "Second Language Learning And Transfer Theory: A Theoretical Assessment." *Language Learning* 19(1969):55–86.

47 Jarvis, Gilbert A. "A Comparison of Contextualized Practice Particularized Referents Vs. Practice With Generic Meaning." Unpublished Ph.D. Dissertation. Lafayette, Indiana: Purdue Univ. 1970.

48 Jespersen, Otto. *How to Teach a Foreign Language*. London: Allen and Unwin, 1904.

49 Joll, Leonard W. "Three Important Levels of Comprehension," in J.A. Figurel,ed., *Forging Ahead in Reading*. Proceedings of the Twelfth Annual Convention. Newark, Delaware: International Reading Association, 1968.

50 Jonas, Sister Ruth Adelaide. "The Twinned Classroom Approach to FLES." *Modern Language Journal* 53(1969):342–46.

51 Kaufman, Maurice. "Will Instruction in Reading

Spanish Affect Ability in Reading English?" *Journal of Reading* 11(1968):521–27.

52 Keitel, Helmut A. "Development and Dissemination of Materials for the Teaching of World History in a Foreign Language (German)." *Modern Language Journal* 54(1970):112–15.

53 Kendall, Harvey L. "Lexical Cues on the Blackboard:A Stimulus to Oral Participation." *Die Unterrichtspraxis* 2,ii(1969):21–24.

54 King, Janet K. "A Reading Program for Realists." *German Quarterly* 42(1969):65–80.

55 Kingston, Albert J. "The Psychology of Reading," 425–32 in J. A. Figurel,ed., *Forging Ahead in Reading*. Proceedings of the Twelfth Annual Convention. Newark, Delaware: International Reading Association, 1968.

56 Kirch, Max S. "Evaluation of Audio-Lingual Skills." *Die Unterrichtspraxis* 1,ii(1968):25–29.

57 ——— "Visuals in the Language Laboratory." *National Association of Language Laboratory Directors Journal* 4,ii(1969):32–35.

58 Klin, George. "Our Unrealistic Language Program." *French Review* 42(1969):722–27.

59 Lado, Robert. "Language, Thought and Memory in Linguistic Performance, A Thought View." Paper given at the Third Annual TESOL Convention, Chicago, March 1969.

60 Laffey, James L.,et al. *Research on Reading from "Research in Education."* Bethesda, Md.: ERIC Document Reproduction Service, 1969.

61 Lambert, Wallace E., and John Macnamara. "Some Cognitive Consequences of Following a First-Grade Curriculum in a Second Language." *Journal of Educational Psychology* 60(1969):86–96.

62 Lane, Harlan. "Why Is College Foreign Language Instruction in Trouble? Three Dozen Reasons." Ann Arbor: Center for Research on Language and Language Behavior, Univ. of Michigan, 1968.

63 Lange, Dale L., ed. "1968 ACTFL Annual Bibliography." *Foreign Language Annals* 2(1969):483–530.

64 ——— "1969 ACTFL Annual Bibliography." *Foreign Language Annals* 3:625–73.

65 *A Language-Teaching Bibliography*. London: Cambridge, 1968. [Compiled and edited by the Centre for Information on Language Teaching and the English-Teaching Information Centre of the British Council.]

66 Light, Timothy. "The Reading-Comprehension Passage and A Comprehensive Reading Programme." *English Language Teaching* 24(1970):120–24.

67 Lipton, Gladys C. "To Read or Not to Read:An Experiment on the FLES Level." *Foreign Language Annals* 3(1969):241–46.

68 MacLaughlin, Anabel. "From Dijon to the Classroom." *Wisconsin Journal of Education* 101,iii(1969):11–12,23.

69 Maginnis, George H. "The Readability Graph and Informal Reading Inventories." *The Reading Teacher* 22(1969):516–18.

70 Meiden, Walter, and Joseph A. Murphy. "The Use of the Language Laboratory to Teach the Read-ing Lesson." *Modern Language Journal* 52 (1968):23–25.

71 Mueller, Theodore. "Analysis of the Results Obtained with 'Basic French – A Programmed Course' Academic Year 1968–69 and Comparison with a Traditional Audio-Lingual Course." Bethesda, Maryland: ERIC Document Reproduction Service, 1969.

72 Newmark, Leonard, and David Reibel. "Necessity and Sufficiency In Language Learning." *International Review of Applied Linguistics in Language Teaching* 6(1968):145–64.

73 "New York City Board of Education Syllabus of Minima in Modern Foreign Languages, 1931," 214–15 in Maxim Newmark,ed., *Twentieth Century Modern Language Teaching*. New York: Philosophical Library, 1948.

74 Nixon, Ruth A. "The Visual Adjunct in the Audio-Lingual Approach to the Teaching of Foreign Languages." *Dissertation Abstracts* 30(1969):624A(Florida State).

75 Ohman, Richard. "Grammar and Meaning," xxxi–xxxiv in William Morris, ed., *The American Heritage Dictionary of the English Language*. Boston: Houghton Mifflin Co., 1969.

76 Oliva, Peter F. *The Teaching of Foreign Languages*. Englewood Cliffs, New Jersey: Prentice-Hall, 1969.

77 Orr, David B., et al. "Self-Pacing Behavior in the Use of Time-Compressed Speech." *Journal of Educational Psychology* 60(1969):28–31.

78 Ort, Barbara A., and Dwight R. Smith. "The Language Teacher Tours the Curriculum:New Horizons for Foreign Language Education." *Foreign Language Annals* 3(1969):28–74.

79 Palmer, Harold. *A Grammar of Spoken English*. Cambridge: Heffer, 1924.

80 Pimsleur, Paul, and Johann F. Struth. "Knowing Your Students in Advance." *Modern Language Journal* 53(1969):85–87.

81 Politzer, Robert L. *Performance Criteria for the Foreign Language Teacher*. Technical Report N. 1A. Stanford, California: Center for Research and Development in Teaching, 1969.

82 ——— and Louis Weiss. "Developmental Aspects of Auditory Discrimination, Echo Response and Recall." *Modern Language Journal* 53(1969):75–85.

83 Potts, Marion. "The Effect of Second-Language Instruction on the Reading Proficiency and General School Achievement of Primary-Grade Children." *American Educational Research Journal* 4(1967):367–73.

84 Purdom, Boyd A. "An Analysis of Listening Skill Development Using the Midwest Program on Airborne Television Instruction." *Dissertation Abstracts* 29(1969):3046A–3047A(Peabody).

85 Rallo, John A. "A Cooperative French Program:A New Approach." *Foreign Language Annals* 2(1969):474–76.

86 Renshaw, J. Parke, "Basics of a Strategy for Language Teaching." *Hispania* 53(1970):67–70.

87 Rivers, Wilga. *Teaching Foreign-Language Skills*. Chicago: Univ. of Chicago Press, 1968.

88 Robinson, Boyd E. "Use of the Initial Teaching

Alphabet in English as a Second Language. Classes for Spanish Speaking Adults." *Dissertation Abstracts* 30(1969):1806A–1807A (Univ. of California-Los Angeles).

89 Rosenbaum, Eric. "The Foreign Language Reading Lesson." *Die Unterrichtspraxis* 2,ii(1969): 16–20.

90 Ryding, William W., and Jean S. Sareil. "Literature in Second-Year College French:The Use of Transformations." *Modern Language Journal* 52(1968):191–94.

91 Saavedra, Barbara H. "Applied Research Center, El Paso Public Schools." *Modern Language Journal* 53(1969):97.

92 Samuels, Marilyn,et al. "Communicational Efficiency of Children Schooled in a Foreign Language." *Journal of Educational Psychology* 60 (1969):389–93.

93 Samuels, S. Jay. "Attentional Processes in Reading:The Effect of Pictures on the Acquisition of Reading Responses." *Journal of Educational Psychology* 58(1967):337–42.

94 Schramm, Wilbur. "Implications of the New Technology for Language Teaching," 41–56 in *Language Development:Selected Papers from a Ford Foundation Conference on the State of the Art.* New York:Ford Foundation, 1968.

95 Seymour, Dorothy. "The Difference Between Linguistics and Phonics." *Reading Teacher* 23(1969):99–102.

96 Shankman, Florence V. "Games Reinforce Reading Skills." *Reading Teacher* 22(1968):262–64.

97 Shawl, James R. *A Definition of One Level of Achievement in the Reading and Writing of Spanish.* Final Report. Washington, D.C.: Office of Education, U.S. Bureau of Research, 1969.

98 Smith, Alfred N.,Jr. "Reading Instruction in English and in Modern Foreign Languages:A Comparative Study." *Dissertation Abstracts* 29 (1968):1489A(Ohio State).

99 Smith, Paul. "Teaching Vocabulary." *Modern Language Journal* 53(1969):531–37.

100 Smith, Philip D.,Jr. "An Assessment of Three Foreign Language Teaching Strategies and Three Language Laboratory Systems." *French Review* 43(1969):289–304.

101 —— *A Comparison Study of the Effectiveness of the Traditional and Audiolingual Approaches to the Foreign Language Instruction Utilizing Laboratory Equipment.* Supplementary Report. Washington, D.C.: U.S. Office of Education, 1969.

102 Stewart, John. "How and When—Literature in the Foreign Language Curriculum." *Bulletin of the Modern Language Association* 25,iii(1969): 38–40.

103 Sticht, Thomas G. "Some Interactions of Speech Rate, Signal Distortion, and Certain Linguistic Factors in Listening Comprehension." *AV Communications Review* 17(1969):159–71.

104 Taylor, Stanford E. *Listening:What Research Says to the Teacher,* No. 29. Washington, D.C.: American Educational Research Association, 1964.

105 Valdman, Albert. "Programmed Instruction Versus Guided Learning in Foreign Language Acquisition." *Die Unterrichtspraxis* 1,ii(1968):1–14.

106 Valette, Rebecca M. *Directions in Foreign Language Testing.* New York:MLA Materials Center, 1969.

107 —— *Modern Language Testing: A Handbook.* New York: Harcourt, Brace and World, 1967.

108 —— "The Pennsylvania Project, Its Conclusions and Its Implications." *Modern Language Journal* 53(1969):396–404.

109 —— "Some Conclusions to be Drawn from the Pennsylvania Study." *National Association of Language Laboratory Directors Newsletter* 3,iii(1969):17–19.

110 Van Valkenburg, John. "Learning Through Listening:Implications For Reading." *Dissertation Abstracts* 29(1968):1692A (Rochester).

111 Westphal, M. Elizabeth. "Some Psycho-Acoustic and Intellectual Correlates of Achievement in German Language Learning of Junior High School Students." *Modern Language Journal* 53(1969):258–66.

112 Witkin, Belle R. "Auditory Perception—Implications for Language Development." *Journal of Research and Development in Education* 3(1969):53–71.

113 Wood, Fred H. "The McCluer Plan:An Innovative Non-Graded Foreign Language Program." *Modern Language Journal* 54(1970):184–87.

114 Young, Eleanor C. "Vitalizing the Reading Skill." *French Review* 42(1969):578–81.

5

Strategies of instruction for speaking and writing

Introduction

Alfred N. Smith
Utah State University

Speaking and writing are the two productive skills. The foreign language teacher often thinks of the teaching of these skills in terms of several levels of development: (*1*) a controlled, mechanical level; (2) a semicontrolled level; and (3) a level of free expression. The mechanical level involves learning pronunciations, spellings, grammatical forms, word order, and meaning in a fixed context which attempts to order and control the various learning problems. At the semicontrolled level the student may be invited to express his own ideas in a speaking or writing activity. He does so, however, within the confines of the specific structures and vocabulary items being studied. Finally, the student engages in free conversation and composition in which he selects randomly, but appropriately, from his entire knowledge of the language. Each level of development requires different strategies of instruction. "Strategy" is used broadly to designate any procedure, technique, activity, or exercise used by the teacher in presentation or by the student in learning and practice.

Speaking and writing: productive skills

The purpose of this chapter is to review strategies of instruction for speaking and writing. In accordance with the theme of this volume, this review will be restricted to strategies which attempt to individualize learning in these skills. At this point it is necessary to delineate what individualization may denote in connection with speaking and writing instruction.

Purpose of the chapter

First, individualization occurs when the student is allowed to pace his development in speaking and writing according to his own learning rate. Students may be subjected to the same teaching methods. They may also be required to do the same speaking and writing exercises. *Time* is the variable factor here which provides for different rates of progress.

Individualization with the productive skills

Secondly, the student may be permitted to design his own approach to a speaking or writing problem by employing devices best suited to his own way of learning. In this case, all students may be given the same performance objectives to fulfill. For example, they may be asked to learn the written forms of a verb in the present tense in order to use them correctly in the blanks of a list of sentences. For practice, students have at their disposal various written explanations, drill sheets, tapes, and, of course, the teacher. Each student progresses as he sees fit. One student may wish to copy each verb form a number of times; another may elect to go directly to the drill sheets; still another may study the forms in the text and then attempt to write them as dictation from the tape. The variable which permits individualization here is *mode of learning*. A detailed description of the use of performance objectives in the teaching of foreign languages is in Steiner (33) and in her article in this volume.

All students do not study languages for the same reasons. As they become more proficient in the basic skills, they seek experiences in the language which conform to their *individual* goals. A student interested in theater or the performing arts will not need the same kinds of speaking skills as the student pursuing a career in diplomacy or politics. A student interested in journalistic reporting at the international level will need different writing skills than a student involved in literary criticism. Instruction which recognizes each student's purpose for studying the language is also individualized.

Why do students study a foreign language?

Finally, any activity which leads to the oral or written expression of a personal thought, idea, or feeling in the foreign language is, in a sense, individualized.

Individualizing speaking and writing instruction may be thought of, then, in terms of providing for individual learning rates, individual modes of learning, individual goals, and the expression of personal thoughts and feelings. This review will attempt to summarize and evaluate strategies of instruction for speaking and writing in which individualization occurs in one or a combination of the ways described above. The review is restricted to information which appeared in the professional literature during the year 1969, although references to earlier or more recent publications may at times be required.

There are three main sections to the chapter. They deal with strategies of instruction described in (*1*) teaching materials; (2) programs of instruction and course descriptions; and (3) general literature on methods of teaching foreign languages.

Teaching materials

This section discusses the treatment of speaking and writing in foreign language textbooks published in this country in 1969 and early 1970.

In general, recent textbooks continue to be audiolingual in their orientation. Learning to *speak* the language is no less a goal than in previous years. Dialogues and pattern drills are still the principal means of introducing and practicing the spoken language. A greater emphasis on writing is immediately noticeable. Little or no delay is recommended in the presentation of the written language, although the listening-speaking-reading-writing order is still observed. Most of these books are conceived to respond to the arrangement of the typical classroom situation which is, for the most part, graded and lockstep in nature. There is, therefore, little provision for different learning rates among students incorporated in these materials. In a preface to the student in a new first-year text, the learner is actually cautioned against getting out of step in this way: "Do not go faster than your teacher; be content with the lesson of the day, and do not go ahead in the book" (de Petra, 22).

Foreign language texts

One of the most anticipated texts of the year was probably the second edition of *A-LM, Level One* (24). In the procedures outlined in the teacher's edition, there is hardly any mention of providing for individual differences. A note to the teacher on page 153 is one of the few hints in the text that different writing activities might be necessary for students of different capabilities. There are, however, certain features which do facilitate the individual learner's task and personalize the material.

Revised "A-LM, Level One"

For the speaking skill, these aspects of the text are considered noteworthy:

1 Systematic and detailed instruction in pronunciation is provided. There are reviews of the most troublesome sounds at regularly spaced intervals in the text.

2 The dialogues and dialogue lines are short and manageable.

3 There are take-home discs containing the basic dialogue and supplement of each unit. These discs allow for complete individual practice when available to all students.

4 The reading notes following the supplement are an aid to students without take-home discs. These notes help individuals working on their own to remember certain pronunciations in the dialogue and supplement.

5 The pattern drills, including the ones in the teacher presentations as well as those in the text proper, are numerous and varied in nature. There are many activities which elicit personal reaction: (*1*) In the Free Response drill, the stu-

dent responds to personalized questions. (2) The student finishes a sentence with his own idea and the vocabulary of his choice in the Free Completion exercise. (3) The Free Substitution drill leads the student to produce original sentences by replacing key words in the model sentence with words of his choice. (4) The student is asked to react spontaneously to questions and statements of the teacher and other students in Rejoinder drills.

6 The recombination material at the end of each lesson provides opportunities for more liberated speaking experiences. A conversation stimulus is presented after the students have handled several dialogue variations. A brief description of the situation is given and the first line of the conversation is suggested. The students then construct the rest of the conversation.

The student is exposed to writing after the completion of Unit One, which serves as a phonological introduction to the language. The first writing activities involve copying in preparation for dictation which is used to reinforce the study of sound-letter correspondences. Both the exercise book and the text provide grammatical exercises and spelling drills which are assigned in conjunction with the oral work covered in class. Although there are challenging exercises in sentence construction and paragraph and dialogue rewriting, there is little opportunity for the student to become personally involved in his writing experiences. There is, of course, the possibility of using some of the free response activities described above as written assignments.

Introduction to written language

The early introduction to writing and its use as a reinforcement to oral learning represents a shift in audiolingual thinking. The reading/writing lag recommended in the first edition was supported primarily by linguists (Politzer, 23) who predicted pronunciation deterioration and other interference problems with premature exposure to graphic forms. The authors of the present edition have modified this notion perhaps in light of the psychological theorizing of Rivers (26) who argues in favor of the "judicious" use of the written language as a visual support from the beginning of instruction. This change in position may also be the result of recent research findings which fail to show significant linguistic gains for audiolingual students who receive prereading and writing training (Lange, 16; Smith, 31; Smith & Baranyi, 32). At any rate, the reviewer sees this change

116

as a step away from methodological rigidity and as an acceptance of the individual learner's psychological needs.

Chez les Français (Langellier & Levy, 17) is a new addition to the Holt four-skills series for secondary schools. There is no aspect of this text which provides for individualization of instruction. However, the text does give the series an additional track for students who do not quite measure up to the Level II text, *Parler et Lire*, after their Level I experience. The book was developed as an alternate Level II text for use by students who received Level I instruction in the Holt elementary sequence or with *Ecouter et Parler* in grades 7 and 8. It could easily be used in a multilevel program with slower Level II students, while the faster ones are grouped to proceed directly to *Parler et Lire*. Thus, in a small way, this text represents an effort to recognize differences in achievement that develop early in language learning.

The "Holt materials": a new addition

The format of the text is modeled largely after its predecessor, *Parler et Lire*. In fact, much of the material is identical. The first two chapters are completely new and are a review of the vocabulary and salient grammar points of *Ecouter et Parler*. Speaking and writing activities, mainly in the form of answers to questions, are based on the conversations, scenes, narratives, and photograph descriptions. There is a variety of grammatical exercises for oral drill and written homework in the text and in the student workbook. These exercises are highly controlled with no occasion for original response. There is a conspicuous lack of personalizing activities. Aside from the role-playing substitution drills in which students follow the exact sequence of a story or conversation, there are no opportunities for students to relate what they learn to their own lives. Personal reaction to the textbook material in the form of free or even semicontrolled oral or written composition is absent.

At the beginning of this section it was stated that 1969 textbooks continue to be audiolingual in their orientation. Beginning college texts are no exception, although more emphasis on cognitive processes and less attention to memorization and rote practice are significant innovations. Intellectual understanding of grammatical operations, meaningful communication, and creative, personal use of the language are stressed. Speaking and writing activities are less contrived. Some of these exercises are expressly designed to permit the individual to respond more honestly and in keeping with his personal reality.

Speaking and writing/Smith

The presentation of grammar and the accompanying pattern drills in two new Spanish texts are particularly good examples of this tendency. In both *Voces y Vistas* (Osborne, Tilles, & Pérez, 21) and *Curso Básico de Español* (Wolfe, 37), simple grammatical explanations precede the speaking drills. There is repetition of model forms and sentences, and in *Voces y Vistas* simple substitutions are occasionally used. The bulk of the drills, however, are conversational in nature. That is, they are mainly response drills requiring answers to questions or logical rejoinders.

Two new Spanish texts and "personal response"

In most audiolingual drill work, the response drill is reserved as a culminating exercise to be used only after intensive practice with rapid-fire substitution and transformation drills. In audiolingualism, automaticity is a prerequisite to conversation. The audiolinguist would fear hesitation and error on the part of a student who had not been adequately conditioned for a response drill. This is, no doubt, a valid criticism of the procedure being described.

It must be noted, however, that these exercises are carefully graded. They develop around a single point of emphasis, and each drill has sufficient items to set the pattern. Of course, there are complicated combinations of structures required in the more advanced drills. The response in this drill is fixed to the extent that it makes use of a certain language pattern. At the same time, it is open-ended in two respects: (1) the student may respond either negatively or affirmatively; and (2) he may apply or eliminate any restriction to react truthfully to the reality of the context. The following drill on the imperfect tense from *Curso Básico de Español* (Wolfe, 37) illustrates these features:

1 *¿Sabía Ud. español el año pasado?*
  No, no lo sabía.
2 *¿Y sus padres?*
  No, ellos no lo sabían tampoco.
3 *¿Y su hermano?*
  No, él no lo sabía tampoco.
4 *¿Y la profesora Equis y yo?*
  Sí, Uds. lo sabían.

Teachers are instructed to change the names in these exercises to fit the situation at hand.

These authors are attempting to take the oral practice of grammar out of the artificial context of contrived drills and to restore the dyadic aspect inherent in authentic language behav-

118

ior. It is their hope that the drill function is being performed but in a way that is not devoid of communication and meaning.

A special feature of the *Curso Básico* text which individualizes to an extent is "drilling in pairs." Some of the drills are designed for choral use with the entire class. Many of them, however, are intended to be conversation drills between two individuals. The class is divided into pairs of students. They can go through the drills twice exchanging roles as respondent and interlocutor the second time around. The teacher is free to help individuals and make corrections.

Probably the most serious effort to individualize foreign language instruction has been made by the authors of programmed materials. Such materials are not new to the foreign language teaching scene. The list of programmed materials compiled by Fiks (9) in an ERIC Focus Report is impressive. This list, by the way, gives important information about each program, including a description of the course objectives. A student or teacher interested in obtaining basic or supplementary programmed materials in speaking and writing should consult this publication.

Programmed learning and individualization

One of the few programmed courses to appear in 1969 is the course for college students entitled *Basic German* (Ruplin & Russell, 28). This series integrates a programmed laboratory course with regular class sessions. Although the teacher is encouraged to use the class sessions as he sees fit, he is supplied with a manual containing all the frames of the program, suggestions for classroom activities, and supporting drills. The program itself presents both phonology and structure (orally and in written form) via tapes and the student text called an "Access Book." The answer spaces in the book are chemically treated. When they are rubbed with a special marker, there is visual confirmation of the response. If the answer is correct, a gray striped pattern on the written response appears. If the answer is wrong, a yellow mark appears. The observant student will soon discover that with a little squinting the gray stripes are detectable in the proper light, chemicals notwithstanding. After this discovery, the student who has no scruples about cheating the program may find his incentive as well as his learning efficiency significantly reduced. Immediate confirmation is one of the few ways motivation can be built into programmed materials. When this element can be anticipated, the challenge disappears and boredom is likely to ensue.

A programmed course for college German

119

Most programmers who know anything about languages would probably assert that individualization of instruction is ideally suited for programming. Valdman (35) is convinced that the preparatory activities in language acquisition (presentation of and drill in the basic elements of phonology, morphology, and syntax) can and should be performed by programmed materials. That students can gain remarkable phonological control through programmed materials has been a frequent observation of F. Rand Morton (18). Another frequent observation is that an effective programmed course cannot be totally "teacher free." The "preparatory activities" of which Valdman speaks must be followed by meaningful application in real communicative situations. Even in the most expensive, ideal programmed systems where branching and instantaneous adaptation are possible, certain language skills remain nonprogrammable. For instance, in his intricate diagram of the possible sequences to be followed in programming the communication skills, Bung (4) has placed *free speaking* and *free writing* in the area of nonprogrammable skills.

What language learning activities can be programme[d]

Aside from programmed materials just discussed, the degree to which recent texts have provided for individual differences in speaking and writing is negligible. It is apparent from this review that teachers who are concerned about this problem will have to seek guidance and solutions from other sources. One source of valuable information would be current foreign language programs and courses where individualization is being tried. The next section is a discussion of such efforts.

Programs of instruction and course descriptions

Certain foreign language programs utilize a multiple approach to individualization. These programs combine partial programming, laboratory instruction, team teaching, nongrading, and flexible scheduling as coordinate elements in the individualizing process. Other programs make use of a single system which provides individualization of a more limited and specialized nature. Computer-assisted instruction and certain laboratory instructional systems are examples. Finally, there is the specialized foreign language course which "individualizes" the curriculum, so to speak. These courses (history, music, journalism, etc., taught in the foreign language) attempt to recognize the different interests, talents, and needs that individuals bring to foreign language study. This section will review the nature of speaking and writing instruction in such programs and courses.

The McCluer Plan (38) is an experiment in individualizing through a multiple approach. The first edition of the Holt materials *Entender y Hablar* have been adapted for use in this program. Each unit of instruction has three distinct phases. The first phase trains the student in listening comprehension. He does not speak until he can pass a self-test indicating total comprehension of the basic dialogue sentences and the question-answer combinations based on them.

Phase two is called "vocalization." The student's task in this phase is to develop correct pronunciation habits. He works on his own in the laboratory with tapes and work sheets. He repeats the basic dialogue sentences after the tape, first without seeing them and again with the book open. He then studies a work sheet on pronunciation. This sheet describes sounds, contrasts them with English, and gives instructions on how to pronounce them. The student refers to this sheet during home practice to refresh his memory about certain pronunciations. When he feels he can read the material accurately and at normal speed, he takes a pronunciation test in the laboratory. If he passes, he goes on to the third phase.

The activities in the final phase are intended to give the student practice in all four skills. The object is to recombine and expand the learnings of the first two phases and to develop accuracy in reading and writing. There is individual and group work at this level. The individual activities are completed at home. Typical speaking and writing assignments involve learning to say the basic dialogue sentences in response to the English equivalent, learning to spell the basic dialogue sentences and the pattern practices, translating the pattern practices, preparing fill-in work sheets on certain grammar points, and giving oral responses to taped questions and comprehension exercises in the laboratory. For the small group activities, students are of necessity placed with those who are progressing at similar rates. Group work is largely conversational with occasional dictations given in turns by different students. The speaking practice includes reading conversations to check pronunciation, asking and answering questions based on a conversation or a report (one student is chosen to be the teacher), making up conversations using previously learned materials, playing games, and doing chain drills. A group test is administered after this phase.

The McCluer Plan

The phases of the McCluer Plan

There are no research data available concerning the effectiveness of this program. The director reports normal problems on the part of students and teachers in adjusting to their new roles. On the whole, the initial reaction is enthusiastic and encouraging (Wood, 38).

The procedures used in the practice of speaking and writing in the McCluer Plan are not always the ones most highly recommended by foreign language teaching specialists. The use of the pattern practices is particularly curious. Since the Holt materials offer a complete taped program, why were these exercises not programmed for use as oral drills in the laboratory? Their purpose is to develop fluency in speaking. It is very puzzling that these exercises were used solely for translation and in written homework assignments. Surely the constraints imposed on the presentation of materials in programming and individualizing do not necessitate a complete turnabout in methodology. Translation is used abundantly in all the phases to cue spoken and written responses. Translation has its place, to be sure. But an excessive dose could lead to the establishment of a compound system of languages in the learner. One wonders how the small conversational groups functioned when pattern practice was omitted and when English was the point of departure for so many of the preparatory activities.

Are the phases useful in the individualization of the productive skills?

In an experimental intermediate college French course described by Everett (7), students designed their own programs and set their own goals. The activities of the course were organized according to skill areas. Every day there were simultaneous offerings in each skill in different rooms. A schedule listing rooms and activities was distributed weekly. Students then planned a course of study to meet their individual skill needs and goals. Those who wished to develop conversational skills attended this hour. Others who needed more work in reading or writing chose those areas. There was also the possibility of attending several skill areas during the hour. The activities were individualized, and dropping in or out presented no problem. There were, of course, certain basic requirements to be fulfilled by all students. Tests on grammar were given every two weeks. The test could be taken, however, at any time in the two-week period. Trial tests over the material to be covered were made available for self-examination. French majors and minors were expected to develop certain levels of proficiency in all the skills. The ambitious student was also able to petition for credit in

An individualized intermedi college program

composition and conversation at the third year level by doing extra work which met established standards.

Conversation was greatly facilitated with this arrangement, because only those who "felt like talking" participated. Groups were formed when different levels of conversational ability were noticed. Conversation was also possible on a one-to-one basis. The teacher's role was to serve as an aid, catalyst, listener, and sometimes speaker. The report did not indicate how topics for discussion were selected or what preparation was required on the part of the student.

In the writing section, students had the advantage of working individually with the instructor and having their work corrected immediately. Students could request no grade on written work which was just practice. In this way they were able to check their progress regularly without the discouragement of a possible low grade. The time could also be used by students to receive consultation and correction on outside writing activities. Again the author makes no mention of how topics and assignments were chosen and made.

This type of course provides the latitude that most college students feel is lacking in present curriculum offerings. It is also in keeping with some of the recommended changes in foreign language requirements that Jakobovits (14) has proposed. Foreign language departments might hear fewer objections about requirements if they began organizing their courses along this line.

An experiment by Shepherd (30) at the high school level was conducted to determine ways of individualizing instruction in advanced courses. The grammar points of each unit were itemized. On an outline listing these items, the student checked off each point by indicating the date of mastery. This check list was kept in a personal file which the teacher examined each day. When all the items had been covered, the student arranged to take the test on that unit.

Individualization of an advanced course, high school level

Writing activities were assigned regularly. There were frequent compositions based on the reading material. At first they were simple imitations. As the course progressed, they became more difficult. By the end of the course, essays of more than 400 words were being written. Grades were not given. Emphasis was placed on correction and revision.

A special written exercise was introduced to counteract the dulling effect on creativity caused by the routine of grammar study. Students were asked to keep a journal in their personal files. Every day they wrote something of their own invention. They were encouraged to express something of personal importance and to avoid clichés and pat phrases. The teacher read these daily and made appropriate written response when possible. No corrections were made, but students soon learned that poorly written entries did not communicate. The teacher would note grammatical difficulties common to the journals and structure remedial work accordingly.

The use of computer-assisted instruction (CAI) has proved successful with certain aspects of language learning. Because the computer to date is unable to receive and *evaluate* a spoken message, its use as a teaching device is limited mainly to writing activities. Even response to a listening activity presented on tape must be made graphically. Rosenbaum (27) has outlined the types of exercises most suitable for CAI. One set of exercises is designed to develop the student's linguistic *competence*, i.e., his knowledge of the way the language operates. Rosenbaum considers substitution and transformation drills, paired sentence exercises, and translation as activities which will foster this development. Another set of exercises is necessary to develop skill in performance. Rosenbaum suggests dictation as an exercise appropriate for performance in the writing skill.

CAI

The contribution a computer program makes to individualization is optimum when it contains mediational and supervisory systems which provide relevant feedback and optional paths for students. Such systems were in operation in a program designed jointly by IBM Research and the language instruction staff at the State University of New York at Stony Brook. This program was used in an experiment to evaluate CAI with first year German classes. The mediational system was programmed to evaluate the student's response with feedback pointing to specific trouble spots. Rather than simply receiving confirmation in terms of "right" or "wrong" the student was forced to analyze his mistakes. Rosenbaum gives this example of the response-feedback process (27): The student's first translation of "We will not send the package to them" is typed to the computer. Several tries with subsequent feedback result in the correct translation.

Contributions of CAI to individualization

First Response:	Nous n'enverrez pas la paquet a les.
Feedback:	Nous ne – – – – enverr– – –1– paquet.
Second Try:	Nous ne leur enverront pas le paquet.

124

Feedback: Nous ne leur enverron– pas le paquet.

Final Response: Nous ne leur enverrons pas le paquet.

Compared with non-CAI groups (audiolingual courses with conventional language laboratory) the CAI groups performed significantly better in reading and writing and "roughly as well" in speaking and listening on the MLA Foreign Language Cooperative subtests (Rosenbaum, 27). The good showing of the CAI groups in the oral/aural skills is surprising considering the fact that these areas were not stressed due to the computers' inability to handle these skills.

The classroom teacher may see little that is applicable to his program in the above description. It is not very likely in any class he undertakes to individualize that he will have the assistance of IBM Research and a staff of professionals trained in computers and programming. It is important to remember, however, that a simple computer program can be written and implemented by a single teacher at minimal cost. An example of such an effort is CARLOS (Computer-Assisted Review Lessons On Syntax), a computer project set up by Turner (34) at Dartmouth College.

CAI applications to the classroom

The computer in this project was used as the source of written homework assignments and grammar review lessons for three second year Spanish courses. The program was also available to other students who needed review or were preparing for examinations in other courses. The student using CARLOS types his student number, the lesson, and the section he is to prepare. He is presented with a problem to which he types a response. A correct answer is confirmed immediately. The computer can anticipate up to two errors. For example, the student is asked to give the *yo* form of *sentar* in the present. He writes: *sento*. The computer, programmed to anticipate this error, replies: "Try again. Remember *sentar* is like *pensar*." Hopefully this hint puts the student on the right track, and he produces *siento*.

Computerized programs, like programmed learning, require discipline and honesty on the part of the learner. The student is on his own and must regulate his pace in light of accurate and continual self-appraisal. Some students have difficulty accepting this responsibility. Others are quite inept at assessing their own progress. Becoming a self-sufficient learner is no doubt the hardest and perhaps the most valuable lesson the student learns in individualized instruction.

Responsibility of students in a CAI program

Courses in other subject areas given in the foreign language offer obvious benefits to the individual student. The foreign language suddenly becomes more relevant because it is being used to gain information in an area of special interest. A compilation by Ort & Smith (20) describing courses of this nature makes it clear that such offerings are feasible additions to most high school programs and are generally quite successful.

Courses in subject areas

In what ways can these courses contribute specifically to the development of speaking and writing skills? If the course can meet a requirement in another area of the curriculum, it is possible for a student to be enrolled in two courses taught in the language: the regular foreign language course and the special area course. The student's time speaking and writing the language is thus doubled. Frequently, the language teacher and the special area teacher cooperate in a team teaching arrangement. This allows for more individual attention. The procedure for grading compositions in a course on government taught in French illustrates this point (Ort & Smith, 20). The paper is graded first for content by the specialist in government. Language usage is then checked by the French teacher. An English teacher proficient in French gives it a third reading for organization and development.

Elective courses in foreign languages will be offered for the first time in 1970–71 to intermediate and advanced students at Marshall-University High School in Minneapolis (6). The increased variety in course offerings will give the student a chance to fashion his language learning experiences according to his interests and needs. Courses which offer special training in speaking and writing include conversation and composition at several levels, grammar review, phonetics and spelling, journalism, correspondence, culture and civilization, and German theater workshop.

Elective courses

In a similar view, Logan (see his article in this volume) has already offered individualized courses within the German program of Live Oak High School in California. This program allows students to use their language skills in searching out and getting information in a large number of minicourses related to specific interests. Speaking and writing skills are used to obtain information. They are also developed beyond basic proficiency levels in specialized courses where vocabulary and structure become quite utilitarian, as in courses with commercial and business interests, driver training, and the like.

Most of the programs and courses described in this section are not true research projects. They are "try-out" experiments intended to explore the adaptability of individualized instructional practices to foreign language teaching. It is clear that speaking and writing activities can be individualized. Whether this leads to higher achievement in these skills is not known. More experimentation is needed.

General literature on methods of teaching foreign languages

This section will review classroom procedures relating to individualized speaking and writing activities found in books on methods of teaching, reports, and journal articles.

An examination of the principal books on foreign language teaching published in 1969 uncovers little information on individualizing speaking and writing. Grittner (12) devotes an entire chapter to a general discussion of teaching machines, programmed learning, and self-instruction. He does not discuss the development of the different skills within these frameworks, however. Feldman & Kline (8) and Oliva (19) mention the language laboratory as a means of individualizing. The usual comments are made that the laboratory provides more individual speaking time and liberates the teacher. There is no description of techniques for teaching speaking and writing in the laboratory.

All three books underline the importance of activities that lead to oral and written self-expression. These authors would agree that these experiences should be reserved for students who have excellent control in the language. Grittner enumerates the following techniques for teaching free composition: personal letters, pen pals, business correspondence, foreign language newspapers, minutes of foreign language club meetings, light verse, short stories, and critical essays. Oliva recommends impromptu talks and dialogues as effective ways of stimulating free speaking. He also considers extracurricular activities in the foreign language as excellent opportunities for additional speaking practice. Clubs, social affairs, assembly programs, skits, plays, films, meals are situations which can provide for different interests and ability levels.

The authors of a publication edited by Hester (13) describing the "verbal-active method" advocate the cultivation of personal

Methods texts

127

expression at every level of foreign language instruction through the use of regular oral and written composition. Oral compositions are assigned after structure and vocabulary have been presented and practiced in question-answer exercises. The compositions are based on the material just learned. They are usually short, allowing students to concentrate on organization and correct usage. Students are encouraged to be original. After the oral presentation, students ask each other questions on what they have just heard. Written composition is handled in much the same way. Students are cautioned to stay within the limits of their knowledge in the language. The use of dictionaries is forbidden. Only mistakes that students should know how to avoid are corrected. Sentences which need rebuilding are done so using only words and structures students know. The best parts of students' papers are occasionally read to the class.

The "verbal-active method"

The authors claim excellent results. They do not deny that the element of error is unavoidably introduced with these composition activities. They feel that this is minimized, however, by the control inherent in the teaching method itself and immediate correction. The authors are convinced that the skill developed in using the language imaginatively and the personal satisfaction the student derives from saying what *he* wants to say are worth the minor errors. Besides, leading the student to discover and correct his own mistakes can be used as a valuable teaching technique.

An obvious disadvantage of this method is the time required for oral presentations and paper grading. With a class of 40 students, it would be impossible to hear an oral composition from every student after each lesson. The only solution would be to hear only certain students each time, making sure that everyone participates in the question-answer period.

Most teachers feel the need to provide liberated speaking experiences for their students. Creating original dialogues is an activity that teachers frequently use. The teacher must realize that this procedure requires careful preparation and motivation. Schwartz (29) describes the step-by-step progression necessary to take the student from contrived speech to liberated dialogue. Variation of the memorized dialogue is the first step. Here the students replay the dialogue with minor substitutions in vocabulary and structure. Adaptation is the next activity. The dialogue is modified to fit the individual student's reality. Names, places, relationships, descriptions are changed by each student to reflect

Liberated speaking

128

his personal situation. The technique of expansion is then used to enlarge the situation by incorporating previously learned linguistic elements into the dialogue structure. The final step is the spontaneous generation of a conversation between two students.

Gahn & Rickel (11) have used liberated dialogues at the junior high school level. They outline the procedures teachers may follow in organizing this final step: (1) Students are placed in small groups of four or five. This grouping may be left to the students or directed by the teacher. (2) Each group selects a chairman. (3) Talking in the groups is kept at a low level so that disturbance is minimal. (4) Students are encouraged to build dialogues around specific grammar points. (5) Ideas may come from memorized dialogues or other sources such as films, plays, stories, comics, and home and school situations familiar to the students. Students memorize these conversations and present them before their class and other classes.

Liberated dialogues; role playing

These creative activities are highly motivating experiences. The role-playing that occurs can have some therapeutic value. Acting out conflicts and recreating relationships makes foreign language learning relevant and personally helpful. Reinert (25) recommends recording these dialogues. In this way they can easily be replayed for correction and kept for future reference.

A video tape recorder can add still another dimension to this activity. "Freezing" the action, replaying, and playing the action without the sound are advantages which Berwald (2) lists.

Free speaking activities can also be based on conversational topics of interest to students. Kersten & Ott (15) suggest preparing the student in the language he needs to converse about school athletic events, dances, the home environment, shopping, tours, weekend activities, and relationships with friends. Gardner (10) explains an oblique approach to conversation in which an experience common to all students is used as a point of departure for discussion. The teacher plays the role of catalyst and mediator. Imaginative reactions to pictures, posters, and other visual stimuli can produce interesting composition and conversation (Blomberg, 3).

Free speaking and student interests

The small group is probably the kind of framework best suited for the development of communication skills. Ciotti (5) has devised a theoretical construct using small group instruction as a means of taking the student from controlled to liberated discussion. The point of departure is a cultural narrative. The group progresses through three speaking stages ranging from total control to noncontrol. In the process progressive networks of interaction and structural modifications are used to facilitate both the psychological and linguistic development of the group.

Free composition can be motivated in several meaningful ways. Wheaton (36) enlisted the students' help in planning a course relevant to their interests. A broad theme was selected. Each student chose a subject for research and all available materials on the subject were collected. These papers were saved as sources of information for future classes. Students were studying individually. They were writing about relevant issues which they identified themselves.

More meaningful compositio

Agatstein (1) describes a similar attempt to make conversation and composition more relevant. He asked students to make a list of five or ten topics which interested them most. Ranking these topics quickly revealed the most popular one: student revolt. Reading materials were gathered. Instruction in vocabulary and grammar related to the topic was begun. Many discussions and composition activities resulted.

How one provides for the individual is the perennial question. The efforts to individualize speaking and writing activities described in this section indicate that a few foreign language teachers have been seeking answers. More teachers need to follow their example.

References, Strategies of instruction for speaking and writing

1 Agatstein, Michael. "*La Révolte des Jeunes* or An Experiment in Relevancy." *French Review* 43(1970):637–40.
2 Berwald, John P. "The Videotape Recorder as a Teaching Aid." *French Review* 43(1970):923–27.
3 Blomberg, John. "Give Them a Better Chance." *Hispania* 52(1969):881–84.
4 Bung, Klaus. "Towards Truly Programmed Language Laboratory Courses." *Audio-visual Language Journal* 7(1969):5–17.
5 Ciotti, Marianne C. "A Conceptual Framework for Small-Group Instruction in High School." *Foreign Language Annals* 3(1969):75–89.

6 "Course Descriptions, 1970–71, Marshall-University High School (Minneapolis, Minnesota)," in Lorraine A. Strasheim,ed., *Foreign Language: A New Apprenticeship for Living*. Bloomington: Indiana Language Program, in preparation.
7 Everett, Aaron B. "A New Look for Intermediate French." *French Review* 43(1969):72–80.
8 Feldman, David M., and Walter D. Kline. *Spanish:Contemporary Methodology*. Waltham, Massachusetts: Blaisdell, 1969.
9 Fiks, Alfred I. *Foreign Language Programmed Materials:1969*. MLA/ERIC Focus Report 7. New York: MLA/ERIC, 1969.

10 Gardner, Stephen H. "The Oblique Approach to French Language Teaching." *French Review* 43 (1970):795–99.

11 Ghan, Zoe Ann, and Kathryn Rickel. "The Liberated Dialogue, or 'Let the Kids Make Up Their Own Dialogues'." *Foreign Language Annals* 3(1970):237–40.

12 Grittner, Frank M. *Teaching Foreign Languages*. New York: Harper and Row, 1969.

13 Hester, Ralph M.,ed. *Teaching a Living Language*. New York: Harper and Row, 1970.

14 Jakobovits, Leon A. "Research Findings and Foreign Language Requirements in Colleges and Universities." *Foreign Language Annals* 2 (1969):436–56.

15 Kersten, Caesar S., and Vesperella E. Ott. "How Relevant Is Your Foreign Language Program?" *Modern Language Journal* 55(1970):9–13.

16 Lange, Dale L. "An Evaluation of Pre-Reading Instruction in Beginning French in Secondary Schools." *Dissertation Abstracts* 27(1966): 1710A(Minnesota).

17 Langellier, Alice, and Sylvia Narins Levy. *Chez les Français*. New York: Holt, Rinehart and Winston, 1969.

18 Morton, F. Rand. "An Experimental Approach to the Language Requirement (The College of Artesia Bilingual Program)." *Modern Language Journal* 55(1970):20–25.

19 Oliva, Peter F. *The Teaching of Foreign Language*. Englewood Cliffs, New Jersey: Prentice-Hall, 1969.

20 Ort, Barbara A., and Dwight R. Smith. "The Language Teacher Tours the Curriculum:New Horizons for Foreign Language Education." *Foreign Language Annals* 3(1969):28–74.

21 Osborne, Robert E., Solomon Tilles, and Carlos Pérez. *Voces y Vistas*. New York: Harper and Row, 1970.

22 de Petra, Yvette. *La Clef, Introduction au Français Elémentaire*. New York: Holt, Rinehart and Winston, 1970.

23 Politzer, Robert L. *Teaching French, An Introduction to Applied Linguistics*. Waltham, Massachusetts: Blaisdell, 1965.

24 Ray, Marilynn, Katia Brillié Lutz, and Consulting Staff. *A-LM, French, Level One*. Second Edition. New York: Harcourt, Brace and World, 1969.

25 Reinert, Harry. "Creative Lab Usage." *National Association of Language Laboratory Directors Journal* 4,i(1969):57–63.

26 Rivers, Wilga M. *The Psychologist and the Foreign-Language Teacher*. Chicago: Univ. of Chicago Press, 1964.

27 Rosenbaum, Peter S. "The Computer as a Learning Environment for Foreign Language Instruction." *Foreign Language Annals* 2(1969):457–65.

28 Ruplin, Ferdinand A., and John R. Russell. *Basic German, A Programmed Course*. New York: Meredith Corporation, 1969.

29 Schwartz, Leon. "The Other M's:Manipulation and Mastery." *French Review* 43(1969):81–92.

30 Shepherd, W.E. "An Experiment in Individualiz-

ing Advanced French." *Foreign Language Annals* 3(1970):394–99.

31 Smith, Philip D., Jr. *A Comparison of the Cognitive and Audiolingual Approaches to Foreign Language Instruction*. Philadelphia: The Center for Curriculum Development, 1970.

32 —— and Helmut A. Baranyi. *A Comparative Study of the Effectiveness of the Traditional and Audiolingual Approaches to Foreign Language Instruction Utilizing Laboratory Equipment*. Final Report, Project No. 7-0133:OEC-1-7-070133-0445. Washington, D.C.: U.S. Department of Health, Education and Welfare, Office of Education, 1968.

33 Steiner, Florence. "Performance Objectives in the Teaching of Foreign Language." *Foreign Language Annals* 3(1970):579–91.

34 Turner, Ronald C. "CARLOS:Computer Assisted Instruction in Spanish." *Hispania* 53(1970): 249–52.

35 Valdman, Albert. "Toward a Better Implementation of the A-L Approach." *Modern Language Journal* 55(1970):309–19.

36 Wheaton, Marjorie. "Brain Washing, Anyone?" *French Review* 43(1970):805–11.

37 Wolfe, David L. *Curso Básico de Español*. New York: Macmillan, 1970.

38 Wood, Fred H. "The McCluer Plan:An Innovative Non-Graded Foreign Language Program." *Modern Language Journal* 55(1970):184–87.

6

Curricula for individualized instruction

Introduction and overview

Gerald E. Logan

Live Oak High School
Morgan Hill, California

Specific curricula for individualized learning of foreign languages seem to be undergoing implementation at an almost explosive pace across the nation, as appears evident by the frequency of the topic in the programs of foreign language meetings during the current school year. The appearance of such curricula in print in any great proliferation, however, is yet to follow. And, of course, long-range evaluation of such programs with regard to attitudinal and cognitive objectives is almost totally absent from the literature in the field.

But the topic seems to dominate the scene and to have as much impact on current foreign language educational practice as did the audiolingual discussions and materials of the late 1950s and early 1960s. Therefore, an investigation of what work has been done in this area recently is certainly in order.

A "curriculum" for individualized learning might seem to many to be a contradiction in terms, since true individualization in the purest sense of the concept would mean a unique approach, content, and set of objectives for *each* student based on his particular aptitude, interests, and goals for learning the language. However, it turns out on examination of the few programs appearing in print and on interviewing additional teachers conducting individualized learning programs that what is meant by individualization is subject to broad and varied interpretation.

The major categories of individualization

The main types of individualization fall into at least seven categories. The most common method of learning on an individualized basis involves the learning rate. Students are allowed to pace themselves, taking as much or as little time as is necessary to master a particular skill or body of material. In some programs this can mean promotion from one level of language skill to another in more or less time than the normal year. In others, students must finish the assigned material by the end of a term, so that any variation of time must occur within fixed limits. Most of the programs to be described in the main portion

Seven categories of individualization

133

of this chapter fall into this category of varied learning rate or self-pacing.

A second type of individualization involves independent study. Here the role of the teacher is minimal. The student works on his own with printed and recorded materials, often unsupervised, and meets with a teacher when he needs help or evaluation.

A third and quite common means of individualization results from interest and ability grouping. Some schools accomplish such individualization by grouping students within a traditional class. Others offer a great many foreign language courses, including minicourses, from which students can choose. Individualization thus becomes a matter of which courses or sections a particular student chooses in order to make up his total program.

A fourth category concerns individualization through remedial and/or enrichment grouping. Students needing more time to master certain concepts form one group and receive extra drill. The main body of the class continues at an average rate. The students needing the least time form a group for the purpose of enrichment.

A fifth type of individualization results when students learn their language skills and practice them with materials and content of their own individual choice according to their specific interests. This type of individualization occurs mainly at more advanced levels of language learning.

Interdisciplinary courses are becoming increasingly popular and provide a sixth means for individualization. Advanced students in some schools may choose to study biology in German, art history in French, or geography in Spanish.

A final category results in those schools which combine several of the above techniques. Several of the school programs to be described allow students to work independently at their own rate using materials of their own choice earning as few or as many units of credit as an evaluation of their accomplishments seems to merit.

Materials

The materials used in these individualized learning programs also fall rather easily into seven categories. The most common material consists of a standard foreign language text. Very few teachers simply hand the student the text as it appears from the publisher if the student is working at his own pace. Instead, the teacher provides a set of written behavioral objectives toward

Categories of materials

which the student is to work. Also necessary is a set of steps or guidelines or directions for the student to follow in reaching these objectives. These directions provide the student with the proper sequence for doing such things as phonic drills, grammar exercises, recorded drills, reading, vocabulary work, listening comprehension, self-testing, etc. Some students on independent study with a standard text are provided with a teacher's manual for their guidance.

The other six categories include programmed materials, computerized material, original teacher-constructed materials, and special learning packets such as "Unipac" and LAPS (Learning Activity Packages). These packages contain a statement of the concept to be learned, a pretest, a sequence of learning activities, and a post-test. Each package typically focuses on only one particular concept or skill.

Scheduling

There is no general trend or pattern discernible as far as matching particular types of individualized learning with certain types of scheduling is concerned. Programs are operating with traditional scheduling, modular scheduling, flexible scheduling of various types, nonscheduling (where students work independently and structure their own time, which may vary from day to day), and "demand" scheduling. The latter type is a fairly recent innovation. Teachers fill out an order each day requesting that certain groups or classes or even individuals meet the next day for designated lengths of time. The requests are processed through a computer, which works out the next day's schedule based on the teachers' demands. Students then plan their day's program based on the schedule for that particular day. Such scheduling can become truly flexible, allowing for variations in time and grouping on a day to day basis.

Schedule patterns

Staff and room utilization

Individualized instruction programs take place in traditional classrooms, in "language islands" where materials and realia and decor are arranged to effect an isolated bit of the target language culture, and where the student sees and hears only the target language, and in language complexes. The latter usually consist of one large central room adjacent to laboratory facilities and smaller rooms and offices. Rooms with movable walls also serve the same purpose.

Specific programs and problems
in individualized learning

The programs with individualized learning at beginning levels described in the literature include the McCluer Plan in Spanish and French in the Ferguson-Florissant school system in St. Louis County, Missouri, using standard textbooks accompanied by detailed behavioral objectives and well spelled-out activities for reaching the objectives (Phelps, Barrett, et al., 62); a program at Nathan Hale High School in Seattle, Washington, where students are taught by teams in groups of varying size under very flexible scheduling (Arendt, 3); a program in French, Spanish, and Portuguese in Hughson, California, using an open laboratory concept and Learning Activity Packages with students in ungraded groups (Arendt, 3); an ungraded German program at Live Oak High School in Morgan Hill, California, involving first and second level students using original teacher-constructed materials (Logan, 50); an independent study program in Chinese in the Tucson, Arizona, public schools (Hooker, 43); a program in German at Mountain View High School in California using an ungraded "language island" concept (McLennan, 54); a program of independent study in French, German, and Spanish for selected eighth graders at Townsend Junior High School in Tucson, Arizona (Bockman, 7); a new program at Marshall-University High School in Minneapolis offering a great number of regular and minicourses in Chinese, French, German, Russian, and Spanish from which students can choose an individual combination (30); an independent study program in German and Chinese at Pacific Grove High School in California (Kohn, 45); a first-year programmed German course at the University of Rochester, which has a 5-year history (Clark, 18); a continuous progress program in first-year French and German at High School North Campus in Abbington, Pennsylvania (Gougher, 36); programmed learning in foreign languages as used in the Tacoma, Washington, public schools (Macias, 51); a programmed Spanish course in the Lindenwood College for Women in St. Charles, Missouri (Morton, 56); the computer-assisted program of individualized instruction in Russian at Stanford (Suppes & Jerman, 75); and a continuous progress program in French, German, and Spanish in the West Bend, Wisconsin, public schools. There are, of course, many other programs of which the profession is not yet aware.

A listing of individualized programs

136

The problem of individualizing content

The content of any of the curricula at the beginning levels allows for very little student choice. In fact, almost all the programs mentioned above consist of standard texts—or at least the textbook concept—which were developed with the standard class in mind. The research results available from educational psychology, which show that different students need different approaches, have not been utilized in developing any text or curriculum. Any program based on the fact that some students learn best visually, some aurally, some through analysis, some through imitation, etc., must rely on the teacher to adapt a standard set of materials to each student's particular learning pattern. It is hardly conceivable that any such ideal individualization of materials is taking place.

The need for multiapproach materials has been stated and restated, perhaps most notably in 1967 by Roger A. Pillet (63) of the University of Chicago. But in reality, largely because of commercial considerations, materials are constructed on the assumption that foreign language skills have a sort of objective, autonomous existence all their own. With sufficient application *Need for multiapproach* all students should be able to acquire these skills in the same *materials* manner. There exists also the assumption that the science of linguistics will come closer and closer to closing the gap that separates us from the one ideal method, and thus the ideal text. Also in 1967 a forecast made for the future of modern language teaching indicated that scientific analysis and new technology would result in "the most efficient way of learning" the foreign language (Cioffari, 16). This same article discussed the use of a master lecturer broadcast through means of closed-circuit television. Little was suggested for the necessity of tailoring this new linguistic knowledge and technology to individuals, as though there were one most efficient method that would apply to all.

This latter concept is the reality which shapes the curricula. The teacher is therefore not only "the sole agent in a position to *Influences on the curriculum* collect data on the responses of individual students to various instructional devices," (Pillet, 63) but also the only one, under present circumstances, either to produce the multiplicity of materials for individual needs, or else to supplement present texts with a variety of instructional strategies. A teacher does not have the time—nor usually the skill—to produce such materials. Therefore, the only dimension of individualization taking

137

place to any great degree at the beginning levels of foreign language learning involves the *rate* of learning, or self-pacing.

Contributions to individualizing through motivational materials tailored to a variety of interests are also lacking at the beginning levels. Cultural material consists of whatever is integrated into, or, more likely, tacked onto, the text. We get only hints that individual teachers may be capitalizing on students' interests by varying the content of the materials through which students acquire the linguistic skills. More likely, however, if they are doing anything at all, such individualization consists of allowing the students to do a supplementary report or two in an area of their own choice and interest.

Materials for student interest beginning levels

At the intermediate level of foreign language instruction we find much the same pattern, although a few schools offering individualized instruction do allow their students to spend part of their time, at this level, working with the language in areas of individual interest. Such programs consist of individualized reading and listening, pen and tape pals, special interest conversation groups, and, as evidenced by some college catalogs and high school curricula, independent study programs or individual contract systems (Dusel et al., 23; 30; Logan, 50).

Intermediate level

It is at the advanced levels of foreign language learning that most individualization involving content takes place. At this level the basic skills have been acquired by most students. An almost unlimited variety of reading and listening materials is available for this level. Individualized and independent study and research for majors in foreign languages have always been a part of college and university programs. But individualized work involving class-size groups of students meeting regularly under the supervision of a teacher is still quite limited. The vast majority of teachers, even at advanced levels, are still putting groups of students through the same paces in lockstep fashion. Examples of the increasing number of exceptions at the secondary level are the advanced French program at Coronado High School in Scottsdale, Arizona, where 17 students were given much latitude in individualized reading and writing and oral and lab work within a standard class period, free from teacher lecturing and domination (Shepherd, 70); the seminar classes at Nathan Hale High School in Seattle, based on a study contract which includes a reading list, study plans for each unit of work, dates for group meetings and films, and performance criteria (Arendt, 3); the completely individualized and ungraded program

Advanced level

in German at Live Oak High School in Morgan Hill, California, where students have a choice of 40 areas of study, including several of a vocational nature, and where the teacher and the student plan the approach and content and objectives in individual conferences throughout the year (Logan, 50); and the planned program at Marshall-University High School in Minneapolis, which lists more than 100 courses and special interest minicourses in Chinese, French, German, Russian, and Spanish (30).

Schools accepting the individualized learning concept find that they can offer a much richer curriculum in a given language than they could when they were operating under the standard class concept. In most school or college systems the number of courses offered is usually limited by the enrollment or expected enrollment in the courses contemplated. Thus, if the ratio of students to teachers is not 30 to 1, or 25 to 1, or 15 to 1, etc., the course is not given. But we now find small schools able to offer any number of "courses" on an individualized or independent basis. The number of such courses is limited only by the materials available in a given school, and by the availability of written or oral instructions for mastery of the course skills or content. Some means of evaluating the student's mastery of the material is also usually necessary. As a result small high schools can offer advanced placement programs, vocational courses, travel courses, terminal courses, or courses for college-bound students. Each student enrolling in such courses can be further accommodated by varying the specific content to meet his particular needs. For instance, a college-bound student might choose to use the same text series he will be using in the college of his choice.

A richer curriculum

The problem of oral work

The biggest problem in the individualization of instruction concerns oral work at all levels. Drilling presents little trouble, since recordings in a variety of forms are available and can be used on an individual basis. Listening comprehension is also only a minor problem. Commercial tapes and comprehension tests are readily available. Many teachers prepare such materials themselves. Whether homemade or commercially constructed, they are always conveniently available for individual use.

But live conversation or communication can be difficult in an individual or independent learning program. Mountain View

Techniques for producing communication

High School solves this problem to a certain extent by volunteer native speakers who come into the language center regularly for conducting small conversation groups or to converse with individuals (McLennan, 54). Live Oak High School requires every student to spend 50 minutes per week in conversation groups of 4 or 5 students. These groups are conducted by a teacher whose mother tongue is the target language, and by a paraprofessional, born and raised with the target language, and hired by the school district on the basis of competitive examinations. Both are part of a 3-man team in the German language center (Logan, 50). Both schools also use teaching assistants, who are advanced language students, to give extra oral practice, often on a one-to-one basis, for beginning level students. In the Coronado Advanced French Program the teacher conducts oral practice and conversation with small groups or individuals (Shepherd, 70). Also typical in advanced classes are individual oral reports. All programs encourage oral discussion among students using the target language. A theoretical model for small group conversational practice which takes students through a controlled stage, a partially-controlled stage, and a noncontrolled stage approaching free and natural communication has been proposed by Ciotti (17).

The problem of packaging the curriculum

When it comes to "packaging" the curriculum the most common method, at least at the basic levels, is to provide a set of steps or instructions to the student which indicate the activities he is to perform. These directions most commonly refer to a standard text. Directions usually include general or specific behavioral objectives for the phase or unit under consideration, the sequence and details of each oral, written, or reading exercise to be followed in reaching these objectives, and the form of evaluation which the student can expect. *The McCluer Plan* (Phelps, Barrett, et al., 62), the Live Oak program (Logan, 50), the Pacific Grove program (Kohn, 45), the Nathan Hale program (Arendt, 3), and the Hughson program (Arendt, 3) are all examples of this approach.

Use of behavioral objectives

Programs where the text itself is actually arranged as a step-by-step progression in all the skills—in other words, programmed materials—do not seem to be widely known or distributed, although there are summaries of the materials available. An ERIC report lists approximately 50 programmed courses in the

Programming

major languages and a few of the minor ones. The report also contains a bibliography and a list of publishers (Fiks, 27).

Programming would appear to be the best solution to so much duplication of effort by so many overworked teachers, as long as individualization continues to remain mainly a matter of self-pacing through a fairly standard sequence of materials. But publishers are not likely to enter the field on a large scale until the individualized approach is more common. The best that can probably be expected from publishers in the near future are supplementary sets of instructions or steps designed to allow individualization of their standard text series. There is literature available on programmed materials and curricula of a local nature in German (Clark, 18), Russian (Makarova, 53), and Spanish (Morton, 56). Theoretical knowledge for teachers interested in programming materials themselves is available (Barrutia, 4; Bung, 11,12).

Computerized programs are also on the horizon (Allen, 1; Feldhusen & Szabo, 26; Freudenstein, 33; Suppes & Jerman, 75; Rosenbaum, 69). But these are not presently of use to teachers in general. Machines which incorporate all the skills and every technological aid in immediate evaluation and diagnosis and redirection imaginable (including evaluation of the written word) are under experimentation. But even with such technical assistance, it should be emphasized that the individualization possible is largely a matter of rate. Capitalization on a student's particular set of interests, motivation, learning abilities and disabilities, etc., will apparently remain for a long time a task for the teacher guiding the use of or administering whatever programs he finds available. Publishers can hardly be expected to produce the myriad of programs which would be needed to meet all the individual needs. The only possibilities the author sees of an outside source of such individualization are of three main types:

Computerized programs

Three ways in which publishers may help

1 A set of materials could be published, recorded, or computerized which would help the learner approach linguistic mastery through several possible paths. These tracks would be carefully predetermined as meeting the needs of the more common subgroups of students, such groups being based on either the best learning psychology for the student, his interests, or both.

2 A set of materials could be composed of a number of small

141

compatible modules to be put together in different combinations. Each student's particular course or sequence then would be determined by the teacher, a diagnostic test, or computer analysis.

3 "Unipacs" could be used for individualizing learning, should the selection and variety of such units ever become great enough for categorization and subsequent selection and arrangement like the modules mentioned above.

Random learning might be an individualized answer for a highly motivated or inquisitive student. The ultimate randomization and individualization of the curriculum, however, leaves the realm of formal school learning as it presently exists. Such a plan might consist of turning the student loose on his own in a country where the target language is used.

The problem of a sufficient variety of materials

If an individualized curriculum is to provide for continuing motivation and is to meet the particular needs of each student, it must contain something more than a standardized core or text. Especially attractive to students, according to teachers who have a great selection of materials from which students may choose, are authentic books, magazines, records, etc., from the countries in which the target language is spoken. Locating such materials is a major problem. One especially useful listing of source materials for foreign language teachers has been compiled by Chamberlain (15). Other possible sources of materials are consulates, state or national education departments, ministers of culture, educational publishing firms abroad, individual teachers or school systems, business firms in the U.S. with branches abroad or foreign businesses with products sold here, advertising agencies, newspapers, foreign and domestic travel bureaus, foreign chambers of commerce, and foreign railway, airline, or shipping companies. These agencies, even if they can't always provide materials themselves, can often serve as invaluable contacts or mediators for contacts in obtaining materials of great interest to specific students.

Sources of materials

Sets of school texts used in various countries, the latest popular records, job information, travel information, posters, school magazines and newspapers, children's books, realia, business and government publications, teen-age and college age magazines, catalogs, hobby books, flags, etc., have become part of the learning materials and environment of schools which take the

Foreign materials

time to write letters to such agencies, or to persons whom the agencies are able to interest in establishing contact with American students or teachers (Logan, 50).

For those with budgets which allow for such things, the usual foreign sources of magazines, newspapers, films, video tapes of TV programs, records, books, and other educational materials should not be overlooked. Money can be saved by contacting other teachers in one's language area to find out what students will really use or read if they have a choice. Teachers seem to be relatively unable to predict what students will really like, choosing often, it seems, what they think students ought to like. Two recent articles concerning this problem are available. One, by Lange (47), concerns the use of newspapers and magazines. In addition to explaining teaching techniques, the article contains a useful bibliography. The other article, by Krogmeier & Shryer (46), contains a checklist and some results concerning what teen-agers want to know about Germany. Much of the information is applicable to other languages.

The problem of scheduling

Scheduling of classes, especially at the secondary school level, is undergoing great change and experimentation, and often has a great bearing on providing for an individualized learning curriculum. The traditional 50-minute class, meeting 5 days per week in the secondary school, or perhaps fewer days per week in the colleges, is still common. Innovative programs such as the Coronado French program (Shepherd, 70), most of the Live Oak program (Logan, 50), the McCluer program (Phelps, Barrett, et al., 62), and many others take place under traditional scheduling. However, one shouldn't let the term "traditional scheduling" be misleading. Students and teachers are often not assigned to these traditional blocks of time in a traditional way. Some schools assign all teachers and all students at one level to the same block of time so that the advantages of team teaching can be used and the flexibility of having several rooms available can be exploited (Phelps, Barrett, et al., 62). Others assign a team of teachers to each period of the day in which the language is being offered. The students are also assigned in equal numbers to each of these periods without regard to level of language proficiency (Logan, 50). This ungraded type of classroom allows for the advantages of team teaching. In addition it reduces the emphasis on level and implements the concept of continuous

Types of schedules

143

progression from level to level at any time that achievement warrants. A further advantage of having ungraded classes is the assistance, tutoring, and leadership which can be provided by advanced students for students at more basic skill levels.

Flexible scheduling and "demand" scheduling present particular problems and advantages. The Mountain View individualized program actually resulted from the school's instituting such scheduling. Because of the irregularity of class meetings and inevitable schedule conflicts on some days causing students to miss an occasional class, self-pacing individualization with emphasis on achievement rather than attendance was the only solution, according to the teachers in the department (McLennan, 54). A particularly useful article concerning flexible scheduling and the foreign language curriculum has been written by Robert Politzer (64) of Stanford. He explains the use of flexible scheduling in making small group and individual instruction easier to initiate. If flexible scheduling is used not for its own sake in order to appear innovative, but "is used to solve very specific instructional problems, to fill very definite and well perceived needs, then it can, indeed, become an important instrument in the improvement of instruction."

Flexible and "demand" scheduling

Still other schools, on both the college and high school level, use no scheduling at all. In these cases students are on independent study, individual contracts, or even in a type of correspondence course. They are assigned to a particular teacher, but meet this teacher only when they want help or are ready for some form of evaluation. Live Oak High School has such a program. It is called there the Individual Contract System. Its initiation has allowed many students to continue their foreign language learning who would ordinarily have had to drop out because of a full schedule of required subjects (Logan, 50). The Marshall-University High School minicourses provide much the same opportunity for students with crowded schedules (30).

The problem of articulation

Articulation between various aspects of a local curriculum and articulation with "outside" curricula deserve a few words. Actually there should be little problem in articulating within various aspects of the curriculum in a particular school or system if behavioral objectives (Bockman, 8; Steiner, 72) for each phase of progress have been worked out, or if a common text series or set of materials is used. Few, if any, schools or school sys-

144

tems give a teacher complete independence to go his own way. However, articulation problems will arise if individualization becomes more than a matter of the learning rate at the basic levels before the basic skills, structures, and vocabulary have been learned. In cases where a student acquires the skills in a different sequence and by using a different content and vocabulary than other students, the problems in articulation are obvious. Since most such innovation still lies in the future, teachers and coordinators must be aware of the problems that *could* be encountered and plan carefully to avoid them. One must be certain that sequences designed to meet the needs of a particular student can be carried through until all the basic skills have been acquired; or, at least, that there are transfer points at which the student can fit easily into another stream. The profession has observed the rather devastating effect that a lack of articulation can have on a student when he comes into foreign language classes from other school systems which use different texts and methods. In individualizing instruction, a lack of articulation can also become an internal problem.

Internal problems of articulation with individualized programs

Several schools are facing this problem now. Live Oak High School is offering 17 courses in German (Logan, 50). Marshall-University High School in Minneapolis will offer many mini-courses in French, German, Russian, and Spanish. Most of these courses will be available for advanced students only (30). The programs parallel those of colleges and universities where a variety of courses are offered after the basic common sequence has been learned. Several of these courses, however, are offered at an early stage to meet the needs of certain categories of students in order to keep them in the language by making it relevant to them.

Two examples

A sampling of such courses in the two programs reveals a commercial course in German available to students after three semesters of study (Logan, 50), a journalism course in French in which students develop writing skill by composing articles for a school French newspaper (30), a random choice course available after one year of language study for those students wanting to strengthen their first level foundation while shopping around to determine on which path they wish to continue in the language (Logan, 50), technical readings in Russian (30), a Spanish course called "Writing for Fun" with a prerequisite of two semesters of Spanish (30). A large number of the courses at all levels in the Marshall-University High School plan are minicourses, requiring students to attend anywhere from a total of one hour to four hours per week per course. Most are scheduled as regular class sections, but some of the courses can be independent study. In both the Marshall-University and the Live Oak programs students may enroll in more than one course during the same semester, and can earn varying totals of credits or partial credits in the foreign language. Selection and preparation of materials for these courses poses a real problem in articulation, since the students enrolling in them have not as yet acquired all the basic skills, and they often have a quite limited vocabulary.

Articulation with curricula in schools outside the local systems actually becomes easier with an individualized curriculum. If the local program has a clear idea of what it expects of students in terms of behavioral objectives (Bockman, 8; Steiner, 72), placement testing can take care of the problems which might arise. Each student entering the program can be placed exactly where he belongs. The frustrations encountered by placing a student at the beginning of level one or level two, when he is well beyond the one and not really ready for the other, are largely eliminated.

External articulation

The colleges seem to make much more use of placement testing than do the secondary schools. The College Board Achievement Tests, Advanced Placement Tests, and the Modern Language Association's proficiency tests are often used, as evidenced by a survey of college catalogs. But the literature in the field — or the lack of it — indicates that these same colleges have few lower division individualized programs with which to take full advantage of such placement testing.

High school–college articulation

Much more frustrating for the teacher, especially the secondary school teacher preparing an advanced class for college, is the articulation problem with the colleges and universities. From an advanced class of 20 students, it is typical in a great many localities across the country that very few go on to the same university or college. Each of these colleges is likely to have quite different expectations, texts, approaches, and goals for its own program. Setting up a single curriculum for a class which will give each individual student the best preparation for "his" college is a futile experience. Many conferences and panels have been held on just this problem. The usual resulting prescription is pressure for conformity of instruction and content at all levels. Individualization of instruction *can* solve this problem in one stroke, even if such individualization occurs only at the

146

secondary level. Students working independently can become familiar with the methods and materials used at the college they will be entering.

Articulation trends in the traditional sense are the antithesis of individualization, and the ultimate result of such trends would be a national lockstep operation in each language. The motivation for such articulation, the concern for the student who has to transfer horizontally or vertically in our school systems, may be laudable. But a more obvious and more acceptable answer to the problem of articulation in a multivalued and heterogeneous society would seem to be individualization rather than conformity.

The problem of classroom space and arrangement

The availability and arrangement of classroom, laboratory, and office space for an individualized curriculum would, as is to be expected, present one picture if the ideal were available, but presents something else when we observe the actual conditions under which most programs are operating. Very few teachers have or will have much more than a standard classroom available to them at the elementary or secondary levels. Colleges or universities are usually better equipped for the type of flexibility required in individualizing instruction.

A study of some of the typical programs now in operation (Logan, 50; McLennan, 54; Phelps, Barrett, et al., 62) reveals that the common basic facilities usually include tables and chairs for individual and small group work, access to a laboratory or laboratory equipment, and storage space for a wide variety of materials. The form these facilities take will vary according to the type and extent of the program, and according to the school and the ease with which teachers in such schools can get their requests honored. The most common housing is a standard classroom with the furniture rearranged. Some are fortunate enough to have an adjoining language laboratory. Others have recording and listening equipment in several individual booths or on tables or counters in the regular classroom. Where two or more teachers have been able to pool their efforts as a team (Logan, 50; Phelps, Barrett, et al., 62), especially if they have adjoining rooms or a large dividable room, the possibilities become greater for approaching the ideal.

According to interviews with several teachers using individualized instruction, the ideal setting would consist of one large

Facilities needed for individualization

147

room for the main study and presentation activities, a second room for quiet individual study, with individual study carrels, one or more smaller rooms for seminars or small conversation groups, an office or two with enough room for individual conferences and storage of records, tests, and files, and individualized laboratory facilities, either in booths in the larger room, or in a separate room easily accessible to the students from the main study center.

The laboratory facilities should contain individualized equipment such as tape recorders, Audio-Flashcard machines or Language Masters, cassette players, listening posts, record players, slide or film viewing posts, and, in more elaborate facilities, computer terminals. The materials, both printed and recorded, that are to be used in the laboratory should be readily accessible, since many students will need to use different materials and equipment at the same time and on a moment's demand.

Language laboratory facilit

The main language center should contain tables and chairs, have a reading corner with magazines and newspapers published in the target language, dictionaries, and other reference materials readily available to the student. Walls and shelves should be full of posters and realia to create a cultural island. There should be a manned testing center in one of the rooms or corners with a complete supply of tests for all phases, levels, and skills so that students can be evaluated when they are ready.

The problem of using the staff most effectively

Utilization and deployment of staff in an individualized curriculum has been mentioned before, but it would seem appropriate at this point to discuss the problem more extensively. The most efficient arrangement in larger schools is for the staff in particular languages to combine its talents and facilities to operate as a team (Arendt, 3; Logan, 50; Phelps, Barrett, et al., 62). This arrangement allows for development and manning of the types of facilities just described. It also allows for specialization. Motivational, recreational, and such other large group activities as may be part of the program can be presented by the more extroverted member of a team. Other roles which might best be filled by a specialist (either one person devoting his time entirely to this activity or, in smaller teams, assuming two or three "specialist" roles) are those of a laboratory director, a conversation group leader, a testing director, a producer of materials, a diagnostician and tutor for individuals with special learning problems, a

Utilization of staff with described facilities

148

phonetician, a librarian, a locator and purchaser of materials, an overall coordinator, a director of extracurricular activities, a counselor in charge of individualizing student contracts, a counselor in charge of appropriate placing of incoming students, someone having knowledge of study abroad possibilities, a director of student or paraprofessional aides, a director of remedial, gifted, or special interest groups, a test evaluator or person in charge of grading, credits, etc.

The team need not be limited to the faculty alone. It can be augmented by students with special abilities and talents (Logan, 50; McLennan, 54; Otto, 60; Phelps, Barrett, et al., 62), experts from the community (McLennan, 54), paraprofessionals (Logan, 50), or specialists from other departments outside the particular language under consideration (30; McLennan, 54).

A team of professionals, semi- and paraprofessionals

However, the most likely situation for a great number of teachers attempting individualization will be a "team" consisting of one teacher. In this case what flexibility can be provided? Under the most restricted circumstances individualization may have to be carried out with the teacher in one room, 25 to 40 desks or the equivalent in chairs and tables, and a tape recorder or two. Students work on their own with the teacher moving about, helping individuals, giving tests to those ready for them, addressing the whole group at certain times for motivational, cultural, or recreational activities, working with a small group on a special task or problem, while the others continue working individually, etc. (Shepherd, 70).

The single teacher as individualizer

If non-grading can be achieved the single teacher's flexibility can be greatly increased by prevailing upon advanced students to help beginners and to do other tasks. If the school allows students to serve as student teachers or teacher cadets or teacher aides for credit or for pay, a great new source is opened up (Logan, 50; McLennan, 54; Otto, 60). Colleges have always had this source to varying degrees, and it is now becoming increasingly more common in secondary schools. Even elementary schools use students from upper grades or from neighboring high schools in such capacities. The employment of paraprofessionals or community people can extend the effectiveness of the single teacher even more.

Teachers shouldn't let the lack of facilities or staff deter them from the benefits of individualization. If one thinks back to the old one-room little red schoolhouse with one teacher handling eight grades, one can get somewhat of a picture as to what an

149

ungraded individualized foreign language program might be like. Many educators are looking back to this era—at least educationally, if not financially—with more than just nostalgia. The individualization and self-reliance that was once developed in such schools by a good teacher is getting a second look (Bloom, 6; Brown, 10).

Summary

Individualized curricula appear to be mushrooming as an answer to the lack of relevance for the individual in the standardized curriculum, and to the boredom or frustration felt in the usual classroom by the faster or slower students respectively. The teacher operating at any level of education and bound by tradition, skepticism, or hesitancy because he may not have the ideal setup, but who realizes all is not well in the traditional approach, should take courage in the knowledge that there are teachers successfully operating individualized programs under the most limited of circumstances.

Programs are being offered which consist of only one beginning or one advanced class in a standard classroom with a single teacher. Programs are also being offered which include hundreds of students and teams of teachers in large language centers or language "islands." The sources available vary from standard texts to unlimited selections of printed and audiovisual materials. Equipment for implementing such curricula varies from a tape recorder or two to standard language labs to very elaborate individualized computerized learning systems. The individualized programs are operating in traditional 50-minute class periods, in flexible and modular scheduling arrangements, under conditions of demand scheduling, and under independent study or contract systems with no scheduling in the usual sense. Basic curriculum content varies from standard textbook fare to original materials especially programmed for individualization, and from uniform fare for all students, but self-paced, to programs (usually at the more advanced levels) offering what is essentially a separate curriculum for each student.

Looking ahead

For the immediate future it appears quite safe to predict a very dramatic increase in the individualized type of learning situation. This increase will demand important changes in the profession.

Teacher training in foreign languages will certainly have to be restructured. The teacher trained to dominate the class constantly, the master drill sergeant, operating in terms of group activities and results, will have to give way to the diagnostician, the educational guide who can determine which students operate best alone, which need more concrete illustrations and explanations than provided basically, which need more approval and reinforcement, which need more motivation, which need many repetitions of drills and explanations. This new teacher must know how to accomplish this diagnosis and to formulate curricula to meet these needs.

The traditional idea of the textbook will also need to undergo change. The textbook as we know it is built on the assumption that there is one best content and approach for all students. A textbook can't be written for each individual student, but small packets or modules of materials, arrangeable in many ways depending on the needs and interests of individual students, are possible. The stress on relevance will require that much of the content be based on mass-media types of communication rather than on textbooks. Such an emphasis will be necessary because of the ever-accelerating rate of change and the need to remain in constant touch with current events in order to stay up-to-date and relevant. The eternal values in the classical literature of the past which we used to feel we could rely on for relevance no longer have the power with students they once seemed to have. In fact, in this day and age the "eternal values" no longer seem to guarantee remaining very eternal. All values appear to be in question and doubt. The students want to be in touch with the "now" of the countries whose languages they are learning. Newspapers and periodicals, films, video tapes of current TV programs, current records and tapes, direct foreign audio and visual hookups, periodicals especially for students—done in a modern style like the "Scholastic" publications (15) now available at the secondary level in certain languages—may take the place of the "basic text."

Teachers conducting individualized learning programs will need to contact each other and evaluate what is happening. Newsletters dealing with individualized instruction and designed to serve as clearinghouses and exchanges of ideas on the subject will begin to appear across the country. At least one is already in the late planning stages. Collecting manuscripts and answering inquiries are Bockman (7,8) and Gougher. Gougher (36), of West Chester State College in Pennsylvania, is a pioneer in the individualized learning field, having conceived the Optimum Learning Rate Program for Moravian Seminary for Girls in 1964. He has since been working successfully with several schools and colleges on the project in Pennsylvania and Delaware.

Finally, it is safe to predict that achievement, rather than time or hours spent in a curriculum, will become the standard criterion for determining the level of education reached. This will require a complete reevaluation of the present practices of grading and of awarding credits or units. If we require a minimum level of performance before allowing a student to pass from one phase of the curriculum to the next—that is, if learning for mastery is to be our strategy or goal—grading in the traditional manner hardly makes sense. If we allow varying amounts of time to reach mastery, the idea of hours spent in class as the basis for awarding credits or units toward graduation will also need to undergo change.

Evaluation of achievement

The foreign language field is exciting and challenging. It is obvious that future articles written on individualized curricula will be based on a sifting of a *surplus* of research and reports in the field rather than on a frantic search for the few available reports in existence at present.

References, Curricula for individualized instruction

1 Allen, John E.,III. "Computational Contributions to Language Teaching," 12–13 in Maurice Silver,ed., *Proceedings:Thirty-First Annual Foreign Language Conference at New York University*. New York: New York Univ. School of Education, Department of Foreign Languages and International Relations Education, 1965.

2 Anon. "Better Teaching through Criterion-Referenced Testing." *Pi Reports* 2(1968):n.p.

3 Arendt, Jermaine D. "New Scheduling Patterns and the Foreign Language Teacher." [To be published in *Foreign Language Annals* 4(1970):October issue.]

4 Barrutia, Richard. "Intrinsic Programming of Foreign Languages," 237–51 in Joseph S. Roucek,ed., *The Study of Foreign Languages*. New York: Philosophical Library, 1968.

5 Benardo, Leo U. "Individual Differences in Foreign Language Learning in the Junior High School," 12–14 in Marvin Wasserman,ed., *Proceedings:Thirty-Second Annual Foreign Language Conference at New York University*. New York: New York Univ. School of Education, Department of Foreign Languages and International Relations Education, 1966.

6 Bloom, Benjamin S. "Learning for Mastery."

UCLA Evaluation Comment 1,ii(1968):1–12.

7 Bockman, John F. *Evaluation of a Project: Independent Foreign Language Study by Selected Eighth Graders at Townsend Junior High School Using Programmed Materials.* Tucson: Tucson Public Schools, 1969.

8 ——— "The Use of Behavioral Objectives in Foreign Language Teaching." *Forum* 16,ii(1969): 3–10.

9 Boggs, Roy A. "The Pennsylvania State University Foreign Language Survey:A Summary for Teachers of German." *Unterrichtspraxis* 2,ii(1969):140–43.

10 Brown, Frank B. *The Appropriate Placement School:A Sophisticated Nongraded Curriculum.* New York: Parker Publishing Company, 1965.

11 Bung, Klaus. *Programmed Learning and the Language Laboratory.* London: Longmoc, 1967.

12 ——— "Towards Truly Programmed Language Laboratory Courses." *Audio-Visual Language Journal* 7(1969):5–17.

13 Carroll, John B. "Individual Differences in Foreign Language Learning," 3–11 in Marvin Wasserman,ed., *Proceedings:Thirty-Second Annual Foreign Language Conference at New York University.* New York: New York Univ. School of Education, Department of Foreign Languages and International Relations Education, 1966.

14 Cavanagh, Peter, and Clive Jones,comps. *Yearbook of Educational and Instructional Technology 1969/70 Incorporating Programs in Print.* Englewood Cliffs, New Jersey: Educational Technology Publishers, 1969.

15 Chamberlain, Jane S.,comp. *Source Materials for Teachers of Foreign Languages.* Washington, D.C.: National Education Association/Department of Foreign Languages, 1968.

16 Cioffari, Vincenzo. "Developments in Modern Language Teaching—A Summary and Forecast." *The DFL Bulletin* 7,i(1967):11–13.

17 Ciotti, Marianne C. "A Conceptual Framework for Small-Group Instruction in High School." *Foreign Language Annals* 3(1969):75–89.

18 Clark, William H. "First-Year College German Through Programmed Instruction." *Unterrichtspraxis* 2,ii(1969):58–60.

19 ——— *Using Programmed Foreign Language Courses in Secondary School with Specially Trained Teachers. Final Report.* Rochester, New York: Univ. of Rochester, 1968.

20 Dodge, James W. "Machine-aided Language Learning," 311–41 in Emma M. Birkmaier,ed., *Britannica Review of Foreign Language Education, Volume I.* Chicago: Encyclopaedia Britannica, 1968[1969].

21 Dusel, John P. *Implications Regarding Possible Elimination of Foreign Language Requirements in Colleges and Universities.* Sacramento: California State Department of Education, 1969.

22 ——— *State Surveys and Language Dropout.* Sacramento: California State Department of Education, 1969.

23 ——— et al. *Foreign Language Dropouts:Problems and Solutions.* Sacramento: California State Department of Education, 1970.

24 Etten, John F. "Flexible Programming in Student Teacher Preparation." *Peabody Journal of Education* 46(1969):215–17.

25 Fearing, Percy. "Nongraded Foreign Language Classes." *Foreign Language Annals* 2(1969): 343–47.

26 Feldhusen, John F., and Michael Szabo. "A Review of Developments in Computer Assisted Instruction." *Educational Technology* 9,iv(1969): 32–39.

27 Fiks, Alfred I. *Foreign Language Programmed Materials.* MLA/ERIC Focus Report 7. New York: MLA/ERIC, 1969.

28 Fleury, Dale F. "Independent Study:Foreign Language Seminars." *National Association of Secondary School Principals Bulletin* 53,338(1969): 90–99.

29 *Foreign Language:A Guide to Curriculum Development.* Dover, Delaware: State Department of Public Instruction, 1968.

30 *Foreign Language Newsletter* 8,v(1970):2–28. [Minneapolis: Minneapolis Public Schools, Department of Foreign Languages.] [Mimeo.]

31 *Foreign Language Problems Study Committee: Report.* Modern and Classical Language Association of Southern California, 1970. [Mimeo.]

32 Forrester, Jean. *Teaching Without Lecturing.* London: Oxford Univ. Press, 1968.

33 Freudenstein, Reinhold. "Informationen aus dem Computer. Ein neues Zentrum für den Fremdsprachenunterricht." *Die neueren Sprachen* 18(1969):187–88.

34 Garvey, Catherine J.,et al. *A Report of the Developmental Testing of a Self-Instructional French Program.* Washington, D.C.: Center for Applied Linguistics, 1967.

35 Glatthorn, Allan A., and Pauline L. Edwards,et al. *An Interim Report on a Continuous Progress Program in French I and Spanish I.* Abbington, Pennsylvania: High School North Campus, 1967.

36 Gougher, Ronald. "Learning of German at Optimum Rates." *Unterrichtspraxis* 3,i(1970): 142–43.

37 Grittner, Frank M. "A Critical Re-Examination of Methods and Materials." *Modern Language Journal* 53(1969):467–77.

38 ——— ed. "What's New in Wisconsin:Innovative Foreign Language Programs." *Voice of the Wisconsin Foreign Language Teacher* 7,i(1967):33–42.

39 Grobman, Hulda. *Evaluation Activities of Curriculum Projects:A Starting Point.* Chicago: Rand McNally, 1969. [AERA Curriculum Evaluation Monograph 2.]

40 Hernick, Michael, and Dora Kennedy. "Multi-Level Grouping of Students in the Modern Foreign Language Program." *Foreign Language Annals* 2(1968):200–04.

41 Hibbard, Allen. *Modular Scheduling and Modern Foreign Languages.* Presented at the Spring Conference of North Dakota Foreign Language Association. [ERIC Document Reproduction Service: ED 030 353.]

42 Hoelzel, Alfred. "Foreign Language Objec-

tives:Myths and Realities." *Bay State Foreign Language Bulletin* 13,ii(1968):2–6.

43 Hooker, David M. "Chinese Language Instruction in Tucson Public Schools:Independent Study." *Arizona Foreign Language Teachers Forum* Jan(1968):n.p.

44 Johansen, Patricia A. "The Development and Field Testing of a Self-Instructional French Program." *Linguistic Reporter* 11,vi(1969):13–27.

45 Kohn, Arnold. *Individualized Study Program.* Pacific Grove, California: Pacific Grove High School, 1969.

46 Krogmeier, Shirley, and Margaret Shryer. "What Do Teen-Agers Want to Know About a Foreign Culture?" *Unterrichtspraxis* 2,ii(1969):185–87.

47 Lange, Dale L. "The Use of Newspapers and Magazines in the Classroom." *Unterrichtspraxis* 2,ii(1969):148–53.

48 Langer, Phillip. "Minicourse:Theory and Strategy." *Educational Technology* 9,ix(1969):54–59.

49 Lipton, Gladys C. "Changes in Objectives and Curriculum," 17–18 in Maurice Silver,ed., *Proceedings:Thirty-First Annual Foreign Language Conference at New York University.* New York: New York Univ. School of Education, Department of Foreign Languages and International Relations Education, 1965.

50 Logan, Gerald E. *German Curriculum.* Morgan Hill, California: Morgan Hill Unified School District, 1969.

51 Macias, Cenobio. "Programmed Learning as Used in the Tacoma Public Schools," 160–62 in Jerrold L. Mordaunt,ed., *Proceedings:Pacific Northwest Conference of Foreign Languages, Twentieth Annual Meeting, April 11–12, 1969.* Victoria, B.C.: Univ. of Victoria, 1969.

52 Mackey, William F. "Trends and Research in Methods and Materials," 69–83 in H.H. Stern,ed., *Languages and the Young School Child.* London:Oxford Univ. Press, 1969.

53 Makarova, G.T. "Nekotorye problemy programmirovannogo obučenija russkomu jazyku inostrancev." *Russkij Jazyk za Rubežom* 1(1969):62–67.

54 McLennan, Robert. *Handbook for German Students.* Mountain View, California: Mountain View High School District, 1969.

55 Moore, J. William. "Instructional Design:After Behavioral Objectives What?" *Educational Technology* 9,ix(1969):45–48.

56 Morton, F. Rand. *Terminal Revision of the ALLP-II Programmed Spanish Language Course.* St. Charles, Missouri: Lindenwood College for Women, 1967.

57 Naber, Richard H. "Dial Access Information Retrieval Systems, Circa 1967." *Illinois Journal of Education* 59,iii(1968):51–54.

58 Neagley, Ross L., and N. Dean Evans. *Handbook for Effective Curriculum Development.* Englewood Cliffs, New Jersey: Prentice-Hall, 1967.

59 Ort, Barbara A., and Dwight R. Smith. "The Language Teacher Tours the Curriculum:New Horizons for Foreign Language Education." *Foreign Language Annals* 3(1969):28–74.

60 Otto, Frank. "Individualizing Instruction Through Team Teaching." *Hispania* 51(1969):473–75.

61 Perren, G.E. "Testing Spoken Language:Some Unsolved Problems," 107–16 in Alan Davies,ed., *Language Testing Symposium.* London: Oxford Univ. Press, 1968.

62 Phelps, Florence, and Martin Barrett,et al. *The McCluer Plan.* St. Louis County, Missouri: Ferguson-Florissant R-2 School District, 1968.

63 Pillet, Roger A. "Individualizing Instruction: Implication for FLES." *The DFL Bulletin* 5,ii(1967):3–4.

64 Politzer, Robert L. "Flexible Scheduling and the Foreign Language Curriculum." *The DFL Bulletin* 7,i(1967):6–8.

65 Popham, W. James,et al. *Instructional Objectives.* Chicago: Rand McNally, 1969. [AERA Curriculum Evaluation Monograph 3.]

66 Rallo, John A. "A Cooperative French Program:A New Approach." *Foreign Language Annals* 2(1968):474–76.

67 Reinert, Harry. "Creative Lab Usage." *National Association of Language Laboratory Directors Journal* 4,i(1969):57–63.

68 *Report of the First Annual Conference:Flexible Scheduling and Foreign Language Teaching.* Bridgeport, Connecticut: Proceedings of the Annual Conference of the Department of Foreign Languages, Univ. of Bridgeport, 1968. [ERIC Document Reproduction Service: ED 029 528.]

69 Rosenbaum, Peter S. "The Computer as a Learning Environment for Foreign Language Instruction." *Foreign Language Annals* 2(1969):457–65.

70 Shepherd, W. Everitt. "An Experiment in Individualized Advanced French." *Foreign Language Annals* 3(1969):394–99.

71 Spokoini, Hilier. "New Directions in the Teaching of Common Western Languages:Programmed Instruction," 22–27 in James Stais,ed., *Proceedings:Thirty-Third Annual Foreign Language Conference at New York University.* New York: New York Univ. School of Education, Department of Foreign Languages and International Relations Education, 1967.

72 Steiner, Florence. "Performance Objectives in the Teaching of Foreign Languages." *Foreign Language Annals* 3(1970):579–91.

73 ——"Teacher-made Tests:Vital in the Foreign Language Classroom," 75–78 in Pat Castle and Charles Jay,eds., *Toward Excellence in Foreign Language Education.* Springfield, Illinois: Office of the Superintendent of Public Instruction, State of Illinois, 1968.

74 Stevens, Thomas C., and Raul Diaz-Carnot. *Adaptation of the ALLP-II Spanish Self-Instructional Program (F. Rand Morton, Univ. of Michigan) to Class Sessions. Final Report.* Conton, Missouri: Culver-Stockton College, 1968.

75 Suppes, Patrick, and Max Jerman. "Computer Assisted Instruction at Stanford." *Educational Technology* 9,i(1969):22–24.

76 Terwilliger, Ronald I. "Multi-Grade Proficiency Grouping for Foreign Language Instruction."

The Modern Language Journal 54(1969):331–33.

77 Turner, Ronald C. *CARLOS:Computer-Assisted Instruction in Spanish at Dartmouth College.* Hanover, New Hampshire: Dartmouth College, 1968. [ERIC Document Reproduction Service: ED 025 972.]

78 Unwin, Derick, and John Leedham,eds. *Aspects of Educational Technology.* London: Methuen, 1967.

79 Wiencke, D. *Independent Study:Pathescope Berlitz German Language Series.* Minneapolis: Minneapolis Public Schools, 1969.

80 Wiley, W. Deane, and Lloyd K. Bishop. *The Flexibly Scheduled High School.* West Nyack, New York: Parker, 1968.

7

Media
in foreign language teaching

Introduction: the technological revolution

Jermaine D. Arendt

Minneapolis Public Schools

Today's children and youth live in a world which has seen much of another generation's science fiction and dreams become reality. Man has hurled himself into space and set foot upon the moon. He flies in aircraft that carry more passengers than live in many a small town. Almost every family has one automobile and many have two or more. Add to that motor scooters, trail bikes, snowmobiles, and boats and motors as other devices that provide entertainment and education.

For under ten dollars the child, himself, can buy a set of small portable two-way radios. He is also likely to own a transistor radio, a cassette tape recorder, and an inexpensive camera.

Besides one or more high-fidelity record players and radios, a family owns at least one television set. Much of the technological world which a child knows he knows primarily through television viewing. He probably meets the ubiquitous computer on television for the first time as it grinds out predictions of election outcomes long before all returns are in. For better or worse, like many of the other technological marvels mentioned above, television has become a major factor in the education of youth. Culkin (18) says that the average high school graduate has spent approximately 15,000 hours viewing television as opposed to 10,800 hours in school.

Electric media and youth

How have the schools reacted to the technological revolution? According to their severest critics, school practices seem to be oblivious of the clicking, clacking, "do not fold or mutilate," flashing lights reality of our multimedia world. And youngsters have responded by "turning on" to other experiences but "dropping out" mentally, if not physically, from what happens in school.

Reversing the common criticism that much present home environment is poor and is also responsible for failure in school, Marshall McLuhan (52) compares the home and school and charges that the school comes off a poor second:

There is a world of difference between the modern home environment of integrated electric information and the classroom. Today's television child is tuned to up-to-the-minute "adult" news . . . and is bewildered when he enters the nineteenth-century environment that still characterizes the educational establishment where information is scarce but ordered and structured by fragmented, classified patterns, subjects, and schedules.[1]

Postman & Weingartner (59) pick up the McLuhan theme in their new book. Tracing the rapid development that electric media have undergone in a little more than one hundred years, they show that print no longer has a monopoly on information delivery: photography (invented in 1839), telegraph (1844), telephone (1876), phonograph (1877), movies (1894), radio (1895), television (1923), and talkies (1927) also serve as sources of information. *Importance of electric media*

They apply the Whorf-Sapir hypothesis to media. Electric media are new languages that "structure our perception of reality" and we need to learn their languages for our own survival. Media study becomes critical in education.

> In a world of high speed, complex, simultaneous, total field change, the conventional, pedestrian, academic modes of analytic, linear segmentation and explication itself comprises a threat to our survival . . . . We have new languages to learn if we don't want to talk ourselves to death.

Thus the schools should use and analyze electric media: (*1*) for more effective presentation of information and (2) so that youth will understand media better.

Aren't electric media being used in education? What of educational television, language laboratories, educational films, filmstrips, and so on? Such media are, of course, being used, *Electric media and education* but in McLuhan's overstatement there are some truths. Since schools are heavily book oriented, electric media are likely to be in short supply. In addition, many educators are unaware of or even belligerent about the technological revolution.

This paper will discuss how foreign language teachers and some of their colleagues in other fields are using technological media as reported by practitioners in recent publications. It will explore the possibilities of media use, as well. Above all, however, it will explore the problems of software, the film, the taped program, the transparency, as opposed to the hardware.

---

1 From *The Medium is the Massage*, by Marshall McLuhan, Quentin Fiore, and Jerome Agel. Copyright © 1967 by Marshall McLuhan, Quentin Fiore, and Jerome Agel. By permission of Bantam Books, Inc.

Debes (19) has published an article of great importance for foreign language educators. Dealing with a concept he calls "visual literacy," he explains important visual skills we need to have in order to deal with our environment:

> Visual literacy refers to a group of vision-competencies a human being can develop by seeing and at the same time having and integrating other sensory experiences. The development of these competencies is fundamental to normal human learning. When developed, they enable a visually literate person to discriminate and interpret the visual actions, objects, and symbols, natural and man made, that he encounters in his environment. Through the creative use of these competencies, he is able to communicate with others. Through the appreciative use of these competencies he is able to comprehend and enjoy master works of visual communication.

It is difficult to see how the foreign language learner can acquire these competencies except through foreign residence or through learning with electric media. For the foreign language teacher the use of electric media is likely to be especially rewarding since there is no other means by which the movement, the sounds, and the excitement of foreign life can be brought to the student in school.

Visual literacy and learning with media

Hocking (41) takes the position that audials and visuals can substitute for a foreign experience building a cultural island (see also Grundstrom, 35) and an experiential base for learners. The impact of modern media is synergistic, he says; that is, the effect is greater than the sum of its parts (Hocking, 38).

Hocking agrees with those who point to alienation of youth from school. Speaking directly to foreign language teachers, he charges that traditional courses contribute to the high dropout rate from foreign language classes. Support for Hocking's position comes from Bloom (11) who claims that 90–95% of all students can master what we teach if we give them time, use diagnostic teaching, and use a variety of teaching materials and methods.

The variety of materials, including electric media, enables students to learn in their own way, to do, in the idiom of the day, "their own thing" within the general boundaries of the learning

159

task and at their own speed. Bloom further stresses the affective benefits of learning mastery. The results, he says, are increased student interest in the subject, an improved self-concept, and the likelihood of a lifelong interest in learning.

However, the use of modern media does not automatically ensure success. It is the quality of the medium and the way it is used that determines its effectiveness. When tape recorders and language laboratories were in their infancy, great benefits were predicted to accrue from their use. Now after some years of use of these electromechanical devices the profession is somewhat *Media are only media* wiser. One study by Smith (74) shows no significant benefits resulted from use of language laboratories in a number of Pennsylvania schools. This study is reviewed in another section of this chapter as well as in the chapter in this volume by W. Flint Smith, chapter 8. At this point, it would be useful to remember that the teacher is also a medium of instruction. He may be good, bad, or indifferent. The same applies to a textbook, a tape recording, a film, or any other medium.

According to Lemler (49) if media use is to be successful the teacher needs to believe in media. He needs to recognize their contribution to instruction in terms of realism, concreteness, directness, and variety. In choosing media Lemler suggests the *How to choose media* following criteria:

1 To what objective(s) will the material offer a definite or unique contribution?
2 Is its content accurate? Is it appropriate to its purpose?
3 Is its content relevant to the maturity, experience and needs of learners?
4 Is the nature of the medium appropriate to the learning task?
5 Does the material meet reasonable standards of technical quality?

Using media — major new publications

The most important single 1969 publication concerning itself with media in foreign language teaching is the Northeast Conference Report, entitled *Sight and Sound: The Sensible and Sensitive Use of Audio-Visual Aids in Foreign Language Teaching*, edited by Edgerton (23). This is the first major attempt in many years to help foreign language teachers use such aids.

The Northeast Conference Report is divided into six major sections covering the following topics: Nonprojected Visuals, Sound Recordings, Slides and Filmstrips, Overhead Projectors, Motion Pictures, and Television.

Nonprojected visuals. This section (Frazier, 32) describes the wide range of teacher-made and commercially available posters, charts, maps, and the like. Specific suggestions regarding teaching techniques are also provided. The chapter is especially useful for teachers in that the visuals described are inexpensive and are generally easily prepared for a specific instructional need.

Sound recordings. The chapter (Arendt, 4) on sound recordings assumes that the reader knows a considerable amount about using recordings. It notes that dissatisfaction with present materials is widespread. The writer states that ideas about foreign language methodology are again being challenged and that these challenges impinge on the use of tape materials. Other factors that call for a modification of the use of tape materials include the increased emphasis on self-instruction.

Slides and filmstrips. The section on slides and filmstrips (Hayden, 36) begins with a simple description of the medium. Teacher-produced and commercially available materials are discussed. Teaching strategies are suggested and additional readings listed.

The overhead projector. This chapter (Wrenn, 85) has a wealth of information on purchase, production, and use of transparencies. A number of production processes are described. Advantages and limitations of the overhead projector are included.

Motion pictures. The writer (Grundstrom, 35) provides technical information regarding the medium and compares it with other media. He points out that film can show language use in the full context of gestures, expressions, and actions. Finally the writer suggests how one selects and uses films.

Television. Considerable technical information (Sheehan, 69) is provided regarding various types of equipment. Advantages of video tape over film are noted. Sources of prerecorded video tape are listed and ways of utilizing television are suggested. Finally, the possible role of television in teacher training is indicated.

Demonstrations

Each of the six sections in the 1969 Northeast Conference Report (Frazier, 32; Shryer, 71; Capretz, 14; Wrenn, 85; Edgerton, 24; Sheehan & Willis, 70) is followed by a carefully described demonstration of the use of the medium. Most of these demonstrations were filmed for the conference and the resulting films have now been made available for sale or rent (Dodge, 21). They are examples of exciting creative teaching that deserve to be shown and discussed at state and regional conferences, and in formal teacher education programs.

Northeast Conference films

Audiovisual aids as media

The major shortcoming of the report is that through its title and separate papers, it somehow fails to present an urgent case for use of media other than the teacher and a textbook. It needs to be followed by writings that demonstrate the use of media in teaching groups of various sizes: large group, small group, and particularly in individualized instruction. The report clearly reflects the inadequately defined role of various components in an instructional system.

Shortcomings

Machine-aided language learning

A second major resource on technology in foreign language learning is that by Dodge (22). The Dodge article is a highly useful summary of literature of the previous year on the subject, covering research, equipment, and software. The section on the rapidly growing body of experimentation with computer-assisted instruction is particularly valuable.

Britannica Review

The Pennsylvania study

A third major work on media in foreign language learning is the already-mentioned report by Smith (74) on the language laboratory. This study failed to show any significant benefits from the use of the language laboratory in schools involved. A flood of responses have attempted to explain the results. Major arguments are raised against the study by Valette (82), who questions the appropriateness of the measuring instruments administered and of the ways in which language laboratorics were used. Hocking (39) raises questions regarding the condition of the laboratories, training of teachers to operate the laboratories, and the apparent failure of some teachers to use the equipment at all. Aleamoni & Spencer (1) charge that recommendations made in the Smith report regarding future purchases and use of language laboratories are either irrelevant to the report findings or in contradiction with them.

Failure of the Pennsylvania studies?

The Smith study seems to have erred in the same direction as the earlier report by Keating in organizing a massive, sprawling study in which controls were not possible. The question is not whether the mere presence of a language laboratory or any other technological medium will improve learning. Nor is it valid to test the effectiveness of a medium if usage is of a kind known to be ineffective. It makes sense to develop the best possible use of the medium and then test its use. However, instead of rejecting the medium if results are unsatisfactory, the real student of learning will revise his materials and techniques to develop ways to use the medium successfully. Smither (75) and Banathy & Jordan (6) have shown that the language laboratory and electronic classroom can be integrated successfully into language courses by this process.

Television and film

A final major publication relating to media in foreign language instruction is a bibliography by Svobodny (77). This report with abstracts is compilation of important research and studies especially in the use of film and television since World War II. Research cited is particularly supportive of attempts to teach foreign languages by television.

Film and TV research bibliography

Software

Ideally, according to Grittner (33), learning materials should include a wide range of components. These "integrated" materials should include visuals which are basic, not supplementary. Such materials now exist for a number of languages and are available commercially from American and foreign publishers. No list of such materials can be satisfactory since no one can say which will fit specific programs.

Suggestions for development of "integrated materials"

Grittner makes a number of suggestions for development of integrated materials for German. They are equally valuable for development of learning materials in other languages. Many of the suggestions may also serve teachers as criteria for selection of materials.

The suggestions indicate:
1 That the "software" be developed before the hardware or concurrently with it.
2 That materials be field tested with a representative cross section of pupils before they are marketed.

163

3 That materials incorporate the latest in testing techniques to aid the teacher in evaluating student progress in the acquisition of skills.

4 That materials be available in a number of formats to accommodate the small low-budget schools, as well as the large well-financed school districts.

5 That all audio materials and equipment observe standards of quality.

6 That quality standards be established and observed for all visual presentations used . . . and that they be in color.

7 That the content be psychologically suitable to the age of the learner.

8 That provisions be made for the heterogeneous make-up of a typical class by developing both remedial and enrichment units.

9 That materials be multisensory, including single concept films, records, tapes, slides, motion pictures, filmstrips, charts, pictures, transparencies, and video tapes.

10 That the culture of the country, modern and past, be depicted.

11 That visual and audio materials be integrated with the "system."

12 That student tests should have topical material with utterances that are short enough to commit to memory.

13 That there be ample, interesting and varied pattern practice.

14 That each unit should have an illustrated grammatical generalization for the lesson.

15 That student homework materials be constructed so as to provide interesting, varied practice on the basic material.

16 That programmed self-testing materials be included in the package.

17 That a teacher's manual be provided to explain the basic principles of the course and outline each lesson in brief.

18 That student tests and teacher keys should be provided with testing tapes.

A major problem for any foreign language department intending to purchase integrated materials is the expense. A secondary school which buys only a basic text for its students spends about one-third to one-half as much for materials as one which also purchases tape recordings, workbooks, flashcards, filmstrips, films, and tests.

Major problem 1: Expense

A second major problem may be the rapid obsolescence of some material due to changes in fashions, technological advances, and the inexorable march of world events. Last year's fashions and last year's foreign minister require explanation time that could be better spent in other ways.

2: *Rapid obsolescence*

A further problem in the use of integrated materials is that they change the role of the teacher. He suddenly finds himself spending more time arranging for a lesson because he has to arrange for and test out audiovisual equipment; he needs to preview the films and filmstrips before showing them; and he is sometimes delayed by equipment breakdown. Most important, he has to adjust to letting the component take over some of his role as presenter.

3: *Role of the teacher*

Finally, it is possible to pay much more for integrated materials and find them very unsatisfactory. Course content is not automatically improved when presented by a technological medium. This fact has all too often been ignored by makers of educational films of all kinds. When Elton Hocking (40) calls educational television "the last of the cottage industries," he is alluding to the "Amateur Hour" atmosphere that pervades so much of this medium because each school district wants to develop its own programs. Another reason that some integrated materials are unsatisfactory is that some components may be poor or even nonexistent. Finally, with the sizable investment required for integrated course materials, many publishers have been particularly reluctant to revise materials when revision was needed.

4: *Expectations*

Not just commercial houses are working on multimedia approaches. Sister Jonas (44) reports the development of materials that focus on the affective domain in foreign language learning. Her project, federally funded, stresses interpersonal relationships between American elementary school pupils and pupils of the same age in France. Classes exchange slides, tape recordings, drawings, and letters. She reports high enthusiasm in both the class participating in the exchange and one which simply uses the materials sent from France.

National media projects

In England, the Schools Council (57) is developing new courses in French, German, Russian, and Spanish in a project remindful of the development of the revolutionary Glastonbury materials in the United States. One striking difference is that the British are initially producing multimedia packages rather than the stark print and tape combinations that were developed in the United States.

Sweden, too, has developed a most intriguing course, *Swedish for Immigrants*, which deserves to be studied for its creative use of television, sound recordings, slides, and printed text. The Swedish development team working under Ake Anderson (2) focuses on actual human rather than belletristic aspects: the need for friendship, for making a living, for finding shelter, and so on. Directed at immigrants and foreign workers who need to learn Swedish to live and work in Sweden, it is modern and youth-oriented.

Smaller multimedia packages

The various media demonstrations which were a part of the 1969 Northeast Conference Report mentioned earlier are examples of how a teacher can analyze a learning problem or unit of work and integrate media in the teaching-learning program. Shryer (71), for example, used graded audio tape recordings and readings to build up aural and oral skills leading ultimately to the ability to comprehend much of a difficult feature film. Regenstreif (Ann Arbor Board of Education, 3) has developed a series of minicourses using slides and tapes for students to study as an enrichment in independent study time during the school day. Rallo (63), on the other hand, has outlined a course which employs team teaching, large and small group instruction, and independent study. Slides, filmstrips, and films are used not only for large group instruction but also for independent study as regular assignments and for makeup work. Kirch (47) indicates that a wide number of commercially available visuals are integrated into courses at the University of Delaware. He recommends them for vocabulary learning, structure practice, and dialogue memorization.

Audials and visuals in a learning problem

A common pattern in language programs is rather heavy use of sound recordings during the first two years of high school language instruction (or the first two semesters of college instruction). After this beginning period, use of recordings falls off quickly and classes become predominantly print-oriented. The result is that oral-aural skills often decline among students who continue their studies. According to Belasco (8) substantially more practice of a type different from dialogue practice and drill is important if students are going to achieve aural competence. He calls for the use of recorded materials typical of those which confront listeners in the foreign culture: recordings of interviews, newscasts, speeches, popular songs, excerpts from plays,

Use of sound recordings

and so on. Such materials, carefully chosen, provide an opportunity for structure study and advanced practice.

Nelson (56) urges increased use of short-wave radio even for beginning courses.

Schmidtlein (67) and Koepke (48) give extensive suggestions on teaching radio plays in intermediate and advanced classes.

The contextual drill

A major characteristic, perhaps the hallmark, of audiolingual foreign language courses has been the attempt to teach grammar through so-called pattern drills. Such drills typically call for the learner to manipulate an utterance according to a suggested model, thereby "internalizing" the grammar. Critics claim that early student enthusiasm quickly turns to boredom under the unrelenting drill which has little relationship to actual communication.

European language teachers have attempted to write more lifelike exercises for language laboratory practice. Smith (73) and Roeske (64) describe the so-called contextual drill in recent articles. Roeske says of contextual drills:

> In the context forms, an interior situational relationship does exist; the single language laboratory exercise is embedded in a conclusive, self-sufficient, and meaningful situation. The pupil is given some kind of prefamiliarizing experience outside the laboratory. During the practice in the lab the pupil himself takes over a part of the situation, takes part mentally in it and feels that it is addressed to him . . . .

The following is an extract from a situational listening exercise and pattern drill, *At London Airport* (Institut für Film und Bild, 5):

Examples of contextual drills

1. Plane thundering in
2. Dialogue (first: listening and comprehension in normal speed)

Announcer: We are at London Airport. Keith and Daisy are also here. They're waiting for their plane to New York.

Reception Hall Loudspeaker:
        Flight 717 to New York
        Flight 717 to New York

Air Hostess: Come on, you two, that's your plane.

(The children step forward a few steps)

Keith (excited):	Look, Daisy! There's a small plane.
Daisy:	Can you see where the small plane's going?
Keith:	It is going to Edinburgh. And there's a big plane.
Daisy:	Can you see where the big plane's going?
Keith:	It is going to Berlin. It's a B.E.A. plane.

(Plane thundering off)

	Oh, there's a big airliner.
Daisy:	Can you see where the big airliner's going?
Keith:	It's going to Africa—to Cairo. Oh, no, to Cape Town. It's a B.O.A.C. liner.
	And there's a very small plane.
Daisy:	Can you see where the very small plane's going?
Keith:	No, I can't see where it's going. . . . Oh, yes, now I can. It's going to Scotland—to Glasgow.
	And there's a very big airliner.
Daisy:	Can you see where the very big airliner's going?
Keith:	It's going to the Continent. It's a Lufthansa liner.
	It's going to Cologne in West Germany.

....

Daisy:	Can you see where the big airliner's going?
Keith (annoyed):	It's a Pan American. Ugh!
	You ask and ask and ask:
	Can you see where that plane's going?
	Can you see where that plane's going?
	Can you see?
	Can you see?
	Can you see?
Loudspeaker:	Flight 717 to New York
	Final call!
	Flight 717 to New York
Air Hostess (impatiently to the children):	
	Your plane! The big airliner's your plane.
	Come on!

(The children run off)

Loudspeaker:	Final call! Flight 717 to New York.
(Plane)	

3. First Drill (without any effects—three-phase system)

Announcer:	All right! Now listen and repeat what Daisy says.
	You repeat what Daisy says:
Keith:	Look, Daisy! There's a small plane!
Daisy:	Can you see where the small plane's going?
Keith:	It's going to Edinburgh. And there's a big plane.
Daisy:	Can you see where the big plane's going?
etc.	

As a further exercise the boys in the class will take over the girl's role in the conversation thus practicing over and over the basic sentence and modifying it slightly as necessary in the context. The response is confirmed each time on tape.

The following is a second example of the contextual drill, this time for the purpose of practicing the third person singular with the present tense—*What Dick Does on Uncle Henry's Farm* (Institut für Film und Bild, 25):

(The telephone rings, receiver being taken off)

Ann:	This is Ann speaking. My number is 187 309. Who is speaking, please?
Dick:	(phone voice) This is Dick speaking. Hello, Ann.
Ann:	Hello, Dick.
Dick:	Ann, next week you are coming to our farm, so I'll tell you what I do here every day.
Ann:	Oh, fine, Dick.
Dad:	What does Dick say?
Ann:	Oh, he's telling me what he does every day.
Dad:	Good, you must tell me what he says.
Ann:	Oh, yes, Daddy, I will. Well, Dick, begin. I'm listening.
Dick:	I get up at seven.
Ann:	He says he gets up at seven.
Dick:	Then I rush to the bathroom.
Ann:	Then he rushes to the bathroom.

Announcer:	Now you tell Daddy what Dick says.
Dick:	First I stretch my arms.
Ann:	First he stretches his arms.
Dick:	I wash with cold water.
Ann:	Hoo! He washes with cold water.
Dick:	Then I brush my teeth.
Ann:	Then he brushes his teeth.
Dick:	Then I dress quickly.
Ann:	Then he dresses quickly.

....

Dick:	In the evening I lie on the sofa and read a book.
Ann:	In the evening he lies on the sofa and reads a book.
Dick:	Well, that's all, Ann. I hope you will like it here. See you next week, Ann. Good-bye, Ann.
Ann:	Good-bye, Dick.
(receiver being put down)	
Dad:	Well, I say, Ann. You will have a good time on Uncle Henry's farm!

Independent study

For about the last ten years schools have shown an increasing interest in independent study as a part of, if not the entire, instructional program. The so-called Trump Plan (80), suggesting a division of instruction into large group, small group, tutorial, and independent study, gave considerable impetus to development of self-instructional programs.

In their present form most foreign language materials, whether integrated or not, are not suitable for use in programs depending largely on independent study. Teachers find, furthermore, that organizing for independent study is a formidable task. They may:

Integrated materials and independent study

1 Create guides and work sheets to accompany existing materials.
2 Develop independent study kits on their own. Such kits are often called Unipacs or Learning Activity Packages (LAPS) and so on.
3 Use programmed courses or programmed sequences.

A study by Linck (50) of independent study programs in all subject areas shows that the school library is the most important facility for independent study. Study areas consist mainly of reading areas and dry (i.e., not equipped with audiovisual equipment) carrels. An examination of foreign language materials used in self-instructional programs indicates that they, like those in other subject areas, are largely print-oriented though they are often correlated with taped materials.

Importance of school library

Unipac

As described by Kapfer & Swenson (45), the Unipac is a carefully written instructional package relying largely upon independent study. It will contain objectives stated in behavioral terms, a pretest, a series of activities, a post-test, and other "quest," that is, enrichment and individual interest activities. Because the Unipac is usually produced at the school or school district level by a teacher or team of teachers, it is often duplicated by a method that prevents satisfactory production of photographs. Limited integration of other visuals and sound recordings is usually attempted. As revision of existing Unipacs takes place perhaps writers will begin to incorporate more audiovisual materials into their activities.

Unipac

The Nathan Hale contract plan

Fleury (30) has described a plan for independent study using the contract system for intermediate level students. Nathan Hale High School students in Seattle, using a study guide, texts, and tape recordings, work largely on their own.

Independent study plans

The McCluer Plan

Materials produced by the Ferguson-Florissant (Missouri) School District (26) likewise depend largely on print materials with considerable support from tape recordings. In this program the teacher plays an important role as monitor, tutor, and small group leader.

The danger with many independent study programs is that the best audiovisual aid, the teacher, is withdrawn from constant contact with students and verbalization about language is substituted for him. Skillful use of technological media could fill this gap, but the media cannot be a return to the "Amateur Hour" attempts of which Hocking complained. As Arendt (4) observed in the Northeast Conference for 1969, too much is expected of tape in many classes. It needs to be given interesting tasks to perform and in the process be combined with other me-

171

dia to be most effective. However, Fearing (28) and Cannaday (13) remind us that tape has an important role to play in permitting individual pacing and providing variety in learning. Fearing illustrates how so-called out-of-sequence students, those with out-of-school language experience, and very rapid or slow learners can work independently with tape and text materials in ungraded programs. Cannaday suggests remedial exercises, special language laboratory projects, and multiple programming for individualizing instruction with tape.

Berman (10) suggests that teachers can easily create an "autolecture" by combining cassette recordings and overhead projectuals which students manipulate themselves in a study center.

Most independent study programs rely on individual pacing to deal with individual differences among students. Individually prescribed instruction (IPI) depends on determining, by diagnosis and often in conference with the learner, what will be an appropriate study program for him. Mitzel (54) points out that IPI is easiest to set up with print materials, but that it is most likely to be successful with a wide variety of media appropriate to student achievement levels. The learning program should be available to the learner at times convenient to him. According to Mitzel the slow student may take three to five times as long as the rapid learner to finish the same material.

Programmed learning

Foreign language teachers, like those in many other subject areas, have been stimulated by the work of B. F. Skinner and other pioneers of programmed learning. Fiks (31) lists a sizable number of programs available for use in foreign language instruction. However, use of programmed materials has remained on a small scale, not at all approaching the massive adoption envisioned by its advocates in the early 1960s. Valdman (81), who has considerable personal experience with the development and use of programmed instruction, no longer is optimistic about its future in language learning. He feels that whole courses cannot effectively be given over to programmed learning and suggests it be used for only limited teaching tasks. Language goals, he feels, cannot be described in the precise terms which programmed instruction requires. He cites the following disadvantages for programmed learning:

Programmed learning suggested for limited use

1 Students miss the teacher-student relationship, and teachers, on the other hand, experience difficulty in maintaining

172

a feeling of true urgency when daily opportunity for students to communicate with the teacher and other students is lacking.

2 There is a built-in monotony in the use of programmed materials due to the sameness of the learning tasks and the surroundings in which learning takes place.

3 For most students, reinforcement by a machine is not sufficient to provide a high level of motivation and there is a necessity for "public" reinforcement.

4 Self-instruction does not provide the opportunity for the student to transfer habits and repertories learned by dialogue with a machine and in artificial drills to the natural communication situation. One might say that natural communication is not programmable by definition since, in the normal use of language, one can seldom predict the responses of one's interlocutor.

5 The acquisition of a foreign language is a long and arduous task. Programmed learning exacerbates this problem because it makes the learner keenly aware of his degree of progress and the distance that separates him from stated goals. It is for this reason that programs that stress audiolingual skills are more likely to adversely affect student motivation than grammar-translation oriented programs.

Valdman suggests in place of complete self-instruction a system he calls "guided learning." Components for his system are the language laboratory, teacher aides, native speaker aides, and master teachers. The precise form of materials for this learning is not suggested nor is it clear whether the author sees a need for teaching machines which provide more than an audio signal.

Guided learning

Bung (12) has exactly the opposite view from Valdman. He favors further attempts to develop "true" programs which he states: (*1*) contain all information the student needs; (2) reduce the need for monitoring; and (3) include presentation and acquisition activities. Bung calls for programs that adapt to different kinds of learners. The teacher, according to Bung, caters to the emotional needs of the learner and need not even coordinate his efforts with a good machine program because the program will not presuppose human intervention.

Another viewpoint

Though admittedly rare, programmed courses are in use. Clark (17) reports use of a commercial German program at the

University of Rochester. He says that achievement by students in programmed classes is comparable with that in conventional classes. Furthermore, he notes a gradually increasing percentage of students who select the programmed course rather than conventional courses.

Morton (55) reports continuing successful use of a programmed course developed years ago. At the College of Artesia, programmed instruction is used to prepare students for an apparently exacting language requirement. Unique in the school is *Programmed courses in use* that one foreign language, Spanish, is required for all students, in an attempt to develop a significant degree of bilingualism in all graduates. The programmed instruction course can be taken at the student's own pace and leads in the upper division to required courses in the student's major which are taught in Spanish.

Ornstein (58) notes the difficulty of programming foreign languages and states that no successful programming attempt dispenses with human intervention. All first year French at the University of Kentucky is "program assisted".

Sweet (78) has described what appears to be the most sophisticated attempt to program a foreign language. He notes the need to provide materials to cope with the different learning styles of learners. In his programmed Latin course, *Artes Latinae*, he includes diagnostic tests, a graded reader, filmstrips, movies, a programmed text, and taped program.

Role of the teacher

Both educational television and teaching machines were introduced with much fanfare. Apologists cited studies to show that students learned as much from these technological media as in regular classes. The impression conveyed was that the teacher at best would lose his central role in instruction and at worst could be dispensed with. Many teachers reject this change of role, and all, perhaps, can be counted on to fight suggestions of their supposed obsolescence.

The almost total demise of televised FLES which suggested that anyone who could turn on the television set could supervise FLES learning is indicative that teachers are resistant to any changes that seem to downgrade their importance.

A more sensible approach would admit that media can do some things better than the teacher but that students rarely can learn for extended periods without a live teacher. A long-term observer of television and other media says "the best television instruction depends upon the teacher" (Hocking, 40).

If media take over the responsibility of presentation of much material from the teacher what is left?

How do media mix with the human element?

Grittner (33) says it is the teacher's job to lift the students above the materials, to teach divergent thinking, to diagnose the students' strengths and weaknesses, and to prescribe proper materials and learning activities.

Interaction of instructional elements

Cannaday (13), speaking particularly of the language laboratory, notes that that medium cannot plan, program, select, guide, interpret, analyze, define, relate, react, or communicate, suggesting therefore the necessity for teacher-media-student interaction.

Walton (84) has prepared an extensive role definition for the teacher who works with computer-assisted instruction. It is in the main applicable with all media. The teacher in a computer-assisted classroom will:

Teacher's role with computer-assisted instruction

1 Become manager of the learning process.
2 Identify learning deficiencies, diagnose learning difficulties, and prescribe corrective treatment.
3 Be concerned about understandings, attitudes, and appreciations as learning outcomes rather than factual knowledge and routine skills.
4 Devote energies to helping students develop character, social maturity, communications skills, lasting perceptions and insights, and creative inclinations.
5 Work to develop new curriculum materials, continue himself to learn and to share his new learnings with more students than he otherwise would.

Ianni (42) notes the following major modes in the teaching-learning sequence: (1) storing up facts; (2) questions and answers; and (3) continuous interplay of minds and emotions in which the development of values, style, individuality, and ability to ask new questions is the hoped-for end result. Media can do the first two; a live teacher must do the third.

A master teacher need not always be present where students are learning from media. Differentiated staffing arrangements would release the professionals from purely monitoring activities by employing paraprofessionals as lab assistants and clerical assistants.

Learning environment

For many years the foreign language classroom was a relatively barren space in which the teacher and the blackboard were the primary, often the only, audiovisual devices. Bergquist (9) describes how the classroom itself has become a lively medium housing often a large assortment of realia: sculpture, musical instruments, flags, and so on. Bulletin boards, maps, charts, and murals increase the impact. Now with a programming center, listen-respond student stations, and other electromechanical devices added, the facility is often termed an "electronic" classroom.

The Foreign Language Resource Center

Increasing interest in individualizing instruction has led to design of a new facility, the Foreign Language Resource Center (FLRC), as described by Rallo (63). The FLRC promises to combine taped recordings with other media including print and nonprint materials in a new setting more stimulating than the conventional language laboratory atmosphere. Arranged to provide individual and group learning spaces the FLRC provides opportunity for browsing, viewing, reading, thinking, discussing, writing, and typing that makes language learning exciting. Displays include real objects, posters, charts, and maps. The following equipment may be available in the center: tape recorders, record players, activated earphones, individual slide and filmstrip viewers, short wave radio, portable blackboards, 8-mm and 16-mm small group projectors, foreign language typewriters, and duplicators.

Functions of the FLRC

The FLRC may begin as a corner of a classroom or the library. Later on a satellite room may be needed to house the growing collection and provide study room for the growing number of pupil users.

For large departments Fearing (27) suggests a design combining teacher office spaces, an open resource area, carrels, and a quiet study lounge. See Figure 1.

The Language Center

For the college or university the English have developed an entirely new concept, the Language Center (Sculthorpe, 68). These service centers take on the primary responsibility for lan-

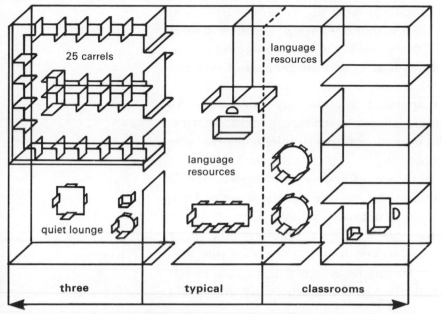

25 carrels

language resources

quiet lounge

language resources

language resources

three   typical   classrooms

FIGURE 1. Foreign Language Resource Center

guage instruction for the entire institution, working closely with all departments to develop courses tailored to departmental needs. Foreign literature courses may be taught in the center, but they are more likely to be taught in the humanities department. The center develops its expertise in language teaching and learning and can purchase the electromechanical equipment it feels is necessary for its work (Sculthorpe, 68).

Systems approach

As we have seen, members of the profession have called for integrated materials for teaching foreign languages. Some publishers in turn have produced components of many kinds to accompany basic texts. Other merchants of instructional materials have made films the primary medium with print materials, tapes, and so on as supplementary elements.

Banathy (6) and others are calling for a more systematic analysis of learning problems as well as a systematic attempt to solve such problems.

A systems approach to education defines an instructional problem and describes in behavioral terms what students will be able to do when they have solved the problem (i.e., usually learned a body of material). Materials, equipment, instructional strategies are organized in what appears to be the most rational

Systems approach: working definitions

177

manner to achieve the objectives. Next the system is tried out, and then it is revised where it is found wanting. Successive uses of the system will lead to further revisions since on-going evaluation and upgrading of the system is an integral part of systems analysis.

Carter (15) defines the approach another way: one states the need, defines objectives, identifies constraints, generates alternate systems, selects the best alternative, implements the system, evaluates, and modifies.

Components of the system are, of course, field tested. Media must be evaluated. Sometimes the relative effectiveness of various media may be under test (Higginson & Love, 37).

Ianni (42) criticizes educators who, he says, often talk about an educational system but who "continue to search for that single revolutionary device or technique which will make it possible for all children to read quickly, think efficiently and study painlessly." *Criticisms and successes*

Banathy & Jordan (7), on the other hand, describe how semi-programmed exercises, combined with regular class instruction in a classroom-laboratory, achieved superior results over conventional instruction without electromechanical equipment.

Careful application of systems analysis to the teaching of foreign languages is rare. However, as more and more sophisticated electric media are introduced into instruction, systems analysis is the only hope for successful integration. The computer is one such medium.

Student media productions

If media have an important role in presenting language and culture, what of the other great objective stated by Postman & Weingartner, that of helping youth to understand media and how they affect us? How do we learn the "languages" of media?

Some things can be learned from studying the use of a medium as an art form. Here the teacher must, first of all, understand the work of the great directors, as well as the work of great artists of the printed word. If *explication de texte* is used in studying literature, why not an *explication de film*?

Even more exciting, however, is the students' attempt to use the medium for their own productions. They can try techniques to produce the effect they wish to create. Is black and white or color film better for their purposes? How do they get satisfactory sound? Sound effects? *Student-created production*

Lukner (51) relates how his German classes have successfully and enthusiastically tape-recorded German radio plays. Grittner (34) suggests ways in which language classes can produce slide-tape descriptions of their community for possible exchange with classes overseas. He also describes ways in which video tape, overhead projectuals, short-wave radio, filmstrips, art prints, commercial films, and even the flannel board can be used by students in creation of their own productions.

Fearing (29) and Katz (46) have both produced films involving students in all phases of production.

Computer-assisted instruction (CAI)

The dramatic, direct and indirect, impact of television on education was noted earlier. But every bit as awe-inspiring is the development and growth of data processing. Man has just scratched the surface of its potential. Inevitably educators came to recognize an unusual potential for education and currently a large number of schools and colleges are using the computer for instruction. A small number are using the computer for language teaching.

DeLay & Nyberg (20) are critical that so much computer-assisted instruction only provides a more flexible rate for students to do the same thing they have always done with books.

Walton (84), however, suggests that the potential of the computer is much greater. It is currently being tried in various combinations of the following applications:

Applications of CAI to learning

1 As a way of selecting material for the individual appropriate to his level of knowledge.
2 As a means of sequencing instructional material to fit an individual's background of knowledge.
3 As a tutor/driller in reading, foreign language, and mathematics instruction.
4 As a help in expanding and mastering English and foreign language vocabularies.
5 As a tool to help students in completing homework assignments.
6 As a retriever of information from the library.
7 As a monitor of an individual student's learning progress.
8 As a diagnostician to pinpoint individual learning difficulties.
9 As an organizer and executor of remedial instruction.

10 As a controller of the pace of instruction.

11 As a way of introducing course material the teacher has not had time to present.

Other less conventional uses are suggested by Walton:

1 As a conversationalist engaging individual students in dialogue for a number of hours a week.

2 As a motivator and stimulator to ease the marginal learner into learning and succeeding in learning.

3 As a sight-raiser to make it feasible for a given student to cope with more difficult material than he otherwise could.

4 As a popularizer of previously unpopular material.

5 As an aid in teaching exact pitch to singers.

6 As a coach in perfecting pronunciation and enunciation.

Thompson & Waterhouse (79) indicate the motivational impact of computers. They experienced lines of students waiting to use teletype machines, the necessity of keeping buildings open in the evening, on weekends and holidays, and during the summer to meet the demand.

Suppes & Jerman (76) divide computer-teaching programs into two types: drill and practice, and tutorial.

Drill and practice

This type of program supplements classroom instruction. It may include branching, evaluation, and review. Typically, a unit of work will be preceded by a pretest. On the basis of pretest results students will be assigned one of a number of lessons. The next day's work will then be assigned on the basis of the previous day's work. A post-test will be given at the end of the unit. Students may work at the lesson at their convenience; they may bunch their work, they may make up absences, and they may move at their own best speed.

Tutorial

The tutorial program assumes the burden of instruction. It may provide for remedial help or for skipping ahead. It may consist of special supplementary units or full course sequences.

Criteria for computer-assisted programs are suggested by Suppes & Jerman (76):   *Criteria for CAI programs*

1 Curriculum content should be satisfactory.

2 Material should be appropriate for the student population.

3 The system should have a low response time.

4 Terminals should be easy to operate, efficient, and reliable.

5 The system should provide feedback to the teacher on student performance.

Three configurations are typical of computer-assisted instruction: *Configurations of CAI*

1 Teletype, telephone line, and computer.

2 Teletype, telephone line, computer, slide projector, and tape recorder.

3 All of the above plus cathode-ray tube, film, and light pen.

Unfortunately for language teachers the second and third configurations are less reliable then the first. However, Ruplin & Russell (66) use the first configuration to teach writing. In this program, oral work is performed in class with a live teacher and also in the language laboratory.

Rosenbaum (65) notes that in contrast to the typical classroom situation, students learning foreign languages by computer get much opportunity to practice. In a typical 50-minute period stu- *Actual uses of CAI* dents and computer may interact 40 to 50 times. In the Stony-brook program a wide variety of exercises were used in CAI and the computer actually allocated tasks according to pupil proficiency. The computer-taught students performed as well as their controls in speaking and listening and excelled in reading and writing.

Poulter (60) suggests using the computer to score frequent audio tests given in the language laboratory, thus improving motivation and providing constant feedback.

Miller (53) says the computer can do more than score tests; it can count correct responses and record scores on an answer sheet. It can analyze educational experimentation. In addition, it can improve teacher-made tests by providing an almost immediate item analysis and a frequency distribution of scores.

An Oregon project called Computer Based Test Development (COMBAT) uses the computer to store and retrieve educational objectives and test items for English, social studies, science, and mathematics teachers in the greater Portland area (Walter et al., 63). Test items are contributed originally by teachers. Later, items on a given subject may be retrieved upon demand and after examination and selection by the classroom teacher are printed out in ditto masters for duplication in the teacher's school. Ultimately the project staff intends to have an item difficulty and discrimination index based on an on-going analysis. The index will be considered by teachers when they request a test.

Programmed learning vs. computer-assisted instruction

Early experimentation comparing programmed instruction presented through textbooks with that presented through teaching machines usually showed no learning differences that justified use of the machine. The computer is, however, a much more sophisticated machine than the early black boxes used in programmed instruction. Programmed instruction has the following shortcomings, according to Suppes & Jerman (76):

Shortcomings of programmed instruction

1 Programmed instruction does not make sufficient allowance for individual differences.
2 Stimulus items are not dependent upon student response.
3 Frames are often redundant to the point of boredom.
4 Reinforcement is not really immediate.
5 Hints are not easily available.
6 Evaluation is difficult.

Computer-assisted instruction, on the other hand, does provide immediate reinforcement. The student is stopped when he makes an error and cannot continue until he corrects his error. Hints can be stored in the computer memory. Branching can be automatically built into the program. An approximation to dialogue between machine and learner is also possible.

Advantage for CAI

Teacher education

The role of technological media in foreign language teacher education can be divided into two parts: (*1*) using media to help the prospective teacher to learn the second language, and (2) helping the prospective teacher learn how he can effectively use media in his own teaching.

Two roles of media in teacher education

Admittedly the areas overlap. If college and university teachers use media naturally and skillfully, they will serve as models for undergraduates who, in turn, are likely to adopt the techniques.

However, as Hocking has indicated (41), college departments have not often recognized the value of machine-aided learning. Thus it is unusual to find electric media used to make the unique contributions they can make. If used at all, they are likely to be employed to teach at one time more students than previously. Indeed the teaching may well be done by the one professor who dares to sit before the camera and do what he has always done in the classroom. The medium saves money for the institution but provides no unique cultural or linguistic benefits. Such an employment of the medium might well turn a great many undergraduates against both language and media.

Specific courses in use of media in foreign language teaching are also sadly lacking. Despite the best efforts of the Office of Education to encourage their inclusion, media components were not often present in EPDA and NDEA institutes. Normal teacher education programs are even less likely to include media education.

Using media in foreign language teacher education

Films have been used extensively in methods classes for lesson demonstration and presentation of other information about language teaching. A list of many of these can be found in Chamberlain (16). The new Northeast Conference films, *Sight and Sound in Foreign Language Teaching*, which were mentioned earlier, are a welcome addition to this list. These films aid the methods teacher by bringing into the classroom some of the best practitioners in the country.

Use of media for demonstrations

The methods teacher can, as well, show foreign language films in his methods class for the purpose of acquainting his students with them. After showing a good film, he has the further opportunity of leading a discussion on developing a good unit of work built around the film.

Equally valuable is practice in developing appropriate visuals to accompany a "bare bones" unit so typical of textbooks. Capretz (14), Frazier (32), Edgerton (24), Wrenn (85), Hayden (36), and Arendt (4) in the 1969 Northeast Conference Report suggest many teaching ideas, including the use of filmstrips and transparencies in dialogue learning, using slides in teaching literature, and developing listening exercises.

Developing use of media in teaching materials

In the previous section some of the possibilities for student work with media have been presented. Before the teacher can undertake leading such an activity he must, himself, have some skill with media production. The methods teacher can provide opportunity for working on productions similar to those suggested by Lukner, Grittner, and Fearing. Only after he has produced similar works is the classroom language teacher likely to have the courage to engage his students in creative media production.

Silverman (72) notes that helpful publications and general courses on film-making (i.e., not directed to foreign language teachers alone) are available in many colleges and universities. He suggests a series of tasks for the teacher in learning about film-making.

The video tape recorder (VTR) in teacher education

The video tape recorder offers many of the same opportunities as film in the student production of skits and plays. Actually it simplifies considerably the problem of production of such works where lip synchronization is important.

More exciting to the teacher trainer is the use of the video tape recorder for demonstration and evaluation of segments of live teaching. Lessons can be videotaped to demonstrate a technique and then replayed at any time in the future as desired.

Use of VTR for demonstration and evaluation of teaching

Supervision of student teachers has often in the past included the use of audio tape to record part or all of a lesson for eventual replay and discussion with the student teacher. Many experienced teachers occasionally will make audio tape recordings for self-evaluation purposes. Valuable as this type of recording is, it suffers from its inability to present visually as well as aurally what went on. Video tape with its combination of sight and sound is vastly superior.

Sheehan (69) at the Northeast Conference demonstrated how one may videotape a student teacher's teaching and then shortly afterward replay the lesson tape discussing with him the procedures he used. A great virtue of the VTR is that its coverage of the lesson is so complete that student teachers can benefit from self-evaluation rather than having to depend largely upon a supervisor's recall and criticism of events that took place during the lesson.

Pusey (61) reports that the University of Colorado has integrated media into both language instruction and teacher education. A beginning university French class learns from a film-text course and serves as the demonstration class for methods students. Films are also used to demonstrate teaching strategies and to teach linguistics and culture. Video tapes have been recorded by the same author for demonstration purposes but also to record micro-units taught by methods students for subsequent evaluation. He particularly noted the value of video tape for studying kinesics, that of the foreign culture and that of students in the classroom.

184

Itkonen (43) has also used the video tape recorder in his methods class. Video tape demonstrations were introduced primarily to counteract the predominance of traditional demonstrations viewed by student teachers in their student teaching. In the Itkonen program both traditional and audiolingual demonstrations are presented; then methods students imitate the demonstrations.

Summary and conclusions

1 Youth live in an electromechanical world and are accustomed to learning from and with electromechanical devices.
2 After the total immersion provided by electronic media, typical classroom learning may seem overorganized, compartmentalized, unexciting, and meager.
3 Technological media multiply the impact of information by providing it in context.
4 More learners can master subject matter if they can learn at their own rate in their own way.
5 The school needs to help youth understand what media are doing to them and why.
6 Electronic media offer an opportunity to help the student become visually literate in a foreign culture.
7 The production, selection, and use of media must be carefully planned to produce the desired benefits.
8 A steadily growing literature is available to those who wish to integrate a wide variety of media into foreign language courses.
9 Many sets of integrated materials are now available commercially. Models are also available for teachers who wish to create their own integrated units.
10 Some new kinds of exercises promise to improve the use of audio recordings.
11 A wide range of independent study materials are being tried in schools and colleges. They range from simple worksheets to computer-assisted instruction.
12 The role of the teacher is changing. There is no evidence that the teacher can be replaced, only that he should be used where he is maximally effective. Where other media or paraprofessionals can do the job better, they should be used.

13 The classroom has given way to the "electronic classroom" and perhaps the language laboratory must give way to the foreign language resource center.

14 In some universities the foreign language department is disappearing in favor of the language center, a kind of service department.

15 The foreign language textbook is giving way to integrated materials. Integrated materials in turn are likely to be developed in the future as a result of a careful analysis of resources needed to reach objectives.

16 Students can learn a great deal about media and a foreign language and culture by producing their own media in foreign language classes.

17 Major efforts are being made to develop instructional programs for presentation by computer. A number of foreign language courses are already being used successfully.

18 If media are to be used successfully by language teachers, teacher-preparing institutions must incorporate media into their programs, as well as instruction about and practice in using media.

References, Media in foreign language teaching

1 Aleamoni, Lawrence M., and Richard E. Spencer. "An Evaluation of the Pennsylvania Foreign Language Project." *Modern Language Journal* 53(1969):421–28.

2 Anderson, Ake. *Swedish for Immigrants*. Stockholm: National Board of Education (in preparation).

3 Ann Arbor Board of Education. *End of Grant Report for the Foreign Language Innovative Curricular Studies*. Ann Arbor: Board of Education, 1969.

4 Arendt, Jermaine D. "Sound Recordings," 28–45 in Mills F. Edgerton,Jr.,ed., *Sight and Sound: The Sensible and Sensitive Use of Audio-Visual Aids*. Reports of the Working Committees of the Northeast Conference on the Teaching of Foreign Languages. New York: MLA Materials Center, 1969.

5 *At London Airport*. Tonband 386. Munich: Institut für Film und Bild, n.d.

6 Banathy, Bela H. "Current Trends in College Curriculum:A Systems Approach," 105–40 in Emma M. Birkmaier,ed., *Britannica Review of Foreign Language Education, Volume 1*. Chicago: Encyclopacdia Britannica, 1968[1969].

7 ——— and Boris Jordan. "A Classroom Laboratory Instructional System (CLIS)." *Foreign Language Annals* 2(1969):466–73.

8 Belasco, Simon. "Toward the Acquisition of Linguistic Competence:From Contrived to Controlled Materials." *Modern Language Journal* 53(1969):185–205.

9 Bergquist, Violet E. "New Developments in the Foreign Language Classroom," 118–26 in George E. Smith and M. Phillip Leamon,eds., *Effective Foreign Language Instruction in the*

Secondary School. Englewood Cliffs, New Jersey: Prentice-Hall, 1969.

10 Berman, Arthur I. "Seminar/Autolecture." *NEA Journal-Today's Education* 57,ix(1968):33–36.

11 Bloom, Benjamin S. "Learning for Mastery." *UCLA Evaluation Comment* 1,ii(1968):1–12.

12 Bung, Klaus. "Towards Truly Programmed Language Laboratory Courses." *Audio-Visual Language Journal* 7(1969):5–17.

13 Cannaday, Robert W.,Jr. "Language Laboratory: Valuable Instructional Aid," 127–66 in George E. Smith and M. Phillip Leamon,eds., *Effective Foreign Language Instruction in the Secondary School.* Englewood Cliffs, New Jersey: Prentice-Hall, 1969.

14 Capretz, Pierre. "Combray:A Multi-Media Introduction to the World of Marcel Proust," 61–63 in Mills F. Edgerton,Jr.,ed., *Sight and Sound:The Sensible and Sensitive Use of Audio-Visual Aids.* Reports of the Working Committees of the Northeast Conference on the Teaching of Foreign Languages. New York: MLA Materials Center, 1969.

15 Carter, Launor F. "The Systems Approach to Education:Mystique and Reality." *Educational Technology* 9,iv(1969):22–31.

16 Chamberlain, Jane Scott. *Source Materials for Teachers of Foreign Languages.* Washington, D.C.: National Education Association, 1969.

17 Clark, William H. "First Year College German Through Programmed Instruction." *Unterrichtspraxis* 2,ii(1969):58–60.

18 Culkin, John M. "A Schoolman's Guide to Marshall McLuhan." *Saturday Review* 50(18 March) 1967:51–53, 70–72.

19 Debes, John L. "The Loom of Visual Literacy." *Audio-Visual Instruction* 14,viii(1969):25–27.

20 DeLay, Donald H., and David Nyberg. "If Your School Stinks, CRAM It." *Phi Delta Kappan* 51(1970):310–12.

21 Dodge, James W. *Film Series:Sight and Sound: Media in Foreign Language Teaching.* Northeast Conference, Box 881, Madison, Connecticut 06443.

22 —— "Machine-aided Language Learning," 331–41 in Emma M. Birkmaier,ed., *Britannica Review of Foreign Language Education, Volume 1.* Chicago: Encyclopaedia Britannica, 1968 [1969].

23 Edgerton, Mills F.,Jr.,ed. *Sight and Sound:The Sensible and Sensitive Use of Audio-Visual Aids.* Reports of the Working Committees of the Northeast Conference on the Teaching of Foreign Languages. New York: MLA Materials Center, 1969.

24 —— "Motion-Picture Film:A Demonstration," 96–98 in Mills F. Edgerton,Jr.,ed., *Sight and Sound:The Sensible and Sensitive Use of Audio-Visual Aids.* Reports of the Working Committees of the Northeast Conference on the Teaching of Foreign Languages. New York: MLA Materials Center, 1969.

25 *English for Today.* Band I Tonbänder, 411–18. Munich: Institut für Film und Bild, 1967.

26 *Espanol:McCluer Plan* and *Le Francais:Mc-Cluer Plan.* Ferguson, Missouri: Ferguson-Florissant School District, 1969.

27 Fearing, Percy,ed. *Foreign Language Facilities Workbook.* St. Paul: Minnesota State Department of Education, 1970.

28 —— "Nongraded Foreign Language Classes." *Foreign Language Annals* 2(1969):343–47.

29 —— "Using the 8 mm Film to Bridge the Gap from Drill to Creative Language Use." Unpublished demonstration. Northeast Conference on the Teaching of Foreign Language, 1969.

30 Fleury, Dale F. "Independent Study:Foreign Language Seminars." *National Association of Secondary School Principals Bulletin* 53,338 (1969):90–99.

31 Fiks, Alfred I. *Foreign Language Programmed Materials:1969.* MLA/ERIC Focus Report 7. New York: MLA/ERIC, 1969.

32 Frazier, Brenda. "Non-projected Visuals," 12–27 in Mills F. Edgerton,Jr.,ed., *Sight and Sound: The Sensible and Sensitive Use of Audio-Visual Aids.* Reports of the Working Committees of the Northeast Conference on the Teaching of Foreign Languages. New York: MLA Materials Center, 1969.

33 Grittner, Frank. "Course Content Articulation and Materials," A Committee Report to the National Symposium on the Advancement of German Teaching. *Unterrichtspraxis* 2,i(1969):53–74.

34 —— *Maintaining Foreign Language Skills for the Advanced Course Dropout.* MLA/ERIC Focus Report 1. New York: MLA/ERIC, 1968.

35 Grundstrom, Allan W. "Motion Pictures," 81–95 in Mills F. Edgerton,Jr.,ed., *Sight and Sound: The Sensible and Sensitive Use of Audio-Visual Aids.* Reports of the Working Committees of the Northeast Conference on the Teaching of Foreign Languages. New York: MLA Materials Center, 1969.

36 Hayden, Rev. Hilary. "Slides and Filmstrip," 50–60 in Mills F. Edgerton,Jr., ed., *Sight and Sound: The Sensible and Sensitive Use of Audio-Visual Aids.* Reports of the Working Committees of the Northeast Conference on the Teaching of Foreign Languages. MLA Materials Center, 1969.

37 Higginson, George M., and Reeve Love. "The Role of Media in Field Testing or Whatever Happened to the Simple Life?" *Audio-Visual Instruction* 15,v(1970):35–37.

38 Hocking, Elton. "Audio-Visual Learning and Foreign Languages," 167–89 in George E. Smith and M. Phillip Leamon,eds., *Effective Foreign Language Instruction in the Secondary School.* Englewood Cliffs, New Jersey: Prentice-Hall, 1969.

39 —— "The Laboratory in Perspective: Teachers, Strategies, Outcomes." *Modern Language Journal* 53(1969):404–10.

40 —— "The Sound of Pictures." *Modern Language Journal* 52(1968):143–45.

41 —— "Technology in Foreign Language Teaching." *Modern Language Journal* 54(1970):79–91.

42 Ianni, Francis A.J. "Technology and Culture in

Education." *National Association of Secondary School Principals Bulletin* 54,343(1970):1–8.

43 Itkonen, Raimo J. "Video-Taped Model Lessons in a Foreign Language Methods Course." Paper presented at the MLA Seminar 27, Audio-Visuals in Teacher Preparation, December 1969.

44 Jonas, Sister Ruth Adelaide. "The Twinned Classroom Approach to FLES." *Modern Language Journal* 53(1969):342–46.

45 Kapfer, Phillip G., and Gardner Swenson. "Individualizing Instruction for Self-Paced Learning." *The Clearing House* 42(1968):405–10.

46 Katz, Sheldon F. "Turning the Kids on with Media." *Audio-Visual Instruction* 14,viii(1969):48–51.

47 Kirch, Max. "Visuals in the Language Laboratory." *National Association of Language Laboratory Directors Journal* 4,ii(1969):32–35.

48 Koepke, Wulf. "Das Hörspiel im Sprachunterricht für Fortgeschrittene." *Unterrichtspraxis* 2,ii(1969):1–12.

49 Lemler, Ford L. "The Teacher and Media." *Audio-Visual Instruction* 14,v(1970):47–49.

50 Linck, Norman. "Educational Media and Independent Study." *Audio-Visual Instruction* 15,ii(1970):36–37.

51 Lukner, Roland F. "Unser erster Hörspielversuch, Ein Beitrag zum Deutschunterricht mit dem Tonbandgerät." *Unterrichtspraxis* 1,ii(1968):32–35.

52 McLuhan, Marshall,et al. *The Medium is the Massage.* New York: Bantam Books, 1967.

53 Miller, Marvin M. "The Computer and Testing." *National Association of Secondary School Principals Bulletin* 54,343(1970):41–47.

54 Mitzel, Harold E. "The Impending Instructional Revolution." *Phi Delta Kappan* 51(1970):434–39.

55 Morton, F. Rand. "An Experimental Approach to the Language Requirement (The College of Artesia Bilingual Program)." *Modern Language Journal* 54(1970):20–25.

56 Nelson, Robert J. *Using Radio to Develop and Maintain Competence in a Foreign Language.* MLA/ERIC Focus Report 11. New York: MLA/ERIC, 1969.

57 *The Nuffield Foundation and the Schools Council Foreign Languages Teaching Materials Project and Modern Language Project.* Leeds: The Schools Council, 1969. [mimeo.]

58 Ornstein, Jacob. "Programmed Instruction and Educational Technology in the Language Field." *Modern Language Journal* 52(1968):401–10.

59 Postman, Neil, and Charles Weingartner. *Teaching as a Subversive Activity.* New York: Delacorte Press, 1969.

60 Poulter, Virgil L. "Computer-Assisted Laboratory Testing." *Modern Language Journal* 53(1969):561–64.

61 Pusey, C. Richards. "Teaching Strategies from the Reel World." Paper presented at the MLA Seminar 27, Audio-Visuals in Teacher Preparation, December 1969.

62 Rallo, John A. "A Cooperative French Program:A New Approach." *Foreign Language Annals* 2(1969):474–76.

63 ——— "Foreign Language Resource Center." *National Association of Language Laboratory Directors Journal* 4,iii(1970):15–22.

64 Roeske, Elfriede. "Der Situationsbezug als Prinzip der Sprachlaborarbeit." *Praxis des neusprachlichen Unterrichts* 15(1968):394–401.

65 Rosenbaum, Peter S. "The Computer as a Learning Environment for Foreign Language Instruction." *Foreign Language Annals* 2(1969):457–63.

66 Ruplin, Ferdinand, and John R. Russell. "Towards Structured Foreign Language Study:An Integrated German Course." *Modern Language Journal* 54(1970):175–83.

67 Schmidtlein, Josef. "Unterrichtliche Erfahrungen mit Tb 185 »Zeit der Schuldlosen« von Siegfried Lenz." *Film Bild Ton* 19(April 1969):17–22.

68 Sculthorpe, Mabel A.L. "Language Centres and Language Services in the Universities." [Paper available from author, University of Kent, Canterbury, England.]

69 Sheehan, Joseph H. "Television," 99–112 in Mills F. Edgerton,Jr.,ed., *Sight and Sound:The Sensible and Sensitive Use of Audio-Visual Aids.* Reports of the Working Committees of the Northeast Conference on the Teaching of Foreign Languages. New York: MLA Materials Center, 1969.

70 ——— and Robert Willis. "Demonstration of the Use of Television in the Training of Foreign Language Teachers," 109–12 in Mills F. Edgerton, Jr.,ed., *Sight and Sound:The Sensible and Sensitive Use of Audio-Visual Aids.* Reports of the Working Committees of the Northeast Conference on the Teaching of Foreign Languages. New York: MLA Materials Center, 1969.

71 Shryer, Margaret S. "Using Taped Material in Studying Goethe's *Faust* in High School.A Slide-Tape Demonstration," 46–49 in Mills F. Edgerton,Jr.,ed., *Sight and Sound:The Sensible and Sensitive Use of Audio-Visual Aids.* Reports of the Working Committees of the Northeast Conference on the Teaching of Foreign Languages. New York: MLA Materials Center, 1969.

72 Silverman, Marvin L. "Film-Making in the Classroom." *Journal of Secondary Education* 45(1970):106–12.

73 Smith, David G. "Contextualisation:Towards a More Precise Definition." *Audio-Visual Language Journal* 7(1970):147–52.

74 Smith, Philip D.,Jr. "An Assessment of Three Foreign Language Teaching Strategies and Three Language Laboratory Systems." *French Review* 43(1969):289–304.

75 Smither, William J., and William L. Woods. *An Experimental Restructuring of the Undergraduate Foreign Language Curriculum with Supporting Research in Teaching Techniques.* Project No. 8941, National Defense Education Act, Title VI. New Orleans: Tulane Univ., 1963.

76 Suppes, Patrick, and Max Jerman. "Computer-Assisted Instruction." *National Association of Secondary School Principals Bulletin* 54,343(1970):27–40.

77 Svobodny, Dolly D. *Research and Studies About the Use of Television and Film in Foreign Language Instruction:A Bibliography with Abstracts.* New York: MLA/ERIC, 1969.

78 Sweet, Waldo. "Integrating Other Media with Programmed Instruction." *Modern Language Journal* 52(1968):420–23.

79 Thompson, Keith K., and Ann Waterhouse. "The Time-Shared Computer:A Teaching Tool." *National Association of Secondary School Principals Bulletin* 54,343(1970):91–98.

80 Trump, J. Lloyd. "The Educational Setting for the Language Laboratory." *International Journal of American Linguistics* 28,i,part 2(1962): 124–30.

81 Valdman, Albert. "Programmed Instruction versus Guided Learning in Foreign Language Acquisition." *Unterrichtspraxis* 1,i(1968):1–14.

82 Valette, Rebecca. "The Pennsylvania Project, Its Conclusions and Its Implications." *Modern Language Journal* 53(1969):396–404.

83 Walter, James,et al. "Project COMBAT." *Oregon Education* (16–18 December), 1969 [Reprint].

84 Walton, Wesley W. "Computers in the Classroom: Master or Servant?" *National Association of Secondary School Principals Bulletin* 54,343 (1970):9–17.

85 Wrenn, James J. "The Overhead Projector," 66–82 in Mills F. Edgerton,Jr.,ed., *Sight and Sound: The Sensible and Sensitive Use of Audio-Visual Aids.* Reports of the Working Committees of the Northeast Conference on the Teaching of Foreign Languages. New York: MLA Materials Center, 1969.

8

Language learning laboratory

Introduction

W. Flint Smith
Purdue University

The scope of this chapter is limited to a discussion of articles from professional journals, monographs, research reports, surveys, and similar sources published in 1969 and dealing with the language laboratory or other laboratory-like media used in foreign language instruction. Occasional citations of studies reported in 1968 or earlier have been included where necessary. Three major topics are offered: language laboratory research, including a summary of the reviews of the Pennsylvania Project; tutorial, machine-aided language learning; and innovative equipment. References to television, film-based teaching, and the like have been omitted unless they relate specifically to the language laboratory concept. The focus of the studies reviewed is not so much on the media as on the learning that can derive from their use; thus, the title "Language Learning Laboratory," first used by Jalling (50), should be understood as an inclusive rubric intended to stress the potential for individualization of instruction inherent in a machine-aided learning environment.

Scope of the chapter

Jalling has noted that the international debate on the effectiveness of tape-guided practice has always cited the opportunity for individualized learning as one of its unquestionable advantages. Yet, it is obvious from a reading of the literature that the primary debate, at least in the United States, has focused too much on equipment and only secondarily upon learner activity. This same lack of concern for the student plagued the potential of programmed learning early in this decade and contributed to the demise of scores of manufacturers of teaching machines and to the frustrations of many who toiled to make programming an efficient means of meeting the individual needs of the learner.

The recent years have seen much professional neglect and misuse of the language laboratory. Much of the investment in machine-aided learning has been undertaken on faith, for carefully controlled research has not been profuse (Carroll, 18; Hocking & Smith, 47; Torkelson & Driscoll, 88). There has been a similar misunderstanding of the role of the laboratory by the

Professional neglect and lack of research

public at large (Hedger, 44). Although about one school in four has a laboratory of some type, at least two studies (Crossman, 25; Rhodes, 68) reported that maintenance of equipment is still a fundamental problem and that few high schools use the lab as frequently as twenty minutes per day. Even though teachers tend to rate themselves as having above-average knowledge and training in the use of audiovisual media (Hallman, 41), a survey of lab usage in higher education revealed that effective utilization of the language laboratory is still a paramount problem. Many junior colleges have laboratories, but the question of what to do with them is not clear (Poirier, 63). In the universities there is unanimous agreement that the laboratories should be used to individualize instruction, but although educational technology is viewed favorably, the acceptance and utilization of its basic tenets is too often missing (Esseff, 29). Generally speaking, there has been a drastic and dramatic decline in funds for laboratory hardware at all levels of education; correspondingly, there has been an increase in expenditures for equipment and materials for tutorial and individualized instruction (cassette tape recorders and prerecorded tape programs) as can be seen in the data in Figure 1 compiled by an independent market advisory and research firm (20).

The year 1969 will be remembered as one in which professional and popular interest in machine-guided learning received more attention than at any time since the last Purdue-Indiana University Conference on the language laboratory in 1965. Professional action was found on several fronts. First, the National Association of Language Laboratory Directors *Newsletter* achieved full status as a *Journal* (*NALLDJ*). Now published quarterly, the scope of NALLD *Journal* underscores a conviction by media specialists and educators that machine-aided learning can prove efficient and beneficial to the language student (Dodge, 26). Its pages include articles dealing with the entire range of language instruction mediated by equipment and, in addition, there is a sounding board for ideas and reviews of materials. The NALLD *Journal*, in combination with the sections on "Methods" and "Equipment" in the Annual Bibliography (Lange, 53,54) of the American Council on the Teaching of Foreign Languages (ACTFL), presents a means by which the professional and the practitioner can keep abreast of innovative classroom and laboratory techniques in language teaching, new equipment specifications, and the results of relevant research.

Machine-guided learning an 1969

192

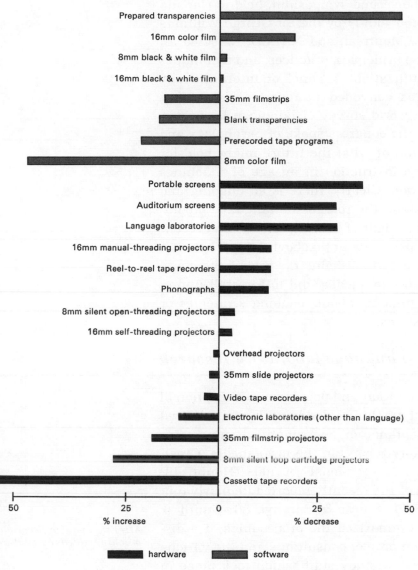

| hardware | software |

FIGURE 1. Audiovisual equipment in schools; % change 1968–69 vs. 1969–70.

Two important conferences involving media in language learning were held in 1969–70, one national, the other reflecting worldwide orientation. On the national level, "Sight and Sound: The Sensible and Sensitive Use of Audio-Visual Aids" was the theme of the Northeast Conference on the Teaching of Foreign Languages, in which many types of hardware and software from nonprojected visuals to audio tapes and television were probed, discussed, and exemplified in detail for the classroom

Important conferences

193

teacher (Edgerton, 28). The second symposium, held in Canada early in 1970 and sponsored jointly by the Sir George Williams University, l'Université de Montréal, and NALLD, reflected an international interest in the principles, practices, and techniques of language laboratory utilization. A panel of internationally recognized authorities was convened to report on the facts, figures, and findings of a world survey of language laboratory usage. Other members of the congress spoke of psychology and the language laboratory and of what the future might hold for mediated foreign language instruction in an age of machines and increasing specialization. Clearly, there is an ongoing and serious attempt to understand the role of the language laboratory and its related media in light of past experience and recent findings in education and psychology (Jakobovits, 49). There is a corresponding dedication to further define the role of the classroom teacher in relation to new media, and to forestall unproductive and polarized arguments about teaching strategies or mediated instructional systems.

Language laboratory research

That there is some polarization and popular misconception of the values and functions of machine-aided learning is evidenced by the rapid popular acceptance of oversimplified summaries and sometimes inflammatory reports in the news media (Gross, 39; Rafferty, 66) and some professional journals (Houpt, 48) with respect to the results of the recently reported Pennsylvania study (Smith, 75,76,77,78,79; Smith & Baranyi, 80; Smith & Berger, 81). Martin (56) summarized the proceedings of a discussion conference between project consultants and the various members of the Pennsylvania study staff which took place in early 1969. The participants noted that the information on the language laboratory had received wider attention than any other aspect of the study, but many felt that the conclusions and recommendations drawn were very vulnerable and open to criticism. It will be the purpose of this section to interpret the results of the Pennsylvania study dealing with the language laboratory and to draw together the conclusions from the various substantive reviews it has generated in an attempt to end further popular misunderstanding of this important longitudinal study. First, however, it will be instructive to delineate the scope of the Pennsylvania Project and to briefly summarize its findings, with par-

Attention paid to research in machine-aided instruction

ticular attention being paid to the role of the language laboratory evaluation within the project as a whole.

Overview of the Pennsylvania Project

The Pennsylvania study had as its major focus an *in situ* evaluation of three foreign language teaching strategies for beginning high school French and German ("traditional," "functional skills," "functional skills with grammar") and three language laboratory systems ("audio-active," "audio-active record," "tape recorder in classroom"). The study was begun in 1965, quite simply, to provide empirical support to popular acceptance of the audiolingual or functional-skills methodology and to further validate the widespread assumption that the language laboratory helps the student assimilate language patterns more efficiently. The three teaching strategies were defined as follows: (1) "Traditional" used textbooks and techniques which reflected an emphasis on general vocabulary acquisition, the reading and writing skills, translation, grammatical analysis and memorization of paradigms. (2) "Functional skills" reflected an audiolingual approach whose representative textbooks and related media stressed the control of a limited vocabulary and fundamental language structures. Emphasis was first placed on speaking and understanding and secondarily on reading and writing. (3) "Functional skills plus grammar" used the essential elements of (2), above, but included the use of grammatical explanations as a supplement to regular audiolingual procedures. The language laboratory systems which complemented the "functional skills" and "functional skills plus grammar" strategies utilized the equipment as follows: (1) "Audio-active" students received 2 25-minute practice sessions each week during which a 10-minute drill tape was played twice. (2) "Audio-active record" students attended 2 25-minute laboratory sessions each week in which they recorded responses to a 10-minute drill tape during the first half of the period and listened to them played back during the second half. In addition to lab practice, all "audio-active" and "audio-active record" groups were to receive guided practice via a tape recorder in the classroom during one fifth of each class period. (3) "Tape recorder in classroom" students received tape-guided practice in their normal classroom for at least 10 minutes of each period, but had no laboratory practice as such. Table 1 summarizes these arrangements. A tape recorder was also present in each "traditionally" taught class, but the teachers

A description of the Pennsylvania studies

195

were carefully and clearly instructed *not* to use it systematically; nor were they to use lab tapes or discs.

Beyond assessment of the effectiveness of strategies and systems, an additional objective of the investigation was to determine which combination of method and equipment would be the most efficacious for learning. Among other variables studied were student and teacher attitudes, teacher proficiency, and the

TABLE 1. Pennsylvania Project: teaching strategies and laboratory systems for Level I and Level II classes.

Traditional	X		
	Tape recorder in classroom	Audio-active laboratory	Record-playback laboratory
Functional skills	X	X	X
Functional skills plus grammar	X	X	X

relationship of each to achievement. The investigation was designed to evaluate these institutions under *typical* rather than optimum conditions in the American secondary school. Since the sample was quite large (over one hundred *classes* in the first-year study) and the design of the experiment exemplary, the outcomes can truly be interpreted as reflecting how well secondary school students typically learn foreign languages in the real world and how media are typically brought to bear in the process. It is important to keep in mind the overall length of the Pennsylvania investigation, for it is unique in its attempt to assess the impact of given language curricula over a four-year period. Table 2 summarizes the chronology of the project.

Variables beyond strategies a learning systems

TABLE 2. Chronology of the Pennsylvania Project.

Project number	Level	Number of students	Year	Reported
5-0683	I	N = 2171	1965–66	Jan. 1968
7-0133	I*	N = 639	1966–67	Oct. 1968
	II	N = 1090	1966–67	Oct. 1968
7-0133†	III	N = 277	1967–68	Aug. 1969
	IV	N = 144	1968–69	Aug. 1969

*replication.
†supplement.

Results

After the first year of study (1965–66) the Pennsylvania Project staff was able to report that there were no significant differences among the respective strategies on any skill except reading, where the "traditional" classes performed significantly better than the "functional skills" classes as measured by the standardized MLA Cooperative tests. No significant differences were observed among the laboratory systems with respect to their relative impact on achievement; the few that did obtain were judged to be random. No optimum strategy-system combination could be detected in the experimental population. Students achieved most in the "traditional strategy" despite individual differences in ability. Initial attitude toward language study was found to be unrelated to later achievement, as were teacher proficiency scores (Smith, 81). Analyses of the data from the replication study and the comparisons undertaken at level II (1966–67) yielded the same results with respect to the effectiveness of the various strategies and media; "traditional" methodology excelled in the "graphic" skills and was as good as "functional-skill" methodology in listening and speaking. The language lab seemed to have no effect on achievement (Smith, 77). Observed after still a third (1967–68) and, in some cases, a fourth year (1968–69) (Smith, 76), "traditional" students performed significantly better than their audiolingual counterparts in both listening and reading achievement, but no influence of prior laboratory experience could be inferred from the data. The results of the comparisons, which were contrary to the expectations of many who had placed much faith and effort in the audiolingual approach and machine-aided learning, have caused a predictable reaction from the profession at large.

Results of strategies and learning systems

The MLJ Symposium

Roeming (70) invited members of the profession to review the voluminous results of the Pennsylvania study in the hope of providing an objective and responsible comment on the investigation as a whole, and in doing so to avoid confusion of the type that surrounded attempts to correct the record after the publication of the Keating Report early in this decade. Roeming noted that confusion was not avoided but felt that the Pennsylvania Project, in the long run, would have far greater impact in aiding the foreign language teaching profession in determining the qualities and limitations of classroom research than in understanding the effectiveness of specific teaching strategies or laboratory systems. Part of the inevitable confusion and controversy is an outgrowth of the review articles themselves, since their authors, at times, overlooked the eighteen months to two years that had elapsed between the inception and reporting of the study; as a result some reviewers introduced criticism based upon literature, techniques, or criteria published *after* the design and implementation had been determined (Smith, 79).

Clark (23) and Aleamoni & Spencer (4) commented on the overall specific merits and shortcomings of the experimental design for the symposium, as did elsewhere Carroll (19) and Wiley (94) for MLA/ERIC on behalf of ACTFL. Independent reviews were offered by Birkmaier & Lange (11), Houpt (48), and Marxheimer (57). For additional bibliography see (5), Martin (56), a supplement to the Report (76), and Valette (92). Valette (91) further reviewed the relative efficacy of the criterion measures used in relation to the vocabulary content of the respective representative textbooks. Otto (61) commented upon the teacher, the school, and the supervisory variables as did Hocking (45), who also reviewed the training for the use of the language laboratory systems. The paragraphs which follow are a compendium of some factors which, in the opinion of these reviewers and others, invalidated any unqualified generalization of the results to schools not included in the experimental population.

Comments on the experiment[al] design

Self-selection of language lab groups

Clark (23) has noted that the Pennsylvania study attempted to control extraneous teacher, student, and school variables through the random assignment of participating schools to one of the combinations of methodology and laboratory systems. In doing so, however, the general requirement that each participating school have a language lab was "overlooked" with reference to the "traditional" groups. This would suggest that schools not having a laboratory but desiring to participate in the project could only have been assigned to the "traditional" strategy. And, if better schools tended to have language laboratory installations, then their assignment to "functional skills" and "functional skills plus grammar" groups might have weighted the school variable (e.g., possession of a language laboratory) differentially among the treatment groups. One probably should not, therefore, extrapolate the "no significant differences" of laboratory

Factor 1: Random assignmen[t] — truly random?

198

effectiveness to all schools, since the initial random assignment was random only within the limits of the self-selected sample.

Criterion measures

A second factor contributing to the nonsignificant differences among the laboratory strategies may have been the overall inappropriateness of the criterion measures available to the investigation (MLA Cooperative Classroom tests) to assess speaking ability and listening comprehension. On the one hand, the ratio of vocabulary between text and test favored the "traditional classes" two-to-one over the audiolingual classes (Valette, 91). On the other hand, the level of difficulty of the listening comprehension and speaking tests proved too hard at the end of the first year for both strategies and systems, and they were only marginally appropriate at the end of the second year, for, on the average, students scored only five to seven points above chance. Smith (76) further noted that the MLA listening and reading tests (Form M) proved to be still too hard for most students even after three full years of foreign language study. Thus, Valette concluded that the contemporary standardized tests failed to demonstrate the significance of any strategy except in the area of reading. Valette further observed that in reading, given the supposed advantages of more vocabulary and the greater number of textbook lessons completed by the "traditional" classes, the "traditional" students actually did much more poorly than one would have anticipated. For example, in comparing the upper five percent of the "traditional" and "audiolingual" classes on the French listening test (Form L) administered at the end of the first year, Valette found that the vocabulary advantage did not help the better "traditional" students; that is, the better students in the audiolingual-oriented classes obtained the higher listening scores. Therefore, the relative insensitivity of the criterion measures may be one reason why the differences between the various laboratory groups were not more pronounced.

Factor 2: The evaluative instruments

Laboratory use

If the outcomes of the analyses of differences in methodologies were not affected by the use of various laboratory systems, then the manner in which the equipment configurations were actually used within the context of the Pennsylvania study becomes a third extremely important factor in understanding the relative effectiveness or ineffectiveness of machine-aided learn-

Factor 3: How were the labs used?

ing. Thus, it is important to know that the teachers were instructed to use the language laboratory in a "lockstep" fashion within two weekly, tape-guided practice sessions. One drill tape was played to the entire laboratory for simultaneous, choral response. There was no use of different tapes for correspondingly different groups of students (Martin, 56). Since the teacher was directed not to individualize instruction in the laboratory (in an attempt to emulate common usage of this media in other schools) it is not surprising that no significant differences were found among the respective systems (Valette, 91). In other words, if the language laboratory is used like a single tape recorder in transmitting a single recorded program to an entire class, it is unlikely that any discernible differences in achievement will be found between students who receive machine-aided practice in a specially equipped room and those who practice similarly via a classroom tape recorder.

On the other hand, the students in the "functional skills" and "functional skills plus grammar" classes were to receive 10 minutes of tape-guided practice each day in the classroom in addition to the 2 prescribed weekly practice sessions. These students had a potential of 100 minutes of practice each week: 2 25-minute massed sessions, and 5 10-minute distributed sessions (Smith, 76). However, the "functional skills" and the "functional skills plus grammar" classes assigned to the "tape recorder in classroom" lab system had only 50 minutes potential each week. From the standpoint of time alone, one would expect the groups having more practice to have a correspondingly higher achievement. Although the data supported this expectation to a degree in listening comprehension and speaking ability after one year of study, there were no significant differences or trends. One must, therefore, look to teacher adherence to the guidelines set by the investigators in attempting to further understand this apparent anomaly.

Teacher adherence

Teacher adherence to the guidelines relevant to each strategy and system becomes a fourth important factor in interpreting the effectiveness of the language laboratory and related media. The participating teachers in the Pennsylvania study received training in the use of the language laboratory in a week-long pre-experimental workshop and three interim sessions which were designed to orient them to the scope and content of the

Factor 4: How effective were teachers with the strategies, labs, and systems?

overall study. Each participant was then visited by a project supervisor several times over the school year and was rated on his adherence to the respective strategy and system combination. Yet the reported ratings invariably reflected only how the teachers performed in the classroom; thus, while the ratings show, on the average, that the "functional skills" and "functional skills plus grammar" students received tape-guided practice in their *classrooms* with a good deal of regularity, the corresponding adherence to the structure and the use of the language *laboratory* was apparently not assessed (Hocking, 45). Moreover, no accounting was made of the *time* the equipment was actually used, and thus one cannot gauge how effectively the labs were applied within the prescribed class-lab schedule; nor was a time analysis undertaken on the use of the classroom recorders. This problem is further compounded since the rating scales were somewhat different for the "traditional" and "audiolingual" strategies and systems, making it impossible to determine directly whether the use of the equipment between the respective methodologies was, in fact, distinct. In short, the seriousness with which the teacher applied the laboratory equipment cannot be estimated from the reports. As a result, the only valid conclusion to be drawn is that students in "language laboratory" systems received more *time* for guided practice than students in "tape recorder in classroom" systems. The added time factor was not significant in bringing about increased achievement in speaking and listening comprehension. Since both the taped materials and their application were dictated by the project guidelines, one can only conclude that it was the structure of the laboratory materials and the mechanical way in which they were used that contributed heavily to the lack of significant differences among the respective groups.

Laboratory grades

A fifth factor related to laboratory use and teacher adherence to strategy is the fact that the investigation did not specify the relative weight or contribution of laboratory performance to six-week or final grades (Smith, 76). Therefore, the seriousness with which students confronted their weekly practice sessions must remain suspect. Lab grades are an elementary but effective extrinsic motivator of student performance; yet this particular technique of encouraging the student to pay close attention to the task was ignored, or at best, uncontrolled.

Factor 5: Lab grades, an effective technique?

Hocking (45) commented that some of the audio-active record laboratories were not separate labs at all; that is, they were parts of laboratory systems that were otherwise audio-active. Nevertheless, they were scored and tabulated separately. Whether the simultaneous, separate, and unequal activities in the laboratory sessions were a deterrent to the investigation is probably a moot point; a small-scale study at Purdue (Hocking, 46) found no differences in achievement among groups divided in a similar manner. More important is the unimaginative usage prescribed by the project: visuals were optional, as were lab quizzes and, presumably, listening comprehension exercises. The students were monitored, but primarily as a means of "keeping order" rather than to provide cogent, individualized correction or corroboration.

Laboratory maintenance

Hocking (45) pointed out, as Martin (56) did elsewhere, that the condition of the language laboratories in the participating schools was not specified. The fact that apparently no quality control or maintenance was required meant that only one school in two had qualified laboratory technicians to maintain the equipment and that only one laboratory in three received periodic servicing (Smith, 75,76). Approximately half of the labs were inoperative ten percent or more of the time during the school year (Smith, 76). Since extremely good models of representative speech are necessary in dialogues, narratives, or pattern drills before the uninitiated student can be expected to decode, encode, repeat, or transform their respective elements, the lack of prescribed preventive maintenance and specification of conditions of the laboratories must be considered a sixth factor detrimental to the unqualified application of the conclusions to other schools.

Factor 6: How well were the labs maintained?

While the general observation by Smith & Berger (81) at the conclusion of the first year of the study that "a more careful and sound policy of language laboratory administration and maintenance [needs to] be immediately initiated" is tenable and justifiable, the corresponding recommendation that "secondary schools should provide a classroom tape recorder for each foreign language classroom for daily use before equipping special electronic classrooms" must be interpreted with the greatest of care. Such a statement will be understood by some to mean that "the language laboratory is no good," and this is completely contrary to the best intentions of the Pennsylvania Project staff. A more balanced viewpoint of the role of the laboratory was presented by Smith & Baranyi (80) at the end of the second year of the investigation and by Smith in a supplementary report published in 1969 (76). The authors reiterated the importance of the classroom tape recorder but tempered their recommendation for the laboratories to read "future educational planning [should] envision the language laboratory in terms of individualized practice in addition to regular classroom instruction rather than as a type of classroom activity." This observation more truly reflected the outcomes of the laboratory aspect of the investigation. It would be patently dangerous, however, to extrapolate from these conclusions that all language laboratories and electronic classrooms are ineffective adjuncts to second language learning. *Machines are machines and nothing more. It is how they are used that counts.* The appropriate software, and to some extent good hardware, were lacking in the Pennsylvania schools, and the results thus were predictable from the beginning.

A "balanced" viewpoint on the role of the language lab

MLA/ERIC and ACTFL analyses

Wiley's methodological review (94) and Carroll's analysis (19) of some of the Pennsylvania data from the first two years of the project shed additional light upon the results of the study. Wiley noted that from the significant initial differences between randomly and nonrandomly assigned audio-active groups, one could infer the existence of social class differences in the communities in which schools were located; one might further conclude that the presence or absence of a language laboratory could be associated with these variables. Thus, if the schools assigned to the "traditional" groups did not have language laboratories but the "functional skills" groups did, any comparisons undertaken would reflect this bias. Since, on the basis of these initial differences, the nonrandomly assigned laboratory groups were dropped by the experimenters from all further analyses regarding systems, the bias to which Wiley referred is probably not an important one as far as the results are concerned. But it does reflect the fact that the assignment of experimental units to the treatment conditions was accomplished only on a partially random basis, and one wonders just how "typical" the language laboratory installations really were. Wiley further cautioned that, taken overall, the findings of the study should be regarded carefully. Although few or no detectable differences were found among strategies or systems, there may have been *true* differences which were too small to detect with the available tests and analytical techniques.

Stowaway variables

Carroll (19) described the presence of a "stowaway variable" (one whose presence is not noted in the design of an experiment but whose effects are disclosed upon later analysis) and commented that too much similarity of the textual materials may have been a variable of this type in the Pennsylvania study. The lack of differentiation among textual materials was by extension also characteristic of the taped audio programs. Hence, the laboratory tapes may be considered a second "stowaway variable" for the audiolingual classes, since they effectively complemented a reduced emphasis on quantity (vocabulary) and a corresponding increased emphasis on repetition, substitution, and transformation of a limited number of basic language structures. One can conclude, perhaps, that time should not be taken away from classroom interaction for the presentation of mechanical noncontextual drills. But since some mechanical drill is necessary, and since most high school schedules do not allow for periods of individual and independent drill, in-class methodology must be more efficiently arranged.

Practice effects

Carroll (19) also summarized several reanalyses of the results from the first two years in which more powerful statistical procedures were applied to the data. Table 3 lists the portions of these analyses that deal with the three laboratory systems as applied to both "functional skills" and "functional skills plus grammar" strategies for the first year. The more stringent analyses still revealed no significant differences among laboratory systems. It is interesting to note, however, a trend with regard to the listening comprehension scores shown in Table 3.

In three of four cases, the adjusted mean scores of the audioactive record groups were the highest among the three equipment groups; apparently, activities involving the recording and playing back of utterances were marginally instrumental in developing the students' ability to understand the spoken word. Just why the same trend is absent for the speaking achievement scores, however, is not clear, given the mutual interdependency

TABLE 3. Analyses of variance and covariance, MLAT and criterion tests.

System	Number of classes	Means		
		(Covariate) MLAT	Listening (adjusted)	Speaking (adjusted)
Functional skills plus grammar classes only				
French				
Tape recorder	3	47.97	21.82	15.55
Audio-active	12	46.04	25.07	14.63
Audio-active record	8	44.84	24.95	13.93
Within-group r		—	0.266	0.655
F-ratio		0.14	0.20	0.40
P		n.s.	n.s.	n.s.
German				
Tape recorder	5	43.74	23.37	14.35
Audio-active	9	48.22	20.59	15.09
Audio-active record	4	46.26	23.86	14.89
Within-group r		—	0.087	0.126
F-ratio		0.28	0.12	0.14
P		n.s.	n.s.	n.s.
Functional skills classes only				
French				
Tape recorder	3	44.28	29.54	15.60
Audio-active	15	49.90	28.21	15.40
Audio-active record	7	49.39	31.19	14.60
Within-group r		—	0.421	0.309
F-ratio		0.72	0.26	0.22
P		n.s.	n.s.	n.s.
German				
Tape recorder	4	45.91	25.65	15.89
Audio-active	10	48.30	18.26	14.63
Audio-active record	5	43.11	27.80	17.48
Within-group r		—	0.012	0.375
F-ratio		0.65	1.49	1.53
P		n.s.	n.s.	n.s.

of these two skills. This apparent anomaly may be related to the fact that the audio-active record students spent only between 25 and 30% of their time actively responding to taped drills. That is, in response to a single four-phase pattern recorded and played back once (stimulus, response, confirmation, response), the student will generally speak but twice during the recording phase: once in response to the initial stimulus and again in repetition of a corroboration or correction. When he plays back his effort, he typically does not correct and rerecord his responses; rather, he tends to *listen* to both the original stimulus and his recorded response. Thus, while he will listen to a total of eight utterances, he will have spoken only on two occasions. The quantity of practice in listening comprehension rapidly increases as a function of the number of patterns the student hears on the taped program. An added practice effect presumably would not exist in an audio-active laboratory or classroom, since students receiving tape-guided practice would actively respond to auditory stimuli 50% of the time, or almost twice as much as their record-playback counterparts. Therefore, one might reasonably expect that speaking scores for the audio-active or the tape recorder in classroom groups would be somewhat higher than for the record-playback group due solely to an added practice effect. This observation is supported partially in three of the four comparisons in the analyses reported by Carroll. On the other hand, Valette (91) observed that the "traditional" students tended to score higher on the "critical sounds" portion of the speaking tests, where the student read aloud an unfamiliar passage and was graded on his pronunciation of certain items. Since the "audiolingual" students read only recombinations of familiar material while the "traditional" students were quite accustomed to reading unfamiliar narratives, the results are again probably an artifact of practice rather than a true estimate of the differences between the systems and the strategy effectiveness.

Practice effects especially on listening

Carroll's exhaustive review of the major aspects of the study (19) led him to six conclusions with respect to the laboratory: First, "the findings with regard to the teaching strategies and laboratory systems are sufficiently solid and replicable to prompt us to rethink both methods and objectives of foreign language teaching." Second, Carroll counselled that although the language laboratory systems as used in conjunction with certain audiolingual texts did not produce the expected facility in oral language skills, one should not abandon language laboratories in secondary school language instruction any more than one should drop all spoken language objectives and go back to "traditional" language methodology (in the older sense of the term). Third, Carroll commented that the study does not reveal what might have happened if machine-aided learning had been used extensively in conjunction with the "traditional" textbooks. Fourth, the investigation does not reveal the degree of interaction between teacher proficiency and the language laboratory; in fact, the teachers' collective expertise seems to have overshadowed any differences which may have arisen from teaching method or language laboratory. Fifth, teachers more proficient in oral language skills tended to teach in the audiolingual classes;

Carroll's six conclusions abo the Pennsylvania studies

206

for that reason, it is possible that the language laboratory equipment and corresponding materials did not have an opportunity to compensate for imperfect oral language skills of less proficient teachers. Finally, Carroll advised that since language practice tapes generally emphasize habit formation rather than the transmission of content, it is possible that current lab materials actually *retard* learning, especially when they are used only to drill and review material already presented in class.

Pennsylvania in perspective

In reviewing the great amount of literature generated by the Pennsylvania Project, one cannot help but formulate an overall opinion about the investigation itself and the conclusions drawn by various other sources. First, and most important, the consumer of this review must keep the Pennsylvania study in its proper perspective. There is no doubt that this longitudinal investigation is one of the most important pieces of research in language instruction in the last ten years, not only from the standpoint of its "textbook research design" and emulation of the typical secondary school foreign language curriculum, but also from the shock effect the results have had on the language teaching profession as a whole. Second, the results of the Pennsylvania study have far-reaching potential when interpreted cautiously and with proper qualification: strategies need to be modified; systems need to be implemented with greater creativity. Decisions must be made to carry these changes forward. This need was revealed dramatically in the responses to a follow-up questionnaire administered by the Pennsylvania staff in 1968 to assess the extent to which the results of the research project had changed the schools' language curriculum and use of the language laboratory (Smith, 76). More than half of the respondents indicated the lab *still* was being used in either one or two half-period sessions per week despite the fact that the investigation had revealed this paradigm to be inefficient and to have little effect on achievement. Finally, one must not look upon the Pennsylvania study as "Peck's bad boy" simply because it came out "wrong" (i.e., contrary to the expectations of the majority), for in the long run it is bound to have a lasting and positive effect on foreign language curricula, methods, and media.

Over a decade has elapsed since the National Defense Education Act (NDEA) was passed by Congress. In the interim hundreds of language teachers have been trained and retrained

Important points to remember in terms of the Pennsylvania studies

in NDEA year-long and summer institutes. Second-generation "audiolingual" and third-generation "traditional" textbooks and materials have appeared, neither as polarized in its respective methodology as was the case early in the sixties. We have learned more of what media can and cannot do for the learner. We have discovered the ills of fixed periods and split schedules. Advances have been made in techniques and in equipment application. To say these past 13 years have been fruitless ignores the growing camaraderie among teachers, increased enrollments, and more and better materials. If many teachers in the sixties were complacent in their acceptance of the tenets of fundamental skill methodology and its shining accouterment, it was because language teaching and language learning had taken on a vibrant and meaningful existence. The Pennsylvania studies have removed us from our tower of false security. It is time to meet the challenge of a new decade.

The real challenge

Small-scale research projects

Several small-scale research projects reported in 1969 yielded interesting information about the potentialities of machine-aided second language learning. Two of these will be considered in some detail, since an understanding of their procedures and results is important in putting them in perspective and in interpreting their outcomes for the classroom situation.

Senior high school study

Smith (83) and Smith & Hocking (84,85), reporting on the same study, investigated the patterns of use and the consequent effectiveness of equipment for tape-guided practice installed within the language classroom (electronic classroom) and in the language laboratory in a senior high school.

Smith explained the rationale of the electronic classroom as follows: (1) it is inexpensive and easy to maintain; (2) it uses already existing space; (3) it is immediately accessible and offers a better chance for frequent and intensive tape-guided practice. Language laboratories are contrasted with the electronic classroom installation in that (1) they are installed in a room apart from the normal classroom; (2) they are expensive to install and costly to maintain; (3) their accessibility depends upon a prescribed schedule and therefore necessitates practice massed in longer units of time.

Rationale for an electronic classroom or a language lab

The electronic classroom (EC) studied by Smith was "wired" as opposed to "wireless." The students had no special booths or tape recorders, but there were audio-active headsets and microphones available at each desk. For the teacher there was a console and monitor intercommunication switches. All of the equipment for the student was retractable to the ceiling. The electronic classroom was therefore immediately convertible for supervised tape-guided practice or for other subject-matter instruction. Language laboratories of two types were also used: record-playback (RP) and audio-active (AA). These three equipment groups (EC, RP, AA) and a control group in each of three languages, French, German and Spanish, formed the basic units of the investigation. Seventy-five minutes per week of normal class time were allotted to machine-guided practice. In the EC groups the teachers distributed practice as they saw fit; in the language lab groups, practice was massed either in 2 35- or 3 25-minute periods. Within each language the instructional materials were identical.

The "W. F. Smith" study

Frequency of use. After one year of instruction, various analyses yielded the following information about the frequency of use: (*1*) the greater accessibility of the electronic classroom equipment did not lead to its greater use; (*2*) median use of the equipment irrespective of equipment group was less than 40 minutes per week; (*3*) the record-playback equipment was used most of all, the electronic classroom the least.

Equipment group effectiveness. The achievement of the respective groups, including that of the control, was assessed with interim tests and the end-of-term Pimsleur Language Proficiency Tests (Form A). The results, evaluated with analyses of covariance, indicated the following: (*1*) In speaking, the record-playback groups scored significantly higher than their control counterparts, although only marginally so. (2) In listening, no statistically significant differences could be detected among the respective groups except in French, where the electronic classroom achieved more than its control counterpart. (3) In reading, marginal significant differences were found favoring the record-playback equipment group over the control for German. (4) No significant differences among groups in the listening and reading skills could be detected from the interim tests, although there was a slight trend toward the record-playback students. Factorial analyses of variance by aptitude and intelligence indicated that there were essentially no significant interactions between these variables and any of the equipment or control groups. The few instances of significance that occurred were for the interim unit tests and these tests were of questionable reliability due to their small number of items.

Conclusions. Although an uncontrolled teacher variable limits the extent to which one may generalize from the Smith study (83) in the strictest sense of the word, the following conclusions seem tenable and applicable to situations where equivalent media are used in language instruction: (1) Excessively truncated or short periods of tape-guided practice may be detrimental to learning. Practice exercise periods should be long enough in addition to being frequent enough to allow the student to gain a meaningful degree of concentration. (2) Generally speaking, the record-playback laboratory, the audio-active laboratory, and the electronic classroom have only marginal effects on achievement when used twice weekly for group choral response. Of the three types of equipment, record-playback has the greater potential for contributing to achievement, audio-active the least. (3) First year language students will probably profit more in terms of total learning if at least a part of their guided-practice session includes the opportunity to record and play back responses. Alternatively, if group choral work is the mode most commonly used, the largest gains may be in auditory comprehension rather than speaking skill, due to the added listening practice afforded in playing back utterances for comparison. Finally, Smith concluded that the best of all equipment installations for the secondary school might prove to be a judicious combination of electronic classrooms and language laboratories, the former for tape-guided classroom practice and the latter for individual study and preparation of taped auditory homework assignments.

Important conclusions for the teacher

Classroom Laboratory Instructional System

Banathy & Jordan (8) reported the results of a longitudinal study including several experiments which investigated the use of a unique Classroom Laboratory Instructional System (CLIS). The purpose of CLIS was to transmit to the learner a greater quantity of well-organized instructional materials than is ordinarily possible in the normal classroom situation. The overriding purpose of CLIS was to increase first the student's overall active participation and ultimately his total language proficiency. The electronic media utilized were similar in function and concept to the electronic classroom described by Smith, above. The materi-

An integrated media and materials program

als were quite different, however. Designed for intensive language instruction (over 180 hours of contact in 6 weeks), they were semiprogrammed exercises comprising at least half of the instructional programs for students of the West Coast Defense Language Institute. Both media and materials were integrated via a composite set of learning experiences which, taken together, formed a well-planned, integrated system. Comparisons of the reading and listening proficiency scores of students who graduated before and after the introduction of the mediated instructional system revealed that those who graduated after the inception of CLIS consistently outperformed their pre-CLIS counterparts. It was obvious that the combination of the teacher, the instructional experience, and the media was instrumental in bringing about superior achievement. The following paragraphs will describe the outcomes and recommendations from the CLIS project in an attempt to transfer the elements of success of this intensive language program to the instructional techniques of beginning classes in schools and colleges.

Guided instruction. The objectives, learning tasks, content, and materials were identical for the CLIS and the non-CLIS groups described by Banathy & Jordan (8). The differential treatment was only in the way these learning experiences were provided, and this difference was fundamental to the success of the CLIS methodology. Each introduction of new structure, each presentation of a dialogue or narration, and each recombination and reading exercise was immediately followed by intensive interaction through the classroom electronic facility in a practice period guided by specially prepared materials and monitored by the teacher. These follow-up repetition and transformation drills, along with guided conversation and question-answer exercises, increased sixfold the amount of time the student actively listened, responded, and interacted in the language. The authors cited these further advantages of CLIS: (1) Classroom interaction is constant and uninterrupted, since the teacher is more than just a drillmaster. He need not organize specific learning exercises *in* the class. Instead, he becomes a manager of learning, a decision-maker, a tutor, and a guide to the learner. (2) The scope and content of the materials presented via tape is more intensive, consistent, and comprehensive than similar material originated by the classroom teacher. No time is lost in hesitation, and more language material can be presented and internalized by the student. (3) The semi-isolation provided by the wear-

211

ing of headphones reduces distraction and increases the student's concentration. (4) The teacher can render extensive individual help to students who require assistance.

Factors for success of CLIS. Three factors seem basic to the successful application of the CLIS techniques to non-intensive instructional situations. First, the amount of time the student can spend with recorded materials is indeed critical, but it is not so critical as the specification and organization of learning experiences. Second, tape-guided practice seems to have its greatest impact on learning when it is not just used to reinforce classroom instruction, but when it forms an integral part of a combination of carefully prepared instructional materials. Third, when appropriate software and hardware are available, they must be applied systematically; that is, the teachers must adopt a positive set to use the equipment and the programs, since the mere availability of media does not mean that they will be used. Finally, in CLIS, the recorded exercises and the media were used whenever the learner reached a stage at which he could optimally benefit from intensive tape-guided practice. Thus, the classroom teacher must learn to recognize these optimum moments when they occur rather than follow a rigidly scheduled practice program.

The Banathy-Jordan study has extremely important implications for the use of media in language instruction, especially in the face of the zero or marginal effectiveness of language laboratories as shown in the Pennsylvania and Smith studies. In effect, Banathy & Jordan have given firm evidence that media work when they are well planned for, systematically used, and applied with superior materials. Furthermore, the results of their comparisons would also seem to indicate that at least audio-activated equipment is to be preferred over a simple classroom tape recorder. Completely enclosed booths such as those described by Hamson (42) are probably not a necessity, but the semi-isolation afforded by the simple headset-microphone combination seems instrumental in providing the student a practice environment in which he can concentrate on taped auditory stimuli.

Implications for use of medi
FL instruction

Lab practice and auditory comprehension

DuFrane (27) attempted to determine the extent to which the language laboratory's contribution to listening comprehension in beginning Spanish could be detected by standardized tests. The achievement of high school students who studied without laboratory drill was compared to that of students who had 2 20-minute laboratory practice periods each week. Both groups also heard master tape material and preliminary pattern practice presented via the classroom tape recorder. Marginally significant differences could be inferred favoring the lab practice group over the control, no-laboratory groups after one year of instruction.

Although several teachers each taught a control and a lab class, thereby controlling for a "teacher effect," the lack of data relevant to how the labs were actually used makes one postulate that a Hawthorne effect may have been operating. Both teachers and students may have reacted to a unique treatment, e.g., the use of a language laboratory. Since the patterns of use of the materials within the laboratory were not reported, it is difficult to know just why the differences were obtained, for similar studies have often shown that practice *per se* can be as ineffective as no practice at all. For example, Politzer & Weiss (64) found a negative relationship between the average number of minutes of laboratory work each week and achievement in auditory comprehension among high school students studying beginning French. The authors concluded that no matter how great the *frequency* of laboratory practice, the *type* of laboratory activity implied in dialogue memorization and pattern drills does little to increase the student's ability to understand the spoken language, and furthermore, can have a negative effect if this type of practice is undertaken at the expense of other types of exercises. Taylor (87) used tapes, language lab techniques, and the principles of programmed instruction to teach the fundamentals of arithmetic to adolescents. Best results were obtained by students who worked with highly structured, programmatic tapes; drill alone made little impact on learning. The learning environment for mathematics seems entirely analogous to any situation where habituated responses are desired. The findings of Politzer & Weiss and Taylor simply reaffirm that unstructured practice of any kind may be stultifying. What is really needed are tape-guided practice sessions that are structured and contain meaningful communication experiences.

Meaningful practice in terms of communication needed in using the language lab

Short-delayed feedback

The importance of receiving feedback on oral responses well within the limits of one's acoustic memory was demonstrated by Chomei & Houlihan (22) in an experiment which assessed the effectiveness of short-delayed feedback (SDP), long-delayed feedback (LDP), and simultaneous feedback (audio-active response). Achievement in listening comprehension, speaking ability, sight reading, dictation, and simultaneous translation was compared among three groups of high school students studying English as a foreign language. One group each practiced with programmatic tapes either in a short-delayed feedback, long-delayed feedback, or audio-activated system. After two months of intensive study, the rank order of the groups in listening and speaking achievement was SDP, LDP, and AA. The authors concluded that the short-delayed feedback students were motivated by the reduced length of time in discovering the correctness of their responses and as a result were more attentive to the task than the other groups. Moreover, since short-delayed feedback is for the student an experience somewhat similar to real communication, correct listening habits were created and, as a result, the SDP students became accustomed to emitting a quick, correct response. The authors later trained the LDP and AA groups in the use of the SDP equipment, and after two months of tape-guided practice, the previous differences among groups had disappeared. In the main, short-delayed feedback equipment is not abundant in schools and colleges. Moreover, one suspects that the practice of having students record and play back responses is not widespread. Nevertheless, the results of the Chomei & Houlihan study give evidence that when the record-playback mode is used, students should record short, discrete utterances (less than one minute) rather than entire exercises. Students will be able to evaluate their own responses more faithfully while their auditory memories vividly retain the sentences and their respective elements.

Short-delayed feedback is mo[re] like a real communication situation

The language laboratory (with or without delayed feedback) and the audio-active electronic classroom as customarily used in second language instruction have traditionally relied upon taped exercises which accompany given textbooks to organize the instructional experiences. By definition, these exercises have been designed both for group and for individual practice, although the former is by far the more common application. What seems important now is to look in greater detail at the organization and content of instructional sequences designed to individualize instruction along the lines of tutorial learning. The Smith, the Banathy & Jordan, the DuFrane, the Chomei & Houlihan, and even the Pennsylvania studies all point in this direction. It

Use of taped exercises contributes to "lockstep" learning for a group of individuals

is clear that language practice tapes structured mainly for groups have not contributed significantly to learning, except in intensive situations. Until now, the equipment for language practice, as well as the materials and group techniques associated with it, have generally tended to aid the *teacher* more than they have helped the language student. The programming of a single taped lesson to all students at one time, the unchanging tempo, the untiring voices — all of these things which have made the tape valuable as a model and as a drillmaster from the teacher's standpoint have also become its major handicap for the student. Such accepted generalizations as "books and pencils have no place in the lab," "the optimum periods of tape-guided practice are twenty minutes in length," and "tapes should never present new materials to the student" are all ripe for reappraisal, according to Arendt (6), especially since the laboratory is being used increasingly for independent and unsupervised study. For this reason, we now turn our attention to some recent studies in creative and individualized tape-guided learning in the laboratory and in the classroom which would seem to have great potential for beginning language instruction, especially from the students' point of view.

Audio-tutorial learning and simulated tutoring

What are they?

Audio-tutorial learning (AT) and simulated tutoring (ST) are highly individualized instructional techniques that have recently enjoyed great success in the physical sciences. In the former, lecture material is presented to the student via audio tapes; in the latter, audio tapes are used to tutor students, systematically, but not necessarily from a remedial standpoint. Interest in individualized training is by no means new. Rather, emphasis on maximum accommodation to individual student characteristics is but a logical outgrowth of programmed learning applied on a less doctrinaire scale (Fiks, 32). Audio-tutorial and simulated tutoring techniques have their origins in cybernetics and cybernetic theory. Both use combinations of media and especially prepared materials of a semiprogrammed nature to "tutor" a single student through an instructional sequence. These techniques thus incorporate Bloom's (12) fundamental precepts of teaching for mastery and the concepts of meaningful verbal

Definitions

215

learning as described by Ausubel (7). First, specific performance objectives are established for the principal concepts that are to be learned from a given unit or lesson. Then, these specific behavioral objectives are used in formulating the instructional sequence which, in turn, forms the basis for qualitative and quantitative evaluations administered during and at the end of each instructional unit. The degree to which the learner acquires fundamental concepts and principles provides the teacher with the necessary feedback to make discrete additions or deletions to reorganize the entire instructional program. In short, tutorial instruction considers the quality of instruction and its effects on the *individual* rather than quantity of material and its effects on random groups of learners. The teacher's efforts are directed toward finding more efficient means of transmitting information so that each student acquires all necessary prerequisites prior to attempting more complex subject matter.

Organization of learning with AT and ST

Efficiency of tutorial teaching

The efficiency of tutorial teaching has been judged in many traditional ways. Differential levels of achievement have been compared with those attained through expository teaching, and student attitudes toward tutorial teaching have been examined. Probably the most critical index of success is the saving in time for the student in achieving criterion performance. In ordinary classroom and laboratory instruction the amount of time the student will have in direct interaction with the teacher or his classmates is quite limited, even where the instructional procedures reflect discussion techniques rather than reception learning. Probably in no other discipline is this as obvious as in language learning, where the amount of individual interaction is extremely critical and the total number of semesters or years the average student will dedicate to the subject is minimal.

Saving in time

Mastery by most

Bloom (12) feels that at least 90% of students can achieve mastery if, as in tutorial teaching, the strategy for learning includes elimination of the restrictions imposed by traditional time limits such as the semester, and if the propensity for having every student at the same place in the book at every moment throughout the year is also abandoned. While some students would take longer than others to learn the material, the great savings in the long run would be that each student would oper-

Time and mastery

ate with *complete* rather than partial information as he studied subsequent units. He would have learned all of the necessary structures and vocabulary to be able to understand the concepts and principles of the new material. As a result, much less time would have to be spent in review to bring the student to minimal criterion performance.

Meaningful reception learning

Another means of increasing the efficiency with which concepts are learned, beyond eliminating prescribed time limits and textbook lessons, is to plan instruction so that each new piece of material can be meaningfully associated with the learner's experiential background. Effective techniques for meaningful reception learning include the use of what Ausubel (7) has called "advance organizers." These organizers introduce the student to the more general concepts to be learned. The instruction then proceeds gradually to concepts of greater and greater specificity. Each new concept or each new behavior is built, first, upon a number of general concepts or principles that have preceded it and, second, upon the degree to which the student has assimilated them into his cognitive structure. Periodic assessment of learning in comparison with stated performance levels allows the teacher to keep a running tally of the learner's progress and to redirect his efforts if needed. Thus, in successful reception learning, it is imperative that a series of advance organizers be planned as an integral part of each tutorial sequence.

Association of learning with learner's background

Tutorial teaching, teaching for mastery, and meaningful reception learning can be summarized in part as follows: (*1*) Performance levels are established for each major subdivision of the learning task. (2) An instructional sequence using a variety of techniques and media is formulated to lead the student to a predetermined criterion. (3) At each level, the learner must demonstrate mastery before he is allowed to proceed to the next major division. (*4*) Each student can control his own pace of learning to a large degree. He will be limited only by the extent and the rapidity with which he assimilates the information and learns to perform the associated behaviors. (5) The student may choose to study only the fundamental concepts to move quickly from one major division to the next, or he may elect to learn the related specifics at each level. (*6*) Remediation can be interjected whenever achievement is found to be below criterion levels. (7) The learning environment provides opportunity for indepen-

A summary

dent study and includes much more individual attention by the teacher.

It is with these characteristics in mind that we now turn to recently reported media-based instructional techniques in language teaching which approximate to some degree the tenets and methodologies of tutorial, mastery, and meaningful reception learning.

Simulated tutoring

The single most creative use of tape-guided practice in the past two years has been reported by Brown (13), who described two methodologies which provide for a more verisimilar communication experience in the language laboratory practice session. The first technique, called "simulated tutoring," involves the recording of the teacher's voice as he tutors a live student *1. "Simulated tutoring"* through the correct pronunciation of a brief dialogue. The teacher and the student (who acts as a foil) are seated face to face and are physically (but not visually) separated during the recording session. The equipment is arranged so that only the teacher's utterances are recorded. The foil's responses give the teacher feedback on the efficacy and the logic of the instructional sequence he has devised; the length of time the foil takes to respond similarly creates appropriate pauses on the mastery tape. When other students use these materials and respond to the teacher's prerecorded utterances, they have the illusion of interacting with a live tutor rather than a taped drillmaster. The sec- *2. "Simulated conversation"* ond technique, dubbed "simulated conversation," involves the student in a situational dialogue (e.g., buying a pair of shoes, meeting people at a cocktail party) in which he is confronted with somewhat unpredictable communications. The exercise is presented via tape recorder after the student has acquired the sentence patterns and situational vocabulary to understand and respond to the conversation. Although the student will be familiar with the sentence patterns and lexical items he encounters, he will not be able to predict the sequence or possible recombinations the tape might present and will thus have to generate his own essentially unique responses. One problem with the simulated conversation technique is providing the student with appropriate feedback, since the tape cannot confirm each of the many possible alternative responses the student might use. Yet the unique value of this technique for the student lies in the very unpredictability, the naturalness, and the realism of the conversation. For this reason, the parameters of acceptable responses must be delineated in some way. Brown advised letting the student go through the conversation two times with suggested responses given, then once without, so that he might have some idea of what responses were appropriate and could learn to produce them with relatively little hesitation. Thus, within the same lesson or conversation, it would become possible to shape both phonetically and culturally the type of response produced by the student. Instruction could be further individualized at the discretion of the teacher.

Simulated tutoring and simulated conversation have a wide variety of immediate application in the facilitation of individualized instruction at both the school and college levels. One of the most obvious uses, one which makes use of Brown's "tutor and foil interaction," is the preparation of tape-guided lessons to supplement given textbook materials. Such tutorial lessons can be made on at least four levels of inclusiveness: (1) to teach both cognitively and audiolingually the formation and application of specific linguistic structures or lexical items; (2) to explain, word-by-word or line-by-line, corresponding narrations or dialogues; (3) to review important and salient concepts of a given unit or units prior to a quiz or examination; (4) to illustrate audiovisually selected cultural aspects (kinesics, for example) of the language group under study.

Application to individualized instruction

The key to successful tutorial learning is the interest and involvement of the student in learning. But foreign language instruction becomes increasingly abstract as the student passes from the fundamental naming and defining structures to those of complex declaration, conjecture, and the like. Visuals, both projected and nonprojected, can be integrated into the laboratory lesson as suggested by Kirch (52), but unless the student's attention is specifically focused on the concepts being presented, the tutorial session lags and his interest-motivation and set to learn are quickly broken. One means of solving this problem is to ask the student to repeat, to transform, or to translate, using cues in both the target and the native language (ask me . . ., tell me . . ., how would you say . . .?) followed by some degree of reinforcement. Arendt (6) recommended the use of work sheets or job sheets for the student. An objective sheet or outline listing the respective concepts on which the guided practice session will focus is prepared for each audiolingual exercise. As he listens to the explanation and exercises, the student can be directed

Key to success of tutorial learning is involvement of the student

to write examples under the respective categories, to underline or encircle, or to fix his attention upon the structural elements or vocabulary listed there. Should he falter, the outline is his crutch; ultimately, the collection of work sheets becomes a convenient student-generated textbook of discrete but highly related concepts to which the learner may refer in preparing for formal or informal evaluations of his achievement. The student's comprehension of each new linguistic structure or concept can be tested as a part of the tutorial lesson by including short quizzes in which performance levels are stated and specific directions are given for remedial and/or supplemental follow-up study with either textbook or live tutor. No less important is the fact that at the end of the hour, both the student and the teacher will have concrete, tangible evidence of a task completed. Finally, self-instructional projects incorporating audio tapes, visuals, and other media can be used to involve the student in a total learning experience. Arendt further showed how students can "contract" to do a number of supplemental units during a marking period or semester, showing their progress through achievement on appropriate evaluative exercises or reports. As such the student undertakes full responsibility for learning. The quantity and quality of his achievement is almost entirely self-determined.

The major benefit of simulated tutoring for the teacher is the time gained for individual face-to-face classroom interaction, for class time no longer has to be used for explication of basic material. A second benefit derives from the processes leading to the organization of the tutorial materials themselves, since each concept must be well thought out and logically presented; thus, the student profits from the careful planning of the taped lesson. A third benefit accrues from the overall collection of tutorial lessons, for specific tapes for extra work or remediation can be assigned as the need arises (for example, to students who have been ill) without requiring extra teacher time. A residual but no less important benefit is the potential for increased utilization of the language laboratory facilities. The tutorial method relies upon individual and independent use of playback equipment for the presentation of the materials. The language laboratory and the school's materials resource center are logical areas for this type of practice. Lastly, the cassette tape player is becoming as common an appliance in students' homes as the ubiquitous record player. This will soon make it practical for the teacher to pro-

Major benefits of simulated tutoring

vide tutorial tapes to supplement textbook homework assignments.

Correcting themes and teaching composition

Phillips (62) has described a unique and innovative use of the simple tape recorder as a means of individualizing instruction in composition classes. No corrections are written on weekly themes; rather, each student is assigned a reel of blank tape onto which the teacher reads aloud the composition and records his comments regarding mistakes in structure, syntax, or vocabulary. Since the "composition tapes" are designed for individual consumption rather than for playing to the class as a whole, the student's tape, along with his theme for the week, is placed in the school's language laboratory or materials resource center. The student retrieves both theme and tape in the laboratory where he listens to a rendering of his assignment and the corresponding corrections. Afterwards, he rewrites specific sentences, paragraphs, or the entire composition according to the instructions recorded throughout or at the end of the tape, and the entire composition is submitted for a second evaluation. The composition may be "tape-corrected" a second time, or a third, at the discretion of the teacher. The advantages of tape-guided composition correction are obvious: (*1*) One cannot write as much or as quickly as one can speak; hence the amount of feedback the teacher can give the student in a fixed period of time is doubled or tripled at the outset. (2) Aside from the personalized tone of the feedback, specific remedial exercises can be incorporated into the tape as necessary. These exercises can vary from audio-lingual drills designed to illustrate a pattern or structure to problem-solving exercises in which the student must refer to specific pages in his text, a dictionary, or similar source book.

Use of tape recorder in writing, especially for correction

Taped corrections need not be limited to compositions, for the technique seems viable enough to be used for any lengthy written homework assignment or even examinations. Until recently, the correction of written work by tape recorder might have been considered impractical and inefficient because of the size and weight of the hardware needed to carry out the technique. The rapid perfection of cassette tapes and lightweight, portable, battery-operated cassette recorders is quickly making this argument untenable, especially since cassette machines are becoming increasingly popular as playback equipment in libraries and resource centers in schools and colleges. One would predict that

221

taped, tutorial corrections will ultimately become widespread for all types of classes in the near future.

The tape recorder talks back

Another innovative technique using the classroom tape recorder was reported by Agatstein (2). Although the tapes involved were played for a group of students, the exercises were directed at specific individuals. Agatstein described his method as follows: A review tape was recorded and played to the classes. As the tape asked factual questions, based upon the week's work, Agatstein pointed to students, who then responded and heard the tape give a confirmation or correction. The process was repeated by other students, who also responded *alta voce*. As the exercise progressed, the voice on the tape began to call upon the students by name, the order and sequence having been previously recorded by the teacher. Agatstein was able to predict who would respond immediately and who would falter; thus, pauses of appropriate length were "programmed" into the tape. Better students needed less time to react and pauses for them were short. Poorer students were given longer pauses and these, in turn, were interspersed with cues and prompts at predictable areas of difficulty. Of course the tape was not infallible, and it over-predicted at times, much to the delight of the class. The instruction was "tutorial" only to a degree. Although the students benefited from the pseudo-individualized nature of the recorded session, the primary benefit was probably one of motivating the group. Nevertheless, making a "tape recorder talk back" would seem to have a great deal of value. In his report, Agatstein presents further recommendations and examples of how classroom teachers can put this technique into practice.

An innovative technique for "individualizing" instruction

Student-recorded dialogues

Reinert (67), Winter (95), and Arendt (6) have described several creative uses of media designed to make language learning more interesting by making students more responsible for what goes on in the teaching-learning situation. For the electronic classroom, Reinert recommended letting pairs or groups of students prepare and record their own dialogues, based upon variations of a dialogue or narrative from a given textbook lesson. Student-recorded dialogues would thus become a technique for giving the students an opportunity to practice their speaking in more natural situations than those where single phrases or utter-

Using the electronic classroom

ances are merely repeated in isolation. Since the preparation of a tape script makes each student an active participant in the work of the group, and since the finished product is to be played for the benefit of all the students or for other classes, Reinert has found that the students are motivated not to treat the task too lightly and, as a consequence, they learn more efficiently. In the laboratory, Reinert recommended splitting the class into three groups of equal size, each of which then would spend a portion of the period working with practice tapes, another portion on an assigned project, such as the construction of a dialogue tape, and a third portion interacting with the teacher. The makeup of each group could be varied, and greater attention could be given to tailoring programs to the needs of relatively small groups of students. One important characteristic of this technique is that students are allowed to progress at their own speed, for grades and credit are based on the amount of work completed and on the extent to which the quality of learning conforms with prescribed performance expectations. Elsewhere, Fleury (33) has suggested the use of taped reading passages in the laboratory as a technique to help the student pace himself while reading and to help him overcome the tendency to translate. Fleury also recommended the use of contracts, group study, individually paced instruction, and the awarding of credit commensurate with demonstrated achievement.

Group work

References on second-language pedagogy

Several major textbooks or collections of references on second-language pedagogy were published in 1968–69 (Bennett, 10; Charest, 21; Feldman & Kline, 31; Grittner, 37; Oliva, 60; Rivers, 69; Roucek, 72; Smith & Leamon, 74; Turner, 89; Walsh, 93). Each has included the customary chapter dedicated to the language laboratory, but one searches almost in vain for examples of concrete application of equipment and supplementary materials. Grittner (37) concluded that the use of the laboratory in the secondary school has been dictated by the complexities of scheduling without regard to whether students were at a point where they could profit from laboratory work. From the practitioner's viewpoint, Grittner's detailed specifications will be helpful in planning a new or replacement installation, but there is precious little information on techniques of application. Turner (89) described the various benefits that can be derived from the close correlation of the language class and the laboratory, but he

Major publications and the language learning laboratory

advised that unless the teacher accepts, both intellectually and emotionally, the fourfold goals of audiolingual instruction, student attitudes and achievement will provide an accurate mirror of the indifference toward tape-guided practice which is sensed in the classroom. On the other hand, Feldman & Kline (31) recommended a library laboratory system and record-playback practice in free periods during, before, or after school hours. With apparent disregard for the materials and the students, they conclude that "it's not the size of the laboratory but rather the quality of the equipment it contains that determines its value." Bennett (10) reflected general universal thinking when he recommended that tapes of ten-minute duration be played at least three times in each lab period as a technique for inculcating habits of automatic response in the learner. Oliva (60), Charest (21), and Claudel (24) referred to the laboratory with the same general palliatives, but made no reference to techniques of application. Rivers (69) also wrote at length about the types and functions of the laboratory and presented suggestions and caveats for the practitioner, but gave no concrete examples for the uninstructed. Mikesell (58) described the qualifications and responsibilities of the media specialist who acts in the capacity of a consultant to schools interested in installing equipment. He also delineated the major steps the specialist should follow in the typical consulting job. Cannaday (15) gave specific recommendations for successful use of language laboratory equipment and materials, and wrote at length on use of the console, scheduling, testing, and administrative procedures. The very comprehensive nature of his presentation makes it a valuable summary for the uninitiated. Langr (55) described the use of the Pennsylvania film series (Cannaday & Gamba, 16) for pre- and in-service training in good laboratory and materials usage for the neophyte teacher, while Glenn (35) reviewed the importance of preparing teacher candidates in the use of media in language instruction. With the exception of Cannaday (15), only rarely do the above authors mention the desirability of assigning daily laboratory grades on a routine basis. Barrutia (9) gave examples of what a teacher might do to effect learning beyond simply playing tapes to the class and monitoring students' responses, suggesting the use of "pronunciation loops" and an "accumulative dialogue drill." Pronunciation loops are made from short sentences, each containing common pronunciation pitfalls. The sentences are recorded by a

Techniques and approaches to learning with media

teacher or a native speaker. The tapes are then cut to the exact length of each sentence; leader tape of equal length is added and the ends are joined together, forming a short but continuous "pronunciation loop." The length of each independent loop is determined by the length of the recorded sentence. When played back on a tape recorder at the beginning of a class or lab period, the pronunciation item becomes an effective repetitive "warm-up" exercise. Pronunciation loops are an excellent means of teaching proverbs or "tongue twisters," too. Accumulative dialogues involve the student more closely in the memorization of representative structures. The technique essentially requires that the student progressively "add a line" to a target-language model and its English equivalent heard on the tape. Reinforcement is provided by the tape's presenting all lines of the dialogue up to the last sentence modeled. The purpose of this technique is therefore to "tutor" the students step by step until the entire conversation has been committed to memory. The final phase presents to the learner one person's part of the conversation and leaves pauses for him to interact as the other person. The accumulative technique, somewhat similar to dialogue repetition drills, would seem to have much to recommend it as a method for giving the individual practice in interacting in short, everyday situations of predictable content and structure, such as registering at a hotel, purchasing a ticket, or ordering a meal. It would appear to be cumbersome, however, when applied to the general lengthy textbook dialogue or similar "didactic" conversations used to list vocabulary words and verb tenses.

Pronunciation loops

Accumulative dialogue drill

Elsewhere Sager (73) wondered whether laboratory exercises should attempt to present a maximum number of structures in the shortest possible time with reduced vocabulary or whether they should spread out learning and syntax by adhering strictly to the principle of contextualization. He concluded that the best type of exercise depends upon the age and motivation of the student. The primary-aged learner can use no other materials than contextual. Hence, the lab cannot contribute much to the young second language learner. Both the secondary school student and the adult learner need contextualized exercises to maintain interest. Taking the main constituent grammatical structures out of context for drill is an advantage, according to Sager, and should be viewed as an integral part of the learning process. The drills themselves, however, should be of the question-answer variety rather than item substitution. Ager (3) observed that

Contextual drills

open-ended and contextually grounded laboratory exercises are probably the most beneficial type for the advanced student who is able to bring his organization and understanding of structure to new materials. Retelling of dialogues and narrations, summarizing news broadcasts, or expressing a context from a different emotional standpoint are some of the techniques that can be practiced in the laboratory. Ager further recommended the use of short "cine-loops" (continuous loops) as visual stimuli for the open-ended exercises. In such a context the student can be required to say more or to change his emotional viewpoint in each successive viewing of the film. Smith (82) reported on the adaptation of the language laboratory and closed-circuit television (CCTV) to simulate a meaningful linguistic environment. Visual stimuli were presented in the laboratory for student-generated narration and commentary. CCTV is the nearest artificial equivalent to the real situations in which language occurs, and the language laboratory affords an appropriate acoustical environment in which students can practice extended narration or commentary. Replaying the video without sound can give the student extended practice in continuous speaking either in imitation of the narrative or through his own unique and novel commentary. Although video playback may be impossibly expensive for many schools, the technique described by Smith should be applicable with films, slides, or even nonprojected visuals. One would predict best results from short-visual models presented intensively to fairly advanced learners. Similar articles by Hayden (43) and Grundstrom (40) discuss respectively the use of slides and filmstrips, and motion pictures, as adjuncts to classroom and laboratory instruction.

Use of media in contextual drills

Computer-aided laboratory testing

The rapidity with which modern electronic computers can process large amounts of data makes computer-aided laboratory testing a distinct possibility, according to Poulter (65) who described a means by which daily or weekly listening comprehension quizzes administered in the language lab can be efficiently used to motivate the student and to provide both teacher and student with a continuous record of achievement. Poulter described five steps in acquiring and making use of the services of independent or institutional computer services and further presented examples of specially designed answer cards for use with marksense pencils. While the technique Poulter described is designed to facilitate measurement of the listening skills, the very rapidity and objectivity with which computer-mediated results are reported makes it a logical extension of the language laboratory concept, especially where laboratory work is assigned on an independent and elective basis. Since the teacher does not have to grade each quiz, his efforts can be directed toward writing and revising the listening comprehension exercises. No less important, according to Poulter, is the reduced degree to which students take their boredom out on the laboratory equipment, for the feedback they receive from the quizzes increases their motivation. Machine-scored tests and objective testing techniques are easily extended to the evaluation of reading achievement. The profession awaits a similar advance, however, in the systematic assessment of speaking ability.

Computer-aided instruction

Computer-aided instruction (CAI) would seem to hold great potential for realizing individualized instruction short of pure tutorial learning. But, although there is much activity in other disciplines, Feldhusen & Szabo (30) were able to report only two cases of direct application in foreign language instruction. Suppes & Jerman (86) commented on CAI and German at Stanford. More recently, Turner (90) has described CAI used as a routine segment of a review course in Spanish syntax. Exercises from a conventional review grammar together with correct answers, predictable errors, and advice to the learner were placed in the computer memory. Students had access to the program on a time-sharing basis. That is, the computer-tutor reacted to student responses only when the learner was actively engaged in interacting with the program, e.g., typing responses on the terminal keyboard. When the student was inactive, i.e., thinking or consulting the textbook, the computer automatically switched its attention to another "active" terminal and, hence, many students and many programs could be presented simultaneously. The computer-mediated exercises were the sole basis for actual written grammar homework, although the language laboratory was used to complement the problem-solving activities of the CAI. Achievement scores indicated that students performing work almost completely on their own outside class with the computer compared favorably with those who did the same work under class supervision of their instructor. In fact, the CAI made possible a de-emphasis of routine written exercises in the class-

CAI and individualization

room and allowed for greater attention to free composition. Turner further discussed the place of CAI in a language curriculum and concluded that costwise, CAI is not as expensive as one might think.

More recently, Rosenbaum (71) and Bung (14) have commented upon similar endeavors. Rosenbaum reported the results of several years of experimentation using the CAI environment as an alternative to supervised interactive activity in the classroom or laboratory. An important aspect of CAI is the increased frequency in the number of interactions the student can experience. For example, Rosenbaum found that active student response using CAI was ten times greater than the typical number of linguistic interactions generated between a teacher and a particular student in a 50-minute class. It is well to keep in mind, however, that "active" in this case meant typing responses to aural and visual cues on a CAI terminal keyboard rather than responding orally. Since computer-based interaction is unique in that each student-generated response can be totally analyzed for its congruence to a model, it is not just the increased frequency of practice that benefits the student. Rather, the combined effects of increased frequency *and* relevance of feedback tend to make each reinforced answer more meaningful. The student not only knows he has made an error, he learns the specific error that has occurred. The overall value of increased practice of this kind was revealed in an experiment in which Rosenbaum and his colleagues sought to evaluate the efficiency of a CAI laboratory as an adjunct to classroom instruction in first-year German. The achievement of a CAI group was compared to that of another which received adjunct instruction in a conventional language laboratory. Two interesting results were obtained: First, although the CAI laboratory emphasized textual rather than aural exercises, there was little difference in speaking and listening comprehension between the CAI group and the non-CAI group. Rosenbaum concluded that this was evidence that the conventional laboratory is relatively ineffective in extending the student's ability to speak and to understand beyond those skills acquired through classroom work. In reading and writing, as expected, the CAI students significantly outperformed their counterparts, since the CAI group had received more systematic practice in syntax and vocabulary. Second, *gains* from the CAI treatment were proportionately larger for students who did poorly than they were for the very best students. The poorer stu-

Experimentation with CAI

dents were able to catch up and stay caught up. Finally, an end-of-term evaluation of achievement revealed that the final achievement scores of the CAI group were more homogeneous than those of the language laboratory students. When one considers the essential components and advantages of computer-aided instruction, the outcomes of the experiment were not in the least surprising. The strength of CAI rests primarily in two areas: (1) remediation (knowledge of results) can be given to the learner with exactitude, so that he will know where to focus his attention when faced with a similar situation; and (2) almost total supervision can be exercised in the learning process. Thus, if the student errs, he can receive partial prompts or be shunted to an alternate series of more discrete steps. Similarly, once criterion performance has been attained, he may skip over redundant materials and use his time more efficiently. Both of these important factors are missing from most programmed learning and simulated tutoring paradigms, where the sequencing of materials is of necessity linear and rather inflexible. But CAI is expensive and, at this writing, almost totally research oriented. Tutorial teaching is inexpensive and immediately applicable. One would suspect that audio-tutorial teaching can attain results on an equal basis with CAI if the instructional environment receives as much detailed planning and structuring, and if the materials are as well programmed. CAI is indeed revolutionary for foreign language teaching, and if it is far, far out of the reach of the general practitioner for the moment, it is well to keep in mind that all good instructional systems are based on several fundamental premises: formulation of objectives, definition of content, and evaluation of achievement. A great deal can be learned, therefore, by observing how these concepts are brought to bear in a complex instructional environment, for while the media may not be available to the teaching profession except in an experimental context, the method may have universal application.

Strengths of CAI

Equipment

Several innovative equipment configurations beyond the ubiquitous reel to reel tape recorder were described during the last year. Devices with unique language laboratory capabilities and/or instant playback were presented by Chomei & Houlihan (22), Johansen (51), Griffith (36) and Adams (1).

Portable Laboratory System

Johansen (51) reviewed the operational sequence and problems involved in creating a new technology for language instruction, and told of a Portable Laboratory System (PLS) capable of both audio and visual display of materials designed for total self-instruction. In brief, PLS was constructed to present audio and visual stimuli and to respond to the student's spoken reply. The device signals the student that the program expects an oral reaction to a stimulus. The program then pauses and waits until the microphone senses that the student has spoken. When the student has responded, PLS interprets the cessation of speech as the termination of the response and automatically advances the student to the next part of the program. Johansen reported that military personnel who studied French phonology, orthography, grammar, and listening comprehension via the programmed multimedia technique were able to satisfy routine travel needs and minimum courtesy requirements after less than 58 hours of instruction. Similar results were noted in another application of the PLS in two semi-intensive academic settings with college-age learners.

PLS and total self-instruction

Instant playback

Griffith (36) commented that there have been many qualitative improvements in the common characteristics of the early language laboratory, but there is still a need for a device which will allow the learner to play back, effortlessly and indefinitely, utterances of any length which cause him difficulty or are of special interest. The lack of this capability, according to Griffith, may cause the poor discriminator to perform worse phonetically than if he had never used the laboratory. The average language laboratory design provides feedback on student-recorded messages after eight to twelve minutes of practice, since global rather than discrete exercises tend to be recorded for playback. As a result, the feedback in the review phase is too global to be of value. The very length of the delayed playback makes it difficult for the student to perceive his various responses objectively and efficiently. Early discrimination training is essential in order for recapitulation practice to be efficient, however, for the learner must know how to make use of this facility. Griffith presented a functional outline specification for a repeater, and noted that the "continuous-loop" and "quick-rewind" devices used here

Feedback with the normal language lab

and there experimentally still need a great deal of refinement. Chomei & Houlihan (22), whose study on the merits of short-delayed feedback was reported above, were able to construct a rapid replay system for individualized use. Their fully automated device was capable of playing back utterances in a fraction of the time normally required in the laboratory. The students' playback tape was of an endless-loop variety and had a maximum recording time of 1 minute 25 seconds. Since the learner depended upon a program played from the console as a model for his utterances, Chomei & Houlihan constructed the console machine to sense and stop itself when the student initiated playback. After a pause of 1 1/2 minutes, the master tape automatically presented the student with the next model. If the student elected not to record and play back, successive models were presented with shorter pauses. Hence, the student might review at his discretion one model indefinitely or none at all.

Short-delayed feedback

Experimental language laboratory

Adams (1) similarly reported on a modification of the control system of the normal language laboratory tape recorder. The experimental language laboratory (XLL) developed by Adams and his associates reduced the cycle of recording and playing back to between one and twenty seconds. The student did not depend upon a console master for stimuli. Rather, each student was provided with his own master tape and his own XLL mechanism over which he exercised full control. Thus, instruction could be completely individualized.

One of the most unique features of XLL was the "records" or audio signals that could be superimposed on the tape either by the student or by the teacher to signal the beginning and ending of recorded messages or drills. Depressing appropriate controls, the student could direct the machine to skip exercises marked by "records" (or to seek the beginning of a previous exercise) and to stop and cue up automatically. Another feature turned on the student microphone and activated appropriate circuits so that the student's responses were recorded, then automatically and immediately played back for comparison along with the model. The XLL can be directed to ignore record-playback and to present the program in a continuous mode with pauses for repetition or transformation, or it can be made to skip over blank parts of the tape. In short, XLL makes it possible to use the language laboratory in several new formats and for many purposes (short-

Instantaneous feedback

delayed feedback, for example) that are either too difficult or impossible to achieve in a conventional lab. The unique control features of XLL would seem to make it especially valuable in tutorial and individualized instruction.

The cassette recorder

The cassette recorder continues in popular acceptance for home use and as a program source in many audio-tutorial situations, notably in the sciences, where native rather than foreign language is the vehicle of communication. Recent improvements in design—independently driven trimotored and electronically controlled tape transports with solenoid pinch-roller operation—have made cassette applicability in language laboratory teaching a definite possibility, especially since dual-channel, touch-button electronics and high-speed (60 inches per second [ips]) duplication equipment are available. But Capretz (17) has cautioned that the cassette tape still cannot guarantee a frequency response of 50–10,000 Hz at the slow speed of 1 7/8 ips. At this writing, few publishers provide language tapes on cassettes, probably since few schools have the corresponding record-playback equipment. Finally, Grosjean & Sawyer (38) did not mention the cassette in their survey of teachers' format preferences regarding publishers' recordings. Laboratory directors continue to prefer master tapes on seven-inch reels of 1/4 inch 1.5 mil tape recorded full-track at 7 1/2 ips.

A useful device?

Radio

Nelson (59) discussed the potential and limitations of using radio in foreign language training and presented information on the best times of the day to receive foreign language broadcasts in various languages. Nelson cited target language broadcasts to help enlarge the beginning student's range of expression beyond the usual limits of the standard language course. For the advanced student, radio is an important technological system which can aid in maintaining comprehension and fluency. Radio recordings provide an excellent means of extending the learner's language world beyond the limits of the language classrooms and laboratory. For example, Garfinkel & Litt (34) used the radio for enrichment in intermediate Spanish classes. Their teacher- and student-made tapes apparently helped maintain a proper attitude toward language learning, although the impact on achievement in auditory comprehension was judged negligible.

Potential and limitations

One useful extension of the radio for the class and the laboratory is to make periodic recordings of news broadcasts, which are then presented as either formal or informal listening comprehension exercises. Radio tapes and radio broadcasts can be especially motivating to the student if the news item is of sufficient interest and importance that he may have heard about it elsewhere.

Conclusion

The "language learning laboratory" is still largely an unfulfilled idea in the American high school if one takes seriously the evidence from research reported in 1968–69; its use in higher education has been similarly unrealized. The potential of tape-guided instruction remains, but it has become increasingly obvious that the fundamental strategy must be *instructional* rather than drill oriented. Both large- and small-scale research have revealed that machine-aided instruction is effective in either of two situations: (*1*) intensive language learning, and (2) semi- or totally individualized learning. The language laboratory and its variations are least effective in an environment which specifies only one or two periods of taped drill each week in which exercises are prescribed without regard to the structure of the materials, the levels of competency of the individual, or his relative position on the continuum of learning—as was clearly illustrated by the outcomes of the Pennsylvania study. Yet the language laboratory can truly become a learning environment. The media are at hand to provide almost any function the teacher needs, from the simple classroom or cassette tape recorder to short-delayed feedback, radio tapes, and computer-aided learning.

More research is needed to assess the effectiveness of innovative equipment such as the cassette recorder or combinations of systems such as the independent study laboratory and the electronic classroom. Real advances, however, must come from the software itself, for there are still no creative taped and visual programs for the learning laboratory which go beyond the repetition, substitution, and transformation exercises that have been so characteristic of the past. The techniques of simulated tutoring and audio-tutorial combined with the tenets of learning for mastery appear to hold much promise for individualizing tape-guided instruction in modern foreign languages. But there will be no progress toward this goal unless the future holds as much dedication and advancement in the design and implementation of software as the past has seen in the application of systems and strategies.

References, Language learning laboratory

1 Adams, E.N. "A Single Station Language Laboratory with Novel Control Characteristics." *National Association of Language Laboratory Directors Journal* 4,ii(1969):12–22.

2 Agatstein, Michael. "A Tape Recorder Talks Back." *French Review* 42(1969):728–34.

3 Ager, D.E. "Open-Ended Exercises in the Language Laboratory." *Modern Languages: Journal of the Modern Language Association* (London) 50(1969):73–78.

4 Aleamoni, Lawrence M., and Richard E. Spencer. "An Evaluation of the Pennsylvania Foreign Language Project." *Modern Language Journal* 53(1969):421–28.

5 Anon. "ACTFL Affairs." *Foreign Language Annals* 3(1969):179–84.

6 Arendt, Jermaine D. "Sound Recordings," 28–49 in Mills F. Edgerton,Jr., ed. *Sight and Sound:The Sensible and Sensitive Use of Audio-Visual Aids*. Reports of the Working Committees of the Northeast Conference. New York: MLA Materials Center, 1969.

7 Ausubel, David P. *Educational Psychology:A Cognitive View*. New York: Holt, Rinehart and Winston, 1968.

8 Banathy, Bela H., and Boris Jordan. "A Classroom Laboratory Instructional System CLIS." *Foreign Language Annals* 2(1969):466–73.

9 Barrutia, Richard. "The Language Laboratory," 79–88 in D. D. Walsh,ed., *A Handbook for Teachers of Spanish and Portuguese*. Lexington, Massachusetts: D.C. Heath, 1969.

10 Bennett, W.A. *Aspects of Language and Language Teaching*. New York: Cambridge Univ. Press, 1969.

11 Birkmaier, Emma, and Dale L. Lange. "What About the Pennsylvania Studies?" *NEA Journal–Today's Education* 58,vii(1969):49,51.

12 Bloom, Benjamin S. "Learning for Mastery." *Evaluation Comment* 1,ii(1968):1–12. [Los Angeles: UCLA Center for the Study of Evaluation of Instruction.]

13 Brown, George H. "Providing Communication Experiences in Programmed Foreign Language Instruction." Professional Paper 35-68. Human Resources Research Offices, George Washington Univ., Alexandria, Virginia, 1968.

14 Bung, Klaus. "Towards Truly Programmed Language Laboratory Courses." *Audio-Visual Language Journal* 7(1969):5–17.

15 Cannaday, Robert W.,Jr. "The Language Laboratory:Valuable Instructional Aid," 127–66 in George E. Smith and M. Phillip Leamon,eds., *Effective Foreign Language Instruction in the Secondary School*. Englewood Cliffs, New Jersey: Prentice-Hall, 1969.

16 —— and Terry Gamba. *Successful Use of the Language Laboratory*. Harrisburg: Pennsylvania Department of Public Instruction, 1965.

17 Capretz, Pierre J. "The Language Laboratory:A Relic of the Past or a Solution to the Future?" *National Association of Language Laboratory Directors Journal* 4,i(1969):32–42.

18 Carroll, John B. "Modern Languages," 866–78 in Robert L. Ebel, Victor H. Noll, Roger M. Bauer, eds., *Encyclopedia of Educational Research*. New York: Macmillan, 1969. [4th ed.]

19 —— "What Does the Pennsylvania Foreign Language Research Project Tell Us?" *Foreign Language Annals* 3(1969):214–36.

20 "The Changing Software/Hardware Market." Venture Marketing Associates, Inc., La Jolla, California, 1969. *Audiovisual Instruction* 14, ix(1969):76.

21 Charest, Gerard J. *Foreign Language Teaching: Basic Guide*. Detroit: Univ. of Detroit Press, 1968.

22 Chomei, Tashiko, and Robert Houlihan. "An Experimental Study of the Effectiveness of a Newly Devised Short-Delay Playback System in a Language Laboratory." *Audio-Visual Language Journal* 6(1968–69):59–72.

23 Clark, John L.D. "The Pennsylvania Project and the 'Audio-Lingual vs. Traditional' Ques-

tion." *Modern Language Journal* 53(1969): 388-96.

24 Claudel, Calvin A. "The Language Laboratory," 219-36 in Joseph S. Roucek,ed., *The Study of Foreign Languages*. New York: Philosophical Library, 1968.

25 Crossman, David. "A Study of the Use of Language Schools in New York State." *Dissertation Abstracts* 29(1968):3908A (Syracuse).

26 Dodge, James W. "Machine-Aided Language Learning," 311-41 in Emma M. Birkmaier,ed., *Britannica Review of Foreign Language Education, Volume I*. Chicago: Encyclopaedia Britannica, 1968 [1969].

27 DuFrane, Daniel L. "The Language Laboratory and First-Year Spanish." *Dissertation Abstracts* 30(1969):1910A (Univ. of California-Berkeley).

28 Edgerton, Mills F.,Jr.,ed. *Sight and Sound:The Sensible and Sensitive Use of Audio-Visual Aids*. Reports of the Working Committees, Northeast Conference. New York: MLA Materials Center, 1969.

29 Esseff, Peter J. "The Language Laboratory and Educational Technology." *Dissertation Abstracts* 30(1969):2416A (Catholic Univ. of America).

30 Feldhusen, John F., and Michael Szabo. "A Review of Developments in Computer-Assisted Instruction." *Educational Technology* 9,iv(1969): 32-39.

31 Feldman, David M., and Walter D. Kline. *Spanish:Contemporary Methodology*. Waltham, Massachusetts: Blaisdell, 1969.

32 Fiks, Alfred I. *Foreign Language Programmed Materials:1969*. MLA/ERIC Focus Reports 7. New York: MLA/ERIC, 1969.

33 Fleury, Dale R. (Mrs.). "Independent Study:Foreign Language Seminars." *National Association of Secondary School Principals Bulletin* 53,338(1969):90-99.

34 Garfinkel, Alan, and Leslee D. Litt. *El eco español·An Enrichment-Oriented Radio Program for Level Two High School Spanish Classes*. Columbus, Ohio: Station WOSU, 1968.

35 Glenn, Leona. "University Labs as a Training Ground for Teachers." *National Association of Language Laboratory Directors Journal* 4, i(1969):15-19.

36 Griffith, B.T. "A Repeater in the Language Laboratory." *Audio-Visual Language Journal* 7 (1969-70):173-79.

37 Grittner, Frank M. *Teaching Foreign Languages*. New York: Harper and Row, 1969.

38 Grosjean, Glen M., and Jesse O. Sawyer. "Format Preferences in Publishers Recordings." *National Association of Language Laboratory Directors Journal* 4,i(1969):68-71.

39 Gross, Martin. "The Critic at Large:The Myth of Automated Teaching." *The Philadelphia Evening Bulletin* (12 Feb 1969).

40 Grundstrom, Allan W. "Motion Pictures," 83-98 in Mills F. Edgerton,Jr.,ed., *Sight and Sound:The Sensible and Sensitive Use of Audio-Visual Aids*. Reports of the Working Committees of the Northeast Conference. New York: MLA Materials Center, 1969.

41 Hallman, Clemens L. "Attitudes of Selected Foreign Language Teachers Concerning Instructional Media in Foreign Language Education." *Dissertation Abstracts* 30(1969):322A (Indiana Univ.).

42 Hamson, Erwin M. "The Closed Booth." *Audio-Visual Language Journal* 6(1968-69):74-77.

43 Hayden, Hilary. "Slides and Filmstrips." 50-60 in Mills F. Edgerton,Jr.,ed., *Sight and Sound: The Sensible and Sensitive Use of Audio-Visual Aids*. Reports of the Working Committees of the Northeast Conference. New York: MLA Materials Center, 1969.

44 Hedger, Brian. "Some Questions about Language Laboratories." *English Language Teaching* 23(1969):132-38.

45 Hocking, Elton. "The Laboratory in Perspective: Teachers, Strategies, Outcomes." *Modern Language Journal* 53(1969):404-10.

46 —— "Experimentation at Purdue University." *International Journal of American Linguistics* 28, i, part II(1962):80-91.

47 —— and W. Flint Smith. "The Language Laboratory in the United States." *Das Sprachabor und der audiovisuelle Unterricht* 1(1969):21-29.

48 Houpt, William P. "The Pennsylvania Foreign Language Project." *German Quarterly* 42(1969): 308-10.

49 Jakobovits, Leon A. "Research Findings and Foreign Language Requirements in Colleges and Universities." *Foreign Language Annals* 2(1969):436-56.

50 Jalling, Hans. "Preliminary Recommendations of the Swedish Research Project on the Use of the Language Laboratories in University Teaching." Centrala arbetsgruppen for SL-forskning: Universite-Spedagogiska Utredningen. [Paper read at the Second International Congress of Applied Linguistics, Cambridge, Sept 1969.]

51 Johansen, Patricia A. "The Development and Field Testing of a Self-Instructional French Program." *Linguistic Reporter* 11,ii(1969): 13-27. [Supplement 24.]

52 Kirch, Max S. "Visuals in the Language Laboratory." *National Association of Language Laboratory Directors Journal* 4,ii(1969):32-35.

53 Lange, Dale L.,ed. "1968 ACTFL Annual Bibliography." *Foreign Language Annals* 2(1969): 483-530.

54 —— "1969 ACTFL Annual Bibliography." *Foreign Language Annals* 3(1970):629-68.

55 Langr, Bernard J. "Using the Pennsylvania Films in Teacher Training." *National Association of Language Laboratory Directors Journal* 4,ii(1969):23-29.

56 Martin, Willard. "A Report on a Discussion Conference on the West Chester, Pennsylvania, Study." *National Association of Language Laboratory Directors Journal* 4,i(1969):64-67.

57 Marxheimer, Edward. "Comments on the Pennsylvania Project:Challenge for Secondary School Laboratory." *National Association of Language Laboratory Directors Newsletter* 3,iii(1969):20-22.

235

58 Mikesell, Norman. "Offering and Using Consultant Services." *National Association of Language Laboratory Directors Journal* 4,i(1969): 43–50.

59 Nelson, Robert J. *Using Radio to Develop and Maintain Competence in a Foreign Language.* MLA/ERIC Focus Reports 11. New York: MLA/ERIC, 1969.

60 Oliva, Peter F. *The Teaching of Foreign Languages.* Englewood Cliffs, New Jersey: Prentice-Hall, 1969.

61 Otto, Frank. "The Teacher in the Pennsylvania Project." *Modern Language Journal* 53(1969): 411–20.

62 Phillips, Robert. "Using the Tape Recorder to Correct Student Compositions." *Hispania* 51(1968):126–27.

63 Poirier, Roger A. "A Survey and Comparison of Foreign Language Instruction in American Junior Colleges." *Dissertation Abstracts* 29(1968): 2156A(Rutgers).

64 Politzer, Robert L., and Louis Weiss. *Characteristics and Behaviors of the Successful Foreign Language Teacher.* HEW Project 5-0252-0103. Stanford, California: Center for Research and Development, School of Education, 1969.

65 Poulter, Virgil L. "Computer-Assisted Laboratory Testing." *Modern Language Journal* 53(1969): 561–64.

66 Rafferty, Max. "Another Teaching Gimmick Failure." *The Post Standard.* Syracuse, New York (3 May 1969).

67 Reinert, Harry. "Creative Lab Usage." *National Association of Language Laboratory Directors Journal* 4,i(1969):57–63.

68 Rhodes, Jack W. "Organization and Administration of Foreign Language Programs." *Dissertation Abstracts* 29(1968):1084A (Univ. of Southern California).

69 Rivers, Wilga M. *Teaching Foreign Language Skills.* Chicago: Univ. of Chicago Press, 1968.

70 Roeming, Robert F. "Critique of the Pennsylvania Project:Preface." *Modern Language Journal* 53(1969):386–87.

71 Rosenbaum, Peter S. "The Computer as a Learning Environment for Foreign Language Instruction." *Foreign Language Annals* 2(1969):457–65.

72 Roucek, Joseph S.,ed. *The Study of Foreign Languages.* New York: Philosophical Library, 1968.

73 Sager, J.C. "The Language Laboratory and Contextual Teaching Methods." *International Review of Applied Linguistics in Language Teaching* 7(1969):217–29.

74 Smith, George E., and M. Phillip Leamon,eds. *Effective Foreign Language Instruction in the Secondary School.* Englewood Cliffs, New Jersey: Prentice-Hall, 1969.

75 Smith, Philip D.,Jr. "An Assessment of Three Foreign Language Teaching Strategies and Three Language Laboratory Systems." *French Review* 43(1969):289–304.

76 ——— *A Comparison Study of the Effectiveness of the Traditional and Audiolingual Approaches to Foreign Language Instruction Utilizing Laboratory Equipment.* Supplementary Report, Project No. 7-0133, Grant No. OEC-1-7-070133-0445. Washington, D.C.: USOE, 1969.

77 ——— "Let's Take Another Look" *NEA Journal—Today's Education.* 58,vii(1969):49–50.

78 ——— "The Pennsylvania Foreign Language Research Project: Teacher Proficiency and Class Achievement in Two Modern Languages." *Foreign Language Annals* 3(1969):194–207.

79 ——— "In Reply to the October, 1969, Modern Language Journal." In Philip D. Smith, Jr. *A Comparison Study of the Effectiveness of the Traditional and Audiolingual Approaches to Foreign Language Instruction Utilizing Laboratory Equipment*: Supplementary Report to Project No. 7-0133, Grant No. OEC-1-71070133-0445. Washington, D.C.: USOE, 1969.

80 ——— and Helmut Baranyi. *A Comparison Study of the Effectiveness of the Traditional and Audiolingual Approaches to Foreign Language Instruction Using Laboratory Equipment.* Final Report, Project No. 7-0133, Grant No. OE-1-7-070133-0445. Washington, D.C.: USOE, 1968.

81 ——— and Emanuel Berger. *An Assessment of Three Foreign Language Teaching Strategies Utilizing Three Language Laboratory Systems.* Final Report, Project No. 5-0683, Grant No. OE-7-48-9013-272. Washington, D.C.: USOE, 1968.

82 Smith, R.W. "Closed-Circuit Television in the Language Laboratory." *Times* (London) *Educational Supplement.* 2801(Jan 1969):253.

83 Smith, W. Flint. "The Language Laboratory and the Electronic Classroom:A Comparison of Their Relative Contribution to Achievement in Three Languages in the Comprehensive High School." *Dissertation Abstracts* 30(1969):1474A(Purdue).

84 ——— and Elton Hocking. "The Fallacy of Accessibility." *National Association of Language Laboratory Directors Newsletter* 3,iii(1969): 10–13.

85 ——— and Elton Hocking. "Student Attitudes: Revisited." *National Association of Language Laboratory Directors Journal* 4,i(1969):51–56.

86 Suppes, Patrick, and Max Jerman. "Computer Assisted Instruction at Stanford." *Educational Technology* 9,i(1969):22–24.

87 Taylor, Ralph C. "An Investigation of the Value of Drill on Arithmetic Fundamentals by Use of Tape Recordings Which Combine Techniques Developed in Language Laboratories with Principles of Programmed Learning." *Dissertation Abstracts* 30(1969):1828A (Univ. of Southern California).

88 Torkelsen, Gerald M., and John P. Driscoll. "Utilization and Management of Learning Resources." *Review of Educational Research* 38(1968):129–52.

89 Turner, E. Daymond, Jr. *Correlation of Language Class and Language Laboratory.* MLA/ERIC Focus Reports 11. New York: MLA/ERIC, 1969. MLA/ERIC, 1969.

90 Turner, Ronald C. "CARLOS:Computer-Assisted Instruction in Spanish." *Hispania* 53(1970):

249–52.

91 Valette, Rebecca M: "The Pennsylvania Project, Its Conclusions and Its Implications." *Modern Language Journal* 53(1969):396–404.

92 ——— "Some Conclusions to be Drawn from the Pennsylvania Study." *National Association of Language Laboratory Directors Newsletter* 3,iii(1969):17–19.

93 Walsh, Donald D.,ed. *A Handbook for Teachers of Spanish and Portuguese.* Lexington, Massachusetts: D.C. Heath, 1969.

94 Wiley, David E. "A Methodological Review of the Pennsylvania Foreign Language Research Project." *Foreign Language Annals* 3(1969):208–13.

95 Winter, Lottie. "Using the Tape Recorder for English Teaching." *English Language Teaching* 23(1969):129–32.

9

Recent developments in the training and certification of the foreign language teacher

Introduction

Howard B. Altman
and Louis Weiss

Stanford University

This review of the state of foreign language teacher education is being written in mid-1970, at a time when many foreign language teachers — at all levels — are finding it necessary to rethink their roles as teachers, as "architects of learning," to use Kai-yu Hsu's phrase (30), as professionals, as humanists. Our predecessor, Richard J. McArdle, detailed the status of teacher education, qualifications, and supervision in the *Britannica Review of Foreign Language Education, Volume I.* His data included most of the main writings through 1968. We have attempted to discuss the literature — published and unpublished — of 1969 and the first half of 1970. We feel simultaneously optimistic and pessimistic as we write; optimistic, because there are some splendidly innovative programs in foreign language teacher training under way at several institutions in the United States; pessimistic, because despite much talk about change, there seems to have been relatively little action.

Our chapter has the following sections:

Temporal and spatial rearrangements in teacher education
The "experience" curriculum
In-service education: retraining vs. advanced study
The training of teachers of English as a second language and second dialect, and teachers for bilingual education programs: special problems
The training of teaching assistants and college teachers of modern foreign languages
Training the teacher of FLES
Developments in teacher certification
The role and responsibilities of the foreign language teacher in the school and in the profession
The role and training of the foreign language supervisor
Training the teacher's teachers
A glimpse into the future

Temporal and spatial rearrangements in teacher education

The state of teacher education in foreign languages in the U.S. during the past two years has been characterized by an ever-increasing fervor for change. McArdle (38) has already cited the motivating and shaping forces — such as the well-known *Guidelines for Teacher Education Programs in Modern Foreign Languages — An Exposition*, compiled by F. André Paquette and published in the October, 1966, issue of the *Modern Language Journal* — which have brought forth a flood of suggestions and designs for altering the preparation of modern language teachers. In the years since the publication of the *Guidelines* no fewer than 150 articles, books, and papers have been written on this topic. One would assume that the content of teacher education programs in foreign languages must be quite different today from its status in 1966.

This is a false assumption. There has, indeed, been much pressure for change, but the desired changes have not been changes of content so much as of form. One can cite numerous examples of rearrangements of the temporal and spatial parameters of foreign language teacher education; the *curriculum*, however, consists largely of exactly the same components as it did prior to the Paquette report.

In spite of pressure for change, little has occurred in teacher education

Perhaps the most universally demanded change has been a lengthening of the period of preservice training by starting teacher education programs earlier in the prospective teacher's academic career. The need for such lengthening is described most forcefully by Sandstrom et al. (65): "The repertoire of skills that an FL teacher must possess is more complex now than ever before, owing to recent advances in applied linguistics, educational psychology, testing, and instructional media. If one adds the additional classroom problems arising from enrolling more diversified populations of students in foreign languages, it becomes clear that considerably more time must be devoted to training prospective teachers."

Lengthening of the preservice period

Williams (79) advocates the beginning of professional education in the prospective teacher's freshman year in college. During that year, the candidate makes weekly visits to assigned high school foreign language classes, where he observes teaching techniques and instructional materials. His professional education that year includes a seminar entitled "Orientation to

Professional education beginning in the freshman year

240

Professional Education." In his sophomore year, the student continues to observe the same classes, assists the teacher, and possibly conducts part of the instruction on occasion. His professional education includes seminars on instructional techniques and a sufficient number of practice teaching episodes for his strengths and weaknesses to be diagnosed. In his junior year, the candidate is involved as a "student teacher," and teaches half-period sessions for one class for an entire semester, serves as a teacher aide, supervises study halls, etc. In the senior year, he becomes a "teaching intern" and conducts one class for a whole semester with only minimal supervision. His professional course work that year might include a course in educational statistics. One may legitimately wonder whether Williams' scheme leaves enough free academic time for the prospective teacher to do advanced course work in his language area!

Pillet (53) writes: "There is a tendency these days to expose teachers earlier to students in the classroom in anticipation that the theoretical work might be better integrated and better received by the students [i.e., the student teachers] after an actual contact with the realities of the classroom."

Study abroad, as part of preservice training, has become almost a *sine qua non*. Benardo (8) advocates a *required* junior year abroad for all prospective teachers of modern languages. Rabura (61), describing a new program at the University of Washington in the training of German teachers, advocates a "spring quarter in Germany" as essential for the training of better qualified teachers.

Study abroad

Overseas programs bridge the gap from temporal to spatial rearrangements. The Committee on Teacher Training of the American Association of Teachers of German has recommended the establishment of a nationwide overseas program for all prospective teachers of German (Deeken, 17). Lee (34) urges the establishment in Britain of training and study centers to which teachers of English from other countries can come for "on location" practice. Sandstrom et al. (65) advocate removing the "methods" courses from college classrooms to public school settings, where the prospective teacher can observe and work with groups of students of various sizes and backgrounds. Glenn (22) feels that a certain amount of foreign language teacher training can be conducted more effectively in the language laboratory rather than in the "methods" classroom. A properly equipped lab is certainly the place for demonstrating the usefulness of audiovisual equipment such as the overhead projector, filmstrip and slide projectors, and other tools which the foreign language teacher finds so helpful. The lab is also the place to learn how to use a lab, which involves everything from proper methods of storing tapes for maximum efficiency to methods of correlating classwork with laboratory work.

The "experience" curriculum

If the basic components of the curriculum in foreign language teacher training are largely what they were prior to the Paquette report, the method of presenting each component and the artificial boundaries separating one from another have been widely rethought in recent years. McArdle (38) discussed in detail the "practice-centered" curricula in foreign language teacher training developed by Robert L. Politzer at Stanford. Not unlike this is the concept of the "performance-oriented" or "experience" curriculum of Sandstrom et al. (65). What all of these terms have in common is the aim of exposing the prospective teacher to at least a modified school environment as the central focus of his professional training. Ideally, and advocated by an increasing number of theorists and teachers, this exposure is no longer limited to working with one master teacher in one school with one basically homogeneous body of pupils, in fulfillment of the "practice teaching" requirement for state certification. Sandstrom et al. (65) and Pillet (53) have stressed the importance of diversified opportunities to work with and observe different foreign language teachers in action and groups of students of various sizes and backgrounds.

Performance curricula in preparing FL teachers

Microteaching, as discussed by Politzer (54) and McArdle (38), affords a modified exposure to a limited school environment and has been used very successfully at Stanford and elsewhere for the purpose of providing training and practical experience for prospective teachers. Politzer feels that microteaching—which involves working with a small corpus of material for a limited time with perhaps half a dozen students, while frequently being videotaped—helps to bridge the gap between theory and practice and, by concentrating on specific aspects of teacher behavior, aids in finding ways to modify that behavior where necessary.

Microteaching

What are the components of the curriculum for training foreign language teachers? First and foremost is work in methodology. Lohnes (35) and Strasheim (74) have pointed to the necessity of language-specific methods courses. Owing to the different problems which teachers of different languages face, the general foreign language methods course is simply too short and too broad in focus to do justice to the idiosyncrasies of teaching one language. Strasheim has recommended a "team" approach in the general foreign language methods course, with personnel from each language department represented in the class, where separate methods courses for each language are not possible.

General FL methods courses

What should course work in methodology entail? The various answers which have been suggested for this question illustrate the blurring of the lines between what have traditionally been the provinces of the methods course, of practice teaching, educational psychology, and the use of audiovisual aids. In discussing methods courses for the training of German teachers, Rabura (60) lists 27 topics to be included, and Altman (2) lists 40! Perhaps a typical list of components is that suggested by the Conference on Methods of Teaching Foreign Languages, held at Butler University, and reported by Strasheim (74):

Suggestions for the content of methods courses

A Instruction concerning the contributions of related disciplines

B Practical and specific information concerning classroom presentation

C Discussion concerning objectives and practical, realistic goals of foreign language study

D Frequent observation of elementary and/or secondary school teaching

E Instruction concerning the purpose, the value, and the use of instructional media, including language laboratories

F Discussion of criteria for the selection of instructional materials

G Evaluation of pupil achievement and means of measurement

H Instruction concerning age levels and articulation

I Discussion on professionalism

J Practice or "bit" teaching during the methods course

Horner (29) lists several prerequisites for the methods course: adolescent psychology, interaction analysis, American secondary education, and knowledge of the language, culture, and civilization which the prospective teacher must teach.

Proficiency in the language(s) to be taught has been stressed by Dusel (19), Girard (21), Lohnes (35), and Rabura (60). Lohnes advocates continuous language training (as opposed to "literature" or "linguistics") into upper-division and graduate programs until the prospective teacher can achieve at least "good" competence in the "four skills" of listening comprehension, speaking, reading, and writing, as measured by the MLA Proficiency Tests.

Language proficiency

Horner (28) has concluded from her observations of student teachers that they have three main weaknesses: they are deficient in their ability to explain and demonstrate simply and convincingly the role grammar plays in verbal communication; they are ill equipped to present a literary excerpt in a relevant and interesting way to young learners; and they lack personal involvement with literature in general and foreign literature in particular. Her solution is three key courses, in addition to the methods course, which should be part of the preparation of every language teacher: (*1*) advanced grammar; (*2*) advanced composition; and (*3*) introduction to literature.

Student-teacher weaknesses

Keppeler (31), on the other hand, feels that there is a justifiable need to de-emphasize "literature" in foreign language programs for undergraduates who plan to teach in the public schools. His suggestion is that the focus of literature-as-a-body-of-knowledge-to-be-internalized be changed to literature-for-conversational-ability. This is somewhat supported by Rabura (60), who advocates a separate third- and fourth-year program in foreign languages for the "teaching majors." These prospective teachers should receive massive exposure to the study of the foreign culture and civilization, and the bulk of their training in literature, which would not be extensive, should deal with modern or contemporary authors. An attempt to construct separate programs to distinguish between the future public school teacher and the future literary scholar has been established in Spanish and Portuguese at the University of Colorado (Keppeler, 31).

Literature in teacher preparation programs

Other components of the preservice curriculum which have been stressed widely are applied or contrastive linguistics (Allen, 1; Benardo, 8; Gefen, 20; Horner, 29; Lohnes, 35; Mordaunt, 42; O'Cherony, 43; Paquette, 46; Pascual, 48; Rabura, 60; Robinett, 63), educational psychology with emphasis on the psychology of language learning (Andersson, 3; Gefen, 20; Rabura, 60), and supervised practice teaching.

Practice teaching, student teaching, intern teaching, practicum, apprentice teaching—these are all synonymous or related terms referring to the phenomenon of placing the prospective teacher before a class and encouraging him to put theory into practice. Zaborowski (81) advocates starting the apprenticeship in the fall, "when the going is truly the roughest." We have already mentioned the trend toward bringing the prospective teacher into the classroom, on both sides of the desk, earlier. Williams (79) has suggested that the student teacher be allowed to conduct a portion of the instruction for one class as early as his sophomore year in college. Andersson (3) insists that the practice teaching be carefully observed and directed by both academic and professional educators. Sheehan (68) advocates the use of closed-circuit television (videotaping) for supervising practice teaching; the apparatus is "silent," the supervisor doesn't have to sit in the last row and take notes (and thereby distract the student teacher). Most importantly, through the use of the split-screen technique, the student teacher can receive immediate feedback on his performance and his class's reaction, and can evaluate himself, "which is a necessary ingredient for real progress and meaningful personal development."

"Student teaching," etc.

The graduate assistantship is another form of practice teaching. It will be discussed in detail in the section of this chapter entitled "The Training of Teaching Assistants and College Teachers of Modern Foreign Languages." Banta (6) laments the fact that the preparation of college instructors is aimed expressly at teaching elementary courses, and that their practice teaching experience is largely also on the elementary level. He describes his satisfactory experiment in allowing two advanced graduate students to take over some of the teaching of his "History of the German Language" course. This gave the student teachers needed supervised experience in teaching an advanced course and was well received by the students enrolled in the course. The Department of German at Stanford University offers a practicum in teaching literature. Here, advanced graduate students can conduct an undergraduate literature course with the close supervision and planning of a graduate professor. Another option is for the graduate student to assist the professor with a graduate course in literature, to collaborate on its planning, and to deliver some of the lectures.

The graduate assistantship as a student teaching experience

In-service education: retraining vs. advanced study

There is widespread agreement among teachers and theorists in foreign languages that the training of the foreign language

245

teacher should not end with the granting of his teaching certificate, but should continue throughout his entire professional career. Benardo (8) and Rabura (60) advocate a lighter teaching load for beginning "teachers in training," perhaps three periods per day plus time spent with a qualified teacher in planning, preparing, and evaluating their own teaching, and in observing the teaching of experienced colleagues.

Continuing education for FL teachers

With the passage of the NDEA in 1958, in-service education became synonymous with "retraining." In the ten years of summer institutes that followed, tens of thousands of language teachers were "retrained." Many of them had just completed their initial training a year or so previously! Retraining, as Corder suggests (15), has had the prescriptive implication that the experienced teacher needed to unlearn what he had learned in his preservice training. Perren (52) uses the term "de-training" to suggest replacing previously learned methods by newer ones. This notion is basically demoralizing. It is also, as is evidenced by the flood of writings on foreign language teacher education in the last few years, no longer the primary function of in-service training. Corder (15) uses the term "advanced study" to refer to the continuous training which professionals receive in their areas of specialization, and which keeps them abreast of the changes in technology and methodology within their specialties. Although some theorists (e.g., Paquette, 47) use these terms interchangeably, we feel the distinction is significant. Indeed, it is of interest to note that recent NDEA Institutes were called "Institutes for Advanced Study." Corder defines the aims of advanced study in foreign language teaching as follows: "to take selected teachers with sound initial training and a history of successful classroom experience and qualify them to assume major responsibility for decisions of language-teaching policy in all its aspects: its materials, its methods and its training in a wide variety of conditions, financial, human, and technical."

NDEA—retraining

"Advanced study"

Girard (21) suggests three functions which the further training of foreign language teachers fulfills: (*1*) to fill in the gaps in incomplete basic training; (*2*) to refresh periodically the teacher's knowledge of the language; (*3*) to develop the teacher's special fields of interest. Deeken (17) adds that not only the teacher's knowledge of the language—and this includes native speakers!—needs to be updated periodically, but also his contacts with the whole culture of the country whose language and culture he teaches. This "renewal" can best be accomplished through pro-

Functions of advanced stud

fessionally sponsored programs of summer studies abroad and through intensive workshops in the U.S. It is still unfortunately true that in some cases the teacher's need to improve his language skills, or to update them, may consume all the time he has available for formal in-service training during the early years of his teaching career.

Pillet (53) states that in-service training, to be effective, must be self-generating. Whether the teacher needs remedial work in language skills or advanced training in using new electromechanical media, he must see the need for this additional professional exposure, or it will probably not be very successful.

Teacher must see need for advanced study

Smith (70), in discussing the in-service training of teachers of English in developing countries, writes: "One discounts at one's own peril the importance of any one of certain key factors in in-service training. The first is care in selection; the second, intensive and practical training of staff; the third, intensive training of students, with no time for boredom to develop and affect morale; the fourth, provision of tools of the trade; the fifth, careful and detailed advance planning; the sixth, adequate follow-up."

What should be the curriculum for in-service education? Theorists are less specific here than when discussing the curriculum of preservice training. There is unanimous agreement (Gefen, 20; Rabura, 61; Deeken, 17; Benardo, 8) that all teachers of modern foreign languages periodically need fresh exposure to the living language and culture of the target country. This exposure can best be received "on location." Deeken (17) has urged the German-teaching profession to design programs which allow more of the experienced teachers of German to go to Germany periodically to engage in in-service training. There is also a consensus that those teachers who need pedagogical or methodological retraining should be encouraged to get it. "Retraining" here would suggest exposure to course work in methods of teaching their language(s), in the psychology of language learning, in the application of linguistics to language teaching, etc. As far as the components of advanced study are concerned, nothing very different from the above has been specified. Rabura (61), in discussing a model M.A. program in German for 25 experienced teachers at the University of Washington, outlines their 36 credit-hour program as follows: language skills, 9 credit hours; methods of teaching foreign languages, 9 hours; culture, civilization, and literature, 9 hours; linguistics, 9 hours; plus a spring quarter in

Curriculum for in-service education

Germany, with concentration on the culture and civilization of Germany and Austria.

Altman (2) has described a seminar in in-service education for intern teachers of high school German, which he has conducted at Stanford University. The focus of the seminar was on learning by doing. Over an entire academic year, each intern was responsible for preparing and *demonstrating* five technical skills of teaching German. Basic "methods course" topics were broken down into minimal units for this purpose. For example, three reports dealt with the presentation of different types of songs in the instructional program: folk songs, *Schlager*, and Germanized versions of popular American songs. Interns prepared for their demonstrations by reading materials in professional journals, by visiting the classes of experienced German teachers in the area to see these techniques being utilized, and by trying them out in their own classes. An excellent feature of the seminar was the frequent presence of a visiting high school teacher of German, who served as a guest "authority" for the evening, commented on the presentations, and discussed his own high school program.

An in-service program for intern teachers of German

In-service education need not be limited to formal course work at a university or to summers spent in study and travel. Pillet (53) points to the periodic "institute" days some secondary schools hold to upgrade the morale and effectiveness of the staff. In northern California, many German teachers are members of local German Teachers Workshops (GTW's), which hold monthly meetings for in-service education and professional camaraderie. Programs are planned which deal with practice-centered issues in teaching German: evaluating new textbooks, discussing techniques for teaching literature, etc. No academic credit is given for participation in such sessions, but this has not detracted from the attendance.

Periodic in-service education

The training of teachers of English as a second language and second dialect, and teachers for bilingual education programs: special problems

Almost one-third of all the writings on foreign language teacher education in the past two years deals exclusively with the topics in this section. The teaching of English as a second language and second dialect in the United States, and the teaching in bilingual education programs, have become major undertakings, with problems and concerns not always shared by those who teach "foreign languages" to American students.

What kind of training is needed by teachers of English as a second language or second dialect? Is the same training suitable for teachers of ESL (English as a Second Language) and ESD (English as a Second Dialect)? Robinett (63) has described programs for training teachers of ESL and ESD and feels that their training should not be identical, since the problems they have to face are not identical. According to Robinett, a typical teacher education program for ESL contains three basic components: linguistics, English language, and professional education. These may be organized into five different courses: (1) introduction to linguistics; (2) applied phonetics; (3) modern English grammar; (4) methods of teaching ESL; (5) practicum in teaching ESL. An additional requirement for the program, Robinett feels, should be the knowledge of at least one foreign language. Other possible subjects for the program might include testing, cultural anthropology, English and American literature, contrastive analysis, use of the language laboratory, and preparation of materials.

Training programs for teachers of ESL and ESD — the same?

Robinett itemizes the major points of difference between teaching ESL and ESD: (1) The ESL teacher requires a general knowledge of English dialects; the ESD teacher must be extremely knowledgeable about those dialects which are sociologically differentiated and regionally distributed. (2) The ESL teacher needs "language versatility — a knowledge of sound types and grammatical structures from a variety of languages"; the ESD teacher needs "dialect flexibility — a knowledge of and tolerance for phonological and grammatical systems which differ within the various dialects of English." In the professional education of the teacher of ESD, greater emphasis must be placed on motivational techniques. Methods of teaching vocabulary, phonemic contrasts, and intonation patterns, however, need not be stressed so much for the ESD teacher as for the ESL.

Differences between teaching English as a second language and as a second dialect

Robinett concludes by stating that the field of English as a second dialect needs to develop teacher education programs of its own, "implementing the many sociolinguistic factors which are peculiar to its realm, all the while utilizing whatever may be helpful from ESL. It will then produce teachers who can unselfconsciously accept nonstandard dialects for what they are — a perfectly good means of communication — and who can then proceed to add to the child's inventory of skills another means of communication — the standard dialect of English."

Politzer (55), in discussing the application of foreign language teaching methodology to the teaching of ESD, cautions that not every native speaker of standard English is qualified to teach it, either as a foreign language or as a second dialect. Politzer feels the most important parallel between the qualifications for foreign language and second dialect teachers lies in the area of applied linguistics. Together with Bartley, Politzer has produced (56,57) a practice-centered teacher-training syllabus for teachers of ESD, which is designed along the lines of his previous syllabi, described by McArdle (38).

A practice-centered curricula for teaching English as a second dialect

Allen (1) suggests the addition of communication, rhetoric, oral interpretation, and the humanities to the ESD curriculum. Resources, skills, insights, and information in these fields exist which may prove helpful to second dialect teachers.

If the teaching of English as a second dialect in the U.S. is occupying the energies of many teachers and theorists, many others are concerned with the training and problems of teachers of English as a second language abroad. Marquardt (36) cites some impressive statistics to show the need for training ESL teachers in large numbers as quickly as possible: there are 45 million students of English in the U.S.S.R. alone! Marquardt lists the basic educational objectives in training ESL teachers abroad to work in multilingual communities: (*1*) Attitudes: the teacher of ESL abroad should learn about the culture of the people he is teaching, should learn to respect it, and should develop respect for technology in extending communication. (2) Understanding: the ESL teacher should understand the differences between a native and nonnative learner of English, and should understand that a culture is a complex of message systems. (3) Skills: the teacher needs to be able to find and use contrastive analyses; he should be aware of the sociolinguistic variation among learners; he should be able to select appropriate teaching materials, involve learners in proper activities, and be able to evaluate his and their performance. (4) Habits: the teacher of ESL abroad must observe and make note of cross-cultural interaction behavior and strive to find cross-cultural situations which will help him to understand his students.

Preparing teachers for ESL abroad

Corder (15) has stated emphatically: "If there is anything that a language-teacher may have to unlearn, it is not so much in the area of linguistics as in the field of sociolinguistics and the way he regards his own language." To this Marquardt (36) would add: "and the way he regards the languages of others."

Perren (51) has edited a collection of articles on the training of teachers of ESL in Britain and in Africa and Asia. In his article in this collection, Cartledge (11) cites the fact that, for most teachers of ESL abroad, teaching English to foreign students will never be more than a part-time job, and that the postgraduate training for ESL teachers of adults abroad, which is given in Britain, is quite inadequate.

Perren himself suggests (52) a training program for teachers who will be teaching through the medium of English, but not teaching the language itself. They should take courses dealing with (1) registers of English; (2) the language of the subject; (3) the language of textbooks; (4) progress in English; (5) reading ability; and (6) writing in English.

When we move to a discussion of the training of teachers for bilingual education programs, we move into an area which may well prove of vital importance nationally and internationally. Despite popular misconceptions, bilingual education is *not* the same phenomenon as FLES. Christian (13) has listed two key aspects of bilingual education programs, especially relevant in the American Southwest, where such programs are most numerous: (1) the incorporation of the student, whose parents speak a language other than English, into the standard social and educational system of the U.S.; and (2) the education of all school children in using a second language and understanding a second culture.

Preparation of teachers for bilingual education

To an unfortunately large extent, bilingual education as a phenomenon has become identified with compensatory education for the disadvantaged. Although culturally and linguistically disadvantaged children in the U.S. can and do benefit from bilingual education, Lambert & Anisfeld (33) have indicated the assets of early bilingual training for "advantaged" children as well.

Dugas (18) has detailed the contributions of several fields toward preparation for bilingual education: linguistics, psycholinguistics, sociolinguistics, social psychology, and developmental psycholinguistics. Psycholinguistics supplies information on the nature of bilingualism, and on the differences between compound and coordinate bilinguals. The compound bilingual is one who has a single set of referents for his two languages. The words "dog" and "*Hund*" conjure up the same image for a compound German-English bilingual. The coordinate bilingual, on the other hand, keeps his two languages separate, has learned his languages in different cultural environments, and has at least partially different referents for the two languages. Social

Contributions of different fields to bilingual education

251

psychology supplies information about the nature of the learner, his attitudes, motivation, etc. Sociolinguistics helps one to understand the linguistic "division of labor" in a situation of stable group bilingualism. Finally, the new field of developmental psycholinguistics gives insight into the stages of concept and language formation in children.

Sharp (67) stresses the importance of the teacher's being able to understand the *cultural content* of what his students say. The problems of intercultural communication are perhaps more crucial than linguistic problems for the teacher of bilingual education for Mexican-American grade school children. Such a teacher needs extensive training in the Hispanic system of values and social patterns, and in sociology with an emphasis on Latin-American society. She should also have a knowledge of some of the great achievements of the Hispanic peoples "so that she may teach her pupils to take pride in their noble language."

Teacher's understanding of t student's message

Rodriguez (64) has stated that by 1970 there will be a need for 100,000 bilingual teachers in the U.S., and 90% of them must be competent in Spanish. He draws attention to a National Teachers Corps Project being conducted (1968) at the University of Southern California. The Project is called HILT, for High Intensity Language Training, and Rodriguez feels that this sort of program may well be the first step toward the development of an extensive program for both preservice and in-service training of teachers for bilingual education projects. The program involves 50 beginning Teacher Corps interns who are taught communication skills in Spanish during a 7-week period. No attempt is made to teach them grammar or other related aspects of the language. They are also given an intensive program in the culture of the language, both formally and in association with Mexican-Americans in the area.

Need for bilingual teachers a the National Teachers Corps

The training of teaching assistants and college teachers of modern foreign languages

The traditional approach to the training of graduate assistants and future college teachers of modern languages has generally been one of departmental *laissez-faire*. McArdle (38) refers to the MacAllister Report of 1963, which surveyed for the Modern Language Association the state of college teacher preparation and found that nearly 60% of the departments which responded offered practically no training to their assistants, no course in

Lack of training for TA's no in MacAllister Report

methods, no visitations by supervisors, and no effective means for supervision. The philosophy behind this attitude is probably best expressed by Perren (52): "University teachers as such are not normally trained to teach at all, presumably because it is assumed that their students have been trained to learn." Perren quickly adds, however: "This may be an even more dubious assumption where a second language is used than when the language is the mother tongue."

During the fall of 1969, a survey on the training and supervision of teaching assistants, sponsored by ACTFL and the Association of Departments of Foreign Languages (ADFL), was carried out by M. P. Hagiwara (24). Elaborate questionnaires were completed by 151 departments of foreign languages representing 92 universities in 39 states. The questions were grouped into four major categories: (1) teaching assistantships; (2) preservice training; (3) in-service training; and (4) supervision.

MLA/ADFL study of training and supervision of teaching assistants

The results justify more optimism than the MacAllister Report could, and one can legitimately point to an improvement in the exercise of academic responsibility of many foreign language departments toward the training and supervision of their junior staff members.

Optimistic results

The amount of training and supervision varies widely among responding departments. Generally speaking, small departments (with a mean number of TA's of 4.8) tend to have minimal programs and, as Hagiwara suggests, to depend upon so-called osmotic learning through contacts with senior faculty members. Large departments, on the other hand, with a mean number of 38.3 TA's, tend to have elaborate systems of orientation, preservice training, and clearly defined responsibilities for supervisors, course heads, and experienced TA's.

As far as the rationale for appointment and the status of TA's are concerned, Hagiwara states that the primary criteria for determining eligibility for a teaching assistantship are the applicant's academic records, previous teaching experience, and travel or study abroad. Factors such as financial need, performance on a proficiency test, and recordings made by the applicant are ranked lower by responding departments. "Letters of recommendation" was not listed on the questionnaire as a possible factor, but Hagiwara suggests it would have ranked high if it had been listed. The criteria employed for reappointments of TA's are teaching performance, graduate work, and, less importantly, financial need. Only about 20% of the departments reporting

Eligibility for a teaching assistantship

mentioned that they test the applicant's linguistic proficiency in any formal way, although the fact that over 85% of the departments consider the experience of travel or study abroad as significant in the selection of graduate assistants indirectly suggests the importance of language fluency and familiarity with the target culture. More than half the departments stated that their assistants teach only one course per term, but in a sizable number (almost 40%) TA's teach two courses per term. Stipends for TA's are generally determined according to their experience and the number of courses they teach. The range indicated by Hagiwara is from $1,200 to $4,332 per year. In roughly two-thirds of the departments, assistants teach only first and second year courses.

What kind of preservice training is provided for new graduate assistants? Hagiwara reports that many departments claim to offer formal or informal conferences, workshops, or seminars designed to provide orientation and training for new junior staff members. Among the topics in preservice training which received a high percentage of total affirmative replies are: (1) discussion and explanation of instructional materials; (2) detailed description of lower-level courses taught by TA's; (3) discussion of various language teaching methods; (4) discussion of the role of the language laboratory; and (5) explanation of methods of testing and evaluating student performance. Only about 31% of the departments have the TA's present a microlesson (see Politzer, 54), and even fewer videotape the microlessons. Surprisingly, during the preservice orientation only 28% offer a discussion of the problems of cultural analysis and of methods of teaching culture.

Preservice training for new graduate assistants

What provisions are made for in-service training of graduate assistants? Hagiwara indicates that in-service supervision of the actual teaching done by assistants is neither as complete nor as widespread as the basically theoretical introduction to teaching given during the orientation period. Methods courses exist in fewer than 75% of the departments and courses in applied linguistics in fewer than 65%. The percentage of these departments which *require* such courses of teaching assistants is less than one-third. Ninety-three percent of the departments reported that visits are made to the TA's' classes, but these tend to be made at ever-decreasing frequency over the academic year. In 83% of the departments, a departmental (course-wide) final examination is given in courses taught by TA's, in an effort to

In-service training of TA's

establish a fairly uniform standard of evaluation and measurement in all the sections. In 80% of the cases, TA's are involved in the composition of these examinations.

Hagiwara has elsewhere (23) discussed the training of TA's in French at the University of Michigan. Each new TA attends a three-day workshop prior to the start of classes in the fall. Demonstrations of teaching techniques are given, videotaped microteaching is done by all TA's (in a simulated classroom situation in front of their peers), and lessons are critiqued by the group immediately after the microteach. During the year TA's are encouraged to take course work in applied linguistics. In the fall, one section of every course is taught by an experienced teaching fellow, and this section serves as a demonstration section which new teaching fellows attend at least seven times in the first month.

Specific training programs

Hanzeli (25) has described a similar preservice "internship" for TA's in Romance languages at the University of Washington. The program was obligatory for all new TA's and consisted of thirteen hours of lecture-discussion, seven hours of viewing and discussing films, five hours of demonstration classes, six hours of simulated practice teaching, and five hours of general discussion. The program took place during two weeks in September and TA's were paid an additional half-month's salary for attendance.

Meiden (40) has described the training program for TA's in Romance languages at Ohio State University. The training for the teaching of the first course includes a preservice two-hour orientation session; attendance by the TA's at a demonstration section of the course taught by a supervisor; three full-hour visits and several shorter ones by a supervisor to TA's classes, followed by conferences; frequent meetings of all TA's teaching the course to solve problems, plan examinations, etc.

Training the teacher of FLES

Although much has been written in the past couple of years about the training of teachers of foreign languages for secondary schools and colleges, relatively little has been said about the preparation of foreign language teachers for the elementary school. Theodore Andersson has written (3) that "the greatest single obstacle to the growth of the FLES movement is the shortage of qualified teachers." Andersson cites a 1959–60 survey which showed that, whereas almost 98% of American teacher-training institutions trained foreign language teachers for the secondary schools, only about 24% trained teachers for FLES. There is no reason to believe that these statistics have improved markedly.

Gefen (20) feels that the second language teacher in the primary school must be a primary school teacher in every sense of the term. Accordingly, the ideal person to teach a foreign language to primary school pupils is the regular classroom teacher, who has been trained in the foreign language. Such a teacher, who has demonstrated the necessary aptitude for second language learning, and who has received training in teaching the second language, Gefen calls a "semi-specialist." She may be allowed to teach the second language in her own class and in one or two others.

The ideal FLES specialist

FLES teachers, like foreign language teachers at all other levels, need training. Gefen (20) has suggested a system for the preservice and in-service training of FLES teachers which is quite elaborate. During initial (preservice) training, the future teacher of FLES should pursue course work in: (1) language improvement (pronunciation, intonation; structure of the language; no literary training as such); (2) linguistics (including applied linguistics and phonetics); (3) structure of the second language (to be studied for the teacher's background information, not for classroom presentation); (4) background studies of the history, traditions, and general way of life of the second language speech community; (5) psychology of language learning (involving psycholinguistic studies of first and second language acquisition); (6) methodology of teaching a second language (to be highly practical in orientation; should include use of audiovisual aids and supervised practice teaching); (7) general subjects (other college courses to be studied). This scheme is laudable for foreign language teachers at *any* level, but one may wonder whether it is realistic to expect such an exhaustive preservice training period for teachers in the elementary school.

Pre- and in-service FLES teacher training programs

Gefen's model for in-service training has two components: (1) a part-time course of not fewer than 100 hours of instruction; (2) a full-time intensive course of three months, most profitably spent in the target country. The curriculum for in-service training which Gefen specifies contains the same basic elements as his preservice model. The only major difference is the lack of practice teaching as part of the methodology section.

Otto suggests (45) that teacher-certification programs in FLES should include a special methods course in developing skills and materials especially for teaching elementary school pupils. Since FLES teachers are not always elementary education majors, Otto recommends that a separate student teaching experience in FLES is desirable for elementary education majors and necessary for secondary education foreign language majors and graduate majors in foreign language education. The latter two types of prospective FLES teachers should receive training in child development and elementary education foundations as part of their course of study.

FLES teacher certification programs

Developments in teacher certification

State certification of teachers of foreign languages, and, indeed, of teachers of all curricular areas, has long been a source of much anxiety, frustration, and spleen-venting. There is widespread agreement among foreign language educators that, to cite Andersson (3), "certification should be based on knowledge and proficiency, *however acquired.*"

Some critics advocate removing both certification, which Sheppard (69) has defined as "the attesting to one's competence," and licensure, "permission to practice," from the clutches of the state and having both functions performed by other "authorities." Benardo (8) feels that prospective teachers should be certified and licensed on the joint recommendation of the university where they received their professional training and the local board of education where they plan to teach. Lohnes (35), in describing the preparation of teachers of German, urges that German teachers be certified based on national standards to be set up and verified by the American Association of Teachers of German. To be certified by the AATG, a candidate would have to: (*1*) achieve a minimal score of "good" on the seven parts of the MLA Proficiency Test for Teachers and Advanced Students; (*2*) demonstrate competence on tests of culture and civilization, to be developed and administered by the AATG; (*3*) pass an oral examination before a board consisting of a senior member of the candidate's college department, a representative of a second graduate department or a school of education, a representative of a state board of education or accrediting agency, and a senior member of the German department of a local high school; (*4*) demonstrate a lesson with a college or high

Suggestions for ways of licensing FL teachers

257

school class before the same board; (5) have filed a report from his intern supervisor. If the candidate is deficient in one of these areas, certification can be provisionally approved and that portion of the examination can be repeated a minimum of six months later. Lohnes maintains that under the above system of certification, the candidate need not have majored or even minored in German; he merely demonstrates his proficiency as a professional, *however acquired.*

Douglas Sheppard's recent article in *Foreign Language Annals*, "Certifying Teachers of Modern Foreign Languages for American Schools – 1969," (69) has updated the last comprehensive study of certification in foreign languages, that of Balakian, done in 1961. Balakian reported the tremendous confusion and lack of standardization in types of certificates issued and in the requirements for certification. A decade later, Sheppard reluctantly reports: "The variety of certificates, kinds of endorsement, and divergencies of interpretations are so great that it is not apparent – at least in regard to foreign languages – that either inter- or intra-state standardization is much more of a reality now than it was ten years ago." Incredibly, what is called a "permanent" or "life" certificate in some states is the equivalent of a "provisional" or "temporary" certificate in others.

Certification: a major study

Sheppard reports that the one constant in foreign language teacher certification that everyone acknowledges is that there is no practical way of equating teaching performance with the number of credit hours on a transcript. The number of credit (semester) hours required for the first certificate in foreign languages varies from 15 to 35 depending upon the state; but even these figures are somewhat meaningless in a comparison, since some states give credit to precollegiate training, some to lower-division undergraduate work, some only to junior-senior level courses and above. Sixteen states claim to allow the possibility of certification on the basis of demonstrated proficiency, but half of these add something like, " . . . if the college or university attests to it" (Sheppard, 69).

Seven states in the country – Connecticut, Delaware, Georgia, Nevada, New York, Virginia, and West Virginia, and until recently, Pennsylvania – unequivocally make use of the MLA Proficiency Tests in some capacity for purposes of certification. Sheppard points to the coincidence that Pennsylvania, which was formerly the only state in the nation to *require* that all candidates for certification in a modern foreign language take the

Use of MLA Proficiency Test

MLA Proficiency Tests, dropped its requirement as of June, 1969, at a time when the conclusions of the now famous Pennsylvania Foreign Language Project suggested no positive correlation, and perhaps a negative one, between student achievement in foreign languages and teacher scores on the MLA Proficiency Tests (Smith, 72).

The whole problem of reciprocity in state certification is one of the most aggravating issues. Sheppard is most explicit here: "Let us suppose that a person certified to teach a modern foreign language in the public secondary schools of one state decides to move to another state. Is it likely that he will be allowed to teach at his new residence without further academic preparation? The chances are that he will not, except on an emergency or temporary basis, unless he happens to have moved within a severely limited number of states . . . which have reciprocal agreements. Indeed there is every likelihood that a certificate issued by the state will not be recognized in certain municipalities of the very same state. Not infrequently the applicant will find the skill or knowledge required for the new certification bears no apparent relationship to the teaching field for which he is seeking certification."

Reciprocity in certification among states

Sheppard writes that only 12 states in the U.S. have reciprocal agreements. This figure is updated by a notice from the California State Department of Education, dated May 4, 1970, which lists 22 states that "comprise an interstate agreement on qualification of educational personnel," and an additional 5 states in the process of entering this reciprocity compact. The original 22 states are: California, Connecticut, Delaware, Florida, Hawaii, Idaho, Indiana, Maine, Maryland, Minnesota, Massachusetts, New Hampshire, New Jersey, New York, North Carolina, Ohio, Rhode Island, South Dakota, Vermont, Washington, West Virginia, and Wisconsin. Those states about to enter the compact are Alaska, Kentucky, Oklahoma, Pennsylvania, and Virginia.

Sheppard concludes with a characterization of the current state of foreign language certification:

Present characteristics of FL certification

A Anyone possessing skills badly enough needed can be certified, if only on an emergency basis.

B Generally, requirements for employment (not necessarily for certification) are more severe in suburban and metropolitan areas than rural; persons who move from one state to

259

C Responsibility for training is largely in the hands of college and university faculties, though state departments retain the right of licensure.

D Perhaps the most innovative and exciting development is the search to encourage schools to become training centers, where students, interns, practitioners, supervisors, teacher trainers, and researchers will all work together.

E The tenor in certification still seems to be "wait and see," but mounting pressures for growth and change may not permit this much longer.

The role and responsibilities of the foreign language teacher in the school and in the profession

It need hardly be pointed out that we are in the midst of a revolution in education, inside as well as outside the classroom. Students are no longer content to be mere passive receptacles of facts and ideas dispensed by the teacher; they are demanding greater involvement in the educational process for themselves and a different relationship with their teachers. In such disciplines as English and social studies, teachers are responding to the battle cry of "relevance" and "individualization" with imaginative, innovative programs. If the teacher of foreign languages is to keep up with those in other disciplines—and with his students—he must be prepared to assume a new role. He must, as Paquette (46) has pointed out, make a "declaration of independence." He must "stop viewing himself as a purveyor of facts and an explicator and come to view himself as the designer, constructor, and manager of the learning situation." He must learn to make a candid assessment of his own skills, Paquette asserts, so that he can make the best use of instructional sources to complement his strengths and weaknesses. To this end, Paquette suggests that the teacher become conversant with three important areas: testing research, linguistics, and educational technology. In the area of testing, there is a need for new classroom tests based on performance criteria, rather than tests which compare one student with another. In other words, tests must be designed which give specific information about individual student achievement. To construct, administer, and evaluate

New role for FL teachers

such tests, the teacher needs to be conversant with recent research in the field of measurement. Teachers must also be aware of the newest theories in linguistics, as they apply to the classroom, and must beware of attaching themselves to any one theory of instruction too quickly and too firmly. In these days when the structuralist-transformationalist controversy is still raging, the foreign language teacher must be able to assess each argument carefully, and must know how to choose from each side of the controversy those techniques which will work in his classroom.

In addition to these theoretical advances, the teacher must learn to use the technological advances to their utmost efficiency. The language laboratory, tape recorder, video tape, and films can provide a variety of native speakers, and can present students with direct associations between lexical and structural items and the reality which they represent. They offer the teacher the opportunity to become more than a trainer in the language system as such and offer the possibility of more individualized instruction than ever before.

The FL teacher as a user of technological advances

In his school, the foreign language teacher must be an "expert" to whom students and colleagues can come for professional advice. He serves as a link with, and communicator and interpreter of, a culture and civilization, and he spends his time teaching about this culture largely through the medium of its language. He must realize at all times that his students' conception of "what a Spaniard is like" is largely the portrait that he has painted for them.

The FL teacher as a communicator of the foreign culture

In addition, the foreign language teacher has the responsibility of keeping his profession professional. He must strive to attain and maintain the standards of excellence which the profession has recommended. He must remember that his education does not end when he receives his diploma. He should join and support the professional organizations whose goal is to contribute to his continuing growth. He has the obligation to be aware of the content of the foreign language programs in his district at all educational levels, and to see to it that he does not contribute to a weakening in the chain of articulation. In short, the foreign language teacher's role is perhaps more demanding and exciting in 1970 than it has ever been before. And the demands and excitement show no signs of abating as he heads into the future.

The FL teacher as a professional

The role and training of the foreign language supervisor

If the foreign language teacher has a responsibility for excellence in his school and profession, he cannot do all that is needed alone, without drawing too heavily upon his reserves of time and energy. It is here that the role of the supervisor in both pre-service and in-service training becomes most urgent. If the supervisor is to be effective, he must be well trained in the fields of teaching and supervision and must have a thorough background in linguistics, methodology, and other related fields. Above all, he must be sensitive to the needs and personalities of the teachers he is supervising. Davidson (16) points out that there is an art to providing helpful supervision and evaluation while still conveying a respect for the individual. "The truly effective supervisory operation implies mutual respect, an understanding of objectives, a cooperative effort, and a considerable latitude in role definition."

Sensitive to needs and personalities

This view is reflected by many members of the profession. O'Neill (44), Wladaver (80), and McKim (39), for example, see the role of the supervisor as contributing not only to public relations, curriculum development, and evaluation, but, most significantly, to the professional growth of his staff members. The key to meaningful supervision is the development of an effective teaching corps by means of an active, carefully designed training program.

Responsible for staff development

Weiss (78) has proposed an in-service foreign language teacher training program based upon his concept of the "training supervisor." In this design, the training supervisor is also a classroom teacher who teaches two classes, a beginning and an advanced language class, which serve as year-long demonstration classes to which members of his staff are urged to come often, to observe the supervisor interacting with real students in a real learning situation, to see new or difficult techniques demonstrated, and perhaps, from time to time, to teach the class themselves while the training supervisor observes. During the time when he is not demonstration-teaching, the training supervisor visits teachers in their classes, works with them in team-teaching projects, and on occasion takes over their teaching duties for several days so that they may use the time for observation of other teachers or for curriculum development work.

A specific supervisor training program

Weiss is quick to point out that the training supervisor should have nothing to do with the promotion, salary arrangements, or any other contractual obligations of the teachers with whom he works. Only in this way can he and they feel free to observe and discuss their respective teaching techniques.

Throughout the school year, the training supervisor offers assistance in a program involving three stages of evaluation: video tape evaluation, interaction analysis, and self-evaluation. Frequently, the supervisor-teacher conference breaks down because of misunderstandings due to different perceptions of the same event. Through the use of video tape, both supervisor and teacher can observe the interaction of teacher with students, and students with students, with objective detachment. Interactional analysis, which has been mentioned above and discussed in detail by McArdle (38), has its strength in its objectivity and in the fact that it makes no overt value judgments about a teacher's behavior. By its very objectivity, it keeps the teacher from being defensive about his classroom performance and clears the way for productive supervision.

After enough training, the teacher will be able to reconstruct for himself, without the aid of video tape or of a supervisor's interaction analysis tally sheet, the events which occurred in his own classroom. When the training has reached this point, the teacher will have learned a great deal about his capabilities for handling certain teaching techniques, his strengths and weaknesses, and the skills and characteristics that make up his individual style. When the training supervisor has brought his charges to the point where they are capable of perceptive self-analysis, he has achieved the goals of his training program.

The need for upgrading the status of the supervisor and intensifying his involvement in teacher training is just as urgent at the university level. Hagiwara's new study (24) of the training and supervision of graduate assistants has already been discussed above. What is of interest here is the information he provides about the role, training, duties, and compensation of the departmental supervisor. Of the 129 supervisors and 62 assistant supervisors in his study, Hagiwara reports that over 35% of them did not (yet) have a doctorate, and that 71% of them were in the rank of assistant professor or below. The median year when those supervisors with Ph.D.'s attained them was as recent as 1966, thus suggesting that those charged with the supervision of graduate assistants and with the administration of lower-level

Need for supervisors on the college level

263

courses tend to be relatively young people who hold somewhat insecure positions in their departments. In almost 50% of the cases, their specialization was literature; only about 17% had specialized in methodology. This would suggest that supervisory duties are frequently assigned to persons *not* solely on the basis of their special qualifications for the job.

In compensation for their special duties, supervisors are frequently—though not always or everywhere—provided with released time from teaching responsibilities. For small departments, the average reduction is 1.0 classes per academic year; for medium-sized departments, 1.9 classes; for large departments, 3.3 classes per year. Almost 30% of the supervisors reported receiving no released time for their supervisory duties, implying that these were added on to the normal teaching assignments and scholarly activities expected of faculty members. It comes as little surprise to learn, in view of these statistics, that over 44% of those supervisors responding indicated their dissatisfaction with the reduction they received. *Compensation of supervisors*

Hagiwara's own discussion (23) of the training and supervision of college teachers of foreign languages at Michigan lists the responsibilities of the TA supervisor which indicate an involvement that goes beyond mere class visitation and evaluation. His duties entail: (1) an introductory workshop for new teaching fellows; (2) two workshops on teaching reading; (3) a course in applied linguistics; (4) checking the departmental tests and individually made quizzes; (5) evaluation of new teaching fellows; (6) class visits to those teaching fellows eligible for promotion to a higher level; (7) personal supervision of those deficient in proper teaching techniques; (8) individual conferences with instructors whenever necessary; (9) checking the departmental grade reports. *TA supervisor*

Meiden (40) reports the use of outstanding graduate students as cosupervisors who devote five hours of their thirteen-hour load to supervision. The purpose of using such personnel is not merely to distribute the task of supervision, but also to bring new talent into the supervision process by identifying, recruiting, and training gifted teachers.

Training the teacher's teachers

If the foreign language supervisor is to play an effective role in training foreign language teachers in modern methodology and in the technical skills of successful classroom teaching (Politzer & Weiss, 58), his own training must be elaborate and varied, to say the least. Throughout the country, universities are developing graduate programs in the relatively new field of "Foreign Language Education." The basic goal of this field is to train the foreign language specialist for supervision, teacher training, curriculum development, or a host of other professional activities in foreign language administration and teaching. Most, but not all, of the programs lead to a doctorate in Foreign Language Education (Ph.D., Ed.D., D.A.). Thomsen (77) lists 11 universities in the U.S. which offer advanced degrees in foreign language education. These are: Florida State, New York University, Ohio State, Purdue, Rutgers, Stanford, State University of New York at Buffalo, University of Texas at Austin, University of Washington, Wayne State, and the University of Minnesota. To this list can be added Temple University and possibly others whose programs have not as yet become known. In the past 5 years, according to Thomsen, these institutions have granted nearly 600 master's degrees and 43 doctorates.

FL education graduate study programs

The overall patterns for these degrees seem to be quite similar throughout the country. Admission to a doctoral program in foreign language education is usually based upon two prerequisites: near-native proficiency in one foreign language, with some knowledge of a second one, and at least two years of teaching experience in foreign languages at the elementary, secondary, or university level. The curriculum tends to be flexible enough to allow individuals—whose goals may be as diverse as teaching English as a second language to adults abroad and developing curriculum for use in FLES—to find a comfortable place in the program. In general, all candidates, however, pursue certain basic courses which (1) continue to develop their proficiency in their first foreign language; (2) attempt to give them some proficiency in a second foreign language; (3) give them a theoretical foundation in foreign language methodology, linguistics, psychology, statistical measurement, and research; (4) give them supervisory experience of some sort; (5) give them certification, if needed. Michel (41) and especially Thomsen (77) go into such programs in detail. We can examine only a few specific programs in some depth here.

The overall pattern for degrees in FL education

The Foreign Language Center at the University of Texas at Austin is an example of this kind of program. It is interdisciplinary in that it cuts across the colleges of arts and science,

University of Texas

education, communications, etc., and across departments of language, linguistics, speech, and anthropology, making use of various faculty members as well as the resources of each individual department. This type of organization, as Michel (41) points out, allows for theses and dissertations to be written on topics that refer to the teaching and learning of language, rather than the traditional topics in literary analysis. It puts on the student's committee specialists in literature and linguistics, in language acquisition and language pedagogy. In this way, the center provides the means for, and encourages much needed research on, the teaching and learning of languages, and carries the preparation of foreign language teachers one step closer toward professionalism.

Stanford University's program leading to the Ph.D. in Foreign Language Education, though lacking the extensive interdisciplinary and interdepartmental staffing, is still somewhat similar to that of Texas. Incoming candidates generally have a master's degree in a specific language or in linguistics. Courses are distributed among four core-requirement areas: curriculum, instruction, and supervision; behavioral science studies; normative studies; and inquiry skills. The program is under the auspices of the School of Education, but allows for flexibility in course work and training that may come from outside the School of Education and even outside the areas specified in the core requirements. A strong point of the program is the opportunity for doctoral candidates to supervise the training of secondary school intern teachers in foreign languages and to do research at the Stanford Center for Research and Development in Teaching. *Stanford University*

The University of Minnesota offers both the M.A. and Ph.D. in Foreign Language Education and Research, with emphasis on developing proficiency in conducting, evaluating, and interpreting research in the field of foreign language education. To this end, there is a concentration in the areas of educational psychology, experimental design, and statistics, as well as in methodology and language skills. The doctoral dissertation must be experimental in design. Possible topics for the dissertation include classroom and related problems, evaluation of experimental curricula, evaluation of specific teaching strategies, and teacher training. *University of Minnesota*

The Department of Germanic Languages and Literature of the University of Washington offers a program leading to a Doctor of Arts (D.A.) degree for the preparation of college teachers of *University of Washington*

German and specialists in German teaching. This program has been developed as a parallel doctoral program to the Ph.D. in Germanic literature or philology, the products of which have traditionally prepared for careers in literary or philological research and scholarship, rather than in language teaching and research in methodology. The three main threads of the D.A. program at Washington are linguistics, educational research, and proficiency in German. During the first two doctoral years, candidates have an opportunity to acquire teaching experience on the lower-division level under the close supervision of departmental coordinators. The third doctoral year is an internship, whereby the D.A. candidate observes, assists, and works with professors who teach upper-division courses. The candidate must prepare topics for discussion, as well as schedules and examinations, for third and fourth year classes, and ultimately he may take over the class for short periods under the supervision of a master teacher. This program is unique in providing such massive exposure to the problems of teaching advanced years of college German, a source of embarrassment for many new Ph.D.'s from more traditional programs, since they have had little or no experience with the teaching of junior-senior courses.

Temple University offers a master's degree in Foreign Language Education which is designed to improve the fluency and methodology of the candidates. The program is interdisciplinary, *Temple University* with half of the course work done in the foreign language that the candidate is to be certified to teach and the other half in courses related primarily to the teaching of foreign languages. In the future, Temple plans to go into block scheduling or modules for professional course work, a positive step toward individualizing the instruction of teacher trainees.

The program in Foreign Language Education at Florida State University has been described by Heflin & Leamon in detail (26). In summary, the graduate program leads to a master's degree or doctorate in Foreign Language Education, and graduate *Florida State University* students prepare for administrative or supervisory positions in foreign language work, to teach foreign languages at the junior college or college level, to become themselves trainers of foreign language teachers, or simply to prepare to be stronger, more knowledgeable teachers in the classroom. Course work is offered in the standard areas discussed above, and a special feature of the program is a methods course offering special sections for teachers of French, German, or Spanish. These sections are conducted primarily in the target languages. A special lecture series brings to campus each year distinguished guest speakers in the field of foreign language education.

A glimpse into the future

Despite the enormous discrepancy between the number of changes suggested for foreign language teacher training, supervision, and certification, and the number of changes which have apparently been made to date, certain factors and several budding programs justify an optimistic outlook for the future of foreign language teacher training.

First of all, the collapse of foreign language requirements nationally, while having at times a devastating effect upon local enrollments, has simultaneously caused a great deal of mental and physical effort to be expended on such problems as making courses relevant to student needs, adapting programs in accordance with new thinking in educational psychology, and producing teachers for the "new" students, which Sandstrom et al. (65) discuss. Such thinking can have only salutary effects for future teacher training programs. The sort of training which has produced successful teachers-for-a-captive-audience will not necessarily be successful when the audience can pick and choose, and say "No!" The research going on into the nature of student aptitude, attitudes, and motivation, the attempts to refine procedures for various techniques in foreign language teaching, the concern with individualizing instruction to fit the student's needs, the realization that the "classics" are not always the best reading material for training young people – all of these factors are being taken into account in designing new preservice and inservice teacher training programs in foreign languages.

Attention to the individual student

Secondly, as has been suggested in this chapter, the training and supervision of foreign language teachers is becoming increasingly dominated by knowledgeable, interested experts who specialize, do research, and publish in the fields of teacher training, methodology, applied linguistics, etc. The unkind, and apparently unforgettable, dictum that "those who can not teach, teach teachers," simply isn't true any longer, if it ever was true.

"Experts" in teacher traini

Thirdly, though NDEA Institutes in the "common" languages in the U.S. seem a thing of the past, EPDA – the Educational Professions Development Act – is a thing of the present, and hopefully of the future, too. Although funding in these trying times is not overwhelming, some funds are available for foreign language teacher training programs. A project this year, for example, has been funded at the University of Minnesota, the purpose of which was to involve practicing secondary school foreign language teachers in the undergraduate foreign language teacher training program (Arendt & Lange, 5).

Government support for teacher education

Fourthly, the sheer flood of writings, professional meetings, and challenges to the foreign language teacher training profession has had a significant impact and will doubtless have increasing impact in the future, as the generation of "new" teachers for "new" students begins to reflect upon its training and experiences. The inertia which has preserved the status quo especially in the area of teacher certification is weakening under the continuous barrage of attacks from inside and outside the foreign language profession.

Significant literature

Fifthly, there is reason to believe that programs for training FLES teachers, secondary school language teachers, and college teachers are starting to be aware of one another's existence. Although the problems for the language teacher at every educational level are often different, it is essential that the foreign language teacher at *any* level know the problems and possible solutions for language teaching at all other levels. Only in this way can we really hope for a properly articulated sequence of language learning from FLES through college.

Communication at all levels of FL instruction

Lastly, several programs are going on at major universities in the United States which are so new that they have not yet had an opportunity to be evaluated or to influence the development of similar programs elsewhere. But such events are only a matter of time. For an encouraging and dramatic example, a new teacher training program in German will be under way in the fall of 1970 at the University of Wisconsin. Under the direction of Ursula Thomas, this program is worthy of interest not only for its intrinsic value as an excellent long-range program for the training of teachers of German, but also for its excellence as an undergraduate language program. The department will select high school graduates with three to five years experience in high school German, who express an interest in teaching German. At the university, they will have at least three semesters of course work in other subject areas, taught in German, in addition to the traditional course work for the German major. Their junior year will be spent in Germany. The first interdisciplinary course to be

New teacher training programs

taught in German will be elementary botany, conducted by a visiting professor in the botany department, who is a native German connected with the University of Göttingen. For this course, all materials—textbooks, lab manuals, etc.—will be in German. Charts, diagrams, and pictures will be used extensively and will provide visual aids that are essential in such a course. Among other activities planned for the students' sophomore year is a course in social studies taught in German. The junior year, as stated above, will be spent in Germany. Upon their return to Wisconsin, the students will have three options: they may take their education courses and a block semester of methods and student teaching; they may do a semester's internship as an undergraduate; or they may go on for a master's degree and do a graduate internship.

It is most encouraging to see this attempt on the college level to provide for interdisciplinary instruction taught in a foreign language, and to provide options in teacher training on the undergraduate level for individualizing programs.

Other encouraging signs are the new Doctor of Arts program in German at Washington, which has already been discussed above, and the adoption at many institutions of the concept of the "experience curriculum" which Sandstrom, Politzer, Rabura, and others have advocated. There is still much to be done in modernizing and improving teacher preparation by even the most forward-looking programs, and all too many programs are evidently not forward looking at all; but as we have seen, there are signs on the horizon that the future may fulfill its promise.

References, Recent developments in the training and certification of the foreign language teacher

1 Allen, Virginia F. "Preparing Teachers to Teach across Dialects." *TESOL Quarterly* 3(1969): 251–56.

2 Altman, Howard B. "The Preparation of the High School German Teacher:Practical Training." *Die Unterrichtspraxis* 3,ii(1970):In press.

3 Andersson, Theodore. *Foreign Languages in the Elementary School:A Struggle against Mediocrity.* Austin: Univ. of Texas Press, 1969.

4 ———— "From NDEA to EPDA: Can We Improve?" *Hispania* 52:357–61.

5 Arendt, Jermaine D., and Dale L. Lange. "An EPDA Institute for Cooperating Teachers in German." *Die Unterrichtspraxis* 3,i(1970):160–66.

6 Banta, Frank G. "Graduate to Graduate: Practice Teaching for Advanced Instruction." *Die Unterrichtspraxis* 2,i(1969):44–46.

7 Bell, Paul W. "The Recruitment and Training of Teachers of Bilingual Students in Miami, Florida," 57–60 in Charles Stubing,ed., *Reports:Bilingualism.* El Paso: Southwest Council of For-

eign Language Teachers, 1966.

8 Benardo, Leo U. "Changes in Teacher Preparation," 16 in Maurice Silver,ed., *Proceedings: Thirty-First Annual Foreign Language Conference at New York University.* New York: New York Univ. School of Education, Department of Foreign Languages and International Relations Education, 1965.

9 Brain, Joseph J. "The Role of the Volunteer in Teaching English to Educated Foreign-Born Adults." *TESOL Quarterly* 2(1968):51–56.

10 Bright, J.A. "The Training of Teachers of English as a Second Language in Africa," 14–43 in G.E. Perren,ed., *Teachers of English as a Second Language:Their Training and Preparation.* Cambridge: Cambridge Univ. Press, 1968.

11 Cartledge, H.A. "Training Teachers of Adults," 44–66 in G.E. Perren,ed., *Teachers of English as a Second Language:Their Training and Preparation.* Cambridge: Cambridge Univ. Press, 1968.

12 Castle, Pat, and Charles Jay. "Foreign Language Teacher Training Programs in Illinois," 16–45 in Pat Castle and Charles Jay,eds., *Toward Excellence in Foreign Language Education.* Springfield, Illinois: Office of the Superintendent of Public Instruction, State of Illinois, 1968.

13 Christian, Chester,ed. *Reports:Bilingual Education:Research and Teaching.* El Paso: Southwest Council of Foreign Language Teachers, 1967.

14 Cline, Marion,Jr. "Preparation of Teachers of Disadvantaged," 61–62 in Charles Stubing,ed., *Reports:Bilingualism.* El Paso: Southwest Council of Foreign Language Teachers, 1966.

15 Corder, S.P. "Advanced Study and the Experienced Teacher," 67–94 in G.E. Perren,ed., *Teachers of English as a Second Language: Their Training and Preparation.* Cambridge: Cambridge Univ. Press, 1968.

16 Davidson, Donald K. "Local Administration of the Foreign Language Program." 202–24 in George E. Smith and M. Phillip Leamon,eds., *Effective Foreign Language Instruction in the Secondary School.* Englewood Cliffs, New Jersey: Prentice-Hall, 1969.

17 Deeken, Hans W.,ed. *The Advancement of the Teaching of German in the United States.* Philadelphia: National Carl Schurz Association, and American Association of Teachers of German, 1968.

18 Dugas, Donald. "Research Relevant to the Development of Bilingual Curricula," 23–28 in Chester Christian,ed., *Reports:Bilingual Education: Research and Teaching.* El Paso: Southwest Council of Foreign Language Teachers, 1967.

19 Dusel, John P., et al. *Foreign Language Dropouts:Problems and Solutions.* Experimental edition. Sacramento: California State Department of Education, 1970.

20 Gefen, Raphael. "Initial and In-Service Training for Second Language Teaching in the Primary School," 84–94 in H.H. Stern,ed., *Languages and the Young School Child.* London: Oxford Univ. Press, 1969.

21 Girard, Denis. "La formation et le perfectionnement des professeurs de langues vivantes," 74–94 in Hans Jalling,ed., *Modern Language Teaching:Papers from the 9th F.I.P.L.V. Congress.* London: Oxford Univ. Press, 1968.

22 Glenn, Leona. "University Labs as a Training Ground for Teachers." *National Association of Language Laboratory Directors Journal* 4,i(1969):15–20.

23 Hagiwara, Michio P. "Training and Supervision of College Foreign Language Teachers." *Foreign Language Annals* 3(1969):90–107.

24 ——— "Trends in Training and Supervision of Graduate Assistants." [Unpublished manuscript.]

25 Hanzeli, Victor E. "Internship for Teaching Assistants." *Improving College and University Teaching* 16(1968):110–12.

26 Heflin, William H.,Jr., and M. Phillip Leamon. "The Program in Foreign Language Education at Florida State University." *Die Unterrichtspraxis* 2,i(1969):100–03.

27 Hornby, A.S. "Teaching Practice," 95–114 in G.E. Perren,ed., *Teachers of English as a Second Language:Their Training and Preparation.* Cambridge: Cambridge Univ. Press, 1968.

28 Horner, Lucie T. "Broader Participation in Foreign Language Teacher Training." *Modern Language Journal* 54(1970):250–54.

29 ——— "A Recommended Foreign Language Methods Course and Its Prerequisites," 46–48 in Pat Castle and Charles Jay, eds., *Toward Excellence in Foreign Language Education.* Springfield, Illinois: Office of the Superintendent of Public Instruction, State of Illinois, 1968.

30 Hsu, Kai-yu. "The Teacher as an Architect of Learning." *Foreign Language Annals* 3(1970): 377–82.

31 Keppeler, Frank. "Literature in Teacher Education." [Unpublished paper read at the Modern Language Association Convention, Denver, December 1969.]

32 King, Charles. "A Decade of NDEA Language Institutes." *Hispania* 52(1969):361–68.

33 Lambert, Wallace E., and Elizabeth Anisfeld. "A Note on the Relationship of Bilingualism and Intelligence." *Canadian Journal of Behavioural Science* 1(1969):123–28.

34 Lee, W.R. "Training and Study Centres in Britain," 115–45 in G.E. Perren,ed., *Teachers of English as a Second Language:Their Training and Preparation.* Cambridge: Cambridge Univ. Press, 1968.

35 Lohnes, Walter F.W. "The Training of German Teachers in the United States." *Die Unterrichtspraxis* 2,ii(1969):69–76.

36 Marquardt, William F. "Preparing English Teachers Abroad." *TESOL Quarterly* 3(1969): 31–35.

37 McAndrew, Elizabeth D. "An Analysis and Evaluation of the Program Leading to Teacher Certification in Spanish." Unpublished M.A. Thesis. Austin: University of Texas, 1970.

38 McArdle, Richard J. "Teacher Education, Qualifications, and Supervision," 259–80 in

Emma M. Birkmaier,ed., *Britannica Review of Foreign Language Education, Vol. I.* Chicago: Encyclopaedia Britannica, 1968[1969].

39 McKim, Lester W. "A Case for Supervision." *Hispania* 52(1969):252–55.

40 Meiden, Walter. "Training the Inexperienced Graduate Assistant for Language Teaching." *Modern Language Journal* 54(1970):168–74.

41 Michel, Joseph. *Graduate Education of the Foreign Language Specialist.* Austin: The University of Texas, 1970.[Mimeo.]

42 Mordaunt, Jerrold L. "AATSP Panel on Language Teacher Preparation," 159 in Jerrold L. Mordaunt,ed., *Proceedings:Pacific Northwest Conference on Foreign Languages, Twentieth Annual Meeting.* Victoria, British Columbia: Univ. of Victoria, 1969.

43 O'Cherony, Rosalyn. "Applied Linguistics in Foreign Language Teacher Training Programs." *The Illinois Journal of Education* 57,iv(1967): 4–6.

44 O'Neill, Flora J. "The Role of the Teacher in the Dynamics of Continuing Professional Growth," 20–23 in Theodore Huebener,ed., *Proceedings: Thirty-Fourth Annual Foreign Language Conference at New York University.* New York: New York Univ. School of Education, Department of Foreign Languages and International Relations Education, 1968.

45 Otto, Frank. "A Survey of FLES Teacher Certification Requirements." *Modern Language Journal* 53(1969):93–94.

46 Paquette, F. André. "The Foreign Language Teacher:The Dynamics of Continuing Professional Growth," 4–19 in Theodore Huebener, ed., *Proceedings:Thirty-Fourth Annual Foreign Language Conference at New York University.* New York: New York Univ. School of Education, Department of Foreign Languages and International Relations Education. 1968.

47 ———— "The Training and Retraining of Foreign Language Teachers," 53–66 in Donald D. Walsh, ed., *A Handbook for Teachers of Spanish and Portuguese.* Lexington, Massachusetts: D.C. Heath, 1969.

48 Pascual, Henry W. "The Development of Language Skills for Bilinguals:Needs for Retooling," 47–49 in Charles Stubing,ed., *Reports:Bilingualism.* El Paso: Southwest Council of Foreign Language Teachers, 1966.

49 Past, Ray,et al. "Bilingualism:From the Viewpoint of Recruitment and Preparation of Bilingual Teachers," 45–46 in Charles Stubing,ed., *Reports:Bilingualism.* El Paso: Southwest Council of Foreign Language Teachers, 1966.

50 Pattison, Bruce. "The Literary Element in Teacher Education," 146–63 in G.E. Perren,ed., *Teachers of English as a Second Language:Their Training and Preparation.* Cambridge: Cambridge Univ. Press, 1968.

51 Perren, G.E.,ed. *Teachers of English as a Second Language:Their Training and Preparation.* Cambridge: Cambridge Univ. Press, 1968.

52 ———— "Training to Teach in English," 164–79 in G.E. Perren,ed., *Teachers of English as a Second Language: Their Training and Preparation.* Cambridge: Cambridge Univ. Press, 1968.

53 Pillet, Roger A. "Teacher Education in Foreign Languages:An Overview." *Modern Language Journal* 54(1970):14–19.

54 Politzer, Robert L. "Microteaching:A New Approach to Teacher Training and Research." *Hispania* 52(1969):44–48.

55 ———— *Problems in Applying Foreign Language Teaching Methods to the Teaching of Standard English as a Second Dialect.* Research and Development Memorandum No. 40. Palo Alto: Stanford Univ. Center for Research and Development in Teaching, 1968.

56 ———— and Diana E. Bartley. "Practice-Centered Teacher Training:Standard English as a Second Dialect." *Modern Language Journal* 54(1970):31.

57 ———— *Teaching Standard English as a Second Dialect:Suggested Teaching Procedures and Sample Microlessons.* Research and Development Memorandum No. 61. Palo Alto: Stanford University Center for Research and Development in Teaching, 1970.

58 ———— and Louis Weiss. *Characteristics and Behaviors of the Successful Foreign Language Teacher.* Technical Report No. 5. Palo Alto: Stanford University Center for Research and Development in Teaching, 1969.

59 Prince, J. Roy. "An Institute Director Looks Back." *Hispania* 52(1969):368–375.

60 Rabura, Horst M. "The Preparation of Language Teachers," 154–58 in Jerrold L. Mordaunt,ed., *Proceedings:Pacific Northwest Conference on Foreign Languages:Twentieth Annual Meeting, April 11–12, 1969.* Volume 20. Victoria, British Columbia: Univ. of Victoria, 1969.

61 ———— "Spring Quarter in Germany:A New Concept in Foreign Language Teacher Training." *Die Unterrichtspraxis,* 2,ii(1969):134–39.

62 Reichmann, Eberhard. "Proposal for a Graduate Minor in Foreign Language Teaching." *Die Unterrichtspraxis* 2,ii(1969):77–80.

63 Robinett, Betty W. "Teacher Training for English as a Second Dialect and English as a Second Language:The Same or Different?" 121–32 in James E. Alatis,ed., *Report of the Twentieth Annual Round Table Meeting on Linguistics and Language Studies.* Georgetown Univ. Monograph Series on Languages and Linguistics. Washington, D.C.: Georgetown Univ. Press, 1969.

64 Rodriguez, Armando. "Bilingual Education and the Foreign Language Teacher." [Paper presented at the AATSP National Convention, San Antonio, 1968.] [ERIC Documentation Reproduction Service: ED 030 343.]

65 Sandstrom, Eleanor L.,et al. "Foreign Languages for All Students?" 105–33 in Joseph A. Tursi,ed., *Foreign Languages and the "New" Student.* Reports of the Working Committees of the Northeast Conference on the Teaching of Foreign Languages. New York: MLA Materials Center, 1970.

66 Savaiano, Eugene. "Wichita State University's Involvement in the NDEA Institute Program." *Hispania* 52(1969):375–83.

67 Sharp, John M. "Intercultural Problems and the Teacher of English as a Second Language," 50–53 in Charles Stubing,ed., *Reports:Bilingualism*. El Paso: Southwest Council of Foreign Language Teachers, 1966.

68 Sheehan, Joseph, and Robert Willis. "Demonstration of the Use of Television in the Training of Foreign Language Teachers," 109–12 in Mills F. Edgerton,ed., *Sight and Sound:The Sensible and Sensitive Use of Audio-Visual Aids*. Reports of the Working Committees of the Northeast Conference on the Teaching of Foreign Languages. New York: MLA Materials Center, 1969.

69 Sheppard, Douglas C. "Certifying Teachers of Modern Foreign Languages for American Public Schools–1969." *Foreign Language Annals* 3(1970):609–23.

70 Smith, D.A. "In-Service Training for Teachers of English in Developing Countries," 180–205 in G.E. Perren,ed., *Teachers of English as a Second Language:Their Training and Preparation*. Cambridge: Cambridge Univ. Press, 1968.

71 Smith, George E., and M. Phillip Leamon,eds. *Effective Foreign Language Instruction in the Secondary School*. Englewood Cliffs, New Jersey: Prentice-Hall, 1969.

72 Smith, Philip D.,Jr. *A Comparison of the Cognitive and Audiolingual Approaches to Foreign Language Instruction:The Pennsylvania Foreign Language Project*. Philadelphia: Center for Curriculum Development, 1970.

73 Steinhauer, David. "The Professional Training of Teachers of Modern Languages at the Elementary Level." *Canadian Modern Language Review* 25,ii(1969):22–30.

74 Strasheim, Lorraine A. *Target:Methods*. Bloomington: Indiana Language Program, 1967.

75 Strevens, Peter. "Improving the Teacher's Own English," 206–27 in G.E. Perren,ed., *Teachers of English as a Second Language:Their Training and Preparation*. Cambridge: Cambridge Univ. Press, 1968.

76 Thomsen, Eugene V. "Graduate Programs in Foreign Language Education in United States Universities." [Paper read at the Modern Language Association Convention, Denver, December 1969.]

77 ——— "Graduate Programs in Foreign Language Education in United States Universities." Unpublished Ph.D. Dissertation. Austin: Univ. of Texas, 1970.

78 Weiss, Louis. "The Training Supervisor:An Innovative Concept in Supervision." [Unpublished manuscript.]

79 Williams, Raymond E. "A Proposed Departure from Conventional Programs for the Education of Foreign Language Teachers," 49–54 in Pat Castle and Charles Jay,eds., *Toward Excellence in Foreign Language Education*. Springfield, Illinois: Office of the Superintendent of Public Instruction, State of Illinois, 1968.

80 Wladaver, Donald. "The Role of the Supervisor," 24–30 in Theodore Huebener,ed., *Proceedings: Thirty-Fourth Annual Foreign Language Conference at New York University*. New York: New York Univ. School of Education, Department of Foreign Languages and International Relations Education, 1968.

81 Zaborowski, Elizabeth K. "Some TESL Guidelines for Training Student Teachers," 54–56 in Charles Stubing,ed., *Reports:Bilingualism*. El Paso: Southwest Council of Foreign Language Teachers, 1966.

10

Classics: The teaching of Latin and Greek and classical humanities

Introduction

Gerald M. Erickson
University of Minnesota

To anyone surveying the condition of the classics in 1969, one word is so ubiquitous and recurs so frequently that it seems to characterize the entire situation. The word is change (Hayden, 38). This change is undoubtedly the result of a number of factors, the most apparent of which is the crisis in the secondary school enrollments. Although it must be conceded that this precipitous decline has stirred those few classicists who were still complacent, it does seem, however, that another factor is also present. More than ever before all persons concerned with the teaching of classics have evinced an eagerness to find out what others are doing and a readiness to profit from the experience of others by adapting and incorporating what seems useful for each local situation into new, innovative programs.

Change

This new spirit seems to have set in motion several trends, which, if continued, can be instrumental in insuring that the youth of today will not be deprived of some significant contact with the Greco-Roman heritage:

A new spirit; several trends

1 A recognition of interdependence between teachers of classics at all levels – elementary, secondary, junior college, college, and university.
2 Intensive self-examination by classicists of their objectives, curricula, and teaching methods in the light of twentieth-century needs and realities.
3 A willingness to remove the discussion of teaching method from the realm of polemic and ideology by asking the really relevant question, "Does it work?"
4 An abandonment of a defensive and obsequiously apologetic posture in the advocacy of the values of the classics.
5 A growing realization that all who have an interest in the perpetuation of the humanistic enterprise and its values have a cause in common, which can be fostered best by cooperative action, and that the internecine competition between the modern foreign languages and the classical must be replaced by a mutual recognition of the values and legitimacy of both.

After a brief look at the enrollment figures for 1969, this article will consider the specific trends, programs, ideas, and agencies which exemplify and foster movement toward a renewed viability of classical studies at all levels.

The status of Latin in 1968

Horresco referens.
  (Vergil, *Aeneis*, II, 204.)
Ignis aurum probat, miseria fortes viros.
  (Seneca, *De Providentia*, V, 4.)

The most recent statistics describing enrollment trends for Latin in the public schools have been made available through a study by the Modern Language Association for fall 1968. In the article presenting the results of this study (Kant, 46), enrollment data for 1965 and 1968 are juxtaposed to facilitate the observation of enrollment trends over this three-year period.

Recent enrollment studies: secondary schools

Some of the more salient facts and observations for classics emerging from the study are as follows:

1 Although the total U.S. foreign language enrollment in grades 7–12 increased from 4,494,212 in 1965 to 4,751,080 in 1968, the foreign language enrollments as a percentage of total schools population dropped from 27.4% to 27.17%.

2 The five leading modern foreign languages—Spanish, French, German, Russian, and Italian—accounted for 91.7% of the total language enrollment in grades 7–12, Latin for just over 8%, and the others for less than 0.5%. This represents an increase of 5.6% for the five modern foreign languages over their share of total language enrollments in 1965.

3 Total enrollment losses in Latin over this three-year period were greatest at the first (−36.7%), second (−36.9%), and third (−37.4%) year levels.

4 A smaller, but nevertheless surprising, loss occurred at the 7th and 8th grade levels with a nationwide loss of −28.2%. Only the Plains states (Iowa, Kansas, Minnesota, Missouri, Nebraska, North Dakota, and South Dakota) had an increase (35.7%).

5 Nationwide Latin IV enrollments (−27.7%) decreased less than levels I, II, and III.

6 Considerable percentage increases can be observed in enrollments for Latin V (89.5%) and Latin VI (307.4%), but

total numbers are too exiguous (Latin V, 257, and Latin VI, 83) to warrant any determination of a trend.

7 The Midcast states (Delaware, District of Columbia, Maryland, New Jersey, New York, and Pennsylvania) experienced the most precipitous losses (−48.8%) but still represent the largest concentration of total Latin enrollments.

8 Nebraska has the distinction of being the only state to have an increase in Latin enrollments over this three-year period (16.1%).

9 The totals in the MLA study do not include grades 5 and 6. The considerable progress made in several urban programs is, consequently, not reflected by these figures.

The enrollment situation in institutions of higher education is considerably brighter than in the secondary schools (26). The total number of B.A. degrees granted has remained stable (1,245 in 1965–66 and 1,243 in 1967–68) but the number of institutions conferring these degrees has increased from 286 to 372 during the same period. The total number of M.A. degrees has decreased slightly from 361 to 348, but the number of institutions conferring these degrees has increased from 65 to 77. The number of Ph.D.'s has increased from 63 to 89 and the total of conferring institutions has risen from 23 to 26. The increase in the number of institutions conferring degrees in classical languages is particularly heartening because it seems to indicate that more institutions are currently offering viable majors in Latin and Greek than in 1965.

Enrollments in higher education

The enrollment status of Latin and Greek in institutions of higher education for fall 1968 has been ascertained in a survey by the MLA which is reported by Kant (47).

TABLE 1. Registration in Latin and Greek in institutions of higher education in the United States, 1965 and 1968.

	U.S. total 1965	U.S. total 1968	Graduate 1968	Undergraduate 1968	Junior college 1968
Latin	39,588 (626)*	34,981 (619)	1,459	32,072	1,450 (50)
Greek	19,531 (537)	19,235 (625)	3,190	14,962	1,133 (40)

The figures in parentheses indicate the number of reporting institutions.

Although these data furnish a solid basis for optimism, special attention should be directed to one vulnerable area. The extremely low enrollments in Greek and Latin should be noted in the junior colleges. While the classical languages were experiencing no increase in these institutions, modern foreign language registrations in junior colleges increased nearly two and one-half times the 1960 figure with the number of reporting junior colleges rising from 455 in 1960 to 745 for 1968. It is quite clear that, as the junior colleges continue to account for an increasingly large portion of total undergraduate enrollments, the classical languages in four-year colleges will experience difficulties with enrollments. When students with a modern language or no language transfer from the two-year colleges to institutions offering a four-year program, it will be extremely difficult and impractical for them to begin a classical language. Unless strong and effective efforts are made soon to establish classics programs appropriate to the needs and objectives of junior colleges, an erosion of classics enrollments in higher education will be inevitable.

An optimistic outlook, but . .

Like the "Fall of the Roman Empire" this decline in enrollments has elicited a great deal of speculation about the cause, with each theory adduced having a grain of truth but each being insufficient in itself. Kovach (54) has identified three major factors: (*1*) modern foreign language programs beginning in grade seven or earlier which at the present attract the type of student who, before the introduction of modern languages at that level, most likely would have taken Latin; (*2*) the National Defense Education Act (NDEA), which provided substantial support for modern foreign language programs and extra educational opportunities for modern language teachers, but which excluded teachers of the classical languages; and (*3*) the shift from Latin to the vernacular in the liturgical activities in the Roman Catholic Church.

Three reasons for the enrollment decline

The former tendency to place the blame for our current difficulties on others, notably callous counselors and Philistine administrators, seems to have been replaced by more productive analyses. Increasingly teachers of classics are realizing that "the fault is not in our stars [or counselors], but in ourselves." Phinney (76) for example observes:

Introspection instead of putting "blame on others"

> The narrow training and outlook of some high school Latin teachers are reflected in their principals' concern that Latin instruction should possess wider cultural goals, that instruction in grammar should be more streamlined, that reading

selections should be more varied and extensive . . . Latin teachers, however, are not going to fulfill their principals' desiderata, unless California universities and colleges actively encourage more of them to enroll in graduate classes which will expand their knowledge of Latin, update their teaching methods, and, in general, raise their morale.

A similar observation is made by Cleary (14), who states, ". . . as a profession Latin teachers have shown a resistance to change, an intransigence to all but the *status quo* — to the tried and true — which is unparalleled in the annals of education."

Resistance to change

A trenchant article by Kovach (52) pulls no punches in ascribing much of our enrollment difficulty to failure of many classics teachers "to understand the nature of the changing society in which we live and try to function." The paramount need in classics teaching today is, according to Kovach, a massive infusion of vitality accompanied by a renascent sense of purpose and relevance.

The case which classicists have propounded for justifying the study of the classical languages is another area in which classicists have themselves been a factor contributing to their own difficulties. Too frequently they have accepted the terms of their opponents with the result that the case of Latin has become apologetic, nebulous, and identified with a basically conservative *Weltanschauung* (Roy, 86).

A new, more realistic and promising approach seems to be emerging. One feature of this new approach is a realization of the true nature of educational decision-making — that it is not the result of some objective appraisal of the needs of today's students and tomorrow's citizens, but is rather the result of a complex farrago of unanalyzed prejudices, pressures of special-interest groups, and different philosophies of education, often but dimly perceived. The result is that decisions about curriculum and method often tend to be a reaction to past and present circumstances rather than attempts to provide students with the skills and knowledge they will need in the future.

Curriculum decisions made to provide students with skills and knowledge

The recognition of this hard fact of life is resulting in several salient trends. One is a trend toward the "hard sell." Wolverton (107) writes of "The Classics in the Academic Marketplace." Kelly (49) observes, "Reliable marketing techniques are indispensable if the competition is not to drive our product into premature obsolescence."

The "hard sell"

Another related trend reflects the mood of Juvenal when he began his Satires: *"Semper ego auditor tantum? Numquamne reponam . . .?"* In a scathing and incisive article Parks (72), asserting that classicists must not continue to justify Latin on the terms of its assailants and to remain the victims of a discriminatory criterion of utility which is applied to classical languages but not to unquestioned "sacred cows" in the school curriculum, asks, "Latin or what? Greek or what? What subjects enjoy unquestioned berths in the curricula of our schools and colleges? What are their achievements? What about their practicality? What do they contribute of lasting value? How much time are they afforded?" He answers his own questions by analyzing the worth of the contributions made by the study of subjects which seemingly have "safe berths" in the curriculum.

Classical languages in the curriculum—or what?

English is and has been a must from grammar school to university. Is it possible to estimate the time, the headache, the money and sheer boredom often associated with its teaching? Viewed in terms of sophisticated achievement or in terms of its ability to measure up to critical expectations, the whole enterprise attains a degree of effectiveness which is a constant matter of national concern. Students are legislated into these classes as captive audiences for as many as 16 to 20 years. Yet when we hear them speak, or when we read their latest literary effort we wonder whether 20 years more would make an appreciable difference.

He then juxtaposes the position of the classics to this sorry state of affairs.

What does this have to do with the Classics? Among other things, the fact that the Classics teacher, during the process of imparting his own discipline, is called upon and is generally able to contribute in six to twelve months more language sense than was gained in as many previous years. Certainly, no good classicist begrudges the student the extra effort required to compensate for this deficiency; however, it is only reasonable that he be somewhat disconcerted to have his program called into question when the language experience characterizing his class may be more significant than that in the English class across the hall where no apology is ever needed. Classicists are appalled at the years lavished upon the study of English with so little returns.

Parks also turns his critical pen on the modern languages, not because they are without educational value, but because they have often been advanced for superficial or downright wrong reasons:

If the ends for studying French, Spanish, Portuguese, or German degenerate into mere methods for finding a hotel in Hamburg, a meal in Madrid, or a way around the streets of Paris, then the schools would do well to turn this training over to Berlitz. . . . Spain is no great power today; Spanish as a tool for defense is ridiculous. Spanish, however, has handed down a literary legacy which will forever bear notice. To promote Spanish and Portuguese solely as a means of communicating with the coffee or rubber growers south of the border would be a prostitution of academics. French, German, or Spanish, were they to cease tomorrow as spoken languages, would continue to have a message for perceptive minds — as is the case with the Classical languages.

Modern languages in the curriculum — or what?

Parks then replies with a series of relevant responses to the trite old chestnut which has so often caused classicists to murmur weak, apologetic, and banal responses, "What can you do with Latin or Greek?"

What do you do with History? What do you do with Literature? What do you do with Philosophy? Indeed, if you are not one of the few specialists, what do you do with chemistry, with algebra, with physics, with the history of art? I cannot recall a single instance where I was called upon to make a technical application of algebra, or trigonometry, or physics, or chemistry, yet I do not regret having had them as academic resources. To be reasonable, therefore, let us not make the classical languages a whipping boy because it seems fashionable, or because we have not the imagination to turn the spotlight elsewhere. If the truth were admitted, these languages might prove more practical than most interests, if we were to recognize nothing more than their contribution to clarity of expression.

What do you do with . . . ?

Parks questions the assumption that "What can you do with it?" should be the most important question in curricular decision-making. Rather, he says, the essential question is "What can you be with it?" and concludes: "A society may forgive an educational system which has failed to teach it to do all that it could do, but it will never forgive it for failing to teach it all that it could be."

Erickson (31) also assails the criterion of utility as it has been applied to curriculum decision-making, and in particular inveighs against the mistaken belief that the schools should respond to the "knowledge explosion" by proliferating "practical" courses and attempting to make existing courses more relevant to expanding technology. He makes the following points:

The criterion of utility and the use of technology in curriculum decision-making

1 The ultimate goal of every applied technology is to remove the need to know anything about it on the part of the user of the technology; e.g., a small child can operate an extremely complex electronic device, such as a color television set, whereas fifty years ago the operation of a comparatively simple battery radio required considerable knowledge of electronics.

2 Technology does, however, create a myriad of human needs, chief among which is a need for more effective communication through language – reading, writing, speaking, and listening.

3 Another cardinal need posed by technology is created by the rapid expansion of available leisure time, for which the schools must prepare their students by developing interests in creative pursuits to help individuals find the fulfillment that is increasingly being denied by automation in their employment.

4 The pace of technological change is so rapid that the schools will be incapable of servicing immediate vocational needs, which will increasingly be serviced by training programs in the industries themselves.

5 The emphasis of the schools of the future will have to be on helping students to learn basic skills, to acquire creative interests and abilities, and, as Bruner (11) expresses it, "To learn how to learn."

6 The study of the classical languages has an important and proven contribution to make in this new and inevitable emphasis in education.

It must be admitted that, because of the many variables present, scientific studies for determining the specific contribution that a particular element of the curriculum has made to the development of specific skills and abilities in students are still likely to be inconclusive. This consideration makes the long-range evaluation of the Latin program at the Boston College High School particularly interesting. Duffy (25) reports that some 7,500 questionnaires were sent to graduates of every class from 1910 through 1966. The graduates represented a wide variety of occupations. The responses to two questions were of special interest. To the question, "Did high-school Latin help you?" 1,534 (87%) replied "Yes," 181 (10%) replied "No," and 56 (3%) replied "Don't know." When asked if the school should drop Latin entirely, 143 (8%) replied "Yes," 1,553 (88%) replied "No," and 75 (4%) were in the "don't know" category.

Utility and a study of attitudes

Unaquaeque enim arbor de fructu suo cognoscitur.

One of the salutary trends mentioned in the introduction of this chapter was the recognition by all engaged in the humanistic enterprise that they have a cause in common and must work cooperatively to ensure their retention. The American Council on the Teaching of Foreign Languages (ACTFL) annual convention held in New Orleans on 28–30 November 1969 furnished palpable and gratifying evidence of this recognition. Many speakers from the modern languages indicated their unqualified support of the classical languages. An excellent slide-sound filmstrip developed by Frank Grittner, Wisconsin foreign language consultant, for promoting the study of foreign languages in the schools, had a generous section setting forth the reasons for taking Latin. Equally gratifying in this presentation was the advocacy of foreign language study as a humanistic experience which has value in itself and not as a prelude to tourism.

Support for the classical languages from all foreign language teachers

Another tangible example of support for classics by modern foreign language teachers can be seen in a statement by the National Council of State Supervisors of Foreign Languages, in which the Council gives its unqualified support to the study of Latin in the schools. It is so significant that it will be quoted at length (68):

> The rationale offered for Latin is essentially the same as that for the modern languages; through the study of a foreign language the monocultural and monolingual individual expands the boundaries of his own relatively narrow world to circumscribe a world which is at once more cosmopolitan. It is this very fact of foreign language study which makes languages crucial to the humanities.
>
> That Latin differs in its grammar from most languages

taught in our schools—even radically in the case of English —illustrates again the unique contribution this ancient language can make. Since Latin is one of the highly inflected languages, its contrast with English is especially sharp. The potential of Latin to create general linguistic concepts within the speaker of English makes it an ideal instrument for developing a deeper understanding of language per se.

Although a comparison of enrollment statistics for modern languages with those for Latin would indicate that the modern languages are apparently enjoying a comparative prosperity, there should be little complacency about the future of MFL enrollments. One disquieting feature in the total MFL picture is that, while total foreign language enrollments increased by 5.7% during the 1965–68 period, total public school enrollments increased by 7% (Kant, 46). There are many indications that foreign language programs will be subjected to increasingly vehement attacks by those who have listened to the siren song of the "knowledge explosion" as well as by those who have abandoned education as a primary function of the schools and would have the schools become mere service stations for industry and the status quo.

Complacency should not be the appropriate attitude for MFL programs

As the attack on foreign language study in schools and institutions of higher education develops in intensity, all those committed to the values of foreign language study, indeed all those interested in the preservation of the humanities, must unite in their efforts. Rockwell (85) observes, "Our real enemies—and they are the enemies of far more important things than our subject—are those who have no time or will to consider what good the classics may be."

Curriculum

*Praeterea pro parte sua quodcumque alit auget
Redditur.*
(Lucretius, *De Rerum Natura* V, 257.)

An interesting study was conducted by Papalia (71) on the rate of attrition in foreign language and the reasons for it in four selected New York schools. Some of his major conclusions were as follows:

A study of attrition in foreign language study

1 The survey taken to establish when foreign language study is begun suggested that in agricultural and industrial communities foreign languages began at grade 9.

284

2 Schools situated in the residential communities with a population of 20% or more of professionals, managers, and business proprietors tended to begin the study of foreign languages in the seventh grade or earlier.

3 Schools A and B, situated in districts representing the average socioeconomic communities, had an attrition significantly higher than school D (higher socioeconomic) but lower than school C (lower socioeconomic).

4 School D, situated in a low socioeconomic community, had an attrition in foreign languages significantly higher than schools A, B, or C.

5 The attrition in Latin was significantly higher than that of the modern languages, and the majority of the students discontinued their study at the end of the second level.

6 The critical points in dropping foreign language study occurred at the end of the second and third year levels.

This study adds further confirmation to what many have believed to be true: foreign language study has been and still remains closely associated with the "middle class" and middle class values. A further, more speculative inference can perhaps also be derived: as students tend to reject the middle class values of their parents, they tend also to reject the study of foreign languages as part of that value system.

FL study and middle class values

Many of the innovative and experimental programs described in the following pages represent an attempt to expand the appeal of the classics and to make them more relevant and accessible to students of different ages and backgrounds. Implicit in all the new ideas and programs is the realization that there should not be one stereotyped curriculum model in classics and that ideally each school should construct a curriculum which is carefully adapted to the needs of the students in that area. These should range from traditional academic programs, where they are successful and flourishing, to the most radically innovative, where the need seems to exist.

New directions

Many obstacles bestrew the path toward this greater flexibility:

Obstacles to new directions

1 Although many commercial Latin texts have included additional authors in their II and III level Latin texts, Caesar continues to be identified with Latin II and Cicero with Latin III. Cleary (14) has some interesting comments on this persistent mortmain:

"What is needed for Latin to survive is major surgery: the transplantation of new methods and approaches and the massive transfusion of new ideas, authors, and teachers into the corpus.

"Let us first address ourselves to the problem of the approaches to take at the intermediate level, in other words, 'What do the young demand of literatures, specifically Roman literature?' Essentially four things: that it be relevant and speak to their lives and the times in which they live; that it be personal and show them that in an increasingly mechanized and depersonalized world the individual still counts for something; that it be sophisticated and offer an intellectual challenge, not easy solutions to the problems of our times; and that it be interesting and enjoyable—hopefully even a joy. Yet the traditional second year curriculum speaks in none of these ways to the modern student. Consider the various gaps current among the young today: generation (they don't trust anyone over thirty, that is, anyone in authority), credibility (they believe little of what is said, less of what is written), communication (understanding is impossible, they say, for although the same words are used, different things are meant or else no attempt at communication exists at all and, as the song goes, the sounds are those of silence).

"Caesar and Cicero, as traditionally taught, reflect those gaps. The military structure, an arm of the establishment, is viewed in an anti-war age with suspicion and distrust by those whose lives may, after all, soon be on the line. And the young, since this is an age of revolution in which the minority asserts itself, find it easier to identify with the radical Catiline than with Cicero and the power structure."

2   State and national Latin examinations, although instituted with the commendable purpose of setting standards and giving some objective measure of competence, but which also dictate both curriculum and method, enforce a rigidity and conservative bias which is not consonant with the need for flexibility and innovation. As Papalia (71) observes in his New York study:

"Most teachers were aware that the amount of content they required was not satisfactorily adjusted to student differences, but they felt that there was little they could do to change these circumstances so long as the State Regents Examinations continue to be given at the end of the third year in the three and four year sequences."

3 Teacher training programs for Latin teachers frequently do not provide the language skills and competencies needed for curriculum changes.

4 Teachers of classical languages, as Kovach (52) points out, often tend to be inflexible and uninterested in change:

"They (Latin teachers) do not understand — or even know about — the 'new look' in modern English grammar, cannot discuss or interpret a single, complete literary work of ancient Greece or Rome in any language, do not realize that Latin is a language and a means of communication, not just a cipher for encoding and decoding, and truthfully — and saddest of all — do not feel competent to cope with curricular change in their own chosen field."

Latin programs for foreign languages in the elementary schools

Kovach (54) has pointed out and discussed the controversy which was raised by Levy about the desirability of FLES programs for Latin. Some observations on the value and nature of FLES programs may be appropriate here:

Value and nature of FLES programs in Latin

1 There is now general agreement that foreign language programs must extend beyond the traditional two-year curriculum, if most of the values of foreign language learning are realized. The acquiescence of Latin teachers to a two-year curriculum is probably a causal factor in the nationwide diminution of Latin enrollments. FLES and seventh-grade programs offer an extended classical curriculum which in turn makes possible the achievement of multiple goals of foreign language study.

2 If Latin is to remain a viable option, it must be offered when other foreign language options are presented to students.

3 Much of the apparent superiority of younger children to older students for language learning can, as Asher & Garcia (5) point out, be ascribed to the superior efficacy of the way in which children learn language:

"Children learn the new language in play situations when utterances are synchronized with physical movement. It may also be that adults learn the new language in static, non-play situations in which their kinaesthetic system is not active and synchronized with speech transmission or reception.

"If the difference in language acquisition between children and adults is play versus non-play, action versus non-action, and physical involvement versus non-physical involvement, these variables may partially explain the accelerated learning of the child."

This statement seems to indicate quite clearly that a Latin FLES program can result in significant language learning, if it is multisensory and involves the whole child in the process. Conversely, any Latin FLES which is merely a "watered-down" version of a high school Latin program is probably worse than no program at all.

Although Latin has been taught sporadically in the elementary schools throughout our history, the Airlie House Conference in 1965 (Latimer, 59) and the Oxford Conference in 1967 (Latimer, 58) provided a renewed impetus for expansion of FLES and seventh-grade programs in Latin. Although the numbers of students currently enrolled in these programs have not matched the expectations and hopes of the Airlie House and Oxford Conference participants, several new programs are demonstrating that Latin programs, when well conceived, can serve real needs of students and the public.

Airlie House and Oxford Conferences

One program which is currently attracting international attention is the Latin FLES program in the District of Columbia. Under the inspiring leadership of Dr. Judith LeBovit, this program began in the school year 1966–67 with some 600 students in 20 schools. Table 2 shows the impressive growth of this program.

Latin FLES: Washington, D.C.

TABLE 2. Enrollment in the Washington, D.C., sixth and seventh grade Latin programs.*

Sixth Grade	1966–67	1967–68	1968–69	1969–70	(Projected) 1970–71
Number of students	620	1,240	1,484	2,000	–
Number of classes	23	43	51	54	80
Number of schools	17	39	50	65	80
Seventh Grade					
Number of students	259	535	814	600	–
Number of classes	10	20	31	19	21
Number of schools	5	13	20	19	20

*Statistics supplied by Department of Foreign Languages, District of Columbia Schools.

The program has a large oral component, particularly in the initial stages. Grammar is taught functionally. As students progress through the program, development of reading skill receives increasing emphasis.

The primary aim of this program is not preparation for college but for life. Classroom teachers have observed a marked improvement in communications skills, including reading, among the Latin FLES students.

The innovative program for Latin FLES in the school district of Philadelphia has also attracted international attention (Kovach, 54; Masciantonio, 62). In this program about 1,000 students (mostly sixth graders, but some fourth and fifth graders were included) learned Latin in daily classes of 20 minutes.

Latin FLES: Philadelphia

The objectives of the program were to expand the verbal functioning of children in English, especially through the study of Latin roots and affixes, to teach children to understand and speak Latin, then to read and write it, to contrast and compare classical culture and civilizations with the students' own, and to develop interest in pupils in the study of the classics and humanities. The course, titled *How the Romans Lived and Spoke (Romani Viventes et Dicentes)*, is centered around the everyday life of a Roman family. Multisensory media, including locally produced visuals and tapes, are used throughout the course (Masciantonio, 62). The program has been well received by administrators and is continuing to expand in numbers and scope.

The Latin FLES program which has had the longest history of successful operation was instituted by Gardocki in the Cleveland diocesan schools. The emphasis of his programs has been to provide the opportunity to attend Latin classes outside regular school time. One of his most successful ventures is the Saturday Latin class. In 1969–70 465 students from grades five through eight registered. The students who attend these classes are drawn from public as well as Catholic and Lutheran parochial schools. The students, therefore, go on to attend a variety of high schools in the area. Gardocki reports in a letter to the author that students who have completed the eighth grade level of this program have been quite successful in getting advanced standing in area high schools and have performed well in advanced high school programs.

Latin FLES: Cleveland

A conference on the teaching of Latin in inner city elementary and high schools was held at the University of Pittsburgh on 23 and 24 April 1970. This conference, which was jointly funded by the National Foundation for the Arts and Humanities, the Pennsylvania Department of Public Instruction, and

University of Pittsburgh Conference on inner city programs

the University of Pittsburgh, was attended by some thirty Latin teachers and administrators.

Representatives from three Latin FLES programs described the objectives, curriculum content, and approach to teaching in their respective schools. The organizer of this conference, Harry Avery of the University of Pittsburgh, reports in a letter to the author that all the programs aroused a considerable amount of frank and free discussion among participants. The administrators who participated in the conference suggested that these and other Latin programs should be described in periodicals which would be read by administrators and not just in publications for classics teachers. They seemed confident that administrators would consider such programs with open minds, but stressed the need for more "hard data" on results in addition to subjective appraisals. Representatives from Philadelphia and Washington assured the administrators that the desired "hard data" are now being collected.

Mrs. Eula Cutt described the Latin Heritage Program which she inaugurated and developed at Northwestern High School in the inner city of Detroit. The emphasis in this program is not so much on language as on the whole cultural complex which has been transmitted from antiquity. A curriculum guide for this program is now available (Cutt, 18).

All speakers at the Pittsburgh Conference presenting these programs emphasized the favorable response from both students and parents. One speaker suggested that blacks were "tired of being experimented on" and welcomed a program which, although innovative in approach, represented a traditional and prestigious facet of American education.

All those responsible for this conference should be commended for their initiative and concern. Many more such efforts for interpreting the values of the classics and the aspirations of classics teachers to administrators and other curriculum decision-makers are urgently needed.

Although the Latin FLES programs described above quite rightly emphasize the immediate benefits to be derived by students from these programs, the probability exists that many of the students in these and similar programs will wish to continue their study beyond the elementary levels. This creates the possibility for extended classics curricula with the potential for successful attainment of the multiple goals which can be established for these programs: a high level of competence in the

Extended classics curricula

target language (Latin), extensive experience in the literary interpretation of texts, a more thorough grounding in classical civilization, and the learning of transfer techniques for efficient language acquisition through the accelerated learning of a "spin-off" language (a Romance language or Greek) by applying concepts and skills already acquired in learning the primary target language, Latin (Erickson, 30).

A program for incorporating the "spin-off" principle into an extended classics curriculum, instituted by Richard Scanlan in the Edina-Morningside schools (Minnesota), included the intro- *The "spin-off" principle* duction of modern Italian and classical Greek along with advanced placement Latin at the fourth- and fifth-year levels (Kovach, 53).

Another advantage of an extended curriculum is that, particularly if the enrollment in the program is sufficiently large, it is possible to identify the different needs, interests, and abilities of students enrolled and to create courses and options which pro- *Possibility of individualized* vide for these differences. A multitrack four-year program *programs* introduced in the New Trier school district (Illinois) according to Albert (1) does meet these varying needs.

A new experimental syllabus for Latin in New York (101) may succeed in loosening somewhat the stranglehold of the Regents Examinations. The new publication is replete with valuable, reasoned suggestions for the improvement of both course content and teaching method. It is not prescriptive but resembles rather a useful guide to aid the creative teacher in developing his own course of study. It would be a valuable addition to any Latin teacher's professional library.

The Cultural Language Study Program now in the Cleveland *Cultural Language Study* Heights-University school district combines an introduction to *Program* Greek civilization and culture with an exposure to the Greek language during the first half of the seventh grade. A similar combination of Roman civilization and culture with an exposure to the Latin language constitutes the second half. Lessons are developed around concepts relevant to the ancient world and to the present. The well-designed and explicit course guide written for this curriculum by Schwartz & Tappenden (91) can be an invaluable guide for teachers and others interested in developing similar programs or including aspects of this program in their Latin courses.

The Latin Advanced Placement Program provides an excellent opportunity for advanced students to realize the benefits of

291

an extended classical curriculum. This program, which is open to students in all types of secondary schools, offers three areas for which students may prepare: Vergil, Latin Prose, and Latin Lyric. Normally students in Latin IV and V take AP, but well-prepared and very able Latin III classes are also encouraged to participate. It is possible for an able and motivated class (or gifted individual students) to prepare for two examinations in a one-year period or for three in a two-year period. Because the Advanced Placement Committee has established and maintained high standards for this program, successful Advanced Placement students can receive advanced standing and credit in many of the most prestigious colleges and universities. The Advanced Placement Committee has constantly sought to make this program as useful to teachers and students as possible and has endeavored to be responsive to changing conditions in the schools. Teachers with Latin level III, IV, or V programs may receive a complete description of the new programs along with necessary enrollment information and procedures by writing to either:

Advanced Placement Program

> Francine Robbins T-252
> Educational Testing Service
> Princeton, New Jersey 08540
>   or
> Richard T. Scanlan
> 361 Lincoln Hall
> Department of Classics, University of Illinois
> Urbana, Illinois 61801

The extended classics curriculum, which makes possible the realization of the values of classical studies to more students and introduces the gifted students to realms of inspiration and challenge, is of course the desideratum. An examination of the enrollment statistics, however, points up another urgently needed area of curriculum development.

Analysis of the figures in Table 3 reveals that total enrollments in Latin III, IV, V, and VI constitute only about 14% of total Latin enrollments and about 24% of all enrollments above Latin I. This concentration of Latin students in Latin I and II can be explained by the fact that the majority of Latin programs in the public schools are still two-year terminal programs. These are the programs which are most frequently being "phased out" by administrators.

Two-year programs still exist

TABLE 3. Latin enrollments in public secondary schools, grades 7–12, with breakdown by courses, fall 1968 (Kant, 46).

Grades 7–12 ⎫	212,888
Grades 7–8 ⎬ Course I	20,141
Grades 9–12 ⎭	192,747
Course II	136,246
Course III	29,678
Course IV	11,508
Course V	751
Course VI	295
Total, courses I–VI	392,697

These observations underscore the urgent need for increased efforts in developing a two-year terminal curriculum which will be more efficient in language teaching, more satisfactory as an introduction to classical civilization and literature, and more appealing to today's youth.

A two-year terminal course is needed

Hnatt (42) proposes a three-year program for students whose major interest is not foreign languages or whose intellectual inclination is not toward scholarship. Many of her suggestions are applicable to a two-year program.

Beginning language instruction at the college level, with some notable exceptions, has traditionally been the "orphan" of classics departments. The unwillingness of senior staff to teach at the beginning levels has often resulted in the assignment to these courses of overworked and inexperienced teaching assistants, who are usually pulled between their instructional duties and the demands made on them as graduate students. Circumstances are, however, compelling classics departments to reassess the role of beginning language instruction.

Problems of college curricula and instruction

The decrease in the numbers of students entering college with backgrounds in classical languages, the students' insistent demands for better instruction, and the current assault on language requirements both for undergraduate and graduate degrees will compel classics departments to assign more experienced and better-qualified teachers to beginning languages, to monitor and evaluate these courses, to establish some standardization of objectives, and to reexamine the articulation of the beginning courses with more advanced offerings.

The problems of beginning language instruction at the college level are being felt by most college and university foreign language departments. In a perceptive and succinct paper Lane (56) has identified many of the causes of trouble in college foreign language instruction, all of which are pertinent to Latin and Greek.

This problem is apparently not limited to the United States. Wheeler (103) decries the lack of clearly defined goals in college language instruction in Australia. Davies & Molyneux (19) describe an approach which attempts to make college instruction in Latin at a British university more efficient and more appealing than the traditional program.

Classical humanities and "in-translation" courses

The "identity crisis" facing classicists, classics departments, and, to a lesser extent, Latin teachers in the secondary school is identified in two articles differing in approach but not in candor.

Stock (95) asserts that philologists (i.e., classicists), by defining their role too narrowly and by eschewing contact and interaction with other disciplines, are relegating themselves to an increasingly irrelevant and trivial role. He suggests that the problems to which scholars address themselves should be much broader in scope than can be encompassed by one discipline and that the combined competencies of many disciplines should be employed in the attack on these problems. The announcement of the establishment in 1969 of the Center for the Coordination of Ancient and Modern Studies at the University of Michigan (29) should provide an impetus to the breaking down of artificial barriers between disciplines.

Breaking down of artificial barriers between disciplines

In another article pointing up the "identity crisis," Motto & Clark (67) state that the traditional role of classicists has suffered massive erosion. They further assert that this should not be a source of lamentation:

Traditional role of classicists has suffered

> And yet, paradoxically, all of this suffering and decline has been good for Classics. "Men must learn by suffering," as the Old Testament prophets proclaimed and choruses of Old Men in Aeschylus' tragedies painfully perceive. For one thing, the Classics have just about scrapped the German Methodology imported by the United States in the nineteenth century, that had every language student believing one studies Latin to be able to construe Irregular Verbs, recite Dative of Disadvantage and march in the Subjunctive as if it were a parade ground.
>
> Instead, Classicists now teach a number of courses in translation, participate in humanities seminars, go snacks in inter-

departmental linguistics programs, and in ever-expanding Comparative Literature Departments. Such tensions and expansions have been good for classicists; more and more nowadays one meets Greek scholars who have been reading and thinking intelligently about the *Upanishads, Beowulf*, Goethe, Gide, Nabokov, Paul Goodman.

Courses in translation

This change presents, according to Motto & Clark (67), a great challenge and opportunity to classicists as "whole new areas of study now come within the borders of the ever-expanding universe of classical studies." One aspect of this change that is impressing itself most palpably on classics departments is the growing necessity for offering courses on literature in translation, classical civilization, and mythology. The response by classicists to this demand has varied; some accept assignments in these areas with gusto and creativity; some accept them as necessary evils. There are three good reasons, two very practical and one ethical, why these nonlanguage courses should receive high priority and excellent instruction:

Reasons for the high priority for courses in translation

1 Most administrators are forced by economic considerations to play the "numbers game." Larger enrollments in nonlanguage courses enable departments to retain a diversified staff and to mount specialized language courses, which often have exiguous enrollments.

2 Good teaching in nonlanguage courses can engender a desire to learn more and "recruit" students into language courses.

3 The primary duty of every classicist should be the interpretation of classical civilization. Even though it is granted that language is an essential aspect of culture, it would be an admission of bankruptcy to assert that, if the ancient language were removed, there is nothing of value left to teach.

The growing concern for these nonlanguage courses is reflected in the publications for classicists. Margon (61) views the establishment of an "in-translation" undergraduate major in classical civilization at Yale as a sign of renewal. He then discusses criteria for the selection of translations, with special attention given to the tension between contemporaneity and authenticity in the approach to translation. Dorsey (24) discusses several reasons for failure of many "in-translation" courses to realize their full potential. He also gives what he considers to be the primary function of such courses:

Discussion of in-translation courses in "the literature"

The greatest use of such courses in literature in translation at this juncture in our history must be to reveal conceptual, aesthetic, and especially ethical alternatives to the American value system, or as it is usually called, the American way of life. At a time when the value system is displaying, in areas domestic and foreign, its anti-humanistic effects, we must offer to students—especially the precocious, alienated student—some of the means for developing autonomous norms instead of anomie. For this purpose the studied culture must be contrasted with our own—starkly, subtly, suavely, or shockingly.

Leineks (60) in replying to some of the points made by Dorsey (24) makes some observations on the amount of background necessary for reading classical works in translation and considers some possible thematic approaches for teaching them.

Background for reading classical works in translation especially mythology

Jeffrey (45) reports on a survey which he conducted in Texas. The purpose of the survey was twofold: to ascertain the extent of the respondents' "knowledge" of classical mythology from a test of over 1,105 mythological names, and to elicit their attitudes toward the value of mythology and its proper place in schools and colleges. Schork (89) takes vigorous exception to the conception of mythology implicit in Jeffrey's questionnaire:

> The study of myth is not a genealogical taxonomy nor is it propaideutic to a study of Milton or even Vergil. . . . Mythology can, of course, be justified as a meaningful component of humanistic education; but that justification, I shall argue, must be based on a recognition that myth is a mode of symbolization different from, but not less important or valid than, other systems whose processes and products are traditionally represented in the curriculum of modern schools and colleges.

Schork then elaborates on the unique characteristics of the mythical perspective. He concludes with some practical suggestions for conducting a class in mythology on the college level.

Rexine (83) reviews recent books relevant to mythology. The resulting analyses should be helpful to anyone planning to teach a course in mythology.

According to Kilgour (51), there is a pronounced trend toward making classical civilization an integral part of the Latin course in Scotland, where it had customarily been regarded as peripheral. He also describes movement toward teaching nonlanguage courses in classical civilization.

Schork (90) describes a classical heritage program offered on Saturdays for high school students and teachers. Begun in 1962 by Peradotto and Schork at Georgetown University in the face of considerable skepticism about the number of students who would give up their Saturday mornings and pay a nominal registration fee ($10.00), the program ran for four successful years in the Washington, D.C., area. Schork initiated a similar program in the Minneapolis-St. Paul area with over 250 students in each of two sessions. The response to the same basic program in two separate areas indicates a generally high level of interest in classical civilization and the willingness of high school students to participate in courses which present classical civilization in a popular but not condescending manner.

A classical heritage program

Approaches to teaching the classical languages

Grammatici certant et adhuc sub iudice lis est.
 (Horace, *De Arte Poetica*, 78.)

Trends in Latin teaching method have in general followed the trends in the teaching of modern foreign languages. These trends and the reactions to them are described historically by DeWitt (21) and by Bock & Latimer (9). It is, however, not inaccurate to state that innovative approaches have encountered more resistance from teachers of classical languages than from their counterparts in the modern foreign languages. This conservatism in method is clearly indicated by a survey of a representative sample of the 1,814 secondary school seniors who took the Latin Achievement Test of the College Entrance Examination Board in the December, January, and March administrations for the academic year 1965–66 (Austin, 6). The questions elicited responses about the types of classroom and extra-classroom learning activities these students had experienced in Latin classes. Taken together they may reflect, with a fair degree of accuracy, the methods practiced by Latin teachers. It is recommended that the reader study the entire report. A few observations drawn from the report may, however, give some notion of how little actual classroom practices have changed. The most frequent activity was translation aloud of prepared texts from Latin to English. This technique was used frequently with about 60% of the students in seventh grade and with over 90% of the students in grades ten, eleven, and twelve. Sight work of any kind with unprepared passages was not a common practice. The

Resistance to innovative approaches as indicated by practice

author remarks, "Their results lend credence to the observations made on occasion by college instructors that one of the weaker aspects of secondary school Latin instruction today is lack of emphasis on developing the ability to read moderately difficult Latin at sight." Students did very little writing of Latin except for translation of English to Latin sentences used as exercises. Very few students in grades seven through ten and less than half at any level frequently discussed and analyzed themes and purposes of Latin literature, studied the scansion of poetry, discussed lives of Roman authors, analyzed styles of individual authors, or read English translations of works by Latin authors. Less than 6% of the students at any level *ever* listened to phonograph or tape recordings in the regular classroom, participated in oral drills in the language laboratory, or listened to tape recordings in the language laboratory. Less than 30% of the students at any level *ever* answered in Latin questions about Latin sentences or passages which had been read at sight, or did oral paraphrasing or summarizing in Latin of sentences or passages read in Latin. Less than 10% of the students at any one level *ever* listened to the teacher explain points of grammar or explain vocabulary in Latin, or wrote summaries in Latin of material read in Latin.

The author of this study does, however, suggest that, since Latin teachers are becoming more receptive to new approaches and since more innovative materials are now available, the results of a survey taken this year would probably show a tendency toward more innovation.

The fact remains, nevertheless, that Latin teachers have remained remarkably resistant to innovations in curriculum and method. The following factors may, at least in part, account for this:

Factors explaining resistanc to change

1 The emphasis on the oral component of languages, which is essential in the new approaches, requires a competency which most Latin teachers do not possess.

2 Teachers of classical languages did not have access to federally-sponsored institutes such as the NDEA until 1966.

3 Many of the standardized tests given for ascertaining proficiency in Latin do not measure the attainment of the objectives of innovative approaches. Indeed, many do not measure the ultimate objective of any instruction in classical languages – the ability to read the language with reason-

able speed, comprehension, retention, and with an aware-ness of stylistic and cultural aspects of language.

4 Many Latin teachers have only one or two Latin classes along with other preparations and, consequently, do not have the available time and energy required for the additional preparation and self-instruction demanded by new methods.

5 There has been a marked tendency on the part of teachers of classical languages to react emotionally to new approaches — to regard their assessment as an ideological rather than an empirical issue.

The emotionally charged aura surrounding discussion of innovative methods for teaching Latin and Greek is rapidly disappearing, largely because the recent precipitous decline in enrollments has impressed upon most teachers the need for new approaches to meet the present crisis. Another factor may be that the drop in enrollments has tended to eliminate teachers whose commitment to the teaching of classical languages was half-hearted or opportunistic.

Discussions of method, theory, and practice

Wilkins (104) sets forth in reasoned and orderly fashion the inadequacies of current approaches to teaching classical languages and suggests some necessary considerations for the establishment of a general theory for teaching them. Alyeshmerni (3) points out problems encountered in the application of descriptive linguistics to teaching method when combined with the assumptions of behavioristic psychology. In a rebuttal to Alyeshmerni, Reedy (82) defends audiolingual principles as applied to the structural approach of Waldo Sweet. An informative account of recent innovations and trends in Latin teaching is given by Kelly (49), who summarizes these developments for British readers.

Programmed learning

Waldo Sweet has been and continues to be the foremost innovator in Latin teaching methodology. Perhaps because of his pioneering role his materials (96,97,99) and proposals have been the center of much emotional controversy. Many attacks have consisted largely of recitations of old prejudices. One such attack by Calder (12) clearly indicates that the attacker did not read Sweet's materials or his discussions of their rationale. However, the controversy, now centering primarily on his programmed materials, continues. Bell, who in May 1968 wrote a

Sweet's materials

favorable review of *Artes Latinae*, subsequently retracted his endorsement in a letter to the editor (8), citing the small number of students going on to the second level and the performance of students on the Cooperative Latin test published by the Educational Testing Service as indicative of mediocre results from the program. Meck (65), responding in a later issue of the same journal, cited a high level of continuation to the second level in her classes and pointed out the irrelevance of the test used to evaluate the objectives of *Artes Latinae*. Sweet also reacted, asserting the inappropriateness of the test administered (98). The success of the *Artes Latinae* materials seems to depend, as is the case with all other materials, on the competence and enthusiasm of the teacher.

Hayes gives a brief historical sketch of developing concepts for programmed instruction and discusses the application of "lean" programming to instruction in Latin and Greek (41). Several program-type texts are now available: a rather traditional approach by Morris (66), a review of traditional grammar by Eikeboom (27), and programs by Hayes for both Latin (40) and Greek (39).

Computers and the classics

The burgeoning application of computer technology to the advancement of knowledge has not been without effect on classical studies and the teaching of the classical languages. This application can be divided into two areas: the use of the computer for the search and classification of literary and linguistic data, and the use of the computer as a means for the presentation of instructional material. Exciting applications of both types are currently being employed in classics.

Computer-assisted instruction (CAI)

Computer-assisted instruction in Latin as part of the regular curriculum is already a reality at the University of Illinois for the beginning and advanced levels. The Latin instruction uses the PLATO (Programmed Logic Automated Teaching Operations) system which has been developed at the University of Illinois. Alpert & Bitzer (2) describe the development of PLATO, analyze the educational potentialities of computer instruction, and make some rather startling predictions about the cost of CBE (Computer-Based Education) in the near future. After describing the evolution of the PLATO system through progres-

PLATO

sively sophisticated stages (PLATO III is now in operation and PLATO IV is projected), the authors address themselves to four common misconceptions about the nature of CBE:

Misconceptions about computer-based education

1 "Computer-based education is synonymous with programmed instruction." The authors state that a sophisticated CBE system can surpass the Skinnerian model by giving unique responses to a wide variety of student responses and inquiries.

2 "Since the instructional strategy must be previously programmed in the computer, it must of necessity anticipate all conceivable student responses so as to compare them with 'correct' responses stored in the machine." The authors indicate that "judging routines" can be incorporated into the machine for assessing the validity of responses. The computer can, for example, be programmed to distinguish between conceptual errors and spelling difficulties.

3 "CBE may be useful for the transfer of information but is not of value in the development of critical thinking." "On the contrary," state the authors, "computer-based instruction has often been found to be more effective than standard educational procedures in many learning situations that call for judgment, interpretation of complex problems, and evaluation by the student of the validity of his conjectures."

4 "A computer system used for computer-based education cannot be used in a time-sharing mode for conventional computer programming." The authors' reply to this is that with PLATO IV as many as 200 or 300 terminals will be able to be used for computational computer functions concurrently with operation of the remaining terminals for computer-based instruction. Under this projected arrangement a student will have to wait only 0.2 seconds or less for a response from the computer.

Perhaps most exciting of all is a predicted $0.35 per student hour operational cost for PLATO IV and an initial $1,800 cost per student station, which can be connected to the main computer by telephone lines within a 150-mile radius. The authors emphasize that CBE will not replace the human teacher but will make possible improvements in the total educational program, such as: abolishment of lockstep schedules, expansion of curricular offerings in schools with limited facilities, provision of remedial instruction, reduction in the number of large lecture

Some exciting prospects

classes, more small instructional groupings, and special instruction at home for physically handicapped students.

Three different levels of Latin instruction by CBE have been developed by Scanlan (88) at the University of Illinois: beginning Latin, reading comprehension of Latin literature (Vergil), and a grammar review. Each of these three programs uses the same mode of interface (presentation of materials, student response, and computer reaction to the student response).

CAI at Illinois: Scanlan

Each student station is provided with an electric keyboard as a means of communicating with the central computer and a television screen for viewing information selected by the computer. The keyboard contains a set of keys labeled with alphabetic and numeric characters similar to those found on a typewriter. These are used by the student to answer questions. The computer writes in a designated place on the screen what the student types. In addition, there are also several functional keys with which the student is able to give various commands to the computer: "NEXT" when he wishes the computer to judge the answer he has given to the current problem; he presses "ERASE" when he wishes to erase a mistake; he presses "HELP" or "DATA" or "LAB" when he wishes to use branching materials which may be available on the current problem. The computer can make a complete printout of the student's performance on each lesson or can, at the instructor's option, print out only erroneous responses. Student response has been uniformly favorable to this mode of instruction. One characteristic comment was that the computer was "kind." Apparently this meant that the computer allowed them to work privately, did not allow others to see their mistakes, enabled them to work at their own speed, and provided assistance when needed.

Another significant outcome of this work with computer-assisted instruction (CAI) has been a growing recognition of the disparity in rate and style of learning between individual students; some students would complete a CAI lesson in twenty minutes, while others required two to three hours for the same lesson. One of the most promising aspects of CAI is that by recognizing and providing for these differences, many more students can be helped to achieve mastery of classical languages than is possible under lockstep conditions.

The results of this prodigious effort will not be limited to the campus of the University of Illinois. Current plans call for the establishment in 1973 of 4,000 remote stations, which will be tied to the Educational Research Laboratory at the university. Presumably any school tied to this network will be able to offer to its students any instructional program available in the central facility. Students will then be able to take Latin by computer in those schools where Latin is not taught or will be enabled to continue into Vergil where a limited Latin program is offered.

Other developments with CAI

Stephen V. F. Waite (Kovach, 54) at Dartmouth College has developed a testing program for elementary Latin which stores grades and a summary of results, including which students missed each question.

C. W. E. Peckett (Kovach, 54), the Priory School for Boys, Shrewsbury, Shropshire, England, is employing computers in the preparation of Latin texts for teaching techniques which emphasize reading and recognition, rather than composition.

Gerald Erickson of the University of Minnesota and Richard Scanlan of the University of Illinois are currently using computers for the detailed analysis of Latin readings selected for a two-year terminal program in Latin. The computer analysis will provide a basis for developing an efficient approach to teaching the vocabulary, syntax, and morphology necessary for the effective reading of these selections in the second year.

Robert Black and Gerald Erickson, in cooperation with the Center for the Study of Human Learning at the University of Minnesota, have developed several pilot lessons for using CAI in developing effective skills for reading Latin texts.

Francis M. Wheeler (Kovach, 54), Department of Classics, Beloit College, Wisconsin, has been processing selected Homeric texts and developing a CAI course in Greek.

Huchthausen (44) performed a computer analysis of Latin texts commonly taught in the German Democratic Republic. Although there were many facets of language which were not included in his survey, he did conclude that computer analysis of target texts for vocabulary, syntax, and morphology helps to make elementary Latin instruction more efficient by identifying elements which are customarily included in elementary texts but which are rarely encountered in reading, and by identifying highly recurrent items which need more emphasis and practice than are provided in the textbooks. Huchthausen also compared the effectiveness of current vocabularies and word lists against his computer results and gives some practical suggestions for anyone who is planning to undertake computer analysis of texts for pedagogical purposes.

Kovach (54) has described the growing interest among many classicists in the use of computers for computer analysis of texts for philological, literary, and linguistic purposes. Further evidence of this interest was shown in the American Philological Association Summer Institute in Computer Applications to Classical Studies, conducted at the University of Illinois, Urbana, in the summer of 1969, under the direction of Nathan Greenberg of Oberlin College with the assistance of Stephen Waite of Dartmouth College.

Independent study

The widespread introduction of various modular scheduling arrangements, the growing recognition of highly divergent learning rates and styles among students, and students' demands for more varied modes of instruction have made the development of independent study programs an urgent necessity.

Clark (13) outlines the essentials of an optional independent study Latin program which has been in operation for two years in the Edina-Morningside Public School, Edina, Minnesota. About 25% of the students who are at Latin levels II and III *An optional program* have elected independent study. Since the program is predicated on the assumption that recognition should be given for level of mastery and learning accomplished rather than time spent in the classroom, independent study has enabled this school to incorporate a Latin V program for some of the students into four years of Latin study. Warburton & Chaffey (102) give the characteristic features of a successful approach to Latin teaching under modular scheduling.

Mary D. Wilson, Department of Latin Education, State University of New York at Albany, has planned a course of independent study for Level V students on an experimental basis for the aca- *A program for Level V studen* demic year 1970–71. Suggested areas for consideration are: history, philosophy, literary genres, Roman life as reflected in selected readings, and Roman art and architecture. Each student, with the permission and direction of the instructor, will be able to pursue in depth either the works or influence of one or two authors, or the ideas and philosophies expressed by several Roman writers.

Multisensory instruction

The concept of multisensory instruction for foreign languages is not a recent innovation. It was applied successfully and systematically to Latin teaching by Johann Amos Comenius in the seventeenth century. Recent developments in instructional technology—the overhead, film, slide, and opaque projectors, the tape recorder, and the portable video tape machine—have only made multisensory language learning much more accessible in the classroom. Although many current applications of multisensory teaching of Latin differ among themselves in materials and teaching techniques, all share these basic assumptions (Erickson, 30):

1 Concurrent employment of as many senses as possible in the language learning process results in more efficient and enduring learning than does reliance upon one sensory mode.
2 All new language elements should, as far as possible, be presented in a meaningful context.
3 Physical activity associated with the target language results in more enduring learning (Asher, 4).

There has been a parallel interest in multisensory language instruction in the Soviet Union, where many notable advances in language teaching have already been achieved. Golubev (35) reviews recent Soviet studies and compares language learning by the direct association of target language and pictorial context with language learning by association of target language and native language. He finds that direct association is not only more efficient and enduring but also leads more directly to active generation of new utterances and efficient reading skills. He also questions the assumption that a multisensory approach is efficient only with younger children. Pictorial materials of an appropriate level of maturity must, however, be used with older students.

Developments in the Soviet Union

Edward Woll (106)—now deceased—has given a very succinct description of his application of multisensory principles in the classroom. He wrote, "This program is still in the process of becoming, much more work and thought is needed to bring it to a perfected and complete program, to make it more truly—*A Multi-sensory Approach*." It is a profound loss to all Latin teachers that he was not able to accomplish this goal.

Richard Scanlan of the University of Illinois has developed a series of pictorial materials for making overhead projection transparencies to teach basic Latin structures. These materials are not related to any specific text and can be used as parallel materials with whatever text the teacher is using.

Transparencies

305

A set of pictorial materials for making transparencies is also available from the classics department of the University of Minnesota. Most of these materials were developed for teaching vocabulary and structure in *Principia* and *Pseudolus Noster* (Peckett & Mundy, 74,75; Dennis, 20). Both of these texts are well adapted to a multisensory approach.

The innovative Latin FLES programs in Washington, D. C., and Philadelphia (discussed above) use a multisensory approach.

Norton & Graber (69), with the support of a grant from the American Classical League, have prepared a monograph accompanied by illustrative teaching materials to aid teachers and curriculum planners in fashioning programs for the middle school, grades 5–8. Graber has also prepared a 16-mm film demonstrating the teaching of reading and four 16-mm films portraying seventh, eighth, and ninth grade Latin students actively responding to effective teaching techniques.

The teaching of reading skills

It is disheartening to observe how little has been done in either of the classical languages to define efficient reading of the target language and to identify the skills necessary for effective reading of a text. It is common knowledge that most students and, in many cases, teachers read Latin or Greek at a very slow pace with less than the desired degree of retention. It is also a well-known but unfortunate fact that many students who have done well in beginning language classes doing prepared Latin to English translations and English to Latin sentences encounter great difficulty in attempting to read unfamiliar texts in Latin or Greek. It does appear that a necessary stage in instruction has been omitted. Research and experimentation on the development of efficient reading procedures and effective measurement of comprehension and retention could pay great dividends in increased student performance and satisfaction with the instruction received. The general treatment by Singer (92) and the old but still relevant work by Skiles (93) may provide useful points of departure on this problem.

Little accomplished in development of reading skills

Cracas (17) expresses concern over the lack of a clear definition of reading ability: "There is little doubt in my mind that much of the discussion concerning method could be settled, or at least less confused, by a more precise goal than the ability to read Latin as Latin. Certainly the words 'read,' 'ability,' and

'Latin' must be defined more objectively before there can be a clear understanding of what is being stated." In a lucid and enlightening analysis Cracas compares four linguistic models for the comprehension of the Latin sentence: the traditional, the structural, the transformational-generative, and the stratificational. He concludes, "From this discussion it should be obvious that there is no linguistic model which states how a language should be taught. . . . This is understandable for *linguistics* covers a much narrower domain than language."

Lack of definition of what reading is

Transformational-generative grammar, like other types of linguistic analysis, is not and probably will not become the basis of a teaching method for foreign languages, but new insights gained by the application of transformational analysis to Latin may prove to be useful to the Latin teacher. Kelly (50) discusses the relationship between transformational and traditional grammar and gives a clear demonstration of transformational analysis of the nominal phrase. Keiler (48) applies the concept of deep structure to the verb phrase. Perhaps the most extensive published application of transformational analysis to Latin is by Lakoff (55).

Application of transformational grammar

The reluctance of publishers to set new Greek type for a limited market has tended for almost half a century to limit innovative approaches in the teaching of classical Greek and to isolate such programs when they were tried. This dearth of innovative texts is now alleviated by the recent appearance of several excellent new Greek texts.

Limitations in the teaching of Greek materials

Ruck (87) has written a text which uses "real Greek" *ab initio* and involves the student in use of the language through a wide variety of drills, exercises, and comprehension activities.

A thorough program in elementary classical Greek based on the principles of structural and applied linguistics is now available from McGill University (Ellis & Schachter, 28). These materials, which include loose-leaf text, drill tapes, and a teacher's manual, were developed over a two-year period with substantial subvention from the Ford Foundation.

The Greek program of Hayes (39) using tapes and printed text, begins with Koine Greek and makes a transition to the Attic Greek of Plato in the later stages.

A novel approach to teaching classical Greek is an intensive interim course reported in a letter to the author by Ray Larson, St. John's University, Collegeville, Minnesota. After a brief introduction to language discovery procedures using an Aztec dialect the teacher informed the students that he would play the role of a "native informant" who knew how to express ideas in Greek, but had no knowledge of formal grammar. The students were then presented with the task of constructing a grammar of Greek on the basis of their questions and observations. Larson reports that at the end of the term students had created a basic description of the language, had learned quite a bit of Greek, and had discovered a great deal about the nature of language. Larson concludes his report with a revealing statement:

> The grammars produced in this experiment were more logically organized than traditional Greek grammars. The categories of traditional grammars were derived from a Latin model, not from direct observation of Greek usage. Our grammars, though far from complete in detail, are based on a sounder scientific procedure and are therefore truer to the facts they are intended to interpret.

Although the study of Greek has become vestigial in many sections of the nation, there are indications of a renewed interest in Greek at the secondary as well as the college level. Masciantonio (63) reports the formation of a Greek curriculum committee, which has a mandate to develop an appropriate Greek curriculum for the Philadelphia schools. An example of a thriving and vigorous Greek program at the Boston College High School is reported by Donaher (23).

Zuntz (108), in a somewhat acerbic review of a popular traditional text, points out both its fundamental as well as trivial inadequacies and in comparison with this text describes his own course, based from the outset on "real" Greek, on induction of rules, and on the application of historical and comparative linguistics "as a help in comprehending and grouping the Greek phenomena."

This reworking of methods and objectives for teaching Greek along with the apparent renewed student interest in things Greek should bring forth a resurgence in the study of the Greek language in the colleges and in the schools.

Teaching the literature

Multa magis quam multorum lectione formanda est mens.
  (Quintilian, *Institutio Oratoria* X, i, 59.)

Today's students present teachers with a challenge that must be answered in school curricula. They demand relevance. This demand should not be equated with contemporaneity. What they ask is that whatever they are learning should create new awareness, new sensitivity, new perspectives, new insights — something which will perceptibly affect them now and can be applied to their lives. No longer will many of them memorize rote forms, march laboriously up and down the hill with Caesar's legions, write inane sentences, and memorize seemingly interminable rules and exceptions solely on the putative promise that some day at the end of this arduous journey they may perceive the recondite treasures embodied in the language. Nor will they countenance the study of a language which is treated as a mask which must be stripped off to get at the meaning.

The "new" student and literature

These considerations dictate that from the very inception of language study students must be made aware that form and content are inextricably fused, that knowledge of the target language can convey to them something that is not available to them in translations, that the reading of the literature can be both an emotional and an intellectual experience. These considerations dictate that literary criticism, broadly conceived, must be an integral facet of language instruction from the very beginning.

Although it is conceded that the techniques of literary criticism can be applied to any work of literature, including Caesar, it is apparent that some types of literature are more amenable to classroom treatment from the standpoint of literary criticism than are others.

The early introduction of lyric and elegiac poetry into the Latin curriculum offers several advantages:

Advantages of early introduction of lyric and elegiac poetry in the curriculum

1 These poems frequently treat themes that are part of the adolescent's life.
2 The relationship between form and content is most easily perceived.
3 Most of the poems are comparatively short and can be read and discussed as an entity. This genre avoids the protracted treatment of a single work over an extended period of time during which students tend to lose sight of the unity of the work as well as the sense of immediacy and tension that shorter works can provide.

Cleary (14) advocates the early introduction of poetry into the Latin curriculum. A reader produced under his direction by the Latin workshop held at Ohio State University in the summer of 1969 gives a prominent place to lyric and elegiac poetry (15).

Two recent texts are specifically designed for introducing students to literary criticism. Hornsby (43) and Balme & Warman (7) have written texts designed to help and encourage the student to apply his critical faculties to classical literature in a disciplined and productive way. *Introduction to literary criticism*

An excellent point of departure for the teacher who would like to introduce literary criticism but has had little training or experience in this area would be Quinn (79,80). Porter's (78) discussion of musicality in ancient poetry should prove to be particularly useful.

Much assistance is available to the teacher for a Vergil class. Some recent and valuable books are Quinn (81), Poeschl (77), Otis (70), Commager (16), and Distler (22). The journals abound in useful articles for Vergilian criticism; two examples of productive approaches are Wilson (105) and Hands (36).

Teacher education

Facile remedium est ubertati; sterilia nullo labore vincuntur.
(Quintilian, *Institutio Oratoria*, II, ii, 6.)

The currently developing nationwide teacher surplus has in all probability affected Latin teachers as well, with the result that no general shortage of Latin teachers exists except in a few isolated local situations. This consideration should lead to an increased emphasis on the quality of the teacher education programs now existing to ensure that future Latin teachers possess the necessary competencies and background for functioning within what will be a rapidly changing field where teaching excellence will be requisite for the survival of the classical languages. *National surplus*

Classics departments throughout the nation are now appearing to manifest greater concern over their role in the preparation of Latin teachers. Evidence of this can be seen in the annual meeting of Big Ten classics chairmen held in November, 1969, in which discussion of teacher education and the consideration of possible cooperative efforts for improving undergraduate and graduate teacher education programs as well as sponsoring in-service workshops were the main items on the agenda. Another evidence of concern was the inclusion of a pedagogical presentation at the December meeting of the American Philological Association in Los Angeles. *Concern for preparation of teachers*

Rexine (83) proposes that centralized efforts should be made to study Latin teacher supply and demand, to ascertain their preparation in classics, and to determine how much Latin is really taught. He also proposes an expansion of MAT (Master of Arts in Teaching) programs and closer coordination and cooperation between institutions offering them.

In September of 1969, directors of federally sponsored EPDA (Education Professions Development Act) Institutes and Fellowship Programs in Basic Studies (government terminology for regular academic subjects) received a letter from the U.S. Office of Education informing them that, with the exception of the second year of some two-year programs already begun, all Basic Studies Programs were to be discontinued at the end of the 1969–70 academic year to effect an eight million dollar budget cut.

The loss of the Basic Studies programs under the EPDA constitutes a grievous blow to the humanities and other traditional disciplines in the schools. Each EPDA program made a sincere attempt to select its participants with the "multiplier effect" in mind so that each participant would be able to conduct workshops and be an agent of salutary change upon return to his school, thus extending the impact of these programs beyond the relatively few people who could be selected as participants. Though the support given to Basic Studies programs was so modest that "token" support would not be an inappropriate description, the very fact that the federal government was supporting classics and the humanities for the schools was a valuable asset in the advocacy of the value and ultimate usefulness of these subjects. Some comparison may be helpful for putting the amount of expenditures required for all of these programs in perspective. Slater (94), using data from Harvey (37), calculates that it costs two million dollars for every 24 hours of operating one aircraft used to defoliate vegetation in Vietnam. The total Basic Studies program represented an expenditure equivalent to four days' defoliation. To ponder the future of a nation that observes such priorities is a frightening task.

The results of protracted efforts by classical organizations to get federal subvention for classical languages comparable to what was provided for the modern languages by the NDEA, and of the long hours spent by classics departments in preparing compendious proposals for submission to the Office of Education, have been largely wiped out by this one letter.

The first federally funded program for the support of Latin teaching began in 1966 at the University of Minnesota where 40 Latin teachers selected on a national basis attended a 6-week

Effects of the canceling of the EPDA Basic Studies Program Institutes and Fellowships

Description of institute programs

311

institute, which concentrated primarily on teaching methods and materials for Latin at the 7th and 8th grade levels. This institute was supported through the National Foundation for the Arts and Humanities.

Minnesota

A second National Foundation for the Arts and Humanities Latin Institute was conducted at the University of Minnesota in 1967. The purpose of this two-week institute was to familiarize persons engaged in the preparation of Latin teachers with new developments in the psychology of language learning, teaching methods, and materials.

A third summer institute was conducted with the support of the EPDA at the University of Illinois in 1968 for 35 Latin teachers selected on a national basis. The primary concentration of this institute was on teaching methods and materials for facilitating the transition from elementary Latin to the reading of unadapted Latin authors.

Illinois, 1968

The summer of 1969 saw an expansion of the number of Latin institutes available to teachers: two were supported by the U.S. Office of Education and two received other types of support.

An Institute for Advanced Study in Arts and Humanities: Latin was conducted from June to August, 1969, at the State University of New York at Albany under the direction of Harriet S. Norton, assisted by Charles Graber. The purpose of the institute was to improve the quality of Latin teachers by preparing them to initiate, develop, and maintain effective programs of Latin for the middle school (grades five–eight). The general objectives were:

SUNY: Albany

1 To familiarize teachers with concepts of *humanitas* contained in Latin literature appropriate to pupils in the middle school.

2 To train teachers to adapt Latin passages focusing on *humanitas* to the middle school child.

3 To acquaint teachers with various approaches and newer technologies applicable to teaching Latin to younger children.

4 To enhance the teachers' background in their subject area by studying linguistic principles of the language, oral interpretation, and Greco-Roman culture through its literature.

Forty teachers, selected primarily from the northeast United States, attended classes in the concepts of *humanitas* in Latin literature, the adaptation of Latin literature, materials and methods in the teaching of Latin, linguistics applied to Latin, oral interpretation of Latin literature, and Roman life and civilization. In addition to these regular classes, participants observed a demonstration class consisting of beginning Latin students about to enter seventh grade. A special laboratory period was set aside for a practicum, special lectures on a wide variety of topics, and a demonstration of audiovisual equipment.

Thirty participants selected from a field of over 500 applicants attended the 6-week Institute for Advanced Study in the Arts and Humanities conducted at the University of Illinois from July to August, 1969, under the direction of Richard Scanlan. The focus of the program was on the selection of appropriate literary material for the third year of an extended classics curriculum beginning in seventh grade or for the second year of Latin study begun at later levels. The objectives of the institute were:

1 To provide for the participants a broader conspectus of Latin literature, a more clearly perceived feeling for variation in style, improved effectiveness in interpreting the literature to students, as well as a sharpened competence in Latin language skills.

2 To provide sufficient introduction to the basic principles of linguistics and the most recent research in this field, with particular emphasis on those elements of linguistics which can be applied to language teaching.

3 To familiarize teachers with relevant aspects of research in language learning.

4 To assist the participants in acquiring the skills, teaching techniques, experience, and materials necessary for teaching the reading of Latin in a new and more stimulating and relevant way.

5 To provide the participants with first-hand experience in developing new materials.

6 To employ a multisensory approach to the teaching of literature.

7 To give the participants an opportunity to learn new teaching techniques and methods as well as to apply them in a practicum situation and thus to profit from an exchange of suggestions and ideas.

8 To make a contribution to the retention of Latin as a significant component of the school curriculum and to the establishment of a longer and educationally richer curriculum in the classical languages.

Participants attended classes in Latin literature, the oral interpretation of Latin literature, the rapid comprehension of Latin literature, and applied linguistics. In the afternoon practicum the participants participated in the development of the new materials for the third year (ninth grade) of an extended Latin curriculum, received and analyzed materials developed for and by the Arts and Humanities Institutes at the University of Illinois in 1968, and investigated techniques which could be applied in more traditional curricula.

There have been two Latin institutes at Brock University, St. Catherines, Ontario, each lasting five days, the first August 25–30 in 1968, and the second August 24–29 in 1969. Anticipating the crisis in classics in the secondary schools in Ontario, which this year has struck with catastrophic results, various officials of the Ontario Department of Education and two of the colleges of education in the province joined with Arthur Kahn of Brock University in planning these institutes at which new methods and techniques for teaching Latin in the secondary schools could be investigated. The programs included lectures by university professors on major figures of Roman literature and on aspects of Roman history, videotaped demonstration lessons, language laboratory practice in pronunciation and in the techniques of reading poetry, panel discussions on administrative problems facing the Latin program, practice in drill techniques and in the use of audiovisual equipment, discussions of new American programs of Latin in the elementary schools as well as various enrichment activities both in the Latin class and extracurricular. Approximately 150 teachers from California to New Brunswick attended the first institute and 100 in a similar geographical distribution attended the second institute. About half of the teachers were from Ontario. A third Brock Latin Institute is projected for the summer of 1971.

Brock University, St. Catherines, Ontario

The Brock University classics department has also been conducting in-service workshops for secondary school teachers. Begun in 1967, they were held in double sessions, morning and afternoon, on four Saturdays each year. The workshops have consistently attracted up to 150 teachers, but the workshop in November, 1969, attracted almost 400 people, including principals, supervisors, and provincial educational administrators.

This series of workshops is similar to the in-service program for Latin teachers conducted by the Texas Education Agency and directed by Bobby W. LaBouve. A syllabus prepared by Mar-

314

garet Forbes (33), who after a career of leadership and labor on behalf of the cause of classics is retiring from teaching in 1970, is the basis of instruction for the preparation of teacher trainers who in turn conduct multiple series of six in-service classes in various parts of Texas.

A Latin workshop for secondary teachers in Ohio was conducted under the direction of Vincent Cleary of Ohio State University in the summer of 1969. The principal objectives were the selection of reading materials for a new curriculum for Latin I and II and the consideration of effective methods and techniques for teaching this literature. Another workshop is planned for the summer of 1970.

During the academic years 1968–69 and 1969–70, the classics department of the University of Minnesota conducted an EPDA Experienced Teacher Fellowship Program for ten experienced teachers selected on a nationwide basis and a Prospective Teacher Fellowship Program for ten recent classics graduates. These programs, which led to the M.A. degree, were designed to prepare teachers for effective teaching in an extended classical curriculum with stress on efficient reading of Latin, oral interpretation of Latin literature, approaches to the humanities, application of literary criticism to the classroom, language learning, teaching methods, and the development of "spin-off" languages (Greek and a Romance language) as part of the advanced stages of the extended classical curriculum.

Although the EPDA institute and fellowship programs described in this section have been terminated, it is hoped that their brief existence may have provided some impetus and guidance for the changes which are necessary for the continued viability of the classical languages and tradition in our schools.

In the first volume of this series, Kovach (54) described professional and service organizations in classics and the contributions which they are making to the promotion of classical studies at all levels. The Joint Association of Classical Teachers (JACT) should also be added to this account. The perquisites of membership in this association, which is open to anyone interested in the teaching of classics, are a subscription to *Didaskalos*, a journal of consistently high quality dedicated solely to the teaching of classics, several mailings, which have useful lists of new publications and news of Association activities, a list of materials available from JACT, and a roster of all members. Details of its activities along with enrollment forms can be obtained from the honorary secretary-general, C. W. Batz, M.A., JACT, 31–34 Gordon Square, London, WC1.

Another publication which should be particularly useful to American classics teachers is *Documentatio Didactica Classica*, an extensive bibliography containing references to new editions of texts, new teaching materials, books on classical themes, and journal articles relevant to the teaching of classics, with rather complete coverage of European sources and partial coverage of sources in Africa and the United States. This publication is a valuable supplement to the *Britannica Review of Foreign Language Education*, and to the ACTFL Bibliography (Lange, 57), which is supported by MLA/ERIC in collaboration with ACTFL and the University of Minnesota. The *Documentatio Didactica* is contained in *Didactica Classica Gandensia*, or is available separately from the same publisher. The current issue, which gives the texts of all papers read at the Frankfort Colloquy, is available from the Editorial Office, St. Petersniewstraat 87, B9000–Ghent, Belgium.

Epilogue

A judgment as to whether these are the "best of times" or the "worst of times" for classics will depend on the perspective of the reader. Some will see in the enrollment trends and the massive changes in curriculum, objectives, and teaching methods of our schools cause for an abject pessimism. It is true that Latin enrollments have dropped precipitously during the three-year period from 1965 to 68 and in all probability have continued this trend since then. It is true that college and university enrollments, although currently showing strength, are threatened by accelerating changes in the organizational structure of higher education. It is true that the traditional Latin curriculum in the schools has been increasingly unappealing both to students and curriculum decision-makers. It is true that even the vestigial prestige of the classics inherited from another era is rapidly disappearing. Those who regard challenge as a threat and change as decay will see cause for pessimism in all of these considerations, and they have a speciously convincing case.

Fortunately, for many other classicists the current situation is, if not a cause for optimism, a challenge fraught with exciting possibilities and a part of a greater struggle in which issues of cardinal importance to our nation will be decided.

Popular interest in Greece and Rome is greater than at any time in recent history; translations of classical literature continue to be produced in great numbers; versions of classical dramas are being presented all over the nation and are well attended; books, articles, and lectures on all aspects of classical civilization are numerous and well received; the film industry is beginning to treat the ancient world seriously. This recent surge of interest is more than a fortuitous occurrence. Most Americans, who had until recently seemed to think that the solution to all problems was merely a matter of the application of "know-how" and doing more of what they have been doing, now find themselves inexorably drawn by events over which they have little control and are faced with the necessity for making decisions about priorities. These decisions, although often necessitated by technology, are not technological decisions; they are ethical and value judgments about how man can on this finite earth establish conditions most favorable to human well-being and the "good life." The attempt to make these generalizations meaningful and specific is (or should be) the central concern of the humanities. Increasingly, the public, and public agencies, will be compelled to choose from a finite series of options the one choice which has the greatest value for human beings. Thus, speculation about the ultimate purposes of life, the nature of true happiness, the claims of "beauty" vs. utility, the definition of morality, and the determination of the bases upon which morality rests has ceased to be a luxury necessary only for those with the leisure and background to consider these matters, and has become a matter of public concern where every man should have an articulate voice in these fundamental decisions. The interest in antiquity is, perhaps subliminally, a reflection of this new awareness.

The resilience of the classical tradition should not be underestimated. In the Soviet Union the study of the classics, which suffered almost total eclipse in the dogmatic enthusiasms of the early post-revolutionary period and received little encouragement under the Stalinist freeze, is now "alive and well," according to a Soviet classicist. Takho-Godi (100) reports that most Soviet universities have classical studies departments and that Latin is taught in all foreign language departments of Soviet teachers' colleges as well as in departments of history. He also notes a high degree of activity at the university level in dissemination of the classical legacy among the adult population and

317

schoolchildren. Takho-Godi also describes the fields of specialization at the various universities and lists some of the more notable recent works of Soviet classical scholars. More awareness of each other and communication between Western and Soviet classicists may prove to be mutually beneficial.

A silent but nevertheless real struggle is going on in our schools today. The real issue, which transcends parochial interest in any specific subject, is being drawn with emerging clarity as curriculum decisions are being made across the nation. The issue is: For what and for whom do the schools exist? One viewpoint is that the schools exist primarily to prepare the student for functioning in the economy. Emphasis on immediately applicable practical skills and knowledge is the natural concomitant of this view. A contending position maintains that the schools must face up to a far more challenging task: that they must help the students to acquire the skills, knowledge, and inner resources which will enable them to find solutions to problems which are as yet unknown or but dimly perceived. Implicit in this challenging task is the necessity for giving much greater attention to developing the human potential of each student by providing significant encounters and involvements with the arts, humanities, and a panoply of human experience and knowledge from the past and present. The ultimate goal of such education must be to create a new generation that is articulate, sensitive, and independent, and armed with that sense of perspective which can be nurtured by transcending the confines of a single culture and a narrow contemporaneity. Classics teachers must become a vital part of a quiet revolution which will ensure that the essential balance between these two conceptions of the role of the schools is restored.

References, Classics: The teaching of Latin and Greek and classical humanities

1 Albert, Ann. "Latin Programs at New Trier High School West." *Classical Journal* 65(1969):175–77.

2 Alpert, D., and D.L. Bitzer. "Advances in Computer Based Education." *Science* 167(1969):1582–90.

3 Alyeshmerni, Monsoor. "Linguistics vs. the Audio-Lingual Approach." *Funditor, Minnesota Latin Newsletter* 95(1970):13–19.

4 Asher, James J. "The Learning Strategy of the Total Physical Response." *Modern Language Journal* 50(1966):79–84.

5 —— and Ramiro Garcia. "The Optimal Age to Learn a Foreign Language." *Modern Language Journal* 53(1969):334–41.

6 Austin, Neale W. *A Survey of the Teaching of Latin in the Secondary Schools*. Test Development Report TDR-69-1. Princeton, New Jersey:

Educational Testing Service, 1969. [ERIC Document Reproduction Service: ED 029 536.]

7 Balme, M.G., and M.S. Warman. *Aestimanda: Practical Criticism of Latin and Greek. Poetry and Prose*. London: Oxford Univ. Press, 1965.

8 Bell, Robert. "Letter to the Editor." *Classical World* 62(1968):98.

9 Bock, Carolyn E., John F. Latimer, and William M. Seaman. "Classical Languages," 146–54 in Robert L. Ebel,ed., *Encyclopedia of Educational Research*. New York: Macmillan, 1969.

10 Bodson, A., and Suzanne Govaerts. "Codification d'un texte latin sur cartes mécanographiques IBM-80 colunnes." *Revue* (International Organization for Ancient Language Analysis by Computer-Liège) 1(1966):1–50. [Corrigenda in subsequent edition. 2(1966):47–48.]

11 Bruner, Jerome,ed. *Learning About Learning: A Conference Report, Working Conference on Research on Children's Learning*. Cooperative Research Monograph 15. Washington, D.C.: U.S. Government Printing Office, 1966.

12 Calder, William M.,III. "Teaching Elementary Ancient Languages, Part I." *Classical Outlook* 45(1968):73–74.

13 Clark, Thomas. "New Latin Program at Edina." *Minnesota Latin Newsletter* 96(1970):7.

14 Cleary, Vincent J. "Beware the Ides of March." *Classical Outlook* 47(1970):78–80.

15 ——— et al. *The Columbus Latin Reader*. Columbus, Ohio: Classics Department, Ohio State Univ., 1969.

16 Commager, Steele,ed. *Virgil:A Collection of Critical Essays*. Englewood Cliffs, New Jersey: Prentice-Hall, 1966.

17 Cracas, Thomas L. "Four Linguistic Models for the Comprehension of the Latin Sentence." *Classical World* 62(1969):255–60.

18 Cutt, Eula G. *Curriculum Guide for Latin Heritage in Secondary Schools*. Detroit, Michigan: Board of Education, 1969. [Mimeo; for a copy send to: Schools Center, Detroit, Michigan 48202, c/o Dr. Naida Dostal, Supervisor of Foreign Language Instruction.]

19 Davies, J.C., and J.H. Molyneux. "An Experimental First-Year University Latin Course." *Didaskalos* 3,i(1969):115–19.

20 Dennis, F.B.K. "*Principia* and *Pseudolus Noster*:A Review." *Didaskalos* 3,i(1969):71–78.

21 DeWitt, Norman J. "Classical Languages," 211–21 in Chester Harris,ed., *Encyclopedia of Educational Research*. New York: Macmillan, 1960. [3rd ed.]

22 Distler, Paul. *Vergil and Vergiliana*. Chicago: Loyola Univ. Press, 1966.

23 Donaher, Brian. "Homeric Academy." *Classical Journal* 65(1969):173.

24 Dorsey, David F.,Jr. "Courses in Literature in Translation." *Classical Outlook* 47(1969):25–26.

25 Duffy, Joseph P.,S.J. "Latin Helps Alumni." *Classical Journal* 64(1968):128–29.

26 *Earned Degrees*. Washington, D.C.: U.S. Office of Education, 1968.

27 Eikeboom, Rogier. *Programmed Latin Grammar*. Glenview, Illinois:Scott Foresman, 1970.

28 Ellis, C. Douglas, and Albert Schachter. *Ancient Greek:A Structural Programme*. Montreal: McGill Univ., 1969.

29 Else, Gerald F. "A New Center." *Classical Outlook* 47(1970):110. [If interested, write to:Professor Gerald F. Else, Director, Center for Coordination of Ancient and Modern Studies. University of Michigan. Ann Arbor, Michigan 48104.]

30 Erickson, Gerald M. "A Multi-Sensory Approach to an Extended Classical Curriculum:Rationale, Structure, and Design for Application in the Classroom." *Dissertation Abstracts* 29(1968): 885A(Minnesota).

31 ——— "The 'Knowledge Explosion' or Let's Say 'So What.'" *Funditor, Minnesota Latin Newsletter* 95(1970):20–23.

32 ——— *Selective Annotated Bibliography for the Multi-Sensory Approach to Latin Teaching*. Minneapolis: Univ. of Minnesota. [Mimeo; available upon request from the Classics Department.]

33 Forbes, Margaret A. *A Syllabus for an In-Service Course in the Teaching of Latin*. Austin: Foreign Language Section, Texas Education Agency, 1969. [Mimeo.]

34 Glickman, Robert J., and Gerrit J. Staalman. *Manual for the Printing of Literary Texts and Concordances by Computer*. Toronto: Univ. of Toronto Press, n.d.

35 Golubev, J.V. "O formirovanii reči na inostrannom jazyke n rannej stadii obučenija (K voprosu o primenenii predmetnoj nagljadnosti)." ["Concerning Foreign Language Speech Development at an Early Stage of Instruction (On the Question of the Application of Subject-Visuals)."] *Inostrannije Jazyke v Škole* 1(1969):38–47.

36 Hands, Donald. "The Aeneid for High School Students." *Classical Bulletin* 45(1969):69–70, 74–75.

37 Harvey, Frank. *Air War-Vietnam*. New York: Bantam Books, 1967.

38 Hayden, Hilary,O.S.B. "Strategy for Change." *Classical World* 62(1969):1–4.

39 Hayes, Walter M.,S.J. *An Introductory Greek Program*. Chicago: Loyola Univ. Press, 1966.

40 ——— *An Introductory Latin Program*. Chicago: Loyola Univ. Press, 1966.

41 ——— "Lean Programming, Latin and Greek." *Classical Journal* 65(1969):307–09.

42 Hnatt, Luciana. "Modified Latin." *Classical Outlook* 47(1969):1–2.

43 Hornsby, Roger. *Reading Latin Poetry*. Norman, Oklahoma: Univ. of Oklahoma Press, 1967.

44 Huchthausen, L. "Recherches statistiques pour l'enseignment du latin." *Revue* (International Organization for Ancient Language Analysis by Computer-Liège) 1(1967):67–82.

45 Jeffrey, Lloyd N. "The Teaching of Classical Mythology:A Recent Survey." *Classical Journal* 64(1969):311–21.

46 Kant, Julia G. "Foreign Language Offerings and Enrollments in Public Schools, Fall 1968." *Foreign Language Annals* 3(1970):400–76.

47 ——— "Foreign Language Registrations in In-

stitutions of Higher Education, Fall 1968." *Foreign Language Annals* 3(1969):247–304.

48 Keiler, Allan R. "Some Problems of Latin Deep Structure." *Classical Journal* 65(1970):208–13.

49 Kelly, David H.,F.S.C. "Teaching Latin in America:Some Recent Observations." *Didaskalos* 3, i(1969):100–09.

50 —— "Transformations in the Latin Nominal Phrase." *Classical Philology* 63(1968):46–52.

51 Kilgour, Andrew. "Towards the Teaching of Classical Civilization." *Didaskalos* 3,i(1969): 134–42.

52 Kovach, Edith M. "A Challenge to Change." *Classical Journal* 64(1969):268–75.

53 —— "Admirandi, Laudandi, Imitandi." *Classical Outlook* 46(1967):109–14.

54 —— "Classics:The Teaching of Latin and Greek," 389–414 in Emma M. Birkmaier,ed., *Britannica Review of Foreign Language Education, Volume 1.* Chicago: Encyclopaedia Britannica, 1968[1969].

55 Lakoff, Robin T. *Abstract Syntax and the Latin Complementation.* Cambridge: Massachusetts Institute of Technology Press, 1968.

56 Lane, Harlan. *Why is College Foreign Language Instruction in Trouble? Three Dozen Reasons.* Ann Arbor: Center for Research on Language and Language Behavior, Univ. of Michigan, 1968. [ERIC Document Reproduction Service: ED 029 544.]

57 Lange, Dale L. "1969 ACTFL Bibliography of Books and Articles on Pedagogy in Foreign Languages." *Foreign Language Annals* 3(1970): 627–73.

58 Latimer, John F.,ed. *The Oxford Conference and Related Activities. A Report to the National Endowment for the Humanities.* Washington, D.C.: American Classical League, 1968.

59 —— *Report of the Planning Conference to Examine the Role of Classical Studies in American Education and to Make Recommendations for Needed Research and Development.* Washington, D.C.: George Washington Univ., 1965.

60 Leineks, Valdis. "Greek Literature in Translation." *Classical Outlook* 47(1970):73.

61 Margon, Joseph S. "Through the Glass Clearly: Teaching Classical Literature through Translation." *Classical World* 63(1970):297–301.

62 Masciantonio, Rudolph. "A Pilot Project for Latin in Elementary Schools." *Classical World* 62 (1969):294.

63 —— "Innovative Materials for Teaching Greek in Public Schools." *Classical Journal* 64(1969): 321–23.

64 —— "New Secondary School Latin Programs in Philadelphia." *Classical World* 63(1970):176.

65 Meck, Agnes. "*Artes Latinae*:An Appraisal After Four Years." *Classical World* 63(1970):267–69.

66 Morris, Sydney. *A Programmed Latin Course.* London: Methuen, 1967.

67 Motto, Ann L., and John R. Clark. "The Classics in Revolt." *Classical World* 63(1969):109–12. [Volume number printed incorrectly as Volume 62(1969).]

68 National Council of State Supervisors of Foreign Languages. "The Role of Latin in American Education." *Classical World* 62(1969):293–94.

69 Norton, Harriet S., and Charles F. Graber. *Colloquamur Latine Cum Pueris Puellisque-Latin in the Middle School.* Albany, New York: Department of Latin Education, State Univ. of New York at Albany, 1968.

70 Otis, Brooks. *Vergil, A Study in Civilized Poetry.* Oxford: Clarendon Press, 1963.

71 Papalia, Anthony. "A Study of Attrition in Foreign Language Enrollment in a Suburban Secondary School." *Dissertation Abstracts* 30(1970): 3199A(SUNY at Buffalo.)

72 Parks, John H. "The Classics in the Curriculum (An Open Letter to Educational Administrators)." *Peabody Journal of Education* 46(1969):331–39.

73 Peckett, C.W.E., and A.R. Mundy. "A Reply to Review of *Principia* and *Pseudolus Noster.*" *Didaskalos* 3,i(1969):79–83.

74 —— *Principia.* Glenview, Illinois: Scott Foresman, 1970. [2nd ed.]

75 —— *Pseudolus Noster.* Glenview, Illinois: Scott Foresman, 1970. [2nd ed.]

76 Phinney, Edward,Jr. "The Status of High-School Latin in California." *Classical Journal* 65(1970): 263.

77 Poeschl, Viktor. *The Art of Vergil:Image and Symbol in the Aeneid.* Ann Arbor: Univ. of Michigan Press, 1962. [Trans. Gerda Seligson]

78 Porter, David H. "Some Sources of Musicality in Ancient Poetry." *Classical Journal* 63(1970): 205–07.

79 Quinn, Kenneth. "The Commentator's Task." *Didaskalos* 2,iii(1968):114–26.

80 —— "Practical Criticism:A Reading of Propertius 21 and Catullus 17." *Greece and Rome* 16(1969):19–29.

81 —— *Vergil's Aeneid:A Critical Description.* Ann Arbor:Univ. of Michigan Press, 1968.

82 Reedy, Jeremiah. "Some Thoughts about the Artes Latinae Program and the Audio-Lingual Approach." *Funditor, Minnesota Latin Newsletter* 95(1970):7–8.

83 Rexine, John E. "A Proposal for Teacher Training in the Classics." Presented at the Univ. of Kentucky Foreign Language Conference. April 1968. [ERIC Document Reproduction Service: ED 026 911.]

84 —— "Classical Mythology:Some Recent Titles." *Classical Bulletin* 45(1968):1–5.

85 Rockwell, Kiffin. "Utility and the Classics." *Classical Outlook* 47(1970):97–98.

86 Roy, D. "Les défenseurs du latin ne sont pas des 'réactionnaires.' " *Revue de la Franco-Ancienne* 163(1969):729.

87 Ruck, Carl A.P. *Ancient Greek—A New Approach.* Cambridge: Massachusetts Institute of Technology Press, 1968.

88 Scanlan, Richard T. *Computer Assisted Instruction.* Urbana, Illinois: Department of Classics, Univ. of Illinois, n.d. [Mimeo.]

89 Schork, Robert J. "Classical Mythology:*Hos Epos Epein.*" *Classical Journal* 65(1969):117–23.

90 —— "Haec Studia Adulescentiam Alunt:A Classical Heritage Program." *Classical Journal*

65(1969):14–19.

91 Schwartz, Betty L., and Jacqueline W. Tappenden. *Cultural Language Study.* Cleveland: Cleveland Heights City School District, 1969.

92 Singer, Harry. "Theoretical Models of Reading." *Journal of Communication* 19(1968):134–56.

93 Skiles, Jonathan. "The Teaching of the Reading of Latin in the Latin Word-Order." *Classical Journal* 39(1943):88–104.

94 Slater, Philip E. "Kill Anything that Moves." *Evergreen Review* 14(1970)79:55–57, 79–84.

95 Stock, Brian. "The Poverty of Philology:The Need for New Direction in Classics and Medieval Studies." *American Council of Learned Societies Newsletter* 20,iii(1969):1–7.

96 Sweet, Waldo E. *Artes Latinae.* Chicago: Encyclopaedia Britannica Educational Corporation, 1968.

97 ——— *Latin Workshop Experimental Materials: Book One.* Ann Arbor, 1953. [Rev. ed. 1956.] [Second revision under new title, *Elementary Latin: The Basic Structures, Part I and II.* ed. by Grace Crawford, Clara Ashley, Frederick Kempner, and Jane M. Infield. Ann Arbor: Univ. of Michigan Press, 1963.]

98 ——— "Letter to the Editor." *Classical World* 63(1970):312.

99 ——— Ruth Craig, and Gerda Seligson. *Latin:A Structural Approach.* Ann Arbor: Univ. of Michigan Press, 1966. [Revised ed.]

100 Takho-Godi, Aza. "Classical Studies in the Soviet Union." *Arethusa* 3(1970):123–27. [Translated S. Rosenburg.]

101 *Tentative Syllabus in Latin.* Albany, New York: Bureau of Secondary Curriculum Development, State Education Department, 1969.

102 Warburton, Joyce, and Mary Chaffey. "Latin Classes in a Flexible Schedule." *Classical Journal* 63(1968):299.

103 Wheeler, J.A. "Defining Aims in University Language Teaching." *Babel–Journal of Australian Language Teachers Association* 5(1969):2–4.

104 Wilkins, John. "Teaching in Classical Languages:Toward a Theory (1)." *Didaskalos* 3,i (1969):168–69.

105 Wilson, John R. "Action and Emotion in Aeneas." *Greece and Rome* 16(1969):67–75.

106 Woll, Edward C. *The Multi-Sensory Approach.* Presented at the Univ. of Kentucky Foreign Language Conference, Lexington, April 1968. [ERIC Document Reproduction Service: ED 019 038.]

107 Wolverton, Robert E. "The Classics in the Academic Marketplace." *Classical Outlook* 47(1969): 13–14.

108 Zuntz, Gunther. "On First Looking into Chase and Phillips. Notes on the Teaching of Beginners' Greek." *Arion* 6(1970):362–73.

11
TESOL

Introduction

Bernard Spolsky
University of New Mexico

In a world of acronyms, TESOL is particularly resistant to attempts at pronunciation, abbreviation, and simplification. TESOL, the teaching of English to speakers of other languages, is the latest of a series of names. The British, more simply, refer to ELT, English language teaching, assuming that you only teach English to people who don't speak it. American practice has moved historically from EFL, English as a foreign language, through ESL, English as a second language, to ESOL. Sometimes, attempts are still made to maintain the distinction between EFL, English as a foreign language, and ESL, English as a second language. As Marckwardt (51) explained, EFL then refers to English taught as a school subject or to adults for much the same purposes that foreign languages are taught in the United States, and ESL means the teaching of English to be used as language of instruction in the school system or as a language of wider communication. ESOL, in this system, means both. One other important acronym, TENES (teaching of English to non-English speakers), is used only in reference to Harold Allen's pioneer survey of the situation in the United States in 1964 (6). In a later section, we shall note other areas of the field with equally awkward labels, such as SESOD, and look for the reality behind them.

Acronyms and their referents

Confusing as these names are, they give a fair picture of the state of the field. TESOL is essentially an unformed area. It represents a new series of attempts to deal with the problem caused by the fact that many children in many parts of the world come to a school that teaches them in Standard English even though they have little or no knowledge of the language. Difficult as is the foreign language teacher's task, it is made somewhat easier by recognizing it for what it is—the teaching of a new language. But the first problem of the teacher of ESOL is usually to make clear to the school system and to the community that there is need for him, that the children he wishes to teach are not just backward or stupid, but speakers of another language. TESOL then necessarily has implications for the full curriculum, exist-

323

ing not just as a single subject, but as a preparation for all. To define a task as large as this, and to find the best methods of accomplishing it, takes time. The literature reviewed in this chapter shows the increasing maturity of the field as it moves from offering panaceas to making a deeper analysis of problems, from quick, easy solutions to long-term plans and approaches.

Theory of TESOL

In a review of the state of the art, Wardhaugh (87) points out the effects of new developments in linguistics and psychology. Ten years ago, language teachers were asked to believe that the linguistic, or audiolingual, or aural-oral method was the answer to their prayers. Generative-transformational grammar cut away the theoretical linguistic base of the method, providing exciting new insights into the structure of English, but not yet showing how these might be applied. Similarly, the ferment in psychological theory produced realization of the complexity of language learning, with no sign of an emerging single view as simple and immediately applicable as had been maintained in the heyday of the audiolingual method. Wardhaugh concludes with a call for extensive research to help settle the basic uncertainties of the field.

Language teaching and new developments

A brief review by Cervenka (22) similarly notes the recognition of the fact that the audiolingual approach was based on an oversimplified theoretical model. The fields of psycholinguistics and sociolinguistics are providing data and theories that will have a major influence on the understanding of language learning and teaching.

Psycho- and sociolinguistics

How to apply the new grammatical information in the classroom is discussed by De Camp (27). Noting the lack of interest that generative grammarians have shown in language teaching application, and the relative inaccessibility to language teachers of most of their work, he advocates workshops and seminars to develop drill materials and explanations based on various insights of generative grammar. Over 30 such transformation drills are presented by Rutherford (65) and used in his textbook (66).

Generative grammar

The relations between linguistics, psychology, and pedagogy are now being extensively discussed. Wardhaugh (86) expects a new unity, like the one that permitted the development of the audiolingual method. He feels it is needed to provide justification for present classroom practice, to give young teachers a new rhetoric to replace the rhetoric of the audiolingual method they no longer can accept. Scott (68), however, calls for no basic revision, but rather a reformation of the present pedagogy in order to accommodate transformational grammar and its notions of competence and performance. The needed revision includes reorganization of ordering in accord with derivational history and the carrying out of deep rather than surface contrastive analysis.

A new unity?

Arguing in favor of more independence for second language pedagogy, Spolsky (77) attempts to distinguish between the applications and the implications of linguistics and psychology. On the one hand, linguistics and its related fields, especially psycholinguistics and sociolinguistics, help lay the basis for a theory of second language acquisition, and ultimately of second language pedagogy. On the other hand, linguistics, especially the part of it concerned with language description, may be applied in the preparation of teaching materials. But the two must be kept separate: a language description has nothing to say about how the material is to be taught. The new understanding of the nature of language and its acquisition, and of the sociological roles of the different varieties, will ultimately permit a better conception of language pedagogy, but there is no point in expecting solutions overnight.

Second language pedagogy

A critical analysis of current views on second language acquisition and bilingualism is offered by Jakobovits (45), together with a program for research into the major problems of second language pedagogy. In a keen and insightful review, he shows the complexity of the basic notions in the field. What does it mean to know how to use a language? He emphasizes communicative rather than linguistic competence. What does it mean to be a bilingual? There are insufficient data to show what constitutes bilingual proficiency. And finally, what does it mean to teach a language? He presents the main student variables (aptitude, intelligence, and motivation) and the teacher-controlled variables (criterion goal, quality of construction, and opportunities for learning). All these factors, plus the sociocultural factors (language loyalty, linguistic composition, biculturalism, and consequence) are further analyzed. Possible strategies of research into the effect of these factors are presented. Jakobovits discusses how behaviorism has continued to dominate American psychology even when its theoretical position has been so

Critical analysis of second language acquisition

strongly challenged. He proposes a research strategy not following the rigorous laboratory tradition, but involving a combination of descriptive approaches using standardized tests, questionnaires, and field observations, and manipulative approaches involving selection and induction of change. In a final chapter, Jakobovits gives details of instruments to be used in a research program. His proposal will hopefully discourage the continuation of the comparative study of various methods, at least until a clearer picture has been developed of the factors that need to be controlled.

One theoretical issue that has continued to generate discussion is contrastive analysis. The doubts about the absolute wisdom and simplicity of the contrastive notion come to the surface in only a few of the papers given at the Nineteenth Georgetown Round Table (Alatis, 4), most participants being satisfied to restate the old orthodoxy or attempt to fit transformational grammar into it. But Carroll (20) reviews psychological research and theory and finds very little in it directly relevant to applied contrastive linguistics, and Hamp (37) calls for starting not with a contrastive grammar, which he finds an empty term, but with error analysis. In this call, he is echoing the proposal of Corder (23) to use a study of errors to understand the learning of general rules. On the key issue of how you go from contrastive description to teaching prescription, Stockwell (79) remarks that it is easier to write a contrastive study than apply one, and points out that his earlier proposal to rank particular problems (Stockwell & Bowen, 80) was based on teaching experience rather than any theoretical position. In the meantime, a study by Brière (17) has started to show the way to an understanding of the nature of interference in the learning of phonology. He emphasizes the importance of detailed phonetic analysis as the basis for comparison, rather than a description in terms of *ad hoc* distinctive features or phonemes and allophones.

Contrastive analysis

Slowly emerging from this work in contrastive analysis is a view of the nature of second language acquisition and of interference and facilitation. There are signs that phonology and grammar are different: that while in the former it may be reasonable to speak of the interference of habits, in the latter the more interesting and important phenomenon probably is the development of incorrect generalizations on the basis both of first language rules and of second language experience. Until we have a more precise theory of second language acquisition, in-

Results of contrastive analysis

terference and facilitation must remain crude concepts. A large gap in present work is comparison at the semantic level, probably the most crucial ultimately for second language teaching.

The fact that so many of these studies are concerned with second language pedagogy as a whole rather than with TESOL alone is a reflection of the close relationship that has continued to be maintained between teachers of ESOL and linguists, and of the basic interest in underlying theory constantly evinced by researchers in the field.

ESOL and bilingual education

The increasing relevance of ESOL to the U.S. national scene is particularly shown by its close association with bilingual education. The recognition of the existence of a large group of children for whom there is a language barrier to education demands a strategy to teach them the standard language (ESOL), and encourages the provision of transitional or maintained education also in the child's language (bilingual education) (Spolsky, 75). The two cannot be separated: any bilingual education program in the United States must include an effective ESOL component, and any ESOL program that ignores the children's first language is likely to be ineffective. The year under review has seen a flurry of practical activity, supported by the funds allocated in accordance with the Bilingual Education Act, and a start on the reasoned study and research required to make such activity meaningful.

ESOL and bilingualism

A most important paper that has cleared the way for intelligent research and thinking is the typology developed by Mackey (50). Bilingual education can be classified according to various dimensions. First are the various possible combinations of languages used in the home, school, area, and country. Within the school itself, a program may use one or more languages for instruction, may aim to transfer students from one language to another gradually or abruptly, or to maintain two languages in equal or differentiated roles, and may favor a standard world language or a national one. Mackey's model produces some hundreds of possible types, a great number of which can in fact be illustrated in actual practice. It permits more meaningful comparisons to be made between various studies of bilingual education, showing that results that seem contradictory can usually be attributed to different types. The greater precision

Dimensions of bilingualism

327

that can now be given to the term bilingual education is starting to bring some order into a field that was fast becoming confused.

A major study of the nature of a bilingual community by Joshua Fishman and others (15) has not only increased our understanding of the complexity of the phenomenon, but has provided a number of valuable instruments and research techniques for further studies. The East Texas Dialect Project (Galvan & Troike, 34) has studied the languages and dialects of the area and incorporated its data and findings directly in curriculum development. Sociolinguistic work like this is making it possible to discover and describe the language situation and develop educational policies based on it.

Bilingualism: a major study

A number of reviews of current bilingual education programs are under way, and their publication should add to an understanding of the relations of ESOL and bilingual education programs, but any basic advances in the field will need to await the funding and carrying out of major research of the type proposed by the National Conference on Bilingual Education (54), the key suggestion of which was a detailed study of factors of the type identified by Jakobovits (45) in an operational setting.

ESOL and American Indians

The specific problems of one non-English-speaking group, the American Indian, have started to receive serious attention. Hopkins stresses the variety in the linguistic situation of American Indians and the importance of English to them (Hopkins, 40). A field study among the Cherokee (Tax & Thomas, 81) reports dramatic improvement when educational development was closely related to the general problem of social, political, and economic alienation, and was accompanied by strong social understanding and support. One Indian-controlled school, Rough Rock Demonstration School on the Navajo Reservation, is developing TESOL as an integral part of its bilingual education program (Hoffman, 39; Pfeiffer, 61).

Specific problems

Much of the activity in the field follows closely the recommendations of a study conducted by the Center for Applied Linguistics for the Bureau of Indian Affairs in 1967 (Ohannessian, 57). Several contrastive studies of Indian languages and English as a guide to teaching English are in preparation; appearing in the period under review were two for Navajo (Pedtke & Werner, 59; Young, 89) and one each for Cree (Soveran, 74), Choctaw

Activity in Indian education

(Nicklas, 55), and Papago (Mathiot & Ohannessian, 52). A major effort to develop English achievement tests for American Indian students is under way (Brière, 16,18).

ESOL and SESOD

Political and educational interest in minority groups coincided with the development of sociolinguistics and its ability to study social as well as regional dialects. One result is the new subfield SESOD, the teaching of Standard English to speakers of other dialects. Its home is unclear (it is claimed by both the National Council of Teachers of English and Teachers of English to Speakers of Other Languages). There are two major issues under debate and study: how different is Standard English from nonstandard dialects, and to what extent are the principles and practices developed in teaching English to speakers of other languages applicable to speakers of other dialects?

SESOD

Many linguists are trying to establish through their research and polemic the notion that nonstandard dialects are highly structured, complete and separate systems, and not just incorrect, inferior, and illogical versions of the standard language (Labov, 47; Bailey, 11; Baratz & Povich, 12). Numbers of studies of what is sometimes called Black English (Houston, 41) are appearing, including descriptions of regional variants such as those of Washington (Baratz & Povich, 12), Detroit (Shuy, 70; Wolfram, 88), and Florida (Houston, 41). An account of a major field study (Shuy, Wolfram, & Riley, 72) provides the model for future research and a picture of the dimensions involved in understanding sociolinguistic variation.

Linguists and nonstandard dialects

There are a number of different positions that might be taken on the language problem of children of lower socioeconomic status. Some educational psychologists present the rather surprising idea that lower class Negro children have no language at all, deriving their notions, as Labov (47) has shown, not just from mistaken views of the structure of language but from inadequate understanding of language use. These impressions of the children's verbal ability are based on formal tests and interviews, situations in which the children are least likely to speak freely. The analysis presented ignores the structure of the dialect itself, taking surface features such as the double negative and labeling them illogical. If the Black English use of negative concord is illogical, so was Old English; if the absence of the

Different views of nonstandard dialects

present copula in Black English is illogical, so are Russian, Hebrew, and Hungarian. A second position is that social varieties
of English are bad and must be corrected; as Shuy (69) points
out, this view is held by the English-teaching profession, which
has traditionally worked to eradicate all locally and socially
identifiable features. The position taken by most linguists is to
propose what is variously called biloquialism and bidialectalism:
the teaching of a second dialect (Abrahams, 3; Baratz & Shuy,
13; Carroll & Feigenbaum, 21; Troike, 82,83). Just as when a
student learns French in school he is not told to stop using English, so when a speaker of a nonstandard dialect is taught the
standard form, he should not be told to stop using his own dialect. Rather, he should learn when to use each, and come to
understand the place and value of each. Given this approach,
the similarity between second dialect teaching and foreign language teaching, between ESOL and SESOD, is readily apparent.

A program to apply standard foreign language teaching techniques to standard dialect teaching has been described by Carroll (21) and Feigenbaum (30). They report the failure of certain
drills, especially the imitation and repetition considered part of
the standard audiolingual methods package, and argue for
minimal-pair drills, appropriateness drills, and grammatical
manipulation. It is clear from this that they have missed many
of the developments in theory of teaching ESOL, drawing their
notions of ESOL methodology from the old orthodoxy.

FL teaching techniques for SESOD

There are a number of arguments against the lumping together
of SESOD and ESOL. Kochman (46) questions whether it is in
fact necessary to teach the standard dialect at all, claiming it to
be "educationally wasteful" and socially impossible of realization. Sledd (73) attacks bidialectalism as being racist and
immoral in its tolerance of white prejudice. We should rid the majority of their prejudices rather than try to compel the minority
to be bidialectal. Virginia Allen, who was early associated with
the application of foreign language teaching techniques to second dialect teaching (8), has recently (7) restated her position in
the light of her experience. She still maintains five points of similarity: the need for contrastive analysis of the student's home
language and the standard dialect; the recognition of the equal
value, in their own domains, of the two systems; the concentration on the structure of the home language and the standard dialect, rather than vocabulary; the need for progression by small
steps; and the importance of habit formation and success in per-

SESOD and ESOL – are they the same?

formance. She also accepts similar drills as suitable. But she emphasizes the importance of recognizing that, for the students, a second dialect is not a foreign language, a position that calls for variation not only of technique but especially of attitude.

There has been a tendency to assume that just to recognize that standard dialect teaching is a language teaching matter will itself somehow be a panacea. But experience and more careful thought are making clear that this is not so. At the very time that the old audiolingual orthodoxy is being questioned in teaching foreign languages, it is rather shocking to find it taking over a new source of activity (and funds). As Sledd (73) points out, the effectiveness of the old methods has never been proved, and their intellectual foundation has been overthrown. There are more hopeful signs, though, as the relevance of sociolinguistics to ESOL is coming to be realized. There is in fact the start of an effect of SESOD on ESOL, as teachers of English as a foreign or second language are coming to understand that they must take into account the general language situation of their pupils. *Language learning in context*
Thus, as it was stated a number of times at the Harpers Ferry Conference on English Teaching as a World Wide Problem (Ohannessian, 56), in any country, English teaching must be seen in the context of other languages in use; it must reflect the sociolinguistic picture. This is the special lesson ESOL has to learn from SESOD—a language is taught in a social setting; and the lesson both have to learn from sociolinguistics—a new language need not be learned at the expense of the old.

ESOL in the world

The Harpers Ferry Conference in 1969 provided an opportunity for some 40 British and American scholars and administrators to talk about the problem of English teaching throughout the world (Ohannessian, 56). In the papers read and subsequent *Harpers Ferry Conference* discussions, it was generally agreed that the limited resources now available needed husbanding and careful application. Careful coordination of activities, based on a detailed analysis of the language teaching situation in the country concerned, is vital. The basic position seemed to be that it is no longer possible to expect to teach English to everyone, everywhere, but necessary to develop priorities for each country. In some, this would involve concentrating efforts on training teachers for the tertiary level.

Reports to the Conference make clear the large number of agencies involved in ESOL activities – the British Council, AID, the U.S. departments of Defense and State, U.S. Information Agency, the Peace Corps, the Ford Foundation, to mention only a few of those that conduct programs or support national activities. Recent descriptions have been published of English teaching activities in Israel (Gefen, 35) and Egypt (Larudee, 48), but none as complete as the major study by Brownell (19) of the situation in Japan.

The "E" in ESOL

Ideas of what is the "English" to be taught to speakers of other languages have undergone great changes in the last decade or so. There are two major aspects to this change. First is our increased ability to recognize social varieties of language. Where in the '40s, linguists and others called for teaching the spoken language rather than the school grammar's concept of the written language, it is now usual to discuss the many varieties that might be appropriate for various situations and purposes (Shuy, 71; Quirk, 63).

Social varieties of language

The second, and more superficially dramatic aspect, has been the triumph of the generative-transformational model of linguistic description. How this should modify the teaching of ESOL is a matter of some debate. Most new work in the analysis and description of English is being done in transformational terms, and is becoming available, in some small measure, in fairly accessible form (Jacobs & Rosenbaum, 43). Some scholars then argue that these grammatical findings are directly (Rutherford, 65) or indirectly (Jacobs, 42) applicable to teaching. The opposite view has been most reasonably stated by Long (49), who, while appreciating the need for deep-structure analysis as a basis for a universal grammar, calls for the continued use of an "intelligent updated traditional surface-structure grammar" as the base for descriptions of English language and especially for ESOL.

Linguistic description

TESOL methods

If this review had been written a decade or so ago, its structure would have been quite different. It would have gone directly from a brief recapitulation of accepted principles of language learning and teaching to a detailed listing of the methods that followed from these principles. It would have referred disparagingly to traditional methods and teachers, and patronizingly to those like Mary Finocchiaro (31) who chose to write a "practical textbook" that was based on experience and that presumed to subject linguists' principles to the test of practicality. But in 1969, with the rejection of the old orthodoxy of the so-called audiolingual, oral-aural, or linguistic method, the question of how to teach English to speakers of other languages is much more open, so that academic theorists and practicing teachers alike can welcome and benefit from suggestions based on practical experience. Thus, the revised and enlarged book by Finocchiaro (32) can freely be recommended as a good place for the beginner in the field to find out what it's about, for the teacher to find ways of improving her teaching, and for the theorist to find a description of sound teaching practice. *A "practical" text*

That stated, there is little new to say about methods. Rutherford (66) has gone furthest so far in developing transformational drills. Hall's "situational reinforcement" (36) puts a great deal of emphasis on "real communication" in meaningful situations, providing drills for talking about going to school or a drugstore. Stevick (78) continues to propose modifications of the old Mim-mem technique that will take the student from single repetition to something like real language. Politzer (62) still finds theoretical justification for going from choral and individual repetition through questions and contrast and pattern drills to question-and-answers. *Methods: very little new*

Basically, however, we seem to be at a stage in methodology of consolidation rather than innovation. Without a theory of second language pedagogy, and good empirical data to test its implications, there is room for reasonable eclecticism, and the textbooks are starting to show this. Neither the language laboratory nor programmed instruction, nor even the computer, has put any teacher out of work. Nor have any studies shown the superiority of any one method. How to teach ESOL remains an open question, left more to the practitioner than a few years ago when theorists knew all the answers. *A methodology of consolidation*

Testing proficiency in English

There have been interesting developments in the theory and practice of language testing in general and English language testing in particular. Two conferences whose proceedings ap-

333

peared in 1968 helped focus attention on the basic issues in language testing (Upshur & Fata, 85; Davies, 25). The publication of the first analytical bibliography of language tests (Savard, 67), prepared by the International Center for Research on Bilingualism, permits teachers and administrators easier access to the tests available. As William Mackey points out in his preface, language teachers have lost their fear of standardized tests. Perhaps it may be felt some have gone too far the other way, leaving them overconfident in the power of the tests to measure language proficiency accurately.

Developments in testing ES(

A central problem is that of validation (Spolsky, 76). What essentially can or does a language test measure? What does it mean to know a language? One answer has been from a descriptive linguistic point of view: to attempt to list all the linguistic items to be known and to test them one by one. A test of items of this sort would be to find out if a student can distinguish between /i/ and /iy/. A second approach is functional (Jakobovits, 44): to call on the student to perform a task involving use of language and assign a grade on his success. Such a task might be "Go to the principal's office and get the class list." If he brings the list, we don't worry what words the student used to the secretary, provided she understood him, and he understood the instruction. A third approach, somewhere between these two, is the use of reduced redundancy as a language testing tool. Working in this area, Darnell (24) has demonstrated a way of handling the normal theoretical difficulty of scoring a cloze by a procedure he calls "clozentropy." He measures a foreign student's performance on a cloze test in terms of the normal responses of a set of native speakers, permitting presumably a more precise functional definition of ability (e.g., this foreign student performs at the 60th percentile of native speakers of English in the first year of an engineering course).

Test validation

One of the principal needs at the moment is for tests of language proficiency for young children. One major project in this area is that of Brière (16,18), who, in the course of developing usable tests for American Indian children, is gathering data that will hopefully advance our understanding of the psycholinguistic basis of language testing.

Tests for young children

The recent publication of a basic textbook by Harris (38) now provides all interested with a valuable introduction to testing English as a second language, and a clear guide for teachers to develop their own tests and to evaluate those prepared by others.

A testing handbook

The rapid growth of the field has led to an ever-growing demand for trained ESOL teachers, but there is little in the way of guidance to those who would set up new programs. The collection of papers edited by Perren (60) brings together the experience and informed opinion of ten British experts. The contributions emphasize the practical, but show good understanding of the key theoretical issues. Of particular interest are the papers of J. A. Bright, describing a program in which a team of three experts had a major effect on retraining intermediate and secondary school teachers in the Sudan; by S. P. Corder, who sets out a program for specialists that consists of theoretical study of linguistics, psychology, and sociolinguistics, descriptive studies of English and other languages, practical study in various techniques, a research exercise, and the study of existing materials; and by Peter Strevens, who presents a model for the evaluation of the aims of training courses.

Models of teacher training in ESOL

In discussing the differences between teacher training for ESOL and for SESOD, Robinett (64) lists three basic components of a teacher training program: linguistics, English language, and professional education. Linguistics she breaks into a general introduction and applied phonetics; professional education into methods and practicum. She then suggests the extent to which ESOL-oriented courses might be modified to suit those who will be teaching speakers of nonstandard dialects.

Basic components of an ESOL teacher training program

Along with the development of programs for specialists in ESOL and SESOD, of great importance will be the modification of general teacher education programs to prepare teachers to recognize and handle students in their classes with a language barrier to education. A good number of universities already have courses in TESOL, but what is needed is to fit TESOL into regular language arts and reading methods courses.

The steady increase in teacher training programs is evident if one compares the listing of programs in 1966 (84) and in 1969 (28). Of the 42 degree and certificate programs listed in the latter, 21 were not in the earlier survey.

Together with this numerical growth has come discussion of the nature of training desirable. A useful step was the survey of 12 university programs undertaken by the Center for Applied Linguistics in 1966 (Ohannessian & McArdle, 58). Of the 12

M.A. programs, all required work in linguistics and TEFL, all but 3 required courses in English language, and only 2 required any practice teaching. The first state department of education to develop regulations for the certification of teachers of ESOL was New Mexico, in 1969. The national professional organization, TESOL, is now planning to develop a set of guidelines on the training of teachers of ESOL, a step essential in professionalization of the field.

Guidelines for ESOL teacher training

In an earlier section, reference was made to the great interest evinced by teachers of ESOL in general language teaching theory. Part of the reason for this is that most specialist TESOL training takes place not in English literature departments, but in independent programs or programs with affiliation with departments of linguistics or education. While the foreign language teacher is often trained in a department that considers the study of literature much more important than the teaching of language, the TESOL specialist is usually trained among those for whom a central concern is the study of language and its acquisition. TESOL specialists tend therefore to be interested in language teaching in general, and not just the teaching of English.

Conclusion

As a field, TESOL is growing both quantitatively and qualitatively. Where a decade or more ago, it seemed to consist of a small number of professionals with a fairly well-established orthodoxy, it is now a growing profession with a great number of beliefs and attitudes. And where the orthodox view once included simple principles, thought to have been derived from linguistic theory, now we have an attempt to develop an independent theory, taking into account the implications of sociolinguistics and psycholinguistics, as well as linguistic theory and behavioral psychology.

Teachers are becoming increasingly professional, their training more complex and their practices more eclectic. Researchers are asking clearer questions, and developing techniques to answer them. And the child who comes to school speaking a language other than Standard English is starting to be recognized as what he is rather than as retarded or a slow learner. Political pressures are helping to make funds available for those active in the field, but how long this will be true is hard to say.

In a time when the cry for "relevance" is all around us (the writing of this review has been interrupted by the National Guard on campus as students declare their own priorities), TESOL can reasonably claim to be relevant to the educational opportunity of a large number of children. The scholarship under review is a fair indication of the importance and urgency accorded to it: the blending of operational programs with long-range research will permit, hopefully, a real advance in quality that matches the increase in quantity.

References, TESOL

1 Aarons, Alfred C. "Training Programs in ESOL and Bilingual Education, 1969–1970." *TESOL Newsletter* 3,i (1969):6–7.

2 ――― Barbara Y. Gordon, and William A. Stewart, eds. "Linguistic-Cultural Differences and American Education." *Florida FL Reporter* 7,i(1969).

3 Abrahams, Roger D. "Black Talk and Black Education." *Florida FL Reporter* 7,i(1969):10–12.

4 Alatis, James E.,ed. *Report of the Nineteenth Annual Round Table Meeting on Linguistics and Language Study*. Georgetown University Monograph Series on Languages and Linguistics, Volume 21. Washington, D.C.: Georgetown Univ. Press, 1968.

5 ――― ed. *Report of the Twentieth Annual Round Table Meeting on Linguistics and Language Study*. Georgetown University Monograph Series on Languages and Linguistics, Volume 22. Washington, D.C.: Georgetown Univ. Press, 1970.

6 Allen, Harold. *A Survey of the Teaching of English to Non-English Speakers in the United States*. Champaign, Illinois: National Council of Teachers of English, 1966.

7 Allen, Virginia F. "A Second Dialect Is Not a Foreign Language," 189–202 in James E. Alatis, ed., *Report of the Twentieth Annual Round Table Meeting on Linguistics and Language Study*. Georgetown University Monograph Series on Languages and Linguistics, Volume 22. Washington, D.C.: Georgetown Univ. Press, 1970.

8 ――― "Teaching Standard English on a Second Dialect." *Teachers College Record* 68(1967):355–70.

9 Andersson, Theodore. "What Is an Ideal English-Spanish Bilingual Program?" *Florida FL Reporter* 7,i (1969):40, 168.

10 Bailey, Beryl L. "Language and Communicative Styles of Afro-American Children in the United States." *Florida FL Reporter*, 7,i (1969):46, 153.

11 ――― "Some Aspects of the Impact of Linguistics on Language Teaching in Disadvantaged Communities." *Elementary English* 45(1968):570–78, 628.

12 Baratz, Joan C., and Edna Povich. *Grammatical Construction in the Language of the Negro Preschool Child*. Washington, D.C.: Center for Applied Linguistics, 1968. [ERIC Document Re-

production Service: ED 020 518.]

13 —— and Roger W. Shuy,eds. *Teaching Black Children to Read*. Washington, D.C.: Center for Applied Linguistics. [ERIC Document Reproduction Service: ED 025 761.]

14 Berry, Brewton. *The Education of the American Indians:A Survey of the Literature*. Columbus: Ohio State University Research Foundation, 1968. [ERIC Document Reproduction Service: ED 026 545.]

15 "Bilingualism in the Barrio." *Modern Language Journal* 53(1969):151–85, 227–58. [Joshua A. Fishman, "Preface," 151; Joshua A. Fishman, "The Measurement and Description of Widespread and Relatively Stable Bilingualism," 152–56; Joshua A. Fishman and Heriberto Casiano, "Puerto Ricans in Our Press," 157–62; Robert L. Cooper and Lawrence Greenfield, "Word Frequency Estimation as a Measure of Degree of Bilingualism," 163–66; Robert L. Cooper and Lawrence Greenfield, "Language Use in a Bilingual Community," 166–72; Robert L. Cooper, "Two Contextual Measures of Bilingualism," 172–78; Martin Edelman, "The Contextualization of Schoolchildren's Bilingualism," 179–82; Tomi D. Berney and Robert L. Cooper, "Semantic Independence and Degree of Bilingualism in Two Communities," 182–85; Joav Findling, "Bilingual Need Affiliation and Future Orientation in Extragroup and Intragroup Domains," 227–31; Judah Ronch, Robert L. Cooper, and Joshua A. Fishman, "Word Naming and Usage Scores for a Sample of Yiddish-English Bilinguals," 232–35; Robert L. Cooper, Barbara R. Fowles, and Abraham Bivner, "Listening Comprehension in a Bilingual Community," 235–41; Stuart H. Silverman, "The Evaluation of Language Varieties," 241–44; Sheldon Fertig and Joshua A. Fishman, "Some Measures of the Interaction Between Language, Domain and Semantic Dimension of Bilinguals," 244–49; Stuart H. Silverman, "A Method for Recording and Analyzing the Prosodic Features of Language," 250–54; Charles E. Terry and Robert L. Cooper, "A Note on the Perception and Production of Phonological Variation," 254–55; Joshua A. Fishman, "Some Things Learned; Some Things to Learn," 255–58.]

16 Brière, Eugène J. *English Language Testing Project for the Bureau of Indian Affairs*. Los Angeles: English Language Testing Project, 1969.

17 —— *A Psycholinguistic Study of Phonological Interference*. The Hague: Mouton, 1968.

18 —— "Testing ESL Skills Among American Indian Children," 133–42 in James E. Alatis,ed., *Report of the Twentieth Annual Round Table Meeting on Linguistics and Language Study*. Georgetown University Monograph Series on Languages and Linguistics, Volume 22. Washington, D.C.: Georgetown Univ. Press, 1970.

19 Brownell, John A. *Japan's Second Language*. Champaign, Illinois: National Council of Teachers of English, 1967.

20 Carroll, John B. "Contrastive Linguistics and Interference Theory," 113–22 in James E. Alatis, ed., *Report of the Nineteenth Annual Round Table Meeting on Linguistics and Language Study*. Georgetown University Monograph Series on Languages and Linguistics, Volume 21. Washington, D.C.: Georgetown Univ. Press, 1968.

21 Carroll, William S., and Irwin Feigenbaum. "Teaching a Second Dialect and Some Implications for TESOL." *TESOL Quarterly* 1,iii(1967): 31–39.

22 Cervenka, E.J. "TESOL: The State of the Art Today." *TESOL Newsletter* 2,i–ii(1968):3–4.

23 Corder, S. Pit. "The Significance of Learner's Errors." *International Review of Applied Linguistics* 5(1967):161–70.

24 Darnell, Donald K. *The Development of an English Proficiency Test of Foreign Students, Using a Clozentropy Procedure, Final Report*. Boulder: Univ. of Colorado, Department of Speech and Drama, 1968. [ERIC Document Reproduction Service: ED 024 039.]

25 Davies, Alan,ed. *Language Testing Symposium*. London: Oxford Univ. Press, 1968.

26 Davis, A.L. "Dialect Research and the Needs of the Schools." *Elementary English* 45(1968): 558–60, 608.

27 De Camp, David. "The Current Discrepancy Between Theoretical and Applied Linguistics." *TESOL Quarterly* 2(1968):3–11.

28 *English Language and Orientation Programs in the United States: Including a List of Programs for Training Teachers of English or a Second Language*. New York: Institute of International Education, 1969.

29 Entwisle, D.R., and Ellen Greenberger. *Differences in the Language of Negro and White Gradeschool Children*, n.d. [ERIC Document Reproduction Service: ED 919 676.]

30 Feigenbaum, Irwin. "Using Foreign Language Methodology to Teach Standard English:Evaluation and Adaptation." *Florida FL Reporter* 7,i(1969):116–22, 156–57.

31 Finocchiaro, Mary. *Teaching English as a Second Language*. New York: Harper and Brothers, 1958.

32 —— *Teaching English as a Second Language*. New York: Harper and Row, 1969. [Revised and enlarged edition.]

33 Francis. W. Nelson. *The English Language*. London: English Univ. Press, 1968.

34 Galvan, Mary M., and Rudolph C. Troike. "The East Texas Dialect Project:A Pattern for Education." *Florida FL Reporter* 7,i(1969):29–31, 152–53.

35 Gefen, R. "The Teaching of English in the Schools of Israel." *English Language Teaching* 23(1969): 274–79.

36 Hall, Eugene J.,et al. *Situational Reinforcement*. Washington, D.C.: Institute of Modern Languages, 1969.

37 Hamp, Eric. "What a Contrastive Grammar is Not, if It is," 137–47 in James E. Alatis,ed., *Report of the Nineteenth Annual Round Table Meeting on Linguistics and Language Study*. Georgetown University Monograph Series on Languages and Linguistics, Volume 21. Washington, D.C.: Georgetown Univ. Press, 1968.

38 Harris, David P. *Testing English as a Second Language*. New York: McGraw-Hill, 1969.

39 Hoffman, Virginia. *Oral English at Rough Rock: A New Program for Navajo Children*. Chinle, Arizona: Navajo Curriculum Center, Rough Rock Demonstration School, 1968.

40 Hopkins, Thomas R. "American Indians and the English Language Arts." *Florida FL Reporter* 7,i(1969):145–46.

41 Houston, Susan H. "A Sociolinguistic Consideration of the Black English of Children in Northern Florida." *Language* 45(1969):599–607.

42 Jacobs, Roderick A. "Linguistic Universals and Their Relevance to TESOL." *TESOL Quarterly* 3(1969):117–22.

43 —— and Peter S. Rosenbaum. *English Transformational Grammar*. Waltham, Massachusetts: Blaisdell, 1968.

44 Jakobovits, Leon A. "A Functional Approach to the Assessment of Language Skills." *Journal of English as a Second Language* 4(1969):63–76.

45 —— *A Psycholinguistic Analysis of Second-Language Learning and Bilingualism*. Urbana: Center for Comparative Psycholinguistics, Univ. of Illinois, 1969.

46 Kochman, Thomas. "Social Factors in the Consideration of Teaching Standard English." *Florida FL Reporter* 7,i(1969):87–88, 157.

47 Labov, William. "The Logic of Non Standard English," 1–43 in James E. Alatis,ed., *Report of the Twentieth Annual Round Table Meeting on Linguistics and Language Study*. Georgetown University Monograph Series on Languages and Linguistics, Volume 22. Washington, D.C.: Georgetown Univ. Press, 1970.

48 Larudee, Faze. "The English Language Institute of the American University in Cairo." *Linguistic Reporter* 11,vi(1969):5–6

49 Long, Ralph. "Linguistic Universals, Deep Structure, and English as a Second Language." *TESOL Quarterly* 3(1969):123–32.

50 Mackey, William. "A Typology of Bilingual Education." *Foreign Language Annals* 3(1970):596–608. [Earlier version given at Conference on Bilingual Education at Univ. of Maryland, 27–28 June 1969.]

51 Marckwardt, Albert H. "English as a Second Language and English as a Foreign Language." *PMLA* 78,ii(1963):25–28.

52 Mathiot, Madeleine, and Sirarpi Ohannessian. "English for Speakers of Papago," 102–35 in Sirarpi Ohannessian and William W. Gage,eds., *Teaching English to Speakers of Choctaw, Navajo, and Papago*. Bureau of Indian Affairs Curriculum Bulletin, No. 6. Washington, D.C.: Bureau of Indian Affairs and Center for Applied Linguistics, 1969.

53 Miller, Mary R. "Teaching English to the Indian of the Plains and the Northwest." *TESOL Quarterly* 2(1968):193–97.

54 *National Conference on Bilingual Education: Language Skills*. Final Report. September 1969.

55 Nicklas, Thurston Dale. "English for Speakers of Choctaw," 1–40 in Sirarpi Ohannessian and William W. Gage,eds., *Teaching English to Speakers of Choctaw, Navajo, and Papago*. Bureau of Indian Affairs Curriculum Bulletin, No. 6. Washington, D.C.: Bureau of Indian Affairs and Center for Applied Linguistics, 1969.

56 Ohannessian, Sirarpi. "Harpers Ferry Conference on English Teaching as a World-Wide Problem." *Linguistic Reporter* 11,ii(1969):1–5.

57 —— *The Study of the Problems of Teaching English to American Indians*. Washington, D.C.: Center for Applied Linguistics, 1967.

58 —— and Lois McArdle. *A Survey of Twelve University Programs for the Preparation of Teachers of English to Speakers of Other Languages*. Washington, D.C.: Center for Applied Linguistics, 1966.

59 Pedtke, Dorothy A., and Oswald Werner. "English for Speakers of Navajo," 41–101 in Sirarpi Ohannessian and William W. Gage,eds., *Teaching English to Speakers of Choctaw, Navajo, and Papago*. Bureau of Indian Affairs Curriculum Bulletin, No. 6. Washington, D.C.: Bureau of Indian Affairs and Center for Applied Linguistics, 1969.

60 Perren, G.E.,ed. *Teachers of English as a Second Language:Their Training and Preparation*. Cambridge: Cambridge Univ. Press, 1968.

61 Pfeiffer, Anita. *The Role of TESOL in Bilingual Education for the Navajo Child*. Chinle, Arizona: Navajo Curriculum Center, Rough Rock Demonstration School, 1969. [ERIC Document Reproduction Service: ED 028 447.]

62 Politzer, Robert L. "Toward Psycholinguistic Models of Language Instruction." *TESOL Quarterly* 2(1968):151–57.

63 Quirk, Randolph. "English Today—A World View." *TESOL Quarterly* 3(1969):23–29.

64 Robinett, Betty W. "Teacher Training for English as a Second Dialect and English as a Second Language:The Same or Different?" 121–32 in James E. Alatis,ed., *Report of the Twentieth Annual Round Table Meeting on Linguistics and Language Study*. Georgetown University Monograph Series on Languages and Linguistics, Volume 22. Washington, D.C.: Georgetown Univ. Press, 1970.

65 Rutherford, W.E. "Deep and Surface Structure, and the Language Drill." *TESOL Quarterly* 2(1968):71–79.

66 —— *Modern English:A Textbook for Foreign Students*. New York: Harcourt, Brace and World, 1968.

67 Savard, Jean-Guy. *Bibliographie Analytique de Tests de Langue:Analytical Bibliography of Language Tests*. Quebec: Les Presses de L'Université Laval, 1969.

68 Scott, Charles T. "Transformational Theory and English as a Second Language/Dialect," 75–92 in James E. Alatis,ed., *Report of the Twentieth Annual Round Table Meeting on Linguistics and Language Study*. Georgetown University Monograph Series on Languages and Linguistics, Volume 22. Washington, D.C.: Georgetown Univ. Press, 1970.

69 Shuy, Roger W. *Bonnie and Clyde Tactics in English Teaching*. Washington, D.C.: Center for

Applied Linguistics, 1968. [ERIC Document Reproduction Service: ED 024 938.]

70 ——— "Detroit Speech:Careless, Awkward, and Inconsistent, or Systematic, Graceful, and Regular?" *Elementary English* 45(1968):565–69.

71 ——— "The Relevance of Sociolinguistics for Language Teaching." *TESOL Quarterly* 3(1969):13–22.

72 ———, Walter A. Wolfram, and W. K. Riley. *Field Techniques in an Urban Language Study.* Washington, D.C.: Center for Applied Linguistics, 1968.

73 Sledd, James. "Bi-Dialectalism:The Linguistics of White Supremacy." *The English Journal* 58(1969):1307–15, 1329.

74 Soveran, Marilylle. *From Cree to English, Part One:The Sound System.* Saskatoon, Canada: Saskatchewan Univ., Indian and Northern Curriculum Resources Center, 1968. [ERIC Document Reproduction Service: ED 025 755.]

75 Spolsky, Bernard. *ESOL and Bilingual Education.* [Paper read at the annual meeting of the American Council for the Teaching of Foreign Language, 29 November 1969.]

76 ——— "Language Testing:The Problem of Validation." *TESOL Quarterly* 2(1968):88–94.

77 ——— "Linguistics and Language Pedagogy Applications or Implications?" 143–55 in James E. Alatis,ed., *Report of the Twentieth Annual Round Table Meeting on Linguistics and Language Study.* Georgetown University Monograph Series on Languages and Linguistics, Volume 22. Washington, D.C.: Georgetown Univ. Press, 1970.

78 Stevick, Earl W. "UHF and Micro-Waves in Transmitting Language Skills." *TESOL Newsletter* 2,i-ii(1968):11–12, 30, 36.

79 Stockwell, Robert P. "Contrastive Analysis and Lapsed Time," 11–26 in James E. Alatis,ed., *Report of the Nineteenth Annual Round Table Meeting on Linguistics and Language Study.* Georgetown University Monograph Series on Languages and Linguistics, Volume 21. Washington, D.C.: Georgetown Univ. Press, 1968.

80 ——— and J. Donald Bowen. *The Sounds of English and Spanish.* Chicago: Univ. of Chicago Press, 1965.

81 Tax, Sol, and Robert K. Thomas. "Education 'for' American Indians:Threat or Promise." *Florida FL Reporter* 7,i(1969):15–19, 154.

82 Troike, Rudolph C. "Receptive Competence, Production Competence, and Performance," 63–73 in James E. Alatis,ed., *Report of the Twentieth Annual Round Table Meeting on Linguistics and Language Study.* Georgetown University Monograph Series on Languages and Linguistics, Volume 22. Washington, D.C.: Georgetown Univ. Press, 1970.

83 ——— "Social Dialects and Language Learning Implications for TESOL." *TESOL Quarterly* 2(1968):176–80.

84 *University Resources in the United States for Linguistics and Teacher Training in English as a Foreign Language.* Washington, D.C.: Center for Applied Linguistics. 1966.

85 Upshur, John A., and Julia Fata,eds. "Problems in Foreign Language Testing." *Language Learning* Special Issue 3(1969).

86 Wardhaugh, Ronald. "Linguistics, Psychology, and Pedagogy, Trinity or Unity?" *TESOL Quarterly* 2(1968):80–87.

87 ——— *Teaching English to Speakers of Other Languages:The State of the Art.* Washington, D.C.: Center for Applied Linguistics/ERIC Clearinghouse for Linguistics, 1969.

88 Wolfram, Walter A. *A Sociolinguistic Description of Detroit Negro Speech.* Washington, D.C.: Center for Applied Linguistics, 1969.

89 Young, Robert. *English as a Language for Navajos:An Overview of Certain Cultural and Linguistic Factors.* Albuquerque: Bureau of Indian Affairs, 1968. [ERIC Document Reproduction Service: ED 021 655.]

12
Trends in foreign language enrollments

Introduction

In his chapter, "Surveys and Reports on Foreign Language Enrollments," in the first volume of the present series, Dusel (8) made use of data from the Modern Language Association's comprehensive national surveys of foreign language enrollments in colleges and public secondary schools for the fall semesters of eight successive years, from 1958 to 1965. Rounding off a ten-year period, the present article adds to its coverage the figures for fall 1968 based on the latest published surveys at both levels (Kant, 13,14) and attempts to present and evaluate data and trends in the light of their implications for the work of the profession.

Since 1961, however, the MLA enrollment surveys in higher education have used, for purposes of statistical comparison, the figures for 1960 rather than those for 1958. The 1960 figures have served as the bases for indexes of growth in all subsequent reports. For the college enrollments, therefore, the ten-year "rounding-off" will not be readily measurable until after the completion of the MLA's 1970 survey.

Richard I. Brod

Modern Language Association

Offerings and enrollments in public secondary schools, fall 1968

The MLA's 1968 survey of foreign language enrollments in public secondary schools (Kant, 13) is the ninth in a series that dates back to 1958, the year of the National Defense Education Act. Despite some inevitable gaps in the data, the report provides a reasonably useful overview of the basic patterns in secondary school language enrollments, including some alarming downward trends.

MLA enrollment studies

In the body of the 1968 report, enrollments in the six leading languages (Spanish, French, German, Russian, Italian, and Latin) are presented in a series of seven tables each. The tables provide data classified by grade level (7–8 and 9–12) and tabulated by course levels, regions, and states, with comparative figures for 1965, and each language's percentages of total school

The 1968 report

TABLE 1. Summary of public high school enrollments in foreign languages with percenta

Year	PSS enrollment	MFL enrollment†	% of MFL's in PSS enrollment	Spanish enrollment	% of Spanish in PSS enrollment	French enrollment	% of French in PSS enrollmen
1	2	3	4	5	6	7	8
1890	202,963	33,089	16.3	–	–	11,772	5.8
1895	350,099	62,685	17.9	–	–	22,757	6.5
1900	519,251	114,765	22.1	–	–	40,503	7.8
1905	679,702	199,153	29.3	–	–	61,852	9.1
1910	915,061	313,890	34.3	6,406	.7	90,591	9.9
1915	1,328,984	477,110	35.9	35,882	2.7	116,957	8.8
1922	2,230,000	611,025	27.4	252,000	11.3	345,650	15.5
1928	3,354,473	845,338	25.2	315,329	9.4	469,626	14.0
1934	5,620,626	1,096,022	19.5	348,479	6.2	612,648	10.9
1948	5,399,452	740,800	13.7	442,755	8.2	253,781	4.7
1958	7,897,232	1,295,944	16.4	691,024	8.8	479,769	6.1
1959	8,155,573	1,564,883	19.2	802,266	9.8	603,733	7.4
1960	8,649,495	1,867,358	21.7	933,409	10.8	744,404	8.6
1961	9,246,925	2,192,207	23.7	1,054,730	11.4	908,082	9.8
1962	9,891,185	2,391,206	24.2	1,137,757	11.5	996;771	10.1
1963	10,750,081	2,781,737	25.9	1,336,105	12.4	1,130,987	10.5
1964	11,075,343	2,898,665	26.2	1,362,831	12.3	1,194,991	10.8
1965	11,611,197	3,067,613	26.4	1,426,822	12.3	1,251,373	10.8
1968	12,721,352	3,518,413	27.7	1,698,034	13.3	1,328,100	10.4

*All foreign language enrollments from 1890 through 1948 are estimated from percentages of the languages in the total high school enrollments giv
William R. Parker, *The National Interest and Foreign Languages*, U.S. National Commission for the United Nations Educational, Scientific, and Cu
Organization, 1957, pp. 52–53. The statistics from 1958 to 1965 are all taken from MLA reports.

enrollments, modern language enrollments, and total foreign language enrollments. Since the various tables do not have space for multiple columns of comparative data for past years, only the figures for 1965, the year of the last previous report, are juxtaposed with those for 1968. Appearing in the introductory section of the report, however, is a summary table which presents data going back to 1890: specifically, enrollment totals for the six languages together with percentages of the total public secondary school enrollment, grades 9–12, for each of the languages.

While on the whole foreign language enrollments continued to grow between 1965 and 1968, a significant downward trend is manifest in the figure for foreign language enrollment as a percentage of public secondary school population in grades 7–12: it fell from 27.4 in 1965 to 27.1 in 1968, thus reversing a trend that had continued unbroken from 1960 (when the percentage was 23.4) to 1965. Total public secondary school enrollment grew

Enrollment growth, but percentage drop, 1965–68

342

of total public secondary school (PSS) enrollment, grades 9–12: 1890–1968.*

German enrollment	% of German in PSS enrollment	Russian enrollment	% of Russian in PSS enrollment	Italian enrollment	% of Italian in PSS enrollment	Latin enrollment	% of Latin in PSS enrollment
9	10	11	12	13	14	15	16
21,311	10.5	–	–	–	–	70,429	34.7
39,911	11.4	–	–	–	–	153,693	43.9
74,252	14.3	–	–	–	–	262,752	50.6
137,299	20.2	–	–	–	–	341,215	50.2
216,869	23.7	–	–	–	–	448,383	49.0
324,272	24.4	–	–	–	–	495,711	37.3
13,385	.6	–	–	–	–	613,250	27.5
60,381	1.8	–	–	–	–	737,984	22.0
134,897	2.4	–	–	–	–	899,300	16.0
43,195	.8	–	–	–	–	421,174	7.8
93,054	1.2	4,055	.1	22,133	.3	617,500	7.8
123,581	1.5	7,513	.1	21,118	.3	639,776	7.8
150,764	1.7	9,722	.1	20,026	.2	654,670	7.6
184,820	2.0	13,224	.1	22,277	.2	695,297	7.5
211,676	2.1	15,832	.2	21,654	.2	702,135	7.1
260,488	2.4	21,552	.2	23,250	.2	680,234	6.3
285,613	2.6	20,485	.2	24,735	.2	590,047	5.3
328,028	2.8	26,716	.2	25,233	.2	591,445	5.1
423,196	3.3	24,318	.2	26,920	.2	371,977	2.9

†The totals of the modern foreign languages (columns 5, 7, 9, 11) do not equal the MFL enrollment totals in column 3, since the column 3 figures include a small number of enrollments for "Other Languages."

7.0% between 1965 and 1968, but foreign language enrollments simply failed to keep pace: in the aggregate they grew only 5.7%. There were, of course, significant growth differences among the various languages: the percentages of growth in Spanish (15.2%), German (27.3%), Italian (10.4%), and "other" languages (92.1%) exceeded that of the total school population; enrollments in French grew in absolute numbers, but too slowly (6.2%) to keep pace; and Russian (−10.7%) and Latin (−37.3%) suffered serious declines.

Tables providing regional and state breakdown of the enrollment figures show that between 1965 and 1968 Spanish had its best growth in the Mideast and Plains regions, German in the Southeast and Plains. Latin, however, suffered its worst losses in the Rocky Mountains and Mideast, including a substantial loss of 63.7% in New York State alone: 33,090 in 1968 compared with 91,146 in 1965. While few inferences can be drawn from such general data, it would appear that the regional growth in

Regional and state enrollment figures

Spanish and German represents a kind of "catching-up" in regions where they had in fact been relatively less well established at the time of the great spurts of general growth in the foreign languages in the early sixties. This is most evident in the case of German in the Southeast, where it grew 295% between 1960 and 1965 (from 4,485 enrollments to 17,717), and another 52.9% between 1965 and 1968 (27,093 enrollments).

The summary table (reproduced above as Table 1) in the MLA report furnishes enrollment figures (in grades 9–12) as far back as 1890, thereby providing a historical perspective for these trends. The table reveals, for example, that growth in German has been rapid and substantial since 1958, and that enrollments have now more than quadrupled since that year. During the same period, Russian, despite a slight loss between 1963 and 1964, underwent steady growth, and had reached in 1965 a level of enrollments more than six times its 1958 figure. Its downward turn between 1965 and 1968 is consequently a development that bears watching. Latin, on the other hand, has been in a decline since 1963, when its enrollments were 3.1% lower than for 1962; by 1964 it had lost another 13.3%; 1965 registered a negligible (0.2%) gain, but between 1965 and 1968 Latin enrollments went down a full 37.1%. The positions of Latin and German are now reversed, and German has replaced Latin as the third leading language in public secondary schools. In 1958, when Latin was still in second place (after Spanish), its enrollments were equal to 7.8% of total public secondary school enrollments and accounted for 32.3% of all FL enrollments in grades 9–12. By 1965 these figures had become 5.1% and 13.4% respectively; by 1968, 2.9% and 9.6%. To some extent, the growth in the modern languages has been at the expense of Latin. Between 1965 and 1968, in grades 7–12, Latin lost 233,502 enrollments; the growth for Spanish alone during the same period was 278,964.

The decline in Latin, of disaster proportions, is by now no longer a secret among classics teachers, but the trend is one that is difficult to fight against on a nationwide basis. Some Latin teachers see the modern languages as their "enemy," and indeed, as indicated above, there is some justification for this view. Yet there is growing evidence that in many schools and districts Latin is still able to hold its own in competition with the modern languages. Kovach, in the first volume of the present series (15), provides a masterful and comprehensive review of innovative programs, research, and improved professional or-

A summary of enrollments, 1890–1968

Decline in Latin enrollments

344

ganization and communication among teachers of Latin and Ancient Greek.

Limitations of the report

Given the difficulties of obtaining data from over 22,000 schools in 50 states and the District of Columbia, and the dependence of the MLA research staff upon the effective cooperation of the various state foreign language supervisors within the limits imposed upon them by local conditions, it is not surprising that the report should be less than perfect. Since 1968 figures were not available at all for Minnesota and Texas, 1967 figures had to be used for these states throughout the report, and in certain tabulations also for Georgia, Massachusetts, and South Dakota. Other isolated gaps in the reports — all duly recorded in footnotes to the tables — left their effects upon the totals. Dusel's warning (8) about the questionable accuracy and validity of census reports, as compared with carefully constructed samples, is certainly justified, but in the absence of anything better, the MLA report must be regarded as at least serviceable. Probably its chief usefulness lies in its analytical tables, i.e., its presentation of enrollments tabulated by language, by state, by course, and by grade level. These figures are of value primarily to those persons who are professionally concerned with local data, such as state supervisors and administrators of local schools and colleges. In this context only short-range comparative data are required, and these are furnished by the tables which juxtapose 1965 and 1968 figures. Long-range trend data, on the other hand, can be found only in the introductory summary table, which presents national totals going back to 1890. Missing in this presentation, unfortunately, are figures for grades seven and eight, and growth trends for the individual languages as expressed in percentages of the total foreign language enrollment. That the data as presented are incomplete and hence potentially misleading will be apparent to every user; yet they will be used, and the MLA will continue to do its best to produce maximally accurate reports.

The 1968 report – less than perfect, but...

As a supplement and corrective to the inherently inadequate census reports, a series of carefully selected samples would serve a real need. These could be both local and comprehensive, on the one hand, and selective and national, on the other. Systematic periodic sampling of discrete key units is normally an

Suggestions for different kinds of enrollment data

excellent source of relatively detailed information about the "hidden" causal factors which may affect the results of a given survey. In the case of enrollments, a close examination of a limited number of school districts might reveal patterns of administrative policy, teaching method or quality, community attitudes, or other similarly intangible factors that could well have an effect upon the growth or decline of enrollments.

No one denies that foreign languages to a certain extent need to be "sold" or "marketed" to a skeptical and occasionally even hostile public, and that the languages are competing on the market with several comparable "products," each with its own selling points. Distasteful though the commercial analogy may be to many teachers, it is clear that an analysis which merely chronicles the decline of a product, without investigating the circumstances or probable causes of that decline, has failed its purpose. Proper analysis may even lead to concrete recommendations for correction and improvement of the faulty product.

Local surveys: two examples

Typical of the limited local surveys which appear occasionally in the literature are two which, coincidentally, provide illustration of the special difficulties of the "marginal" languages. Lèbano (16) reports on the teaching of Italian in colleges in five Great Lakes states: Illinois, Indiana, Michigan, Ohio, and Wisconsin. Despite a discrepancy between the base number of institutions in his present report and that of a similar survey conducted in 1960, Lèbano compares the two sets of data and concludes that there was a considerable increase (more than 50%) in Italian enrollments in the region, which in fact is consistent with the regional data obtained from the MLA reports for 1965 and 1968. Since, moreover, the author's questionnaire encompassed a number of important matters above and beyond the gross enrollment figures (degree offerings, breakdown by course levels, number of majors, graduate students, and faculty members), he was able to pinpoint what he considers a potential threat to the present relative prosperity: the unwillingness of some institutions to support programs in Italian beyond a level appropriate to a marginal field of study. While he is certainly correct in insisting that adequate staffing is necessary to maintain established and flourishing programs, there is no evidence for assuming that faculty appointments alone can automatically create demand sufficient to justify them in less well-established

Italian in the Great Lakes region

346

programs. General or regional enrollment figures are not likely to convince institutions to invest in such programs in the absence of local demand.

The survey by Teitelbaum (27) of FL programs in 64 Long Island school districts also reveals evidence (despite a general increase in enrollments) of an erosion of certain marginal programs in the various districts. The author compares data of 1966 with those of 1968, showing, among other things, a growing abandonment of language laboratories, of advanced placement programs, and, in some cases, of instruction in the less widely taught languages like Latin and Russian. While the latter trend is to some extent counteracted by the introduction of exotic languages like Japanese and Swahili (in one district each), the general trend in the region surveyed has been toward the complete dominance of the enrollment picture by the two leading languages, Spanish and French, which together accounted for 88.9% of FL enrollments in the district in 1968–69, compared with only 78.8% in 1965–66.

The Long Island survey

Making use of his intimate acquaintance with the region, Teitelbaum was able to probe intelligently into policies and practices in the various districts, insofar as they serve to illuminate or explain the trends. His questionnaire, for example, in seeking more extensive information and opinion on the effectiveness of language laboratories, yielded replies which the author (Teitelbaum, 27) summarizes in his conclusion that "ALM and Advanced Placement are incompatible." While such a statement may be of questionable value as a generalization, it merits some attention within the context described by the survey and conceivably might even lead some readers to a productive reexamination of the relevant issues.

College registrations: fall 1968

The 1968 college enrollments report (Kant, 14) reflects the MLA's usual success in obtaining an excellent return on its questionnaire: 2,479, or 95.4%, of the 2,599 questionnaires that were mailed out to the college registrars. The results show continued overall growth, but at a much slower rate than was manifest in the early 1960s, and with isolated instances of actual decline in enrollments. Totals for 1960, 1963, 1965, and 1968 for the five leading modern foreign languages show an overall growth of 74.7% between 1960 and 1968, the period of fastest

Five major languages: growth in college enrollments, 1960–68

TABLE 2. Trends in registrations in the five leading modern foreign languages, 1960–68, by type of institution: totals for U.S.

	1960	1963	1965	1968
4-year	544,317	706,832	848,811	913,505
2-year	51,007	75,088	103,685	126,779
Total	595,324	781,920	952,496	1,040,284

Index of growth (1960=100.0)			Percent growth between surveys		
	1963	1965	1968	1960–63	1963–65	1965–68
4-year	129.8	155.9	167.6	29.8	20.1	7.6
2-year	147.2	203.2	248.5	47.2	38.1	22.3
Total	131.3	159.9	174.7	31.3	21.8	9.2

TABLE 3. Trends in registrations in the five leading modern foreign languages, 1960–68, by level.

	1960	1963	1965	1968
Undergraduate	578,988	752,868	919,059	1,005,778
Graduate	16,336	29,052	33,437	34,506
Total	595,324	781,920	952,496	1,040,284

Index of growth (1960=100.0)			Percent growth between surveys		
	1963	1965	1968	1960–63	1963–65	1965–68
Undergraduate	130.0	158.7	172.0	30.0	22.1	9.4
Graduate	177.8	204.7	211.2	77.8	15.1	3.2
Total	131.3	159.9	174.7	31.3	21.8	9.2

growth (31.3%) having been between 1960 and 1963. Table 2 above shows trend data analyzed according to type of institution: two-year and four-year. Graduate registrations are included in the four-year figures. Table 3 presents the same totals analyzed according to level. Junior colleges are included in the undergraduate figures. All data are from Kant (14), except the figures for percent change between surveys, which were calculated especially for the present report.

Notable are the growth figures for the two-year colleges, and even more striking, the statistical evidence for the spectacular expansion of graduate study in foreign languages in the early part of the decade and the subsequent leveling-off between 1965 and 1968.

Table 4 shows growth patterns for the five leading modern languages individually, Table 5 gives the percentages of the total accounted for by each of them in the years indicated,

Enrollment growth in two-ye colleges

348

TABLE 4. Trends in registrations in the five leading modern foreign languages, 1960–68 (all types of institutions), by language.

	1960	1963	1965	1968
French	228,813	302,226	371,625	388,096
German	146,110	182,609	213,901	216,263
Italian	11,142	16,874	22,920	30,359
Russian	30,570	33,538	33,710	40,696
Spanish	178,689	246,673	310,340	364,870
Total	595,324	781,920	952,496	1,040,284

	Index of growth (1960=100.0)			Percent growth between surveys		
	1963	1965	1968	1960–63	1963–65	1965–68
French	132.1	162.4	169.6	32.1	23.0	4.4
German	125.0	146.4	148.0	25.0	17.1	1.1
Italian	151.4	205.7	272.5	51.4	35.8	32.5
Russian	109.7	110.3	133.1	9.7	0.5	20.7
Spanish	138.0	173.7	204.2	38.0	25.8	17.6
Total	131.3	159.9	174.7	31.3	21.8	9.2

TABLE 5. Trends in registrations in the five leading modern foreign languages, 1960–68, by language: percentage of total.

	1960	1963	1965	1968
French	38.4	38.6	39.0	37.3
German	24.6	23.4	22.5	20.8
Italian	1.9	2.2	2.4	2.9
Russian	5.1	4.3	3.5	3.9
Spanish	30.0	31.5	32.6	35.1

and Table 6 provides the breakdown for graduate registrations.

The figures show a strong spurt of growth for French, German, Italian, and Spanish in the period 1960–63, leveling off steadily in the following years, and in the case of French and German leveling off severely between 1965 and 1968. On the graduate level, in fact, German suffered a significant decline (10.3%) in registrations between 1965 and 1968, and French came virtually to a standstill. The data for Italian show a consistent upward trend on both levels, but those for Russian are erratic, and the raw figures for both languages are essentially too small to permit valid inferences.

Latin, Greek, and "other" languages

Since the ten trend tables in the MLA report deal only with the five leading modern languages, the most notable area of decline,

TABLE 6. Trends in registrations in the five leading modern foreign languages, 1960–68, by language, graduate registrations only.

	1960	1963	1965	1968
French	5,759	10,502	12,449	12,511
German	4,970	8,172	9,218	8,267
Italian	440	640	769	947
Russian	1,952	2,707	2,428	2,418
Spanish	3,215	7,031	8,573	10,363
Total	16,336	29,052	33,437	34,506

	Index of growth (1960=100.0)			Percent growth between surveys		
	1963	1965	1968	1960–63	1963–65	1965–68
French	182.4	216.2	217.2	82.4	18.5	0.5
German	164.4	185.5	166.3	64.4	12.8	−10.3
Italian	145.5	174.8	215.2	45.5	20.2	23.1
Russian	138.7	124.4	123.9	38.7	−10.3	− 0.4
Spanish	218.7	266.7	322.3	118.7	21.9	20.9
Total	177.8	204.7	211.2	77.8	15.1	3.2

that of Latin, is discussed only in the introduction to the report. Latin registrations, which were not reported by the MLA prior to 1965, declined from 39,588 in that year to 34,981 in 1968, a loss of 11%; the figures for Greek went from 19,531 in 1965 to 19,285 in 1968, a decrease of only 1.2%. On the other hand, the most spectacular growth in the entire survey was experienced by the aggregate of registrations in the "other," or less widely taught languages: from 23,281 in 1965 to 32,813 in 1968 – a growth of 40.1%. Of these languages, the most popular are Hebrew, Chinese, Japanese, and Portuguese, which together account for 23,602 registrations, or 71.9% of the total. Table 7 shows growth trends for the languages that had registrations of 1,000 or more in 1968 as well as for the total group of "other" languages.

Specific figures for the Latin and Greek decline

Increases for "other" languages

Regional trends

Ten of the tables (4 through 13) in the MLA report permit the reader to ascertain growth trends in the five leading modern languages, singly and collectively, by region and state. Adjoining the registration figures for each state and regional group are index figures showing growth in 1963, 1965, and 1968 relative to the 1960 figure taken as a base equal to 100.0. Thus, the growth index for the United States as a whole for 1968 is 170.9, and a cursory glance at the table of states reveals which have had an average, greater, or less than average growth since 1960. It

Regional and state enrollment patterns

TABLE 7. Trends in registrations in the less widely taught modern foreign
languages, 1960–68.

	1960	1963	1965	1968
Arabic	541	835	930	1,100
Chinese	1,844	2,444	3,359	5,061
Hebrew	3,834	5,538	8,093	10,169
Japanese	1,746	2,813	3,443	4,324
Norwegian	722	942	803	1,103
Portuguese	1,033	2,051	3,034	4,048
Swedish	622	705	682	1,101
Subtotal	10,342	15,328	20,344	26,906
Other FL's	2,325	4,410	2,937	5,907
Total	12,667	19,738	23,281	32,813

Index of growth (1960=100.0)		Percent growth between surveys	
1963:	155.8	1960–63:	55.8
1965:	183.8	1963–65:	17.9
1968:	259.0	1965–68:	40.1

shows that New England, the Mideast, and the Great Lakes are
below average, the Plains Region has had average (170.8)
growth, and, in ascending order, the Rocky Mountains, the Far
West, the Southeast, and the Southwest (197.2) have exceeded
the average. Widely divergent distribution patterns emerge from
the tables giving figures for four-year colleges alone, for junior
colleges, and for the individual languages, but registration
figures for some states and languages are so small as to render
the indexes meaningless. For example, the apparently spectacular growth of Italian in Tennessee, from seven students in 1960
to 597 in 1968, which may be real, or may simply reflect inadequate questionnaire returns for the earlier years, is interpreted
in the table by the index figure 8528.

Summer school 1969

Printed together with the full text of the MLA's survey report
for fall 1968 (Kant, 14) is a set of six tables presenting foreign
language registrations for summer 1969. Of the 2,149 institutions that reported data for the fall, 879 also reported for the
summer. Total registrations reported were 141,763 (12.5% of the
fall total). Of these, 17,240 were on the graduate level (38% of
the fall total), 13,583 were in junior colleges (10.4% of the fall).
Student contact hours averaged 8.0 in summer, compared with
3.8 in fall, reflecting the use of intensive summer courses.

Summer enrollments

351

Critique of the report

With its relatively high (95.4%) return of questionnaires, the MLA report for 1968 provides a useful picture of foreign language enrollments in the fall of that year. The tables listing comparative figures for the years 1960, 1963, and 1965, however, as Willbern's foreword points out (Kant, 14), are unavoidably less useful, since the data are derived from a different base of institutions in each of these years. In addition, totals reported in the aggregate trend tables (Tables 4, 5, and 6 in the MLA report) are based, for 1960 and 1963, on *all* modern languages, including the "other" or less widely taught, while those for 1965 and 1968 are based on the five leading modern languages alone – a fact which tends to invalidate the accuracy of the indexes of change.

How useful is the report?

A feature of the 1968 survey not found in any previous MLA report is the listing of "student contact hours" alongside the registration figures. Registrars were asked to multiply the number of individual registrations in each course by the number of hours of student attendance per week. Unfortunately, the tabular figures on contact hours are virtually useless, since they are reported *institutionally* only in the case of the "other" languages, in the special institutional table of these languages. For the five leading modern languages and for Latin and Greek, however, contact hours are reported in the aggregate, by state, and no information is furnished which could help pinpoint or interpret the slight deviations from the national average (3.8) which occur among the various states and languages. Though required to collect these data by the terms of its contract with the Office of Education, the MLA would do well to suppress the aggregate totals in the printed tables and replace them with a figure representing the *average* number of contact hours *per student* (i.e. the quotient of the number of hours divided by the number of registrations), or better yet, to omit them altogether and report general patterns and inferences (if any) in the introduction.

Innovations: suggested and actual

Two other innovations introduced by the latest MLA report are worthy of note: first, the wider availability of the reports resulting from their appearance in the pages of *Foreign Language Annals* (13,14); and second, the inclusion of summer school data, in particular the roster of registrations in "other" languages by state and institution. Despite some noticeable gaps in the data, the summer school report provides an interesting general picture that will naturally become more useful as soon as comparative data are made available by subsequent reports.

Enrollments in foreign languages compared with enrollments in higher education

Unfortunately, the MLA reports for 1965 and 1968 fail to provide the figures of total institutional enrollments which formerly (most recently in 1963) were reported both in the institutional directory and in the tables giving aggregate enrollments by states (Marron, Tierney, & Dershem, 19). The data were obtained from college registrars on the same questionnaires that were used to record foreign language enrollment figures. Difficult as these figures are to obtain, they provide the basic yardstick against which the foreign language figures must be measured if they are to have any diagnostic value for assessing strengths and weaknesses in the profession.

1965–68 institutional totals not reported

In the absence of institutional enrollment figures for the specific roster of colleges which responded to the MLA's survey, one turns, for purposes of comparison, to data on growth in higher education enrollments *in general* during the period covered, data which serve to indicate, in a general way, whether or not the growth in foreign language enrollments has kept pace with growth in higher education. The best source of the overall national totals are the annual reports of the Office of Education, entitled *Opening Fall Enrollments in Higher Education*. In Table 8 below, data from the Office of Education reports for 1960, 1963, 1965, and 1968 (28,29,30,31) are compared with the MLA survey figures for the same years. Under MLA surveys, the figure giving institutional enrollments (available for 1960 and 1963 only) represents only those institutions which reported that they had instruction in one or more modern foreign languages (in 1960, 1,661 institutions; in 1963, 1,780). The foreword and introduction to the 1963 report (Marron, Tierney, & Dershem, 19) explain the sources of the 1960 data. No figure is available for the total number of institutions responding to the 1960 survey. Note that the figures for modern language enrollments include "other" modern languages in addition to the five leading languages covered in Tables 2 through 7, above.

Comparison of growth in FL's in higher education with overall college growth

The indexes in Table 8 reveal that while modern foreign language enrollments grew significantly faster than total institutional enrollments between 1960 and 1963, by 1965 they were no

TABLE 8. Trends in enrollments in higher education compared with trends in
modern foreign languages, 1960–68.

	1960	1963	1965	1968
U.S.O.E. reports				
Number of institutions	2,008	2,132	2,173	2,483
Total enrollments	3,582,726	4,494,626	5,526,325	7,513,091
Index of growth (1960=100)	100.0	125.5	154.2	209.7
MLA surveys				
Number institutions responding	–	2,145	2,100	2,479
Number institutions with MFL's	1,661	1,780	1,880	2,120
Institutional enrollments	3,226,055	4,215,251	–	–
Index of growth (1960=100)	100.0	130.6	–	–
Total MFL enrollments	608,749	801,781	975,777	1,073,097
Index of growth (1960=100)	100.0	131.7	160.3	176.3
MFL enrollments as % of O.E.	17.0	17.8	17.6	14.3

	Percent growth between surveys		
	1960–63	1963–65	1965–68
Total institutional enrollments			
(U.S.O.E.)	25.5	22.9	36.0
MFL enrollments	31.7	21.7	10.0

longer quite able to keep pace, and by 1968 had fallen noticeably
behind.

A further source of comparative data are the enrollment reports compiled by Garland G. Parker and published annually in
School and Society (22). These reports, which can be regarded
as complementary to the Office of Education reports, cover accredited institutions only, and only one category of junior colleges. Comparative figures from Parker's 1965–66 report (22)
and his 1968–69 report (23) reveal substantial growth over the
three-year period, but less than is indicated by the more comprehensive U.S.O.E. data. In 1965, 1,100 institutions reported
3,279,162 full-time enrollments, and 4,530,608 (gross) total
enrollments. In 1968, the figures for 1,145 institutions were
4,092,234 full-time and 5,521,963 total enrollments, representing
an increase of 24.8% full-time and 21.9% (gross) total enrollments between 1965 and 1968. In summary, the percentage
growth in total higher education enrollments is more than double
the growth in modern foreign language enrollments (10%) between 1965 and 1968, if one uses *School and Society* reports for
the former set of data; it is more than triple if one makes use of
U.S.O.E. reports. In any case there is ample statistical evidence

A second comparison

TABLE 9. Foreign language entrance and degree requirements, totals for U.S.

	1957	1960	1966
Number of colleges conferring the B.A.	836	898	1,158
Number of colleges with FL entrance requirement	239	267	389
Percent of total	28.5	29.7	33.6
Number of colleges with FL requirement for the B.A.	709	772	1,030
Percent of total	84.8	85.9	88.9

Number of colleges which between 1960 and 1965	FL entrance requirement	FL requirement for the B.A.
instituted	71	47
dropped	32	18
strengthened	–	114
decreased	–	75

of an abrupt and substantial diminution of the role played by foreign languages in higher education between 1965 and 1968.

Lowering of FL requirements for the B.A. and B.S.

In the academic year 1965–66 the MLA, supported by funds from the U.S. Office of Education, conducted its third survey of institutional practices regarding foreign language entrance and degree requirements in U.S. colleges and universities. Previous surveys had been made in 1957 and 1960 (Lund & Herslow, 17; 24). The published results of the 1966 survey (Willbern, 35) were based on responses from 1,158 institutions and gave evidence of a continuing trend toward strengthening both kinds of requirements. *A study of FL entrance and degree requirements*

In addition to a directory of the entrance and degree requirements for each reporting institution, the MLA study provided a summary table with comparative figures for 1957, 1960, and 1966, by region and state, and a series of supplementary lists naming the colleges which had dropped, instituted, strengthened, or reduced requirements since 1960. Table 9 summarizes data appearing in the published report (Willbern, 35).

In the fall of 1970 the MLA began to gather data for a new comprehensive survey of entrance and degree requirements to be published in 1971. Even prior to 1970, however, there was mounting evidence of the widespread instability of foreign language requirements in many colleges (12). In a carefully chosen sample of 275 colleges, 222 of which responded to the questionnaire, Richards & Salas (25) found that some 29% of the in- *Instability of requirements* stitutions reported a downward shift, or weakening, in the requirement: sometimes outright abolition, more often a reduction or an expansion of the options available to students. Isolated private reports tended to confirm the general estimate that this sort of shift was occurring in a significant number—possibly 25 to 30% of institutions. Apart from its likely effects, tangible and psychological, positive and negative, upon college students and teachers, the trend deserves attention for its likely consequences for the role of foreign languages in the curricula of secondary schools. Some of the institutions (e.g., the University of Colorado and Indiana University) which have recently abolished or modified their degree requirements in foreign languages have in fact taken the opportunity to reaffirm their entrance requirements (12); and there is as yet no evidence for assuming that entrance requirements are eroding rapidly.

The 1970 MLA survey will attempt to shed light on these developments, and in its final report will undertake to assess the effects of the changes in requirements upon enrollments in schools and colleges, to the extent that these effects are manifest in the results of the concurrent enrollment surveys. The study will also attempt to ascertain, through a questionnaire directed to foreign language department chairmen, whether, in each chairman's judgment, the changes (if any) in requirements in his institution have come about as a result of declining interest in languages, or dissatisfaction with college requirements in general.

The 1970 MLA study

To judge by a number of informal reports already received from colleges, particularly from relatively well-established "prestige" colleges, it would appear that the trend toward elimination or reduction of degree requirements in foreign languages does not necessarily represent hostility toward language study, but may simply be part of a rejection of the concept of the required, prescribed curriculum. As such, it has more to do with developments in the educational system in general, and with social and cultural conditions in the nation, than with foreign language pedagogy. Since, however, this trend has created a crisis for the profession, economic, at least, if not necessarily existential, it has compelled foreign language departments to reexamine both their mode of operation and their role in American education. In this sense it is a salutary development, but it will certainly require a massive effort on the part of the profession to ensure the continued acceptance by the public of the goals of

Expected results

foreign language study, and the continuing and improving work of the teaching profession in attempting to achieve those goals.

To some extent the sense of present or impending crisis has already done more to promote unity and—more important —unified action in the profession than the many years of complacent prosperity had ever done. The establishment and growth of ACTFL and the strengthening of other existing organizations are productive steps, as are the heroic efforts to revitalize the teaching of Latin and Greek, already noted above. An important breakthrough for teachers of German began with a recent series of leadership conferences which yielded first, a detailed statement of policy recommendations, research priorities, and action programs in the critical areas of student motivation, teacher training, course content, and articulation; and second, a collaboration between the AATG and the National Carl Schurz Association (Deeken, 6) that has proved to be productive, both professionally and financially.

The crisis and professional unity

Implications for the "labor market" in foreign languages

Fluctuations and trends in enrollments unquestionably have significant implications for the most fundamental concern of the profession: earning a living. That enrollments are not the only variable is self-evident; the term "labor market" suggests the existence of a variable of supply as well as of demand. Moreover, there are factors both within and without the jurisdiction of institutional employers which can operate to fix or decrease the number of jobs, even under circumstances when demand would otherwise keep pace with supply. Chief among these factors are first, inflation, giving rise to increased operating costs; and second, cutbacks in direct and indirect government support of education in general, or of the liberal arts in particular. These are the kinds of factors which impel individual institutions to "hold the line," even during a period of population growth, through such devices as increased teaching loads, salary freezes, and failure to fill vacancies. It should be kept in mind that the growth in foreign languages, as reported in the 1968 surveys, for schools as well as for colleges, was sufficiently marginal (i.e., lower than the average overall institutional growth) to encourage institutions to regard their foreign language programs as areas where budgetary cutbacks would be reasonable.

Factors influencing the "job market"

357

As far as supply is concerned, there is little evidence for assuming that the present oversupply would have come into being had demand not decreased so suddenly. On the other hand, the burgeoning (and affluent) graduate programs of the early sixties produced a "generation" of teachers who now constitute a numerous and well-established middle echelon, many of whom are tenured, but still young and far from retirement. The result appears to be a general loss of mobility at all ranks and levels.

A teacher oversupply

It might be assumed, in view of the severe slowdown of growth in graduate enrollments between 1965 and 1968 (only 3.2%), that with fewer teachers graduating, supply may again come into balance with demand; yet apart from its demoralizing aspects, this decline in graduate study itself contributes to the overall decline in the number of students, contact hours, and, ultimately, college teaching positions. Conversely, the relatively rapid growth of enrollments in junior colleges has generally not succeeded in creating new jobs for graduates, especially not for Ph.D.'s, who are seldom trained for the kinds of teaching and the kind of commitment needed in such institutions.

Decline in graduate students

A general reorientation of graduate-level teacher training in foreign languages toward the preparation of junior college teachers might help to restore a partial balance eventually, assuming the decline in enrollments does not continue (as, however, it is likely to do). The general need for college (and secondary school) teachers with better training in language skills, pedagogy, and applied linguistics was long ago recognized by leaders of the profession, including Axelrod (1), Freeman, Mac-Allister (18), Paquette (20), and others, but their warnings were all too often disregarded. In 1966, in his foreword to Paquette's *Guidelines* (20), William R. Parker wrote:

Graduate level teacher training: a reorientation

> The present prosperity of language teachers, to which I made some contributions from 1952 to 1959, is, believe me, basically illusive; it can disappear as dramatically and unexpectedly as it appeared, for it lacks the solid foundation with which this issue of *The Modern Language Journal* is chiefly, and commendably, concerned. That solid foundation is a practical consensus on the effective preparation of future teachers. There is no more important problem facing the profession. . . .

One is tempted to regard the sudden reawakening of the profession, in the face of a decline in its prosperity, as another example of "too little too late."

In the absence of specific projections of growth in foreign language enrollments, it is useful to examine those available for higher education and secondary school enrollments in general. Projections for secondary schools appear in a recent report from the American Council on Education (11) both as numbers of students and, more conveniently, in the form of index figures using 1959 as a base. In that year, total public school enrollments in grades 9–12 were reported as approximately 8,271,000. Taking the 1959 base as 100, the corresponding enrollments for succeeding years are as follows:

General enrollment projections for secondary schools

Year of report	Index (1959=100)	Year of projection	Index (1959=100)
1960	104	1969	160
1961	113	1970	164
1962	122		
1963	132		
1964	138		
1965	140	1975	185
1966	144		
1967	148		
1968	154	1978	186

The figures show a gradual resumption and acceleration of growth until about 1975, when a slowdown is anticipated. It should be noted that figures and projections for secondary school enrollments can and should be studied in the context of total school enrollments, elementary and secondary, public and private; this context is available in the document cited.

For higher education, data based on reports from the U.S. Office of Education and the American Council on Education (11), with the addition of figures showing percent change, are presented in Table 10. The table shows that the deceleration in rate of general growth in higher education that has been manifest in the latter half of the sixties is likely to continue into the seventies, and is in fact a function of a projected noticeable slowdown in population growth. At the same time, the ratio of college enrollments to general population (ages 18–21) will increase, and graduate enrollments will, between 1970 and 1975, regain and surpass the rate of growth they enjoyed between 1960 and 1965.

General enrollment projections for higher education

As far as the academic "labor market" is concerned, there is no reason to expect, on the basis of general statistics alone, either a shortage of teachers or an expansion of employment

TABLE 10. Population ages 18–21 and opening fall degree-credit enrollments, 1960–68, with projections 1970–78 (in thousands).

	Population ages 18–21	Estimated undergraduate enrollment	Ratio of enrollment to population	Graduate enrollment	Total enrollment
1960	9,724	3,227	.33	356	3,583
1965	12,299	4,945	.40	582	5,526
1968	14,321	6,160	.43	768	6,928
1970	14,481	6,533	.45	844	7,377
1975	16,293	8,186	.50	1,157	9,343
1978	16,861	8,979	.53	1,339	10,318

Percent change

	Population ages 18–21	Opening fall degree-credit enrollments		
		Undergraduate	Graduate	Total
1960–65	26.5	53.2	35.4	54.2
1965–70	17.7	31.9	27.8	33.4
1970–75	12.5	25.2	37.1	26.6
1960–70	48.9	103.1	52.8	105.9
1968–78	17.7	45.8	74.3	48.9

opportunities. Cartter & Farrell (2), in examining the likely impact of the military draft upon the supply of college teachers, assess it as a relatively minor factor, given the present general level of military manpower needs. They also review the existing employment situation in college teaching, explain the faulty analyses that even as recently as the mid-sixties had led to predictions of dire shortages of teachers by 1970, and construct a projections model for the next several years. Since the authors' point of view is strictly objective, and not that of an unemployed college teacher, it is not surprising that they assess the situation positively in terms of educational quality:

Academic labor market

> We can look forward to the 1970's with confidence that there will be an adequate supply of available manpower to meet most critical needs in teaching, research and other specialized employment fields. Whereas for the last decade we have needed to channel about half of all persons receiving the doctorate into college teaching to maintain the quality of our staffs, in the 1970's less than a third will be required, and fifteen years from now it may require only one in five.

The authors have no place in the context of their article for a field-by-field assessment of the labor market situation. It is worth noting, however, that the general trend they foresee will unavoidably have a greater impact on fields like English and the foreign languages, where teaching has been the career goal of graduates to a far greater extent than in many other fields. It is clear that enrollment trends in foreign languages are subject to too many variables to permit any kind of prediction here, but the mere fact that their rate of growth at all levels (though not uniformly in all languages) has fallen behind the rate of institutional growth is ominous enough. The drop on the secondary school level is slight, but it demands attention; on the college level the decline (shown in Table 8) in foreign language enrollments as a percentage of total higher education enrollments, from 17.6% in 1965 to 14.3% in 1968, is one that has serious consequences for teachers on all levels. If, as appears likely, the profession will no longer be able to depend on entrance and degree requirements as a means of recruiting its "captive audience," it will need to seek new channels, new forms, and new and challenging opportunities for serving American education and society.

Prediction for the future – impossible, but ...

References, Trends in foreign language enrollments

1 Axelrod, Joseph. *The Education of the Modern Foreign Language Teacher for American Schools.* New York: Modern Language Association, 1966.

2 Cartter, Allan M., and Robert L. Farrell. "Academic Labor Market Projections and the Draft," 357–74 in *The Economics and Financing of Higher Education in the United States. A Compendium of Papers Submitted to the Joint Economic Committee, Congress of the United States.* Washington: Government Printing Office, 1969.

3 Childers, J. Wesley. "Foreign-Language Offerings and Enrollments in Public Secondary Schools, Fall 1958." *PMLA* 76,ii(1961):36–50.

4 ——— "Foreign-Language Offerings and Enrollments in Public Secondary Schools, Fall 1959," 15–33 in *Reports of Surveys and Studies in the Teaching of Modern Foreign Languages.* New York: Modern Language Association, 1961.

5 ——— "Foreign-Language Offerings and Enrollments in Public Secondary Schools, Fall 1960." *PMLA* 77,iv, part 2 (1962):11–30.

6 Deeken, Hans W. *Investigation of the National Potential for the Advancement of the Teaching of German in the United States.* Final Report. Philadelphia: National Carl Schurz Association and American Association of Teachers of German, 1968.

7 Dershem, James F., Gladys A. Lund, and Nina Greer Herslow. *Foreign-Language Offerings and Enrollments in Secondary Schools, Fall 1964.* New York: Modern Language Association, 1966.

8 Dusel, John P. "Surveys and Reports on Foreign Language Enrollments," 415–38 in Emma M. Birkmaier,ed., *Britannica Review of Foreign Language Education, Volume 1.* Chicago: Encyclopaedia Britannica, 1968 [1969].

9 Eshelman, James N., and James F. Dershem. *Foreign-Language Offerings and Enrollments in Public Secondary Schools, Fall 1963.* New York: Modern Language Association, 1965.

10 ——— and Nancy W. Lian. *Foreign-Language Offerings and Enrollments in Secondary Schools. Public Schools:Fall 1961, Fall 1962 and Nonpublic Schools:Fall 1962.* New York: Modern

Language Association, 1964.

11 *A Fact Book on Higher Education* [Pre-print of Issue No. 1, 1970]. Washington: American Council on Education, 1970.

12 "The Foreign Language Requirement:Status Reports." *Bulletin of the Association of Departments of Foreign Languages* 1,i(1969):7–10; ii(1969):9–11; iii(1970):5–10.

13 Kant, Julia Gibson. *Foreign Language Offerings and Enrollments in Public and Non-Public Secondary Schools, Fall 1968.* New York: Modern Language Association, 1970. [Reprinted in part in *Foreign Language Annals* 3(1970):400–58.]

14 —— *Foreign Language Registrations and Student Contact Hours in Institutions of Higher Education, Fall 1968 and Summer 1969.* New York: Modern Language Association, 1969. [Reprinted in part in *Foreign Language Annals* 3(1969):247–304; 3(1970)459–76.]

15 Kovach, Edith M. A. "Classics:The Teaching of Latin and Greek," 389–414 in Emma M. Birkmaier,ed., *Britannica Review of Foreign Language Education, Volume 1.* Chicago: Encyclopaedia Britannica, 1968 [1969].

16 Lèbano, Edoardo. "Survey on the Teaching of Italian in the Central Great Lakes States." *Modern Language Journal* 53(1969):554–60.

17 Lund, Gladys A., and Nina Greer Herslow. *Foreign Language Entrance and Degree Requirements in U.S. Colleges and Universities, Fall 1966.* New York: Modern Language Association, 1966.

18 MacAllister, Archibald T. "The Preparation of College Teachers of Modern Foreign Languages." *PMLA* 79,iv(1964):29–43. [Reprinted in *Modern Language Journal* 50(1966):400–415.]

19 Marron, James M., Hanne Tierney, and James F. Dershem. *Modern Foreign Language Enrollments in Institutions of Higher Education, Fall 1963.* New York: Modern Language Association, 1964.

20 Paquette, F. André. "Guidelines for Teacher Education Programs in Modern Foreign Languages—An Exposition." *Modern Language Journal* 50(1964):323–425.

21 Parker, Garland G. "Fifty Years of Collegiate Enrollments:1919–20 to 1969–70, Part Two." *School and Society* 98(1970):215–224.

22 —— "Statistics of Attendance in American Universities and Colleges, 1965–66." *School and Society* 94(1966):47–63.

23 —— "Statistics of Attendance in American Universities and Colleges, 1968–69." *School and Society* 97(1969):43–61.

24 *Reports of Surveys and Studies in the Teaching of Modern Foreign Languages, 1959–61.* New York: Modern Language Association, 1961.

25 Richards, Henry J., and Teresa C. Salas. "The Erosion of Foreign Language Requirements in College and University Curricula:Some Observable Trends." *Bulletin of the Association of Departments of Foreign Languages* 1,ii(1969):37–40.

26 Teague, Caroline, and Hans Rütimann. *Foreign Language Offerings and Enrollments in Public Secondary Schools, Fall 1965.* New York: Modern Language Association, 1967.

27 Teitelbaum, Sidney L. *The Foreign Language Instructional Program on Long Island: 1969 Survey.* East Meadow, New York: Foreign Language Association of Chairmen and Supervisors, 1969.

28 U.S. Office of Education. *Opening Fall Enrollment in Higher Education, 1960.* Washington, D.C.: Government Printing Office, 1961.

29 —— *Opening Fall Enrollment in Higher Education, 1963.* Washington, D.C.: Government Printing Office, 1964.

30 —— *Opening Fall Enrollment in Higher Education, 1965.* Washington, D.C.: Government Printing Office, 1966.

31 —— *Opening Fall Enrollment in Higher Education, 1968.* Washington, D.C.: Government Printing Office, 1969.

32 Vamos, Mara, and John Harmon. *Modern Foreign Language Enrollments in Four-year Accredited Colleges and Universities, Fall 1958 and Fall 1959.* New York: Modern Language Association, 1961.

33 —— *Modern Foreign Language Enrollments in Four-year Accredited Colleges and Universities, Fall 1960.* New York: Modern Language Association, 1961.

34 Willbern, Glen. "Foreign Language Enrollments in Public Secondary Schools, 1965." *Foreign Language Annals* 1(1968): 239–253.

35 —— "Foreign Language Entrance and Degree Requirements in Colleges that Grant the B.A. Degree:Fall 1966." *Foreign Language Annals* 1(1967):49–70.

36 Wolfe, Warren J. "Foreign Language Entrance and Degree Requirements for the B.S. Degree." *PMLA* 74,iv,part 2(1959):34–44.

Index

A

AA (Audio-active response) 214
AATG (American Association of
  Teachers of German) 257-58
Ability grouping 133
Acronyms 323
ACTFL: see American Council on
  the Teaching of Foreign
  Languages
Adams, E. N. 231
Advanced Placement Tests 146
Advanced study 246-48
Agatstein, Michael 130, 222
Alexander, L. G. 80
Allen, Virginia G. 26, 330
A-LM, Level One (textbook)
  114-15
Alpert, D. 300-1
Altman, Howard B. 9-10, 239-70
American Association of Teachers
  of German (AATG) 257-58
American Council on Education
  359-60
American Council on the Teaching
  of Foreign Languages (ACTFL)
  192
  meetings 26, 28, 283
Applied Language Research Center
  (El Paso, Texas) 87
Approach tendencies 40
Aptitudes 89-90
Arendt, Jermaine D. 157-86, 7
  scheduling 136, 138
  work sheets 219
Artes Latinae (Sweet) 300
Articulation 144-47
Asher, James J. 82, 90, 287-88
AT (Audio-tutorial learning) 215
Attitudes 40
Audio-active response (AA) 214
Audiolingual approach 89-91
  drills 117
  paradigm 96-99, 102
Audio-tutorial learning (AT) 215
Audiovisual materials 142-43, 151
Auditory discrimination 89
Ausubel, David P. 79
Avery, Harry 290
Avoidance techniques 40

B

Banathy, Bela H. 212
  behavioral objectives 45, 50
Banks, Michael E. 100
Barber, William H. 15, 19
Barrett, Martin 143, 147
Barrutia, Richard 224
Bartley, Diana E. 45-46
Basic German (textbook) 118
Becker, James M. 19-20
Becker, Ralph J. 72
Behavioral objectives 35-62, 3-4
Belasco, Simon 166
Benardo, Leo U. 241
Bennett, W. A. 82, 224
Berwald, John P. 129
Bidialectalism 330
Bilingualism 87, 174, 327, 328
  teacher training programs 251
Biloquialism 330
Birkmaier, Emma M. 2
Birmingham, John 21
Bitzer, D. L. 300-1
Black English 329-30
Blomberg, John 129
Bloom, Benjamin S. 150, 51
  mastery learning 159-60, 216-17
Bloom Taxonomy 51, 53
Bockman, John F. 136, 146
Borton, Terry 44
Boston College High School 283
Boyd, Malcolm 23
Boyd's community 23
Bradford, Arthur 105
Breitenstein, P. H. 106
Brewer, Marilynn 66
Brière, Eugène J. 326
Brock University (St. Catherines,
  Ontario) 314
Brod, Richard 12-13, 341-61
Brodinsky, Ben 59
Brooks, Nelson 41, 81
Brown, Frank B. 150
Brown, George H. 218
Bruner, Jerome S. 23, 44
Buckby, M. 94
Bundy, Jean D. 98
Bung, Klaus 173
Burkholder, Rachel B. 100
Burling, Robbins 106
Bus
  education en route 87-88

C

Cadoux, Remunda 37, 39
CAI: see Computer-assisted (aided)
  instruction

Index

Cannaday, Robert W., Jr. 175
CARLOS (Computer-Assisted Review Lessons On Syntax) 125
Carroll, John B. 204–6
Carter, Launor F. 178
Cassette recorder 232
    see also Tape recorder
Cawelti, Gordon 60
CBE (Computer-Based Education) 300–2
Central States Conference on the Teaching of Foreign Languages 16
Certification 9–10, 257–60
Cervenka, E. J. 324
Chamberlain, Jane S. 142
Chastain, Kenneth D. 86
Chez les Français (textbook) 116
Chomei, Tashiko 214, 231
Christian, Chester 251
Cioffari, Vincenzo 137
Ciotti, Marianne C. 129, 140
Clark, John R. 294–95
Clark, Ramsey 22
Clark, Thomas 304
Clark, William H. 59
Classical heritage program 297
Classical languages 10–11
Classroom 72–73, 135, 147–48
    techniques in listening 93–94
Classroom Laboratory Instructional System (CLIS) 210–12
Cleary, Vincent J. 285–86
CLIS (Classroom Laboratory Instructional System) 210–12
CLOZE procedure 104, 334
Coleman, Ben C. 87
College
    book survey 101
    experimental French course 122–23
    foreign language requirements 355–56
    lack of teacher training 252–53
    language centers in England 176–77
    placement testing 146
    registrations 347–61
    requirements of secondary schools 16
College Board Achievement Tests 146
College entrance examination 62–65
College Entrance Examination Board 62–63, 66–67
COMBAT (Computer Based Test Development) 181–82
Communication 25, 139
Comprehension 104
Computer-assisted (aided) instruction (CAI) 124–25, 175, 179–83, 227–29, 300–4
Computer-Assisted Review Lessons On Syntax (CARLOS) 125

Computer-Based Education (CBE) 300–2
Computer Based Test Development (COMBAT) 181–82
Computers 141, 300
Connor, Marjorie W. 91
Contextual drill 167–70, 225–26
Contrastive linguistic analysis 326
Corder, S. P. 335
Coronado High School (Scottsdale, Ariz.) 138
Cracas, Thomas L. 306–7
Cues 101–2
Culhane, Joseph W. 104
Culture, 19, 55, 291
Curriculum 133–52, 285–97
    behavioral objectives 36
    practice-centered 242
Curso Básico de Español (textbook) 117–18
Cutt, Eula G. 290

D

Damore, Anthony P. 58
Dannerbeck, Francis J. 98
Darian, Steven 83
De Camp, David 324
Degrees
    classical languages 277, 315
    foreign language requirements 265, 355–56
DeLay, Donald 64–65
Delco, E. A. 35
Demilia, Lorraine 101
Demuth, Jerry 61
Dialects 329–31
Dialogues 112
Documentatio Didactica Classica (bibliography) 316
Dorsey, David F., Jr. 295–96
Dropouts 72
Duffy, P. 283
DuFrane, Daniel L. 212–13
Duker, Sam 84
Dulin, Kenneth 103
Dusel, John P. 138

E

Ecouter et Parler (textbook) 116
Edgerton, Mills F., Jr. 94
Education, Office of (U.S.) 66, 71, 73
Educational Testing Service 94
Education Professions Development Act (1969) (EPDA) 1
    programs 311, 315
Ehn, Willard 60
Eisner, Elliot 42, 49–50
Eiss, Albert F. 49
Elective courses 126
Electronic classroom 7, 208–10, 222
Elementary school 16, 27
Elsass, Ray 61
English 280, 284, 323, 332

English as a Second Dialect (ESD) 249–50
English as a Second Language (ESL) 249–51
Enrollment 341–61
  classics 276–78
  college 13
  high school 13–14
  placement programs 139
Entender y Hablar (textbook) 120
EPDA: *see* Education Professions Development Act
ERIC/CRIER Center 99
Erickson, Gerald M. 10–11, 275–318
ESD (English as a Second Dialect) 249–50
ESL (English as a Second Language) 249–51
ESOL: *see* TESOL (Teaching English to speakers of other languages)
Ethics 69–70
Evaluation 4, 62–75
Everett, Aaron B. 83, 122
Experience curriculum 242–45
Experimental language laboratory (XLL) 231–32

F

Farr, Roger 95
Fatigue 101
Feldman, David M. 81, 224
  audiolingual approach 96
Fiks, Alfred I. 105, 118
Films 183–84
Finocchiaro, Mary 333
FLES: *see* Foreign Language in the Elementary School
FLICS (Foreign Language Innovative Curricula Studies) 28
FLRC (Foreign Language Resource Center) 176
Folk linguistics 29
Foreign Language Innovative Curricula Studies (FLICS) 28
Foreign Language in the Elementary School (FLES) 17
  Latin 287–90
  multisensory approach 306
  Symposium I 26
  teacher training 255–57
Foreign Language Resource Center (FLRC) 176
Freidenberg, Edgar Z. 18
French
  experimental college course 122–23
  Holt four-skills series 116
  methods 86–87
  registrations 349
  secondary level 55
  study programs 138
Fry formula 101

G

Gagné, Robert M. 107–8
Gahn, Zoe Ann 129
Games 94
Garcia, Ramiro 287–88
Gardner, John W. 30
Gardner, Stephen H. 129
Gefen, Raphael 256
Geis, George L. 57–58
Generative-transformational grammar 324–25, 307
German 163–64
  bilingual program at Univ. of Wisconsin 269–70
  Live Oak High School 126
  registrations 349
  seminar for intern teachers 248
  study programs 139
  world cultures course 86
Gibbons, Maurice 26
Goodman, Paul 15, 20
Gossage, Howard L. 23
Graber, Charles F. 306, 312
Grading 65–66, 123–26
  student teachers 149
Greek 350, 306–8
Grittner, Frank M. 16
  bilingualism 82–83, 95
  evaluation of programs 38
  grouping and scheduling 59–60
  individualizing instruction 56
  integration 163–64
  language laboratory 223
  listening 94
  performance objectives 47
  role of the teacher 175
  techniques for teaching 127
Grobman, Hulda 69–70
Gronlund, Norman E. 51–53
Grouping 59–61
Guided learning 173

H

Hagiwara, Michio P. 253–55
Hamilton, Stanley 93
Harpers Ferry Conference on English Teaching as a World Wide Problem 331
Harris, Theodore L. 95
Hartwig, Hellmut A. 16, 67
Hatfield, William N. 68
Herbert, Charles 53–54
  teacher behavior 46
  testing 42, 64
Hernick, Michael E. 41
Hester, Ralph M. 127–28
Hibbard, Allen 61
High school 16, 21, 139
  articulation 146–47
  behavioral objectives 37–38
  foreign language curriculum 28
  Holt materials 123–24
  MLA enrollment studies 341–45
  reading habits 101

Index

Hills, L. Rust 22
Hills, Penney C. 22
Hnatt, Luciana 293
Hocking, Elton 15–16, 159
Hoetker, James 42–43, 47–48, 59
Holt, John 21, 25–26
Horner, Lucie T. 244
Houlihan, Robert 214, 231
Hoye, Almon G. 56, 60
Huchthausen, L. 303
Hughes, John P. 79

I

Ianni, Francis A. J. 178
Indiana Language Program 26, 28
Indians, American 12
    ESOL 328
Individual Contract System 144
Individualized instruction 15–32
    curricula 133–52
    independent study 170–72
Initial Teaching Alphabet (ITA)
    101
In-service education 9
    college teaching assistants
      254–55
    continuing education 245–48
Institute for Advanced Study in the
    Arts and Humanities 313
Integration
    multimedia 163–65
"In translation" courses 295
ITA (Initial Teaching Alphabet)
    101
Italian 346
Itkonen, Raimo J. 185

J

JACT (Joint Association of
    Classical Teachers) 315–16
Jaekel, Hugo 88
Jakobovits, Leon A. 28–29, 325
    motivation 39–40
    receptive skills 81–82, 88–89
Jalling, Hans 191
Jarvis, Gilbert A. 4–5, 79–108
Jeffrey, Lloyd N. 296
Jerman, Max 182
Johansen, Patricia A. 230
Joint Association of Classical
    Teachers (JACT) 315–16
Joll, Leonard W. 103
Jonas, Sister Ruth Adelaide 87, 165
Jordan, Boris 212
Joyce, Bruce R. 41

K

Kant, Julia Gibson 347–52
Kaufman, Maurice 99
Keitel, Helmut A. 86
Kendall, Harvey L. 105
Kennedy, John F. 18
Keppeler, Frank 244
Kersten, Caesar S. 37–38, 129
King, Janet K. 97, 102

Kingston, Albert J. 95, 102
Kirch, Max S. 93–94
Kittel, Jack E. 55–56, 72
Klin, George 82
Kline, Walter D. 81, 96, 224
Kochman, Thomas 330
Korzybski, Alfred 21
Kovach, Edith M. 287–88, 303–4
    classics service organization 315
    Latin enrollment 278–79
Krogmeier, Shirley 143

L

Labov, William 329
Lado, Robert 79
Laffey, James L. 99
Laleike, Fred H. 55
Lambert, Wallace E. 86
Lane, Harlan 89
Lange, Dale L. 1–14
Langer, Philip 61
Language Center (England)
    177–78
Language laboratory 56, 148,
    191–234
LAPS: see Learning Activity
    Packages
Latin 174, 276–318, 350
    FLES programs 27
Latin Advanced Placement program
    291–2
Lawson, John H. 26, 29
LDP (Long-delayed feedback) 214
Learning Activity Packages (LAPS)
    135,170
Lèbano, Edoardo 346
Lemler, Ford L. 160
Leonard, George B. 23
Lipton, Gladys C. 99
Literature 104–5, 244, 309–10
    how to use media 159–63
Live Oak High School (Morgan Hill,
    Calif.) 139–40
    Individual Contract System
      144–46
Logan, Gerald E. 6, 126, 133–52
Long, Ralph 332
Long-delayed feedback (LDP) 214
Long Island (N.Y.) survey 347

M

MacAllister Report (1963) 252
McCluer Plan 28, 84, 171–72
    Holt materials 120, 122
Machine-aided language learning 8,
    192–95
Macías, Cenobio C. 57
Mackey, William 327
McLennan, Robert 144, 147
McLuhan, Marshall 22, 157–58
Macnamara, John 86
Mager, Robert F. 40, 51
Maginis, George H. 101
Mandel, E. Jules 43–44, 70
Margon, Joseph S. 295

Marker, Gerald W. 15, 19
Marquardt, William F. 250
Marshall-University High School 144–46
Masciantonio, Rudolph 27
Mastery learning 216
Matranga, Edward C. 57–58, 62
Matthews, George T. 35
Mehlinger, Howard D. 15, 18–19
Meiden, Walter 66
Methods of Teaching Foreign Languages, Conference on 243
Mexican-Americans 252
Microteaching 242
Minicourses 61
Modern Language Association (MLA) 341–58
    enrollment report 276–77
    testing 199, 259
Moore, J. William 46–47, 70
Moreno, Edward V. 51, 57
Morton, F. Rand 118
Motivation 39–41, 113, 129
Motto, Ann L. 294–5
Mountain View High School 140
Mowrer, Donald E. 45, 59
Mueller, Theodore 91
Multisensory instruction 304–6

N

Nathan Hale High School (Seattle, Wash.) 138
National Association of Language Laboratory Directors (NALLD) 193–94
National Association of Secondary-School Principals 28
National Teachers Corps 252
Nelson, Robert J. 39–40, 232
Newmark, Leonard 88
New York State Regents Examinations 291
Nixon, Ruth A. 93
Northeast Conference Report 160–62
Norton, Harriet S. 306, 312
Nyman, Stephen 24

O

Ohman, Richard 80
Operational objectives 43–44
Orr, David B. 92
Ort, Barbara A. 86, 126
Ott, Vesperella E. 37–38, 129
Overseas study 241, 247, 269–70

P

Palmer, Harold 83
Papalia, Anthony 284–87
Paquette, F. André 26
Paquette report (1966) 240
Parker, Garland G. 354
Parker, J. Cecil 44, 50
Parker, William R. 358
Parks, John H. 280–81

Parler et Lire (textbook) 116
Pennsylvania Project 73–75, 194
    effects 207–8
    evaluative instruments 199
    individualized practice 203
    laboratory use 200–2
    teaching effectiveness 201
    teaching strategies 195–96
Performance curriculum 43–62
Perren, G. E. 251, 253
de Petra, Yvette 114
Phelps, Florence 143, 147
Philadelphia, Pa.
    school without walls 24
Phillips, Robert 221
Phinney, Edward, Jr. 278–79
Pillet, Roger A. 45, 137, 241
Pimsleur, Paul 39, 83
    testing 42, 63
Pittsburgh, University of
    conference on inner city programs 289–90
PLATO (Programmed Logic Automated Teaching Operations) system 300–1
PLS (Portable Laboratory System) 230
Poetry 309
Politzer, Robert L. 45–46, 89, 96
    audiolingual approach 115
    oral reading 104
    scheduling 144
    teaching ESD 249–50
Popham, W. James 44, 49–51
    grading 65–66
Portable Laboratory System (PLS) 230
Portuguese 87, 350
Postman, Neil 15, 18, 20
    Whorf-Sapir hypothesis 158
Potts, Marion 100
Poulter, Virgil L. 227
Preservice training 240–41
Procedural statements 43–44
Programmed Logic Automated Teaching Operations (PLATO) system 300–1
Programmed materials 59, 105, 118, 150
    compared with CAI 182
    disadvantages 172–74
    ERIC report 140
Project Cram 64
Pronunciation 89, 120
    tapes 224–25
Psycholinguistics 251–52
Purdom, Boyd A. 85

R

Radio 232–33
Rallo, John A. 176
Reception learning 217
Reibel, David 88
Reinert, Harry 38, 129, 222

Index

Relevance 26, 260–61
Renshaw, J. Parke 87
Research
  educational psychology 137
Rexine, John E. 310–11
Rickel, Kathryn 129
Rivers, Wilga M. 16, 85, 98
  audiolingual approach 115
Robinett, Betty W. 335, 249
Robinson, Boyd E. 95, 101
Rodriguez, Armando 252
Roeming, Robert F. 197–98
Roeske, Elfriede 167
Rose, Theodore E. 67
Rosenbaum, Eric 96, 99, 103–4
Rosenbaum, Peter S. 124–25, 228
Rubin, Louis J. 44, 50
Ruplin, Ferdinand 56, 118
Russell, John R. 56, 118
Russian 56

S

Saavedra, Barbara H. 87
Sager, J. C. 225
Samuels, Marilyn 86
Samuels, S. Jay 28, 41, 100
Sandstrom, Eleanor L. 39
Sawyer, Jesse O. 81
Scanlan, Richard 302-3, 313
  overhead projection
    transparencies 305
  "spin-off" principle 291
Scheduling 59–62
  individualized instruction 135,
    143–44, 150
School and Society 354
Schork, Robert J. 296–97
Schramm, Wilbur 89
Schwartz, Leon 128
Sculthorpe, Mabel A. L. 177
SDP (Short-delayed feedback) 214
Secondary school: *see* High school
Second language pedagogy 223, 325
Seelye, H. Ned 50–51, 66
  culture, teaching of 55
SESOD (Standard English to
  speakers of other dialects,
  teaching of) 323
  teacher training programs 9
  TESOL 329–30, 335
Seymour, Dorothy 95
Shane, Harold G. 18, 30
Sharp, Gerald V. 57, 59–60, 66
Shawl, James R. 100
Shepherd, W. Everitt 9–10, 123
  study programs 138, 140, 149
Sheppard, Douglas C. 258
Short-delayed feedback (SDP) 214
Shryer, Margaret 143
Simulated conversation 218–19
Simulated tutoring (ST) 215,
  218–21
Sledd, James 330
Smith, Alfred N. 112–130, 4–6,
  97

Smith, Dwight R. 86, 126
Smith, Melvin 46, 52
Smith, Paul 106
Smith, Philip D. 73
Smith, W. Flint 191–234, 7
Smith, William L. 19
Sociolinguistics 328–29
Software 163–66
Sounds 85
Spanish 57, 174
  computer-aided instruction 227
  experimental group 99
  new textbooks 117
  performance objectives 54–55
  registrations 349
  Teacher Corps interns 252
Speech rate 91–92
Spolsky, Bernard 323–37, 11–12
ST: *see* Simulated tutoring
Stake, Robert 72
Standard English to speakers of
  other dialects, teaching of: *see*
  SESOD
Stanislaus County project 54–55
Steiner, Florence 35–75, 3–4
Stewart, Donald 65
Stewart, John 104–5
Sticht, Thomas G. 91–92
Stock, Brian 294
Strasheim, Lorraine A. 15–33, 41
  evaluation of programs 38
Struth, Johann F. 42, 83
Student-created productions
  178–79
Student teachers 244
Sullivan, Howard J. 49–50, 68–69
Suppes, Patrick 182
Swedish for Immigrants (Anderson)
  166
Sweet, Waldo E. 174, 299–300
Systems approach 177–78

T

Takho-Godi, Aza 317–18
Tape recorder 221–22
Taxonomies 51
Taylor, Stanford E. 86
Teachers
  technological revolution 174–75
Teacher training programs 9, 335–36
  college teaching assistants
    252–55
  pressure for change 240
  use of technological media 183
Teaching English to speakers of
  other languages: *see* TESOL
Teen-agers 19
Teitelbaum, Sidney L. 347
Television 157
TESOL 323–37
  teacher training programs 9–12
Testing 62-68, 146, 334
  computer-aided 226–27
  Holt material 122–23
  listening comprehension 94

Textbooks 151
Total Physical Response Technique
  90–91
Transfer students 278
Transformational-generative
  grammar 307, 324–25
Trump Plan 170
Turner, Daymond, Jr. 223–24
Turner, Ronald C. 227–28
  computer program 125
Tutorial program 180–81
Tutorial teaching 216–17
Twinned classroom 87
Tyler, Louise L. 48–50
Type design 102

U

Unipac (learning packets) 135,
  142, 170–71
United States
  secondary education 30

V

Valdman, Albert 105, 119
  programmed learning 172–73
Valette, Rebecca
  relevancy 37
  taxonomies 51–53
  testing 40, 42, 63–64
Van Valkenburg, John 85–86

Verbal-active method 127–28
Video tape recorder (VTR) 184–85
  supervision of student teaching
    245
Vocabulary 103, 106
Voces y Vistas (textbook) 117
VTR: *see* Video tape recorder

W

Walton, Wesley W. 175
  applications of CAI 179–80
Wardhaugh, Ronald 324
Weaton, Marjorie 130
Weingartner, Charles 15, 18, 20, 158
Weisbord, Marvin R. 18
Weiss, Louis 239–70, 9–10, 89
Whorf-Sapir hypothesis 158
Wiley, David E. 203
Wilmoth, Juanita 60
Wilson, Mary D. 304
Witkin, Belle R. 84, 92
Woerderhoff, Frank J. 86
Wolfe, David L. 117
Wood, Fred H. 84, 122
Woodford, Protase 63, 67

X

XLL (Experimental language
  laboratory) 231–32